700.8996041 WAL
HARROW CAM[illegible]
UNIVERSITY [illegible]
Watford Rd, No[illegible]
Harrow, Middlesex HA1 3TP
KU-249-693

THE CARIBBEAN ARTISTS MOVEMENT 1966–1972

27 0006592 9

THE CARIBBEAN ARTISTS MOVEMENT 1966–1972

A Literary & Cultural History

Anne Walmsley

HARROW CAMPUS LIBRARIES
UNIVERSITY OF WESTMINSTER
Watford Rd, Northwick Park
Harrow, Middlesex HA1 3TP

NEW BEACON BOOKS
LONDON AND PORT OF SPAIN

First published in 1992 by New Beacon Books Ltd.,
76 Stroud Green Road, London N4 3EN, England.

© 1992 Anne Walmsley

ISBN: 1 873201 01 X hardback
1 873201 06 0 paperback

All rights reserved. No part of this publication may be reproduced or transmitted in any form or by any means, electronic or mechanical, including photography, recording or any information storage or retrieval system, without prior permission in writing from the publisher.

Printed by Villiers Publications Ltd., 26a Shepherds Hill,
London N6 5AH, England.

TO ALL THE BROTHERS AND SISTERS IN CAM

‘From this ground of beginning . . . it would be possible for us to nurture a concept of wholeness, of community, and of continuity.’

Edward Kamau Brathwaite

‘This vision of consciousness is the peculiar reality of language, because the concept of language is one which continuously transforms inner and outer formal categories of experience, earlier and representative modes of speech itself, the still life resident in painting and sculpture as such, even music which one ceases to ‘hear’ – the peculiar reality of language provides a medium to *see* in consciousness the ‘free’ motion and to *hear* with consciousness the ‘silent’ flood of sound by a continuous inward revisionary and momentous logic of potent explosive images evoked in the mind.’

Wilson Harris

‘There is a place within, which I call ‘the place of silence’, neither intellectual nor emotional. When we are fortunate enough to make the necessary connection, it helps us to see more clearly, and achieve some sort of inner balance and outward action.’

Ronald Moody

‘The forces meeting in the Caribbean all around the archipelago will eventually, I feel, change this world . . . not in the sense of a big civilisation in one spot, but as the result of the total of man’s experience and groping for the development of his consciousness.’

Aubrey Williams

Contents

Acknowledgements xi

List of abbreviations xiv

List of colour plates xv

Preface xvii

1 **The Background:** Caribbean People in Britain, 1930s–1960s 1

The 1920s and 1930s. The 1940s. The 1950s: the writers; the theatre people; the artists; the students; centres of West Indian activity. The late 1950s to the mid-1960s: pressures in the Eastern Caribbean and in Britain; student migrants, artist residents; groups and associations.

2 **The Beginnings of CAM**, December 1966 – March 1967 35

John La Rose. Edward Kamau Brathwaite. Andrew Salkey. Initiatives for a writers' and artists' group. Early, private CAM meetings. CAM's first public reading.

3 **CAM Goes Public**, March – July 1967 63

CAM meetings, public and private. Venues for CAM. CAM Newsletter and Book Service. Public events, July 1967.

4 **A Wider Audience**, September – December 1967 94

CAM's First Conference: speakers and sessions; conference exhibitions. Conference follow-up sessions. CAM after the conference.

5 **A Broader Context**, January – September 1968 127

CAM in Britain, January – March: organisation; speakers and sessions; outside events. CAM people in the Caribbean: Cuba; Jamaica. CAM in Britain, April – May: public sessions; first CAM art exhibition. CAM in Britain, June – August: public sessions; response to outside events.

6 **Confrontation and Crisis:** The Second Conference, 31 August – 2 September 1968 **157**

The main sessions. Poetry in performance, books on display, art in exhibition. CAM's 'business' meeting.

7 **Grounding in the Caribbean**, October 1968 – December 1970 **190**

The context for CAM in Jamaica: Yard Theatre; early *Savacou;* other CAM-based work. The context for CAM around the Caribbean in 1970: Guyana; Trinidad; Jamaica.

8 **Keeping on in Britain**, October 1968 – December 1970 **223**

A new CAM committee. CAM (UK) activity, late 1968. Public sessions, 1969. The CAM-WISU Symposium. CAM members' other involvements. CAM (UK) activity, 1970.

9 **CAM Continuing:** At Home, 1971–1982 **259**

1971–72. ACLALS papers, *Savacou* poems. Publications and productions. Carifesta '72. 1973–82.

10 **CAM Continuing:** At Home Away From Home, 1971–1982 **283**

1971–72. The new CAM initiative. CAM at Keskidee, 1972. CAM's 'disappearance'. 1973–82.

11 **Postscript** **304**
The character of CAM. CAM in a sequence of movements. The legacy of CAM.

Appendices **323**
CAM Meetings. CAM Conferences. CAM Art Exhibitions. CAM Journals. Manuscripts and oral source material.

Notes **330**

Select bibliography and discography **341**

A selection of work by CAM artists facing **172**

Acknowledgements

Writing this book has to a considerable extent been communal work, in the CAM tradition. I am much indebted to many people:

● the founders of CAM – Edward Kamau and the late Doris Brathwaite, John La Rose and Andrew Salkey – for their encouragement, interest and help all the way through, and for providing access to CAM papers and tapes which they had safeguarded; likewise to Donald Hinds, later CAM newsletter editor and secretary;

● former members of CAM, and people associated with CAM, for giving so generously of their time when I interviewed and re-interviewed them, and for lending me precious archive material;

● many friends in and out of CAM whose kind hospitality helped the book, particularly the interviews, along: in the USA, Andrew and Pat Salkey; in Jamaica, Edward Kamau and the late Doris Brathwaite, Oliver Clarke, and especially Mervyn and Helen Morris; in Barbados, Ann Musgrave; in Trinidad, Therese Mills;

● those who assisted with making the massive amount of oral material on CAM accessible for this research: Carl Kirton for copying all the original reel-to-reel recordings of CAM sessions onto cassettes; Janice Shinebourne for transcribing several of them, and Akua Rugg for transcribing all the rest; Joan Griffiths of the BBC, for providing technical advice and equipment for interviews;

● people who provided ready help at libraries, especially Christiane Keane of the Commonwealth Institute, John Killingbeck of the National Sound Archive, Rod Prince of the West India Committee, and the staff of the British Library and the Reference Section of Wimbledon Library;

● CAM members who have scrutinised the typescript at various stages: Edward Kamau Brathwaite and John La Rose, both of whom gave me abundant comments and suggestions; the late Aubrey Williams whose positive response to an early draft was precious; Errol Lloyd, who provided valuable insights; Sarah White, for her doubly informed editorial assessments and suggestions;

● stalwart help from three people with no previous CAM connection: Katherine Frank, author, teacher and friend, for several readings and constant practical advice; Naseem Nathoo, for assistance with the research and preparation of the typescript in countless ways over a long period, and for friendship and support throughout; and my husband Ron Farquhar, for a close reading, good suggestions and apt encouragement, as well as living with the work for six years;

● the Leverhulme Trust for its Research Fellowship, part-time, from 1985 to 1988, which enabled me to carry out the CAM research far more thoroughly than would otherwise have been possible; to the University of Kent at Canterbury, and in particular Professor Louis James and Dr Lyn Innes, for help with the Fellowship; to Dr Innes and to Dr Stewart Brown for their perceptive comments when they read the completed typescript as a thesis; Louis James's advice on this subsequent book, in early draft and in almost final form, had especial value because of his own active part in CAM;

● the late Mary Helen Scott, my only aunt, who died in 1987; her generosity enabled me to write this book just as her confidence in my work sustained me while she lived.

I am grateful to the following for kindly allowing me to reprint copyright material: Oxford University Press for the quotations from *Rights of Passage* and *Islands* (*The Arrivants*) by Edward Kamau Brathwaite on pp 190 and 209; Michael Gilkes for the quotation from this book *Wilson Harris and the Caribbean Novel* on p 160; Messrs Aitken & Stone Limited for the quotations from *Finding the Centre: Two Narratives* by V.S. Naipaul on pp 11–12; and all the copyright holders of short quotations from printed work whom I have not contacted but of which the full sources are provided in the Notes, pp 330–340. I am especially grateful to the Art Derry Estate, the CLR James Estate, the Bryan King Estate, the Ronald Moody Estate, and the Aubrey Williams Estate, for agreeing that I might incorporate and use material by the late Art Derry, the late CLR James, the late Bryan King, the late Ronald Moody, and the late Aubrey Williams, in the context in which they appeared in the typescript pages seen by the executor of the said estate or by the person concerned before his death. I am also grateful to the following for giving me permission to quote what they have written or said, as included in the typescript pages which I showed to them: Edward Kamau Brathwaite, James Berry, Donald Bowen, Lynette Dolphin, Douglas Hall, Wilson Harris, John Hearne, Donald Hinds, Louis James, Michael Kustow, Christopher Laird, John La Rose, Errol Lloyd, Lucille Mathurin Mair, Marina Omowale Maxwell, Kenneth Ramchand, Robert Reinders, Gordon Rohlehr, Jill Sheppard, Hortense J Spillers, Jon Stallworthy, Henry Swanzy, Jeremy Verity, Clive Wake and Karina Williamson. I much appreciated the generous trust of the many CAM members or people associated with CAM whom I interviewed or was in touch with and who agreed that I might quote material by themselves without checking the details. To the very few people whose words I have incorporated without succeeding in reaching themselves or their heirs, my apologies and sincere hopes that they have not in any way been misrepresented or misquoted.

We wish to thank the following for prints and transparencies of work by Caribbean artists as follows: Bogle L'Ouverture, *Waiting*, by Errol Lloyd; Clifton Campbell, *The Man and the Tightrope* and *The Bird Watcher*; Commonwealth Institute, *Liberty was my Friend* by Winston Branch and *Vision* by Ronald Moody; Karl 'Jerry' Craig, *Tropical Landscape*; Paul Dash, *Figures dancing in a Street*; Althea McNish, *Pomegranate* and *Azul*; Cynthia Moody, *Johanaan*, *The Mother*, *Man . . . His Universe* by the late Ronald Moody; Eve Williams, *Ning-Ning*, *Tumatumari*, and Timehri Airport murals, all by the late Aubrey Williams. Our warm thanks to Andy Keate for taking photographs of *Hosein Festival* and *Manzanilla Moon* by the late Art Derry, *The Lesson*, *The Sisters* and *Richard Small* by Errol Lloyd, and *Visual Idea* and *Warrau II* by the late Aubrey Williams, expressly for this book.

We wish to thank the copyright holders and sources for photographs appearing within the text on the following pages:
Jack Adam, pp 49, 239; James Berry, pp 5, 224; Bogle L'Ouverture, pp 297, 298; British Film Institute, p 13; Anne Bolt, p 16; Edward Kamau Brathwaite, pp 115, 186, 269; Karl Broodhagen and *Savacou*, p 138; Brookside Press, p 71; Syd Burke, p 151, 235; Cochrane Theatre, p 58; Gerhard Cohn, p 115; Andre Deutsch, pp 65, 236; Hiltrud Egonu, p 31; Doris Harper Wills, p 274; Margaret Harris and Dangaroo Press, p 64; Donald Hinds, pp 23, 224; History Department, UWI, Mona, p 97; *Jamaica Gleaner*, pp 191, 199; *Jamaica Weekly Gleaner*, p 285; Maria La Yacona and Grove Press, p 198; Christopher Laird, p 281; Althea McNish, p 81; Cynthia Moody, pp 31, 126, 201; New Beacon Books, pp 36, 86, 122, 155, 213, 234, 239, 294, 290–1, 303; Oxford University Press, pp 39, 75; Andrew Salkey, pp 12, 44, 136, 146; Elizabeth-Ann Seymour Boys, p 271; Barrington Watson, p 270; Denis Williams and Michael Joseph, p 139; Eve Williams, p 73; Woodstock Gallery, p 100.

List of Abbreviations

ACLALS	Association for Commonwealth Literature and Language Studies
ASAWI	African Studies Association of the West Indies
ATCAL	Association for the Teaching of Caribbean, African and Asian Literatures
BCA	British Caribbean Association
BG	British Guiana
CAC	Creative Arts Centre
CAM	Caribbean Artists Movement
CARD	Campaign Against Racial Discrimination
CEA	Caribbean Education Association
CECWA	Caribbean Educational and Community Workers Association
CRE	Commission for Racial Equality
CI	Commonwealth Institute
CWS	Caribbean Writers Series
CXC	Caribbean Examinations Council
GT	Great Tradition
HEB	Heinemann Educational Books
ICA	Institute of Contemporary Arts
IRR	Institute of Race Relations
JBC	Jamaica Broadcasting Corporation
LSE	London School of Economics
LT	Little Tradition
MRR	Mystic Revelation of Rastafari
NHAC	National History and Arts Council
NJAC	National Joint Action Committee (Trinidad and Tobago)
NLWIA	North London West Indian Association
NVCG	New Vision Centre Gallery
NVG	New Vision Group
OUP	Oxford University Press
PNC	Peoples National Congress (BG/Guyana)
PNM	Peoples National Movement (Trinidad and Tobago)
PNP	Peoples National Party (Jamaica)
PPP	Peoples Progressive Party (BG/Guyana)
RAAS	Racial Action Adjustment Society
SNCC	Student Non-Violent Coordinating Committee
TASPO	Trinidad All Steel Percussion Orchestra
UCWI	University College of the West Indies
UWI	University of the West Indies
WIIP	West Indian Independence Party (Trinidad and Tobago)
WFM	Workers Freedom Movement (Trinidad and Tobago)
WISU	West Indian Students Union
WISC	West Indian Standing Conference

Colour Plates

Work by Caribbean artists shown at CAM exhibitions or on view to CAM members

Althea McNish, *Pomegranate*, 1967, panel in plastic laminate. 134 × 65 cm. Collection artist.

Althea McNish, *Azul*, 1967, Jacquard woven textile in wool, produced by Sekers Fabrics Ltd.

Karl 'Jerry' Craig, *Tropical Landscape*, 1970, oil and acrylic on masonite. 91 × 127 cm. Collection artist.

Ronald Moody, *The Mother*, 1958, concrete. Height 130 cm. Leicester Museums and Art Gallery.

Ronald Moody, detail of *Johanaan*, also known as *Peace*, 1936, elm. Height 155 cm. Tate Gallery.

Ronald Moody, *Man . . . His Universe*, 1969, glass resin. Height 104 cm. Leicester Museums and Art Gallery.

Ronald Moody, *Orchid Bird*, 1968, glass resin. Height 95 cm. Collection Cynthia Moody.

Aubrey Williams, *Visual Idea*, 1963, oil on canvas. 114 × 132 cm. Collection Eve Williams.

Aubrey Williams, murals at Timehri Airport, Guyana, 1970 – on west wall *Itiribisi* and *Maridowa* – polymer primer stainers on concrete.

Aubrey Williams, *Tumatumari*, 1970, mural in departure lounge of Timehri Airport, Guyana, polymer primer stainers on concrete [?]

Aubrey Williams, *Ning-Ning*, 1969 (?), birds and animals from Guyanese folklore including: Mama Pig, Carrion Crow Governor, White Horse and Pet Camoodie, oil on canvas. 120 × 150 cm. Guyana National Museum.

Aubrey Williams, *Warrau 2*, 1972, oil on canvas. 74 × 94 cm. Collection Eve Williams.

Art Derry, *Manzanilla Moon*, 1965, oil on canvas. 51 × 41 cm. Collection Irma La Rose.

Art Derry, *Hosein Festival*, 1964, oil on canvas. 75 × 52 cm. Collection John La Rose and Sarah White.

Paul Dash, *Figures Dancing in the Street*, 1965/6, oil on hardboard. 61 × 81 cm. Collection artist.

Errol Lloyd, *Waiting*, 1970, oil on canvas. 61 × 91 cm. Collection Vera Hyatt.

Errol Lloyd, *The Lesson*, 1972, oil on canvas. 61 × 91 cm. Collection artist.

Errol Lloyd, *Richard Small*, 1968, bronze. Height 30 cm. Collection artist.

Clifton Campbell, *The Man and the Tightrope*, 1964, oil on canvas. 152 × 183 cm. Collection artist.

Clifton Campbell, *The Bird Watcher*, 1964, oil on canvas. 76 × 107 cm. Collection artist.

Winston Branch, *Liberty was my Friend*, 1970, oil on canvas. 244 × 244 cm. Leicestershire Education Authority.

Cover picture Ronald Moody, *Vision*, also known as *Male half figure*, 1944, oak. Height 102 cm. Centre for Black and African Arts and Civilisation, Lagos, Nigeria.

Preface

The Caribbean Artists Movement (CAM) came into being and was active at a 'time of crossroads', as Edward Kamau Brathwaite – one of CAM's founders – has called it. The activities and concerns of CAM, and indeed its character, resulted from a particular historical context. In the 1960s, the decade of Independence, ties between Britain and her former colonies were still strong. The cream of graduates from the University of the West Indies still came to Britain for postgraduate study. Thus there was a substantial number of very able, highly educated West Indian students in Britain for a limited period, with leisure to explore ideas together and to organise artistic events. Already in Britain were other talented West Indians, educated in the best colonial tradition, who had come over before Independence, in the 1950s and early 1960s; a few, even earlier. Some came to study, then stayed on and wrote or painted for a living in Britain; others had already worked as writers at home, and came to Britain to gain more experience and wider recognition. But the vast majority of West Indians came from 1947 onwards: to meet the British post-war labour shortage, and at the same time to get a break from the depressed post-war economy in the West Indies. They had limited education and little experience or aspirations in what were then recognised as 'arts'.

CAM's membership was drawn from all three of these categories. Its leadership came initially from the first two, only later from the third. So the themes with which CAM began reflected the major concerns of highly educated, artistically aware West Indians, reacting against generations of European cultural domination. They sought to discover their own aesthetic and to chart new directions for their arts and culture; to become acquainted with their history; to rehabilitate their Amerindian inheritance and to reinstate their African roots; to reestablish links with the 'folk' through incorporating the peoples' language and musical rhythms in Caribbean literature; to reassert their own tradition in the face of the dominant tradition.

In London in the mid-1960s major writers and artists were seeking and developing new forms and language for Caribbean arts: Wilson Harris in fiction, Brathwaite in poetry, Ronald Moody in sculpture, Aubrey Williams in painting. They, and the writers John La Rose, Andrew Salkey and Orlando Patterson, playwright and filmwriter Evan Jones, and critic Louis James, came together to form CAM. The movement drew a wide range of men and women who had been born in the British West Indies but were now living in Britain, from CLR James to Linton Kwesi Johnson.

CAM bridged the transformation of Britain's West Indian community from one of exiles and immigrants to black British. CAM educated, in the widest sense, all who took part in it or were touched by it. It set the stage for trends now dominant in Caribbean arts, especially in poetry with its stress on orality and performance, its use of 'nation language' and the rhythms of everyday speech. It foreshadowed many of the directions of the so-called 'black arts' in Britain.

Perhaps as a result of its very breadth of reach, and what Andrew Salkey – with John La Rose, Brathwaite's fellow founder – called its 'mirage-like structure', CAM is curiously absent in cultural histories of the period, both of Britain and the Caribbean. Those of Britain which deal, for example, with the arts or with student revolt in the 1960s, ignore or marginalise Caribbean and black activity, just as British writers' and journalists' involvement in CAM events at the time was minimal. Books on Caribbean art, dance, and drama overlook the contribution of CAM and the significance of its artists. Critical writing on Caribbean literature scarcely mentions the talks and debates at CAM's public sessions and conferences; bibliographies omit seminal CAM papers, even when they were published in its *Newsletter* or its journal, *Savacou*. The only published accounts of CAM have appeared in Caribbean or black/multicultural British journals. The few references to CAM in books on the development of black arts in Britain tend to be limited and partial. No wonder, then, that the black writers and artists born in Britain after 1960 tend to believe that black arts began in the 1970s, and are almost wholly ignorant of what went before.

Just as the founder-members of CAM consciously named themselves a movement, so they were aware of the historical value of its talks, discussions, exhibitions and other activities. Sessions were recorded from the start, and the tapes have been carefully stored. Notices of CAM sessions and correspondence were filed and carefully preserved. CAM's founder-members always envisaged that its history would, in time, be fully documented and made public.

As the person entrusted with this archive material, my prime aim has been to record what was said and what happened in CAM as accurately as possible, and to attempt to place it in context. I have let others speak whenever feasible, and have tried to confine my own part to that of unobtrusive narrator. Inevitably, though, my linking commentary attempts to disclose a pattern of events and developments. But I have deliberately avoided theoretical analysis of CAM, in the belief that this would constrict and distort it. This documentary history will, I hope, provide information and a framework from which others may write the many related studies which CAM stimulates and abundantly deserves. Such studies might well include a detailed look at the work of leading CAM writers and artists in order to establish whether there was indeed an implicit ideology, a shared Caribbean aesthetic. There is need for surveys and critical analyses of the cultural areas in which CAM members were primarily active, from the historical perspective of 25 years on. And there is need also for an account of the regional character of CAM – its West Indianness and its strong sense of being pan-Caribbean, now apparently and perhaps inevitably, in Britain at least, almost entirely lost or subsumed in 'Blackness'.

Limitations and imbalance should be mentioned. CAM public sessions, including conferences, were recorded regularly from March 1967 to September 1968, spasmodically thereafter, so that public debate is covered more fully in the earlier phases of CAM. Very few private sessions were recorded, nor were the 'warishis' which took place at members' homes after public sessions; it was here, according to those who attended them, that the 'real' CAM happened – hence La Rose's claim that it is impossible to tell the full story of CAM. Similarly, letters record how things were done, by whom, how people and events were regarded; but telephone calls and face-to-face conversations have left nothing behind. While Brathwaite as CAM secretary communicated mainly through letters – dated, with carbon copies – Salkey and La Rose, and, later Donald Hinds and James Berry, did so mainly by phone or by meeting, and thus the picture of how CAM operated may to some extent be unbalanced.

Another prime source of information about CAM is the people who were members, who participated in it, or whose work was touched by it. But taped interviews are unreliable; peoples' memories of what happened 20 or more years ago are often blurred. Those more closely involved with CAM may be tempted to superimpose what they wish had happened. And my research began too late for adequate or indeed any memories by several key people. CLR James was over 80, and aware that he could no longer remember people and events as clearly as before. As he told me: 'I have problems now that four years ago I didn't have. I'm not worrying about it at all but that's how it is.' Ronald Moody had died in 1984, aged 80. A major treasury of CAM memories was lost with the death of Doris Brathwaite in 1986, aged 60; this account of CAM is much the poorer without her.

There is also the limitation that I am not myself from the Caribbean. I cannot write about CAM with the confidence and sense of personal involvement of one's own people making history, evident in, say, Nathan Huggins's account of the Harlem Renaissance. I was not part of the inner circle of CAM in its most dynamic early years; I attended few of its 'warishis' at members' homes. But I was an active member of CAM from 1967 onwards. References to myself are in the third person in order to be less obtrusive. Like so many fellow members, the things I learnt and came to understand through CAM, the working friendships made there, have remained lively and productive. CAM has proved the springboard of much of my subsequent work. The research for this book has involved me in CAM all over again, at a much deeper and more comprehensive level. I hope that some of this shows in what I have written. Most of all I hope that this attempt to present a documentary history will reinforce the CAM experience for those who were part of it, and will give those who were not – and especially those who came after it – something of CAM to encourage their own work.

Anne Walmsley
London, February 1992

1 The Background
Caribbean People in Britain

Artists Movement

The initiatives which resulted in the formation of the Caribbean Artists Movement (CAM) in late 1966 came from three Caribbean writers. Two had recently arrived in Britain – Edward (now Kamau) Brathwaite in 1965 and John La Rose in 1961. The third, Andrew Salkey, had worked in London since 1952. Brathwaite had already spent four years in Britain, as a student at Cambridge in the early 1950s. Once formed, CAM drew in Caribbean people with cultural interests and ambitions who had lived in Britain from the 1920s onwards. Some had come in order to study, some in search of work or better opportunities. Others came because of political pressures at home. Their social and educational backgrounds, their interests and experience, varied widely, and so in consequence did the type of work open to them, and the sort of work which they wanted to do. Moreover the climate and opportunities for Caribbean people in Britain changed with each decade, especially after the Second World War. A glance at some of the leading cultural figures at work in Britain over this 50-year period will both set the scene for the formation of CAM, and introduce its players.

The 1920s and 1930s

For Ronald Moody and CLR James, born in 1900 and 1901, going to Britain was the only option for ambitious young men from black middle-class homes and the best colonial secondary schools. Even Jamaica and Trinidad, the most populous British West Indian islands, had no higher education institutions in the 1920s. The University of the West Indies (UWI), for its first 15 years the University College of the West Indies (UCWI), affiliated to London University, was not opened until 1947; local facilities for professional training followed: Medicine was early, and Law came in 1963 with the establishment of the Faculty of Law on the Barbados campus. Not until the 1950s was there a Jamaica School of Art, not until the 1970s, a School of Drama.

Ronald Moody came to London from Jamaica in 1923, to study dentistry: more because professional training was open to him and expected of him as the youngest of a prominent, middle-class Kingston family, than because he was enthusiastic about this or any recognised career. Alongside his studies at the Royal Dental Hospital, London, he read widely in philosophy – from Plato to the metaphysics of China and India – and haunted the museums and art galleries of London. It was during a chance visit to the Egyptian Rooms of the British Museum in 1928 that – as he later explained – he suddenly knew, without any doubt, that sculpture was the only thing he wanted to do: the result of his response to 'the tremendous inner force, the irresistible movement in stillness, which some of the [Egyptian] pieces possessed'.[1] While still a student, he began experimenting with moulding imaginative faces in plasticine. Soon after he qualified as a dentist in 1930, and had set up in practice in Cavendish Place, London W1, he planned and carved his first sculpture in wood. It was a head, 18 inches in height, in oak, which he called Wohin ('Whither' from the title of a song by Schubert). It was bought by an art critic, Marie Seton, and led to a one-man show of Moody's work in Paris, October 1937, then in Amsterdam, January 1938. Such was the response to his work, especially from French critics, that he decided to move to Paris, where he married Helene Coppel-Cowan, an English painter, and a friend from his early years in London. Two years of prolific, outstanding work and of growing acclaim were cut short when, in June 1940, Paris fell to the Germans. Moody and his wife got out, just in time, leaving everything. Their escape across occupied France was long and arduous, compounded by ill-health. In Marseilles Moody contracted pleurisy, and, when he was scarcely better, made his first unsuccessful attempt to cross the Pyrennees into Spain. He then persuaded his wife to accept repatriation, while he made two further attempts, the third of which was successful. He eventually reached Britain in October 1941.

Harold Arundel Moody, Ronald's eldest brother, had lived in Britain since training and qualifying as a doctor at King's College Hospital in 1910. Because of the racial prejudice and discrimination which he observed and personally encountered in British society, he founded the League of Coloured Peoples in 1931, and was its President until his death in 1947. Ronald, who regarded himself as the rebel, artistic younger brother, something of the black sheep in a family of distinguished, high-flying professionals, admired his brother's anti-racist work, but himself distrusted any sort of political or social activism or alignment. From his early days in London he moved amongst writers and artists, and would have found himself, as a sculptor, relatively cushioned from racial discrimination.

CLR James came to Britain from Trinidad in 1932, encouraged by Learie Constantine, 'an old acquaintance and cricketing opponent',[2] and left, for the United States, in 1938. James's extraordinarily prolific and varied achievements during his initial stay in Britain indicate something of the climate and opportunities open in the 1930s to a black Caribbean intellectual. He remembers how,

> I had written *The Life of Captain Cipriani* in the Caribbean, I brought it to England. I published it in Nelson, Lancashire, where Constantine was. I sent it to the Caribbean. And I sent a copy to Leonard Woolf, and he said, 'I would like to publish this, but not all of it.' I said, 'Go right ahead.' So he took what he wanted and made *The Case for West Indian Self-Government* which, by the way, has had a tremendous effect.

James then wrote, and found publishers for: *Minty Alley* (1936); *World Revolution 1917–1936: The Rise and Fall of the Communist International* (1937); *The Black Jacobins: Toussaint L'Ouverture, and the San Domingo Revolution* (1938), *A History of Negro Revolt* (1938). He also wrote and took part, with Paul Robeson, in a play, *Toussaint L'Ouverture*, at the Westminster Theatre, London, in 1936. The entire compass of his early writing found not just an audience, but opportunities to earn money in Britain. He was able to live from work as a cricket correspondent first for the *Manchester Guardian*. and then for the *Glasgow Herald*.

Meanwhile, James explains, 'I got swept into politics here. I came here in 1932. Hitler came into power in 1933 and the world had been demolished. The contemporary world had been swept into politics, political life. . . . And I had a good historical background, so I was able to move into politics.' He was active in both British and international politics: first in the Independent Labour Party, then in the Revolutionary Socialist League, writing for the paper of the first, and editing the newspaper of the second. He took part in the movement of the unemployed, and made speaking tours throughout Britain. He contributed to the growth of the Trotskyist movement in France, and was one of the British delegates to the founding conference of the Fourth International in 1938. His particular involvement in African politics began when, in 1937, he became editor of the journal of the International African Service Bureau, whose founder and chairman was his childhood friend, George Padmore. He chaired the International African Friends of Abyssinia during the Italian Invasion in 1936, and agitated amongst British workers for action through solidarity.

The 1940s

After the end of the Second World War, in 1945, there began substantial migration from the West Indies to Britain of a social class very different from that of James and the Moody brothers. In 1948 three boats containing a total of around 700 West Indian men and women arrived in British ports, in search of work and a better life. They were mostly in their twenties, with skills and initiative, but with elementary (primary) schooling only and from a working-class background. The British postwar economy was run down and short of labour; jobs were easily found by these and similar numbers of West Indians arriving in 1949 and 1950. Their British passports gave them the right to come to Britain, to live and work there; this was confirmed by the 1948 Nationality Act which granted United Kingdom citizenship to citizens of Britain's colonies and former colonies.

James Berry arrived from Jamaica on the second 1948 boat, the *Orbita*. He recalls, 'My friend came in the June on the *Windrush*, and then I said, look, the next ship, I'll be on it. And I was.' Berry was then about 20, and had already worked for four years in the USA as a contract labourer on farms and in factories. England provided his first chance to meet people from other parts of the West Indies. It also enabled him to meet West Indians from other social levels, as an equal:

> It was really fascinating to begin to meet fellows from the other islands – Barbadians and Trinidadians and so on. The house I lived in, in Somerleyton Road, Brixton, had people who had come over for the first time. . . . And I remember two brothers from Trinidad who were civil servants. They'd come over for six months on that civil servant sort of thing [so-called 'home leave'].

Multiple West Indian occupancy of houses became common as a result of the entrenched racial prejudice of most British property owners.

The Second World War itself had provided working-class West Indians with a chance to come to Britain – with the armed forces. Barrington Johnson (now Bari Jonson) joined up with the Royal Air Force in 1944; he was under age, but his father, who had been through the First World War, encouraged him, knowing that there would be opportunities in Britain for studying and so on which were not available to someone of his background in Jamaica. Jonson followed a course in mechanical engineering at Brighton Technical College, and took dancing lessons. After two years, he abandoned the course and joined *Ballet Nègre*, the London-based dance company formed by Berto Pasuka, a fellow Jamaican.

Meanwhile increasing numbers of middle-class West Indians came over to Britain to study. Those who enrolled at London University in September 1945 included for the first time a significant number of women, amongst them – to read history – Elsa Goveia from British Guiana (now Guyana) and Lucille Walrond (now Lucille Mathurin Mair) from Jamaica, daughter of the Harlem Renaissance writer Eric Walrond; their fellow students came from all the countries of the then British West Indies. In December 1945, 113 such students registered for the first West Indian Students Conference, held at St Peter's Church Hall,

James Berry (centre) and Bari Jonson (right) with friends in London in the 1950s

Belsize Park, and formed the West Indian Students Union (WISU). Its early activities included a deputation to the Secretary of State for the Colonies in November 1946 on the question of the establishment of a West Indian university; a bi-annual newsletter, whose aims included 'to help build up a Caribbean culture of our own'; talks on individual West Indian territories; a study group on the economic history and development of the West Indies led by Dr W Arthur Lewis of St Lucia, then teaching at the London School of Economics (LSE) – of which Goveia wrote at the time: 'This is a field of study entirely new to most of us . . . and we are more than ever convinced that a people must know something of its past in order to plan for the future.'[3]

Pearl Nunez (soon Connor, now Mogotsi) came from Trinidad to Britain in 1948 as a student: first at the Central London Polytechnic, then at London University. But very early in her student life she married the already famous singer, actor and filmstar Edric Connor, and found herself amongst the West Indian intellectual and artistic elite of London:

> I was a courier taking him around when he visited Trinidad in '48. . . . And when I came here, he kind of hosted me and introduced me round, and in no time at all it was a romance. And in no time at all it was a marriage. And there I was, plonked into the middle of his own cultural life, which meant a Caribbean life, because he was very involved with the West Indian and Caribbean people throughout his life here.

Pearl Connor also had an entrée to this Caribbean cultural life in her own right; in Trinidad she had broadcast biographies of distinguished Caribbean people, at the instigation of Beryl McBurnie, the pioneer of dance and founder of the Little Carib Theatre in Trinidad. She came over to London with letters of introduction to the BBC, and was inevitably drawn into work with the BBC Caribbean Service and its weekly programme, *Caribbean Voices*.

This programme had been started by Una Marson, Jamaican 'poet, journalist, editor, broadcaster, social worker, feminist'.[4] Returning to England in 1938, Marson allied herself particularly with Harold Moody's League of Coloured Peoples. She worked with the BBC first as a script-writer and then during the Second World War as producer of a programme called 'Calling the West Indies'. This popular programme enabled West Indian servicemen who were based in London to maintain contact with friends and family back home. Marson's 'flair for organising and wide range of literary contacts in Jamaica soon led to the transformation of the programme into a cultural feature, making use of West Indian artistes and material available in Britain at the time'.[5] By the time Marson returned to Jamaica in 1946, the programme had become an almost exclusively literary magazine, drawing its material from the whole of the West Indies via Cedric Lindo, a Jamaican journalist who forwarded a selection of what he had collected to London. Henry Swanzy, an Irishman on the BBC staff, took over as producer of the programme under its new name, *Caribbean Voices*, in August 1946, and was responsible for it for the next eight years. The half-hour long programme was broadcast from London on Sundays at 23.15 GMT, and heard in the West Indies on Sunday afternoons. It broadcast (and paid for) new writing by West Indians, in the West Indies and in Britain; it applied criticism to the new writing, through editorial selection, comment and critical symposia; it used West Indians in Britain to read and comment on the writing which was broadcast.

Pearl Connor had easy access to *Caribbean Voices*, through her background and connections. James Berry had no such access. The very different social levels of West Indian society at which Berry and Connor moved in Britain also resulted in contrasting experiences of West Indian social and cultural organisations in the late 1940s and early 1950s. Berry recalls:

> I was the secretary of an organisation there [round Paddington] called the Africa and Caribbean Social and Cultural Centre, which was started by Millard Johnson. . . . It was social and cultural, and of course could not help being political. The old man, Norman Manley, when he came over, he came there and talked. And the Kabaka [of Buganda]. Everybody who came over who was important, came and talked. Millard Johnson was political and very active.

Connor remembers less formally organised meetings of friends from their circle in their homes:

> There were a lot of cultural groups, a lot of organisations. I was often invited to what you call, not soirées, but little gatherings. I would say they were quite politicised. They were involved with independence so they were bringing together all the forces belong-

> ing to the country – cultural, artistic etc, who would matter in the future Caribbean nation. . . . A lot of the meetings happened in our house, because we had space and Edric was wellknown.

'Politics' to both groups meant involvement with preparations for the independence of West Indian colonies. Members of the Connor circle 'were concerned with going back, we always meant to go back and contribute, you know. Go back and build a nation, there, not here'. Members of organisations such as the African and Caribbean Social and Cultural Centre were equally concerned with problems which West Indians in Britain were experiencing in their day-to-day lives, primarily in housing and at work. Alongside was a network of West Indian social and cultural groups, organised to promote the welfare of West Indian immigrants, in all the areas of London and the major cities in which they had settled. Both the Berry and Connor types of groups were involved with independence not only 'at home', but also in Africa; leaders from Africa and Asia as well as from the Caribbean spoke to them. Berry considers this unusual at the time: 'Caribbean people had very few links with Africa. But somehow it was developing.' Connor had a similar experience, at another level: 'We were meeting other Commonwealth peoples and a lot of Africans, of course. The Kenyatta trial was going on. Thompson from Jamaica had come for it, and so on. So we were involved with Africa and the Caribbean – our roots, that's to say.' Both types of groups held meetings in the spirit of the October 1945 Fifth Pan-African Congress in Manchester, when CLR James (back in Britain from the USA specially for it) and George Padmore, alongside Jomo Kenyatta and Kwame Nkrumah, pledged themselves to 'the liquidation of colonialism and imperialism'. In its 'Challenge to the Colonial Powers', the congress not only asserted, 'We are determined to be free,' it condemned 'the monopoly of capital and the rule of private wealth and industry for private profit alone.'[6]

CLR James's base throughout the 1940s was in the USA. Ronald Moody spent the 1940s back in London trying to recover his health, and to resume his work. In wartime London there were few opportunities for continuing work as a sculptor. Suitable wood was scarce; so was time, between work as a dental surgeon with the Public Health Department and Civil Defence duties. As soon as the war was over he was able to retrieve the work and tools which he had been forced to abandon in Paris, and to take on a garage in London as a studio. The following year, in May 1946, he held a one-man show at the Arcade Gallery, off Bond Street; amongst the new work exhibited was a portrait of his brother, Harold Moody. Directly afterwards, he gave the first three of a planned series of talks on art on the BBC radio programme, 'Calling the West Indies'. In December he again visited Paris, hoping to arrange an exhibition there. Everything seemed set for more work and more exposure. But in February 1947 he fell seriously ill with tuberculosis. The next three years were dogged by illness; despite frequent attempts to resume work, and invitations to exhibit in London and Paris, not until late 1949 was he able to take up again his sculpture, his broadcasts, and to re-schedule exhibitions.

Towards the end of the war, another Jamaican had settled in London and taken up sculpture. Namba Roy was born in 1910 into the Maroons of Accompong, where his father and grandfather were hereditary carvers and storytellers, and carried on the traditions of their Congolese forebears. Roy had served as a volunteer with the British Merchant Marines until he was torpedoed and invalided out in 1944. He decided to live in Britain rather than return to Jamaica, and made his home in London where, alongside whatever unskilled manual employment was available to him, he set himself to carve in wood and in ivory, to paint, and to write.

The 1950s

The number of West Indians coming to Britain in search of work gradually increased in the early 1950s, with some 2000 arriving in 1952 and a similar number in 1953. Thereafter the numbers rapidly increased, so that by 1958 some 125,000 West Indians had come to Britain since the end of the war.[7] This was the result of continuing impoverished living conditions and poor economic prospects in the West Indies; of stringent restrictions on immigration to the USA in 1952 with the passing of the McCarran Act; of positive encouragement by British industry to West Indians to come over and meet the postwar labour shortage. Although the jobs on offer, or for which West Indians had to settle, were almost always far below those which they were skilled in, prospects still seemed better than what they left behind.

Some of those who came from the Caribbean to Britain as immigrants in the 1950s already had an interest, and ambitions, in writing or in art – the predominant art forms practised by those who later became associated with CAM. They hoped that in Britain they would obtain training and experience, a responsive audience, and opportunities to live by the practice of their craft – all of which were severely limited in the West Indies: small, fragmented, and still colonies in name and in cultural orientation.

The writers

Would-be writers already had opportunities of publication in the West Indies, but on a very small scale. Although there was no publishing house, apart from the short-lived Pioneer Press in

Jamaica, poems and short stories had for some time been published by periodicals such as the *Forum Quarterly* in Barbados, *The Beacon* in Trinidad, *The West Indian Review* and *Public Opinion* in Jamaica, and by some national newspapers in their Sunday editions: the Jamaica *Gleaner*, the Trinidad *Guardian* and the British Guiana *Chronicle*. More regular and significant opportunities came in the 'little magazines' of the region: *Bim*, published twice-yearly in Barbados from 1942 onwards; *Focus*, published in Jamaica in 1943, 1948, 1956, 1960; *Kyk-over-al*, published twice-yearly in British Guiana, from 1945 to 1961. Literary material in the form of short fiction – an extract from a novel in progress or a story – critical essays and articles, extracts from plays, and poems, when submitted to one of these magazines was scrutinised by a distinguished and respected editor – Frank Collymore (*Bim*), Edna Manley (*Focus*), Arthur Seymour (*Kyk-over-al*) – and, if selected for publication, read by an attentive, if small, public. Even more prestige and encouragement resulted when work was accepted by the London-based BBC programme, *Caribbean Voices*, and broadcast to the far wider, radio-listening public of the English-speaking Caribbean.

When George Lamming and Samuel Selvon came to Britain from Trinidad on an immigrant ship in 1950, aged 23 and 27, both had had encouragement from these sources. In addition Lamming, who had left Barbados for Trinidad four years earlier, acted there as an agent for *Bim*, while Selvon worked as a sub-editor of the *Trinidad Guardian*'s weekly magazine supplement during the same period. When they came to Britain, Selvon 'had already written a large part of his first novel, *A Brighter Sun*', whereas, continues Lamming, 'fiction was not my ally, and I had left my poems behind'.[8] This first novel of Selvon's and the books which he and Lamming wrote in London during the 1950s were readily accepted for publication. Michael Joseph published Lamming's novels *In the Castle of my Skin* (1953), *The Emigrants* (1954), *Of Age and Innocence* (1958), *Season of Adventure* (1960) and his extended, autobiographical immigrant's essay, *The Pleasures of Exile* (1960). Selvon's first three novels were published by Alan Wingate: *A Brighter Sun* (1952), *An Island is a World* (1955), *The Lonely Londoners* (1956); his next two by MacGibbon and Kee, *Ways of Sunlight* (1957) and *Turn Again Tiger* (1958). With royalties from a steady flow of successfully published books, fees from serialisation and freelance work for BBC radio, for English newspapers and magazines, Selvon was able to become a full-time writer in 1954 – despite losing more than a year's work when he contracted tuberculosis. Lamming seems to have survived as a freelance writer from the start, thanks to regular and substantial work with the BBC; in addition to frequent appearances as author and as reader on *Caribbean Voices*, he regularly produced programmes for the BBC's Overseas Service.

Edward Kamau Brathwaite and VS Naipaul also came to Britain in 1950, but as students, aged 20 and 18. Brathwaite had won a Barbados government scholarship from Harrison College to read history at Cambridge, Naipaul a Trinidad government scholarship from Queen's Royal College to read English at Oxford. Brathwaite was already contributing poems to *Bim* in Barbados; he continued to write, and to be published, while a student at Cambridge. Stuart Hall and Ian McDonald, who followed in 1951 – Hall to Oxford from Jamaica on a Rhodes Scholarship, McDonald to Cambridge from Trinidad – also began to write as students; as with Brathwaite, some of their work was broadcast on *Caribbean Voices*. Naipaul, however, did not begin to write until he had left Oxford and made his home in London. In 1954 Henry Swanzy was taken off *Caribbean Voices* and Naipaul became its editor and presenter, on a part-time basis, for two years. This provided his stimulus to start writing, and was the economic base from which he wrote the stories later published as *Miguel Street* (1959). Before their publication, he also wrote his first two novels – set, like the short stories, in Trinidad: *The Mystic Masseur* (1957) and *The Suffrage of Elvira* (1958).

Michael Anthony came to Britain in 1954 when he was 23, from a black, working-class family in a village on the east coast of Trinidad. Anthony had been encouraged in his aspirations to be a writer by the *Trinidad Guardian*, which published one of his poems in 1951, and in 1952–3, almost everything he sent it. He had been discouraged by *Caribbean Voices*, to which he was a regular listener: 'I knew, when you sent material up, it got as far as Jamaica, and it came back to you from Jamaica, because we had Mr Lindo there who was sorting these things out. It seemed a very hard task.'[9] However, when he reached London, he tried again. His first poems and his first short story were all rejected. VS Naipaul had just become editor.

> I sent a second story and I had a letter from Naipaul saying, 'Will you come and have a talk with me?' And when I went there he said, 'I didn't call you here because I think your story is marvellous. I called you here because your story shows a little bit of promise and mainly because the work we get from the West Indies is so awful. You seem to have something and I think if you keep on writing short stories you will make it. But I don't think your poems have any future at all.' He was very frank, but he was very courteous and I appreciated his regime because all the stories I sent later on were accepted by him.[10]

The circle of Caribbean writers responsible for *Caribbean Voices* was able to help Anthony develop skills and confidence as a writer, which resulted in his three novels published in the 1960s.

Andrew Salkey, who came from Jamaica to Britain in 1952, aged 24, had had work accepted by *Caribbean Voices* since he was at school. Born into a middle-class Kingston family, he was educated at Munro College, a prestigeous boys' boarding school staffed and run on English public school lines. After leaving school he worked in Kingston; he became part of the inner circle of the city's artistic life and his work was regularly accepted by *Caribbean Voices* via Cedric Lindo. With such a background, when he contacted Henry Swanzy on arrival in London, he recalls:

> They employed me as a freelance person to read stuff back to the Caribbean. And I also contributed as a writer. And that was the way that really I got to know people like Edgar [Mittelholzer] who was already on the programme . . . George [Lamming] and Sam Selvon, John Hearne came later, and Jan Carew, Sylvia Wynter. . . . We operated in the Peter Robinson part of Oxford Street, and then the Langham Hotel, in Portland Place.

This work, with other part-time jobs, enabled Salkey to complete a degree in English Literature at London University. And the *Caribbean Voices* involvement provided the basis of his future wealth of creative work as novelist, poet and anthologiser.

Thus would-be writers arriving in Britain from the Caribbean in the 1950s found a range of opportunities and encouragement open to them, especially if they lived in London. Book publishing was experiencing something of a postwar boom; small, young publishing houses were eager to bring out work by fresh, vigorous, new voices from far corners of the Commonwealth, especially those who used English with the fluency, individuality and verve of West Indians. Publishers found a ready market for books about these writers' tropical home environment and society, despite their containing much implicit and, especially in the work of Lamming, explicit criticism of colonialism. Books which reflected the new phenomenon of West Indians making their home in London also found an audience. The market was as yet mainly in Britain itself.

Meanwhile *Caribbean Voices* continued to provide regular, open access to radio publication. It was also in effect a fledgling school in creative writing, and a broad-based literary club. VS Naipaul has described how he wrote his first attempt at a short story there:

> The Caribbean Service was on the second floor of what had been the Langham Hotel, opposite Broadcasting House. On this floor the BBC had set aside a room for people like me, 'freelances'. . . . People were in and out of the freelances' room while I typed. Some would have dropped by at the BBC that afternoon for the company and the chat, and the off-chance of a commission by a producer for some little script. . . . The freelances' room was like a club: chat,

> movement, the separate anxieties of young or youngish men below the passing fellowship of the room. . . . And I benefited from the fellowship of the room that afternoon. Without that fellowship, without the response of the three men [John Stockbridge, Andrew Salkey, Gordon Woolford] who read the story, I might not have wanted to go on with what I had begun. I passed the three typed sheets around.[11]

John Figueroa was closely associated with *Caribbean Voices*, as poet and critic, until his return to Jamaica in 1953 to take up the post of Senior Lecturer in Education at UCWI. He has described how 'the production of this programme offered to West Indians in London an opportunity to meet English and African writers and to discuss West Indian literature in particular and writing and art in general. Henry Swanzy, for instance, and myself held regular open-house meetings in connection with the programme.'[12] Edgar Mittelholzer, born in British Guiana, replaced Naipaul as editor of *Caribbean Voices* in October 1956; he had just returned to London after four years in Canada and Barbados, a successful professional writer. Two years later the BBC decided that the programme had served its purpose and closed it, in April 1958.

BBC Caribbean Service Tribute to Edgar Mittelholzer, May 1965 (l to r) Henry Swanzy, George Lamming, Andrew Salkey, Jan Carew, Sam Selvon

Caribbean Voices, and the BBC Caribbean Service of which it was part, also provided an important outlet and source of employment for writers and others working in theatre, in London at least. Pearl Connor recalls how 'we were doing plays by Naipaul, Selvon and Salkey'; together with Nadia Cattouse, from British Honduras (now Belize), and Carmen Munro, from British Guiana, 'we were all the early bright brigade of broadcasters'.

Meanwhile Edric Connor 'was always trying to put on [stage] productions'. Pearl recalls how, before venues such as the Africa Centre and West Indian Students Centre were available, he and Horace James, also from Trinidad, used a church hall in Hampstead, or hired a hall near Leicester Square. When the British Council premises opened in Hans Crescent they used its small theatre, mounting plays by contemporary West Indian writers such as Errol John, Errol Hill and Derek Walcott.

Good parts for West Indian actors in stage productions tended to be limited to West Indian plays. Lloyd Reckord, from a middle-class Jamaican background, came to Britain in 1951; he trained and performed with the Bristol Old Vic School for three years, then left to take up a scholarship for further study in the USA. From 1957 onwards he travelled back and forth between Britain and Jamaica, according to specific productions which he was asked to direct or act in. For example, in 1959, he played the lead in *Flesh to a Tiger* by the playwright Barry Reckord, his brother, at the Royal Court Theatre. But even a West Indian play did not ensure parts for West Indian actors. Mervyn Morris, a Jamaican Rhodes Scholar at Oxford from 1958 to 1961, was appalled to find that in a stage production of Errol John's play, *Moon on a Rainbow Shawl*, neither of the principals was Trinidadian, and one was American.

Edric and Pearl Connor at a film premiere in the 1950s

Bari Jonson's experience was different. His work as a dancer took him into the theatre world generally. Although he had no formal training in drama – he could not afford it at the time – he found that when mainstream British productions needed a black actor, 'of course they were glad to have people who could speak and so on on stage. But many times you found that just being black was enough'. His breakthrough on stage came when he played Joseph Asagai in *A Raisin in the Sun* by Lorraine Hansbury, at the Adelphi Theatre in London's West End, in 1959. 'I was the leading black actor from Britain. And I stole the raves, as they say.' After that he stopped dancing; he worked as an actor 'pretty regularly. . . . The opportunities were not necessarily the good parts one would have expected to get, but one made a living at them'. Jonson was not much involved in the West Indian plays produced in London at this time.

Evan Jones, from a Jamaica-Welsh planter family, made his debut on *Caribbean Voices* as a poet; 'Song of the Banana Man' was broadcast in 1952, while he was at Oxford. When he took up residence in London in 1956, he set about making a living as a playwright and scriptwriter, initially for stage, radio and television, from 1961 also for film. He wrote what he was offered or commissioned. There were few requests for West Indian scripts; if there had been more he would, he says, have been glad to do them. Because his prime aim was to be a professional writer, and because he proved himself able to produce scripts on a wide range of material and topics, he avoided being type-cast as a 'black' writer.

The artists

The situation for people coming to Britain from the Caribbean with ambitions and talents as visual artists was different in almost every way from that of writers. At school in the Caribbean, art was a soft option, a non-academic subject, with none of the status of English, whose language and literature were central to the British colonial heritage. People could leave school knowing a good deal about literature: English and American, and classics of European literature. They could be fluent and confident at expressing themselves in English. But they could leave without having looked at or discussed any formal manifestations of the visual arts; galleries of work by local artists were rare, even the concept of being an artist, of making a living as an artist, was almost unknown. After leaving school, opportunities for learning art techniques, of exposure and sales to viewers were very limited. The art training available in the West Indies in the 1950s taught people to express themselves in traditional figurative ways. ER Burrowes's Working Peoples Art Group in British Guiana, Edna Manley's classes at the Institute of Jamaica, Harry Simmons in St Lucia, were amongst the pioneering teachers; the classes and annual exhibitions of the Trinidad and Tobago Art Society likewise played an important role. Art collectors such as Jack Kelshall in Trinidad and AD Scott in Jamaica were also important in fostering the work of local artists. In Jamaica especially, people were encouraged to produce in painting or sculpture a visual response to their own people and environment, equivalent to the 'nativisation of consciousness'[13] which was becoming apparent in literature; both were part of the movement of cultural nationalism in the build-up to independence. After their arrival in Britain, few people had the confidence, or courage, to become artists on their own; most went through rigorous training at an art school, inevitably a training in European art, when they had their first encounter with an overwhelming range of twentieth-century art movements and styles. There were for artists no equivalents of book publishers or magazines or literary agents. The only means of displaying and selling their work to an audience was in a gallery, and very few galleries would risk showing unknown artists from any part of the Commonwealth. Nor was there any sort of equivalent for artists of the BBC *Caribbean Voices*, with the mutual support and encouragement and the ready-made forum for discussion which it gave to writers.

In 1952, Aubrey Williams came to Britain from British Guiana, on six months' leave from the department of agriculture where he was a field officer. He was already a painter. As a child in Georgetown, he was producing drawings and paintings of outstanding promise which drew the encouragement of Mr De Wynter, a Dutch art restorer in the churches of British Guiana, and of ER Burrowes at the Working Peoples Art Group. But it was, claims Williams, while working as an agricultural instructor amongst Amerindians in the interior, that he had his first real training in art:

> It was in the North West District, among the Warrau Indians, that I really stumbled upon art. When I heard the Indians talking about colour and form, and how man makes things according to his own image, I started to understand what art really is. It is at once the evocation of something that has never been in the world before – and yet nothing really new, just rearrangement. During this period I did a tremendous lot of painting which I then destroyed.

He returned to Georgetown into the ferment and tensions of the pre-independence struggle, the earliest and fiercest in the West Indies. All his intellectual friends had joined the Peoples Progressive Party (PPP) which was at the forefront of the struggle, led by Cheddi Jagan and Forbes Burnham. Williams's earlier work on the East Coast was investigated and he was accused of having created farmers' communes, in consequence of his personal friendship with Jagan. Williams was strongly advised by a friend in the PPP to get away to England. The British government, prompted by the Americans, had become increasingly nervous about the radical policies and intentions of the PPP. A few months after the massive PPP victory in the first General Election to be held under universal adult suffrage, British troops moved into the colony; the Guianese constitution was suspended, a State of Emergency was declared, and all the PPP leadership – including many of Williams's colleagues and friends – were put in jail.

Aubrey Williams was 26 when he came to Britain. After an abortive start in agricultural engineering at Leicester – 'Why have you come here? We can't teach you anything', was, he remembers, the comment of one of his teachers – he used the money he had saved to travel and see as much as he could, on the Continent and in Britain. In 1954 and 1955 he was a student at St Martin's School of Art, but he did not sign on for a third year, because he did not want its diploma. Also, he was painting increasingly in an abstract style and considered that the figurative art taught at St Martin's restricted his vision. He held his first one-man show at the Archer Gallery, in 1954, while a first-year student. This gallery, run by Dr Mary Morris in Westbourne Grove, also held exhibitions of work by Namba Roy in 1952 and 1955. Williams had meanwhile married Eve Lafargue, who had joined him from British Guiana; it was she who persuaded him – and enabled him – in the mid-1950s to give up part-time factory and cafe work in order to paint full-time.

A turning point came for Williams when he showed his work to Denis Bowen, the South African painter and teacher, founder (in 1951) of the New Vision Group (NVG). The group was open to any artist interested primarily in non-figurative work and to all nationalities, and provided such artists with opportunities to show their work. Margaret Garlake, in her history of New Vision, explains: 'The practice of giving unknown, young, foreign artists one-man shows was almost unique in London at that time and was only possible because the gallery was a non-profit-making organisation. Few commercial galleries were interested in non-figurative

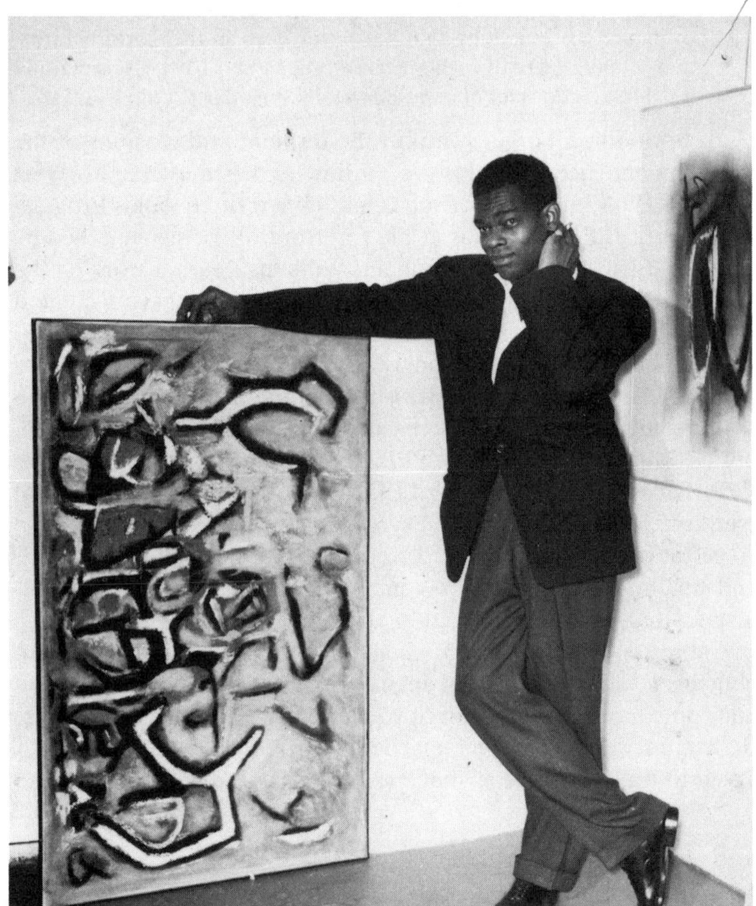

Aubrey Williams preparing for an exhibition at the New Vision Gallery in 1958, with 'El Dorado' propped on the floor

art.'[14] Bowen included work by Aubrey Williams in the New Vision '58 Open Exhibition early in 1958, in all its venues: at the New Vision Centre Gallery (NVCG), two basement rooms at 4 Seymour Place, Marble Arch; at the Coffee Houses in Kingsway and Northumberland Avenue, and at the Polish YMCA. In August 1958 Williams exhibited at the NVCG with one other painter; in August 1959 and November 1960, he held one-man shows there. Exposure at the NVCG, and the companionship and help of other artists in the NVG, were his best possible entrée into the London and international art scene. The 1958 show led to invitations to exhibit in Paris, Milan and Chicago. Williams's work of this period is described as having been 'highly expressive gestural abstraction';[15] it carried titles from the Guiana interior – Arawak, Wanaima, Tumatu Mari – and sold very well. Reviews by British critics tended to stress its exotic character, with references to 'tropical forests and primeval ritual dances'.[16] But Jan Carew – a fellow Guyanese, well established in London as writer and critic since the 1940s – was able to write about Williams's work with insight and understanding.

In the 1950s Ronald Moody, now in better health, also exhibited frequently; as a sculptor, mainly of portraits, he had access to a range of commercial galleries denied to Williams. He held a one-man show in Paris in 1950, and took part in many annual group shows in the West End of London. In 1958 he was elected to the Council of the Society of Portrait Sculptors. Part-time work as a dental surgeon – he was on the London County Council list from 1954 to 1972 – supplemented what he earned as a sculptor. In 1958 the Chelsea Borough Council offered him a purpose-built, low-rent studio where he worked for the next 25 years. His apprenticeship in sculpture was long past; now in turn he gave encouragement and help to Namba Roy as a sculptor in ivory.

Three artists who came to Britain from Trinidad in the early 1950s exemplify the contrast in opportunities in art for people from different backgrounds. Art Derry came in 1954, in his twenties, from a black working-class family in San Juan, a small town near Port of Spain. He had worked there as a commercial artist in advertising, painting in his spare time. In Britain he was unable to get similarly skilled work, and had to take jobs such as sign-writing; as he explains, 'It's just that simply I didn't know anybody.' But he used to paint when he got home, and he started to exhibit in 1956. 'I bought a copy of the *Arts Review* and saw the Hammersmith Galleries advertising for painters and I went out to the Hammersmith Galleries and I got an exhibition.' It was a one-man show, at which he sold 'a lot of work'. The previous year, he had enrolled at the Hornsey College of Art, but soon left, on the advice of one of his teachers, who said: 'You leave this college before you get ruined. You've got a natural way of expressing yourself, and we'll take it out of you before you've finished.' In his early years in London, without formal training and through his own initiatives, Derry found encouragement and response from British selectors and purchasers.

When Althea McNish came with her mother from Trinidad in the early 1950s, to join her father in London, she had a place, and family financial backing, to study at the Architectural Association School in Bedford Square. Instead, she decided to do a course in illustration, commercial art and cartography at the London College of Printing. From there she went on to the Royal College of Art, where she specialised in textile design, followed by a postgraduate scholarship. In Port of Spain she and her family had many friends in the artistic, intellectual middle class; now at her family's home in London, Edric and Pearl Connor, George Lamming and many other writers and artists were frequent visitors. With such ability and opportunities, a secure home in London and good family connections, and an art form which made use of her Caribbean background, she was immediately successful as a textile designer.

> Textiles are something in which you have to hawk your work around, you have to approach people who might be interested in your work. . . . I would have to prepare a complete collection to show to buyers. And several letters were written, some from my father's office, and introductions like this which were extremely useful. And other people like Sir Hugh Casson, he was one of the tutors at the Royal College, liked my work very much, he introduced me to several architects. . . . And of course Liberty's was one of the first people that I saw, and that was an introduction through my father.

Knolly La Fortune came from Trinidad to London in 1954, to take up a teacher's scholarship to study art at Goldsmith's College. Alongside working as a school teacher in Port of Spain, he had been active in art and literature; a member of the Readers' and Writers' Guild, Secretary of the Art Teachers' Movement, and a member of the Trinidad and Tobago Art Society – through which he saw the work of and met the British Guiana-born sculptor, Karl Broodhagen, who lived in Barbados; the England-born sculptress, Edna Manley, wife of Norman Manley of Jamaica; and Dunstan St Omer, the painter from St Lucia. At Goldsmiths, he exhibited paintings and continued to write. He returned to Trinidad in 1957 as a qualified art teacher. But his active support for the Peoples National Movement, led by Dr Eric Williams, in the run-up to Independence, offended the Roman Catholic teaching hierarchy, which blocked his advancement. So he returned to Britain in 1959, for further study alongside teaching.

The students
An exact contemporary of Edward Kamau Brathwaite as a student at Cambridge was Antony Haynes, also from Barbados. They had been together at Harrison College without knowing each other. Brathwaite remembers how Haynes, from a 300 year-old white planter family, was reputed to have one of the two highest IQs in the school, and took a full part in all the Modern Sixth activities. They got to know each other at Cambridge – they were both at Pembroke College. Haynes, who read economics, has a particular memory of Brathwaite: 'I remember his introducing me to modern jazz because, whereas I was interested in classical jazz, he used to play marvellously progressive people worth knowing: Coleman Hawkins, or someone like that.' Ian McDonald, a year later was, like Brathwaite, reading history. He recalls Brathwaite being 'obviously devoted to writing and literature', while Brathwaite recalls encouraging him in his writing, and being responsible for publication of his first poems in Cambridge.

The link between all three students was Bryan King, Fellow of Pembroke College, university lecturer in jurisprudence. King, like Haynes, white, but from St Kitts, had been the British Council representative in Barbados in the mid-1940s, and was passionately concerned with the people and culture of the West Indies. McDonald recalls how King's 'rooms in Pembroke were famous for all West Indians . . . not only in Cambridge, but in London, and all over England. Any West Indian who wanted anything would go to Bryan King'. As Brathwaite puts it, 'Bryan King was our godfather at Cambridge. I like many other Bajans chose not only Cambridge but Pembroke because we had heard of him.' He recalls George Lamming often coming to see King, and their first meeting soon after publication of *In the Castle of my Skin*. Many meetings of the West Indian Society, of which King was Treasurer, were held in his rooms; Brathwaite and McDonald were President in successive years.

Brathwaite's first long poem written in Cambridge is dedicated to Bryan King.[17] His writing of that time found a variety of outlets. Poetry and prose continued to appear in *Bim*; individual poems were accepted by various Cambridge publications, and a selection was included in *Poetry from Cambridge, 1947–50* in 1951.[18] His work was broadcast from time to time on *Caribbean Voices*; in consequence, Brathwaite invited Henry Swanzy to speak about Caribbean writing, in response to a paper by himself, to a group in Cambridge. Swanzy particularly remembered that Brathwaite 'did have a wonderful thing with "The Boy and the Sea", a sort of novella which was prose, which was absolutely brilliant, I thought; you could smell the sea in it.'

Meanwhile Stuart Hall was contributing to *Caribbean Voices* from Oxford, first whilst an undergraduate, reading English, then as a postgraduate student; his research was on the relationship between realism and cultural identity in the late 19th century American novel. He was also active with the Oxford West Indian Students' Society, and in politics, helping to start the *Universities and Left Review* in 1956, which merged with *The New Reasoner* to form *The New Left Review* in 1960.

When CAM was formed, Brathwaite involved all these Cambridge and Oxford contemporaries, and his fellow contributors to *Caribbean Voices* and its producer, in appropriate ways.

Centres of West Indian activity

The West Indian Students Centre in Collingham Gardens, Earls Court, opened in 1955, ten years after the formation of WISU. Until then, student gatherings mainly used the British Council building in Hans Crescent. Non-students, or 'ordinary immigrants', as Donald Hinds once found himself described had to make do with church halls or similar places.[19] The Students Centre had been founded 'in order to fulfil a long-felt need of students, constantly urged upon Governments [of the constituent West Indian countries] by the West Indian Students Union in London'.[20] It rapidly became the focus not just of full-time student activities, but also a popular venue for part-time students and for every type of West Indian social, political and cultural event. Winston (Pony) K Hynam, for many years its warden, recalled how, with time, its purpose altered:

> It was established in 1955 as a 'home from home' mainly for full-time students coming to the UK. As time passed, this was expanded to include part-time students who had taken up permanent residence here, and later still to offer organisations such as CAM, the Commission for Racial Equality [CRE], the West Indian Standing Conference etc a meeting place and facilities, all of which enriched the life of the Centre itself.[21]

Another centre of West Indian activity, cultural and political, developed in London around Claudia Jones and *The West Indian Gazette*, a monthly newspaper which she started in March 1958 with Amy Ashwood Garvey, widow of Marcus Garvey. Its purpose, as Jones wrote in an editorial, was, 'to stimulate political and social thinking amongst West Indians, Africans and Asians in Britain'.[22]

When Claudia Jones arrived in Britain in December 1955, it was her second migration. In 1924, when she was almost nine, she had emigrated from Trinidad to the USA with her mother and three sisters, to join her father who had gone ahead in search of work. Brought up and educated in Harlem, experiencing both the 1930's depression and the discrimination against Afro-Americans in the USA, she aligned herself early with the Communist Party. Its programme seemed committed to radical change, and Claudia Jones was active within it, particularly as a journalist. But in the political climate of the Second World War and immediately after, the US authorities moved to repress her activities. Her arrest in 1948 on a deportation warrant, when she was charged with seeking 'the overthrow of the government by force and violence',[23] was followed by a prolonged trial and then prison for the whole year of 1955. On release, she was deported to Britain: Trinidad refused to have her. Despite poor health, exacerbated by her recent experience, she immediately made links with activist West Indian immigrant groups in Britain, in particular with the Caribbean Labour Congress (London Branch), with the trade unions and the Communist Party. She used her experience of racial discrimination in the USA, her understanding of the race/class correlation, to analyse and attempt to combat the accelerating pressures on West Indian migrants in Britain. For by the mid-1950s, the swelling numbers of migrants were encountering increased discrimination and hostility wherever they worked and lived.

When hostility against the West Indian community, fuelled by extreme rightwing and fascist propaganda, erupted in the Nottingham and Notting Hill riots of late 1958, Jones was amongst those who gave courageous leadership to those who suffered. She 'was able to console and prevent what some people thought would turn into a stampede of selling out and returning to the countries of their origin'.[24] After the riots, she coordinated the first West Indian Carnival in Britain, at Porchester Hall, Bayswater, and was instrumental in bringing the calypsonian, The Mighty Sparrow, to Britain from Trinidad for a series of concerts.

Her promotion of West Indian popular culture was part of a wide range of contacts and interests. Though her aim in the *Gazette* was to reach the 'ordinary immigrant', she claimed: 'It counts among its contributors and supporters many West Indian writers who live in England, trade-unionists and members of Parliament.'[25] George Lamming and Andrew Salkey, regular contributors to *Caribbean Voices* in the early 1950s, wrote for the *Gazette* in the late 1950s: an indicator of the change in orientation of leading Caribbean literary figures, as the demise of *Caribbean Voices* and the birth of the *Gazette* marked the changing climate in Britain.

The *Gazette* as a training ground in writing, and Claudia Jones as a formative influence and political educator, were equally important for young West Indians with scant education and no literary experience – exemplifed by Donald Hinds. Born in 1934, brought up by his grandmother in St Thomas in rural Jamaica when first his stepfather and then his mother emigrated to Britain, he left elementary school early and worked as an unpaid monitor in the school of which his aunt's husband was headmaster. This enabled him to take the Jamaican Local Examination externally. He passed the third year when he was 19, equipping him to work as a probationer-teacher in the Jamaican system. But he had been writing since he was 14, and recalls: 'I had this strange feeling – I wanted to go to university, I must be a graduate and this sort of thing.' He spent 1954–5 staying with his aunt in Mandeville, where he read widely and began to write:

> The Public Library became my own personal library, and I really started reading, and I remember this, I've never been able to repeat it – in 12 months, I read 104 books. They varied in size, from the Gleaner Company's own publications, the Pioneer Press, with Ogilvie's *Cactus Village* and so on . . . to Dickens's *David Copperfield*, not the abridged version, but the massive original, and Charles Reade's *The Cloister and the Hearth*. My favourite writer at that time was Sir Walter Scott: *Rob Roy* and all that. Not that I can stand him now. I was reading then, and writing. I have my first novel which ran through eight exercise books.

WEST INDIAN GAZETTE
AND AFRO-ASIAN CARIBBEAN NEWS
STILL—"No Room At The Inn"
"Miss World" is "Miss Jamaica"
Colour-bar Immigrants Bill Continues
Estate Agent Gets Four Years Jail
Ask your Grocer for ENCONA

Front page of the* West Indian Gazette, *December 1963

In 1955, aged 21, Donald Hinds came to Britain. He was working as a London Transport bus conductor in 1958, and writing a novel about immigrants in his spare time; one day Theo Campbell got onto his bus, and sold him a copy of the *West Indian Gazette*. Campbell, in Britain since serving with the RAF in the War, had moved to Lambeth in 1955 where he opened a record shop, specialising in imported Jamaican popular music, and a travel agency. The *Gazette* was based at his shop, and Campbell had become its sports editor. When Campbell heard that Hinds was a writer, he said, 'Well, if you're a writer, come and see Miss Jones!' Hinds began to contribute regularly to the *Gazette*, and then became its City Reporter, thanks to Claudia Jones's influence and training. He recalls, too, the lively, concerned people connected with her newspaper: 'Claudia was the focal point of everything West Indian at that time. . . . If you spent a lot of time at the *West Indian Gazette* you'd meet almost anybody who was interested in what was going on in this country, including visiting politicians.' Through working on the *Gazette*, Hinds's interest in the conditions and problems of West Indians in Britain became sharpened and politicised; it bore fruit in the early 1960s when he compiled and wrote the book *Journey to an Illusion: The West Indian in Britain* (1966).

CLR James had also been interned for a year on Ellis Island for his allegedly subversive activities and, on release, expelled from the USA two years before Claudia Jones. Back in Britain, from 1953, he was mainly engaged in writing: continuing contributions to the political debate in the USA, presenting his ideas on socialist revolution in *Facing Reality* (1958), and starting the re-examination of his assumptions about human culture which led to the writing of *Beyond a Boundary* (1963). In 1958 he returned to Trinidad at the invitation of the Prime Minister, Dr Eric Williams, as editor of the weekly organ of the Peoples National Movement (PNM). James renamed what had been *PNM Weekly*, *The Nation*. James's biographer, Paul Buhle, writes: 'He assumed the editorship, and Selma James a like responsibility for one essential purpose: the building of the PNM from a partisan force into a body that could transform Trinidad and Tobago.' In addition, 'James sought to entertain his audience, to uplift it spiritually to a new appreciation of Trinidadian and West Indian popular selfhood.'[26] James also became Secretary of the West Indies Federal Labour Party, an alliance of the main socialist and nationalist island parties of the Anglophone Caribbean, and the governing party of the embryonic West Indies Federation.

The late 1950s to the mid-1960s

Pressures in the Eastern Caribbean and in Britain

While in the late 1950s the West Indian community in Britain was devising ways of organising and mobilising itself, cultural and political activists were leaving the Eastern Caribbean in the hopes of finding more space and scope in Britain. The crushing of the socialist independence movement in British Guiana which had caused Aubrey Williams to leave in 1952 was responsible for the migration of many politically and culturally active fellow countrymen and women later in the decade.

The pressures of a comparable, though less widespread, political movement in Trinidad were responsible for the migration of John La Rose to Venezuela in 1958, and then to Britain in 1961. Born in 1927 into a middle-class family of Arima in central Trinidad, La Rose had taken a prominent part in radical political, trade union and cultural organisations in Trinidad since his late teens. Shortly after leaving St Mary's College in Port of Spain – the leading Roman Catholic secondary school – he returned to teach there for almost two years. In 1947 he become employed as a senior executive with the Colonial Life Insurance Company, but his revolutionary political activities prompted his dismissal in the early 1950s. He had been banned from other West Indian islands and from Guyana by the British colonial authorities, a Marxist whom they termed communist. The news of his banning was high profile news in radio and in the newspapers. Other such employment in Trinidad was closed to him. In Trinidad's General Election of 1956 he contested the seat of Arima, his home town, as a candidate of the West Indian Independence Party (WIIP) of which he was

General Secretary. Work as a teacher in Venezuela for about three years enabled him to bring his family to Britain in 1961. He planned to study law so that he could return to Trinidad and work independently of colonial government authorities or employers.

Soon after arriving in Britain, John and Irma La Rose bought a house in Uplands Road, Hornsey, North London. Eric and Jessica Huntley, former political associates of La Rose from Guyana, lived with them there for a short while. Jessica had visited La Rose in Trinidad on her way to London, and there was, indeed, a formal link between the WIIP in Trinidad and the PPP in Guyana. The Huntleys had both been very involved in political work. Eric was an executive member of the PPP; he had worked on *Thunder*, the PPP paper, and sold PPP literature in the rural areas. He had grown up in a working-class family with no books at home, without access to a library, and was, he claims, educated through the PPP. Eric arrived in London in 1956, Jessica in 1957. Eric explains why they came: 'The British troops had landed, the Constitution was suspended, the government was dismissed, the party had split twice, and so the political life was in a sort of doldrums, a sort of dead-end. And I was dismissed from my job, so we thought it best to come abroad to study.'

Ivan Van Sertima came to Britain in 1959. He, too, had been profoundly moved and disillusioned by events in Guyana, though as a younger man, from a middle-class background, his experiences had been very different from those of the Huntleys. Through his father, who was head of Road and River Transport in the interior, a Greek scholar, a close personal friend of Cheddi Jagan and Forbes Burnham, Ivan was drawn, when a teenager, directly into the national movement as the PPP fought for power:

> I became very involved. I began to speak on my father's platform. And we won the election. Then came all the great events which totally consumed me for years, because I just kept brooding again and again on what happened: our 133 days in power, what happened afterwards, how it affected us, you know. . . . It did two things: it revolutionised me, in a way, but it also filled me for a while with the feeling and the fear that we could never really change anything, because the powers that be were overwhelming.

It was through his father, too, that Van Sertima first heard of Wilson Harris – they worked together in the interior. 'There is one poet', he was told by his father, and thought he meant Martin Carter, active in the PPP. 'There is one poet that is very important, and that is Wilson Harris.' Harris, born in New Amsterdam in 1921, was educated at Queen's College in Georgetown and then trained as a land surveyor. After qualifying in 1942, he travelled widely in the coastal areas and the interior of Guyana, and became familiar with its great rivers and waterfalls, dense forests and open savannahs, and equally with the Amerindian peoples who live there. At the same time he was writing stories, poems, essays and reviews, many of which appeared in *Kyk-over-al*, the magazine started and edited, from 1945, by AJ Seymour – himself a poet, critic and editor. Collections of Harris's poems were published in Guyana in 1951 and 1954. He took little part in Seymour's literary group. Because of his work, he was at a remove from the political and literary activity of Georgetown; he regards this as having contributed vitally to his early development as a writer:

> My particular thing was not one which would have appealed to the Guyanese intellectuals. It is true that *Kyk-over-al* published things that I did. . . . Looking back, I am glad that I lived in that way, almost on the margins of the society – I mean, in fact, as I travelled so often into the interior, which took me away from the city, so I lived almost as if one were exiled from the society. But what that did, really, was to stimulate one's profound concerns, because one had to make up one's mind, whether one would pursue this kind of creative thing, despite the difficulties that surrounded it, the fact that people didn't want it. I mean, they were much more interested in Martin Carter's political poems, I don't think they saw this other thing I'm speaking of at all.

Harris did not actively involve himself in politics nor, like many of his friends, align himself with the PPP, during the turbulent years of the 1950s. But he was sympathetic to its cause; he remembers visiting his fellow poet and friend, Martin Carter, under house arrest soon after being released from internment under the State of Emergency.

Ivan Van Sertima did not meet Harris until 1957 or 1958, during the two years which he spent working in the Government Information Service, under Arthur Seymour. By then, he recalls, political hopes had failed and,

> we were full of despair and doubt. And here came someone with a vision which seemed to transcend the political, and yet was deeply rooted in the region. . . . Wilson seemed to present something that made us aware that we were involved in a larger world, and that we were not controlled by or confined to a moment, and that there was something else that could transcend that failure, that could make sense of it.

Amongst Van Sertima's early memories of Wilson Harris are his first attempts at writing a novel, alone in a house in Georgetown, vividly described in a talk to CAM in 1970 (see Chapter 8). Harris's conviction that only by 'moving men away from fixed ways of seeing and feeling', only by developing 'a different kind of consciousness, a different kind of vision', could the past be redeemed, was, states Van Sertima, what led he himself to leave

Guyana: 'I think the great force for me was to find in what way I could rediscover these various strands.'

Harris and Van Sertima met again shortly after arriving in London in 1959. They both worked at the Central Office of Information: Harris for six months, Van Sertima for four and a half years. Van Sertima recalls:

> We had a marvellous opportunity to spend all our lunch time just talking. And I remember those days very well, because Wilson had just finished *Palace* [*of the Peacock*], and he was working on *The Far Journey of Oudin*. . . . The overwhelming thing at that time was the struggle to find new ways of dealing with the complex heritage of the Caribbean.

Harris settled in London and married Margaret Burns, from Scotland, herself a writer. John La Rose recalls meeting Harris in 1961, soon after his own arrival in London; he, too, had been deeply struck by the quality of Harris's poetry in the collection, *Eternity to Season*, when he first read it in Trinidad. In 1962 CLR James was back once more in London, following the break-up of Federation, and his rift with Eric Williams over the Americans' retention of a naval base at Chaguaramas in Trinidad. Hearing from James that he had read Harris's work and was keen to know him, La Rose asked Lionel Jeffreys, a Guyanese, to arrange a meeting. Harris says he remembers the occasion vividly. 'I was immensely struck by the way James had read the [Guyana] *Quartet*, and the way he spoke of it, and his admiration for it. This was startling, because West Indians of his generation would not have been moved in that way.' And James commented:

> A remarkable man in every respect. He is not so easy to read as the other West Indian writers. Don't stop, continue, and you will come to understanding in the end. But he is a very gifted writer, and I don't quite understand – because Harris writes as if he were educated in Germany and is a modern man and he comes from the Caribbean. What a remarkable person!

When the lecture given by Harris at the Students Centre on 15 May 1964, 'Tradition and the West Indian Novel', was published by the West Indian Students Union as a pamphlet, James contributed an introduction.

1961 was the last year in which West Indians could enter Britain freely as British citizens. The 1958–9 riots appeared to confirm to 'official' Britain that British society could not continue to accommodate large numbers of 'coloured' immigrants – the blanket term then used for people from Africa, Asia and the West Indies – and that immigration controls must be imposed. In 1962 Britain's Conservative government passed the Commonwealth Immigrants Act. Organisations formed shortly before or in the wake of the

1958–9 riots fought the 1962 Act in vain.

Early in December 1964, Martin Luther King passed through London on his way to Oslo to receive the Nobel Peace Prize. He spoke at Africa Unity House in Collingham Gardens, two doors away from the Students Centre. Claudia Jones was there, with Knolly La Fortune, her cousin. Afterwards, recalls Pearl Connor, 'Claudia brought him [King] to our house and David Pitt, Edric, myself, and a few very close brothers and sisters of the Movement for Colonial Freedom; for man's freedom, I suppose; for liberation. We met him, yes, he was very mild.'

On 25 December, two months before her 50th birthday, Claudia Jones died. The cause was her chronic heart condition, aggravated by stress. In one of several tributes at her funeral, Dr David (now Lord) Pitt said: 'By the death of Claudia Jones we lost a freedom fighter. . . . She recognised that the coloured community needed to be organised and that they needed a medium of self-expression. . . . Claudia was aware of the importance of getting the host community to understand and appreciate the West Indian culture.'[27] Something at least of what she did and stood for was later continued in CAM.

Two months after Claudia Jones's death, an organisation which she had helped to found was formally launched: the Campaign Against Racial Discrimination (CARD). Instigated by Martin Luther King at meetings on his way through London, it was intended to be an umbrella organisation for existing groups and brought together various Asian and Afro-Caribbean organisations, including the West Indian Standing Conference, and Labour party 'radicals'. Its focus was on Parliament, for the repeal of the 1962 Commonwealth Immigrants Act and for anti-discrimination laws. Richard Small, a law student from Jamaica, in Britain since 1960, was closely involved with CARD from the start. Small came from a professional family in Kingston; his father was a judge, and Richard had been aware, while growing up, of his father's struggle to reach such a position as a black Jamaican, equally of their privileged situation in Jamaican society. In 1964 Richard Small had just completed an LLB degree at King's College, London, but had serious reservations as to whether he wanted to be a lawyer. In addition to studying for his degree, he had been active in West Indian student and community concerns based at the West Indian Students Centre. Small was at this time a personal assistant to CLR James. The opportunity to work with CARD came at the moment when Small's law degree was completed; it reinforced his reservations about completing his legal training. As Press Officer for CARD, he was immediately and fully engaged in speaking and in organisational work.

In February 1965, shortly after CARD was established, another significant Afro-American leader visited Britain – Malcolm X. His visit to France had been cut short by the authorities, who barred him from further visits as an 'undesirable person'. BBC reporters took him on an interviewing tour of Smethwick, near Birmingham, with a large black immigrant population; the BBC was widely criticised for fanning racism in an already tense community. He spoke at the LSE, and at Africa Unity House; he also took part in an Oxford Union debate against the MP Enoch Powell, who was beginning to articulate and broadcast his anti-black immigrant views. Malcolm X's visit, like Martin Luther King's a few months earlier, had a profound effect on Caribbean people in Britain at a time when they were feeling increasingly pressured and unwelcome in Britain.

Student migrants, artist residents

After the 1962 Commonwealth Immigrants Act, the only Caribbean people able to enter Britain freely were students and school children. Those who came to Britain in the 1960s and were later associated with CAM mostly came for professional or technical training or postgraduate study. Facilities at home were still very limited.

Orlando Patterson came from Jamaica in late 1962, a graduate of the Social Sciences Faculty at UWI. After three years of research at LSE, where he was a Commonwealth Scholar, he was awarded a PhD for his thesis on slave society in Jamaica, and immediately appointed an assistant lecturer at LSE. His first novel, *The Children of Sisyphus* (1964), was published to great acclaim. He had been writing and finding local outlets for short stories since he was a schoolboy.

In the early and mid-1960s a number of other UWI graduates, in English and history, came over for postgraduate research at a variety of universities in Britain. Among the English graduates, Kenneth Ramchand, from Trinidad, went to Edinburgh, where he did pioneering research in West Indian literature with his historical and critical study of the West Indian novel. Gordon Rohlehr, from British Guiana, studied at Birmingham for a doctorate on Joseph Conrad; Vishnudat Singh, from Trinidad, at London on DH Lawrence; Maureen Warner (now Warner Lewis), also from Trinidad, studied linguistics at York. These three had been undergraduates together at Mona, and kept in touch with each other in Britain. Brinsley Samaroo was also engaged in research at London University, after doing his first degree in history in India. In 1965 two lecturers at UWI, Mona, came for postgraduate study and research: Don Wilson, in education, at London University; Edward Kamau Brathwaite, in history, at Sussex University.

Amongst the undergraduate students of the 1960s, several had already been to school in Britain. Oliver Clarke, from a prominent white Jamaican farming, business and professional family – Edith Clarke, the social worker and author of *My Mother Who Fathered Me*,[28] was his aunt – went to Sherborne, a public school, and then, in 1964, to LSE as a student in accountancy. Archie Markham came as the teenage child of immigrant parents in the 1950s, from Montserrat, and after a comprehensive school in Ladbroke Grove, went as a student to St David's College, Lampeter. Others came direct from the Caribbean as undergraduates: Wally Look Lai, from Trinidad, to read English at Oxford; Ansel Wong, also from Trinidad, to read English at Hull; Peter Fraser, from Guyana, to read history at Sussex. Christopher Laird, from Trinidad, read for a general degree in London as an external student.

Errol Lloyd followed Richard Small by reading law in London; they came from a similar family background and had been friends in Jamaica. Locksley Comrie, from a black working-class Kingston family, came from Jamaica to study engineering at Brixton Technical College. Students of drama included Marina (now Ama Omowale) Maxwell, born in Trinidad and a recent graduate from UWI in Jamaica, Ken Corsbie and Doris Harper Wills, from Guyana. Corsbie and Wills attended the Rose Bruford School, at Sidcup in Kent.

Faustin Charles came over from Trinidad in his early twenties in order to study philosophy at London University, but soon became absorbed in writing poetry and fiction. Fellow writers Sebastian Clarke (now Amon Saba Saakana) and Linton (now Kwesi) Johnson also came over in the early 1960s – from Trinidad and Jamaica, to join their families in Britain – Clarke, aged 17, Johnson, aged 9.

Winston Benn enrolled at the Sir John Cass College in 1964; he had come over from Trinidad three years earlier, but spent time in the RAF before he decided to concentrate on painting. In 1966 Winston Branch arrived from St Lucia to study at the Slade, and Judith McEachrane arrived from Trinidad to study at the Hammersmith College of Art and Design; she and Christopher Laird were married in London two years later. Clifton Campbell, Karl 'Jerry' Craig and Paul Dash had all come to Britain about ten years earlier: Craig, from a middle-class Jamaican family to study art at the London College of Printing; Campbell and Dash with immigrant parents, from Jamaica and from Barbados, to state schools. When they embarked on art training – Campbell at St Martin's School of Art, Dash at Chelsea School of Art – they were at a greater distance from their Caribbean background than contemporaries who came over directly to study; this resulted in particular problems, later articulated in CAM. Craig returned to Jamaica to work as an artist and art teacher upon completion of his Fine Arts

Diploma in London, but since 1958 had been back in London.

Meanwhile the writers and artists who had come to Britain from the Caribbean had by the 1960s established themselves professionally. Andrew Salkey, like his former colleagues on *Caribbean Voices*, became a published novelist with *A Quality of Violence* (1959), and *Escape to an Autumn Pavement* (1960): the first set in rural Jamaica, the second in London. In 1964, 1965 and 1966 he published novels for children set in the Caribbean with Oxford University Press (OUP). Michael Anthony, likewise, began to publish fiction – with Andre Deutsch – in the 1960s: *The Games were Coming* (1963), *The Year in San Fernando* (1965), *Green Days by the River* (1967), all set in Trinidad. VS Naipaul followed his 1950s fiction with *A House for Mr Biswas* (1961), Mr *Stone and the Knight's Companion* (1963) and *The Mimic Men* (1967): the first set in Trinidad, the second in London, the third in both, all published by Deutsch. *Season of Adventure* (1960), proved to be not only George Lamming's last San Christobal novel, but his last for 11 years. Sam Selvon brought out fewer books than in the previous decade: *I Hear Thunder* (1963), and *The Housing Lark* (1965), set in Trinidad and London respectively. Meanwhile Wilson Harris, after Fabers' initial leap of confidence (thanks to Andrew Salkey's recommendation) in *Palace of the Peacock* (1960), brought out a novel set in the Guyana interior almost each year: *The Far Journey of Oudin* (1961), *The Whole Armour* (1962), *The Secret Ladder* (1963), *Heartland* (1964), *The Eye of the Scarecrow* (1965), *The Waiting Room* (1967). Honours and awards given to these writers during the 1950s and 1960s indicate something of their critical standing in Britain. Lamming won the Somerset Maugham Award (1957), Selvon, a travelling scholarship from the Society of Authors (1958); Salkey, the Thomas Helmore Prize for Poetry (1955), and Naipaul, the John Llewellyn Rhys Memorial Prize (1958), the Somerset Maugham Award (1961), the Phoenix Trust Award (1962), the Hawthornden Prize (1964), and the WH Smith Prize (1968).

But by late 1966, when CAM began, some of the early West Indian writers 'in exile' in London were no longer around – Jan Carew had emigrated to Canada, John Hearne and Sylvia Wynter had returned to Jamaica, Roger Mais and Edgar Mittelholzer were dead. The first writers of the 1950s to gain prominence, Lamming and Selvon, were now less productive. In addition to VS Naipaul and Andrew Salkey, the writers of the moment in Britain were Patterson, Anthony and Harris.

Ronald Moody's work continued to develop, and his reputation to grow. In the 1960s, he held his first one-man show for ten years at the Woodstock Gallery, between Oxford Street and Bond Street. His new work included a 'Reclining Figure' in concrete and

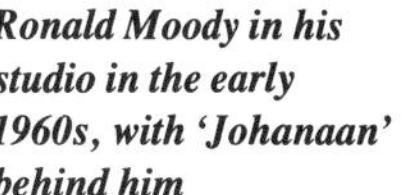

Ronald Moody in his studio in the early 1960s, with 'Johanaan' behind him

fibre glass. As before, his heads and figures carved in wood greatly impressed the critics: 'His work is monolithic, silent and strong.'[29] In addition to further one-man shows at the Woodstock, he was represented in many prestigious group exhibitions including the Royal Academy and the Society of Portrait Sculptors. He continued to experiment with new techniques and materials. In March 1963 he was commissioned to do a piece of sculpture to stand outside the Epidemiological Research Unit at the Mona Campus of UWI: hence 'Savacou', based, after much research, on 'a deity in Carib mythology who became a bird and later a star, and was attributed with control over thunder and strong winds'.[30] The following August the aluminium sculpture was unveiled in London, outside the Commonwealth Institute, and then shipped to Jamaica. The previous October Moody and his wife made a visit to Jamaica, his first since 1923. According to the *Daily Gleaner* he 'expressed delight in the tremendous change in the attitude of people towards art'.[31] At a group show at the Woodstock in 1964 he was introduced to a fellow exhibitor, the Nigerian painter, Uzo Egonu. Despite the 30-year gap in age and their widely different backgrounds and art, a close friendship developed which lasted until Moody's death in 1983. Moody's friendship and sharing of sculptor's skills with Namba Roy was brought to an end with Roy's death in 1961.[32]

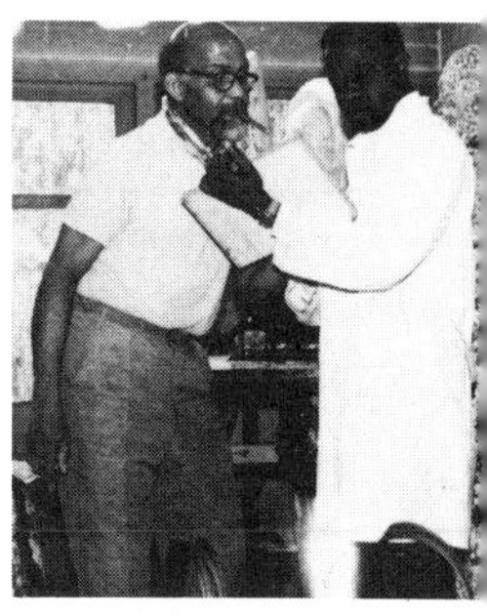

Ronald Moody and Uzo Egonu in 1970 discussing the linocut and woodcut printing presses which they were building together

Aubrey Williams became known nationally and internationally

in the 1960s, with one-man shows in New York, Switzerland and Italy, and in London, at the Grabowski Gallery in Sloane Avenue. But it was as a Commonwealth painter that he now found his greatest exposure and success. In 1963, the first Commonwealth Biennale of Abstract Art was held at the Commonwealth Institute. Williams's work was singled out; one critic found that 'the shapes and strange colours . . . possess an untamed power beneath the accomplished and sophisticated technique. . . . The international cross-currents are more noticeable than native characteristics.'[33] His painting 'Roraima' was awarded the £50 prize, donated by Frank Avray Wilson, a well-known British painter with a particular interest in abstract painting. In 1965 Williams was awarded the Commonwealth Prize for Painting, presented by the Queen. At the Royal Academy Exhibition, *Treasures of the Commonwealth*, part of the Commonwealth Arts Festival, Aubrey Williams's painting, 'Guyana', was exhibited and reproduced in the catalogue; a painting by Frank Bowling – also from Guyana – was the only other work by a British-based Caribbean artist.

Groups and associations

Until the mid-1960s, creative friendships among Caribbean artists in Britain were mainly on a personal basis: Aubrey Williams and Jan Carew; Ronald Moody and Namba Roy. Groups are important to artists as the means whereby they can most easily exhibit their work, and through which they learn and are stimulated by each other. The groups in which Moody and Williams exhibited until 1967 were international or Commonwealth. Each essentially worked alone in his studio – Moody in Chelsea, Williams in Hampstead – with few contacts with other Caribbean artists and intellectuals.

Theatre people, in contrast, essentially work together. Because most Caribbean actors and directors found few opportunities in British theatre, they formed their own drama groups and companies, which in turn encouraged Caribbean writers to write for them. Edric and Pearl Connor's Negro Theatre Workshop was formed from their earlier theatrical group, and based at the office of Pearl's theatrical agency at 6 Paddington Street. When the Africa Centre was opened in its spacious premises in Covent Garden (informally 1962, officially 1964), the Workshop used it for rehearsal and performance of some of its productions. The Workshop took a play by Obi Egbuna, *Wind Versus Polygamy*, to the 1966 Festival of Negro Arts at Dakar, Senegal. Ram John Holder's decision to come to Britain in 1962, after several years in the USA – he first went over from Guyana as a student, then worked as a musician/actor – was partly influenced by hearing from Edric Connor about this Workshop.

Bari Jonson took no part in the Workshop, although he worked with Pearl Connor in a number of ways over the years. By the 1960s he was well established in Britain as an actor and producer. In 1963 he devised *Ex-Africa*, a programme of Afro-American, African and Caribbean literature – with the help of Andrew Salkey and of Shake Keane, poet and jazz musician from St Vincent. *Ex-Africa* was developed from a Sunday night show which Jonson had produced at the Royal Court Theatre. He took it to the Edinburgh Festival, where Carmen Munro and Shake Keane performed in it with him.

The Caribbean Students Performing Group was based at the Students Centre. Jacques Compton, from St Lucia, was responsible for the literature side, Alex Pascall, from Trinidad, for the music and dance. Knolly La Fortune, a member of the group, recalls how his poem, 'The Ballad of Papa Bois', was recited by Compton and himself, with an accompaniment of drums and other music, and how they 'used to give readings, recitations, to different schools and colleges, to Women's Institutes, and of course at the Students Centre'. Concerts by the group, which included performances by the Alex Pascall Singers, and by Raymond McLean, an outstanding dancer trained in Trinidad by Beryl McBurnie, were given at the Commonwealth Institute and raised money, for instance for the Trinidad Youth Movement and Hurricane Janet; they had a concert at St Paul's Cathedral in aid of funds to send the body of Edric Connor home to Trinidad after his death in London in 1968.

Although writers, like artists, work alone, several of those who had come over from the Caribbean kept in touch with one another informally. Wilson Harris recalls how 'Andrew Salkey was vitally interested in having Caribbean writers and so on in his house, and talking about things'. CLR James recalled an attempt to organise something similar to the 1930s Beacon group in Trinidad: 'It was not very dynamic. But we got together, and it was in regard to that that I met George Lamming, and then Wilson Harris, and Vidia Naipaul, though we didn't see too much of Naipaul.' Young, unpublished writers tended only to meet such writers if they were lucky enough to have some personal link. Faustin Charles remembers often going to CLR James's house in Staverton Road, to talk. They knew each other from Trinidad; Charles had introduced himself in 1960 after writing a short article on 'Culture and the Queens Hall' for the *Nation*, of which James was then editor.

Postgraduate students naturally formed groups, as an extension of their field of research and particular interests. Wally Look Lai remembers 'a number of small circles of progressive West Indians in London in the 1960s, all of whom were related in some sort of disconnected fashion to the idea of maintaining a continuing interest in affairs back in the Caribbean'. There was the 'Marxist intellectual milieu around the *New Left Review*'[34] of which Orlando Patterson amongst others was part; Richard Small recalls study groups led by CLR James. Don Wilson and his wife, Betty, have memories of a particular group, also attended by Patterson and by Oliver Clarke:

> In our second year, 1966, we started a discussion group in our house. We were living in Muswell Hill at the time, and myself and Betty with people like Peter Figueroa, from Jamaica – we felt we wanted to get a study group where we would present papers, talk about the Caribbean, talk about Africa, and look at the sorts of problems, developments in Jamaica and in other countries that were related to the Caribbean.

The group used to meet regularly on Sunday evenings, 'have drinks and eats and chat for two, three hours: fairly formal presentation of a paper and then discussion afterwards'. When the Wilsons moved to central London, to a flat in William Goodenough House, Mecklenburgh Square, for their final year, 1966–7, the group continued to meet, by now about 14 in number.

In October 1966 Edward Kamau and Doris Brathwaite also moved into a flat in William Goodenough House. They had spent the first year, 1965–6, living in Brighton, close to Sussex University. But as most of Brathwaite's research material was in London, they decided to move there. Through Peter Figueroa, John Figueroa's younger brother and also a poet, Brathwaite was invited to one of the group's meetings. But he already had ideas far beyond such an academic, exclusive group.

By 1966 London had lost two of its centres of West Indian cultural ferment: *Caribbean Voices* had closed a decade before; *The West Indian Gazette* came to an end shortly after the death of Claudia Jones. But the West Indian Students Centre hosted a variety of cultural activities: lectures, discussion groups, dance and drama performances, activities which, as Richard Small recalls, 'created openness for links with the migrant community . . . [and] were not limited to students'. For some sort of association of West Indian artists and intellectuals, meeting at the Students Centre with its student and, increasingly, immigrant audience, the possibilities seemed limitless.

2 The Beginnings of CAM
December 1966 - March 1967

CAM did not, however, evolve from any group already existing amongst West Indians in London in the 1960s. It was something quite new, born from the first meeting between John La Rose and Edward Kamau Brathwaite, in London, in the autumn of 1966. Brathwaite had returned to Britain the year before – 11 years after he left Cambridge. La Rose had been there since 1961. Andrew Salkey, the essential third of CAM's founders, had lived in London continuously for almost 15 years; the West Indian Students Centre, the institution which enabled CAM to flourish, had existed in London for over ten years. The longer British experience and the wider contacts of Salkey, the established structure and facilities of the Students Centre, provided the perfect complement to the new ideas, the fresh vision, of La Rose and Brathwaite, coming to Britain a decade later.

Brathwaite, La Rose and Salkey, all born between 1927 and 1930, all practising writers, shared enough to create a movement with a remarkably consistent core of policy, and to sustain it as an organisation of vitality and significance for over five years. Yet the social and political structure and traditions of their home islands of Barbados, Trinidad and Jamaica were widely different. Even more marked in contrast was their work, and the context of their work, during the formative years when they were in their twenties and thirties, that is, between the late 1940s and 1966. Links had already been made through their parallel work and interests – between Salkey and Brathwaite and between Brathwaite and La Rose, through literature; between Salkey and La Rose, through politics. When the three met together for the first time in order to discuss the formation of an association of writers and artists, their varied backgrounds and experience, their existing links, all contributed to the dynamism of their ideas.

The particular time at which the three men met together in London was also influential in the formation and nature of CAM. By the mid-1960s, a substantial quantity of West Indian fiction, and some poetry of quality, had been published; several plays by West Indians writers had been successfully performed on the London stage. But their work seemed to be drawing less attention from British critics than in the 1950s, and no West Indian critics were yet being published or heard. Several gifted and single-minded West Indian artists were producing work of high quality, but it too suffered from the lack of informed assessment. There was an evident and urgent need for criticism, and critical criteria, which were appropriate to West Indian art, for an aesthetic which was no longer tied to European art. Individual West Indian writers and artists in Britain were working out new forms of art, experimenting with a new language; they wanted to share their ideas and their new work with each other. West Indians in Britain – student and 'ordinary immigrant' alike – had very little knowledge of contemporary West Indian arts, and constituted a potential audience. All these factors contributed to the birth of CAM, and to the way in which it was set up.

John La Rose

John La Rose

In 1966 John La Rose had started to put into action his long-cherished publishing ideas. He had completed, as 'Antony La Rose', a collection of his own poems, *Foundations*, and this was the first title to appear under the New Beacon imprint in August 1966. He was preparing for publication two books by JJ Thomas: *The Theory and Practice of Creole Grammar* and *Froudacity – West Indian Fables Explained*, first published in 1869 and 1889 respectively, and long out of print. The name 'New Beacon' came from what La Rose regarded as his publishing company's ancestor and inspiration: the *Beacon* magazine of Trinidad (1931–33), and the group around it, which he saw as having had 'a tremendous cultural impact at the time'.[1]

La Rose had begun to think about publishing books in Trinidad in the 1940s and 1950s: new books, and also old books which were no longer freely available. He remembers British publishers rejecting a novel by John Wickham, although several of Wickham's stories had been successfully broadcast on the BBC's *Caribbean Voices* and on radio programmes in Trinidad. He decided 'not just to complain, but to do it oneself'.[2] He recalls how Irma, his first wife, typed out books such as W Arthur Lewis's *Labour in the West Indies* and JJ Thomas's *Creole Grammar* – a labour indeed on a manual typewriter with carbon copies – so that he and his friends in Trinidad could read and discuss them. He became aware of ways in which the people of his country were deprived of information which would provide a sense of continuity with the past, so that 'each generation starts as if nothing had happened before and sets its own agenda'.[3] To republish such works would, he had decided, 'keep the continuities alive'.[4] As a young man, La Rose had made use of the libraries of Port of Spain in order to educate himself about the Caribbean: the Caribbean Commission Library, then under Nancy Wint, and the West

Indian section of the Public Library in Belmont Circular Road. His interest in popular culture had begun while he was at St Mary's College. The teacher preparing him for the Higher School Certificate General Paper was interested in carnival, kaiso and calypso, and drew his attention to their use of creole language. JJ Thomas's *Creole Grammar* – commonly referred to in Trinidad as 'the Patois Grammar' – showed La Rose the value of proverbs, and he began to collect them himself. The purpose behind Thomas's book also impressed him. Thomas had discovered that people brought up in court were convicted because they had difficulty in defending themselves; their creole speech was not understood by, or was mistakenly translated for, the colonial magistrates – hence his interest in studying and systematising the peoples' language. This, to La Rose, exemplified the Trinidadian proverb, 'Sense mek before book'.

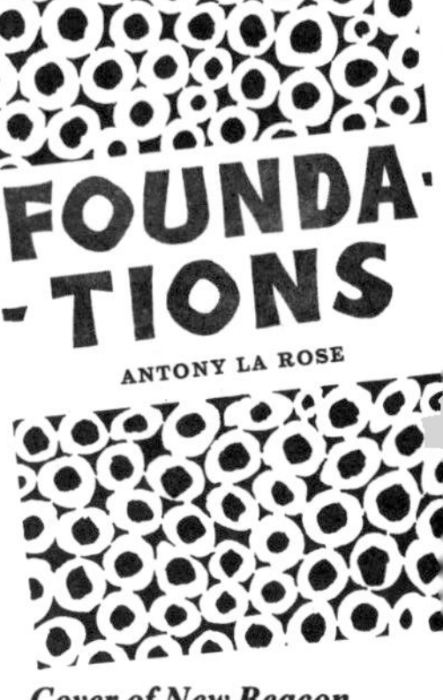

Cover of New Beacon Book's first publication, cover design by Art Derry

La Rose's childhood in Arima, in the 1930s, had given him a broad-based experience of Trinidad society and culture. Arima, on the Mausica River, had names which preserved the Amerindian and French creole past. The nearby community of Caribs spoke Spanish creole and took part in the annual Santa Rosa festival. 'Over the Line', the train line, was Malabar, a village of Afro-Trinidadians. When, on Empire Day, the people of Arima remembered how 'Queen Victoria and Wilberforce freed the slaves . . . no one claimed ancestry from enslaved Africans, not then, in Arima'.[5] Later, in Port of Spain, and later still in Venezuela, where he worked from 1958–61, La Rose studied French and Spanish literature. He had met Venezuela's leading poet, Rafael Cadenas, in Trinidad. A lecture by Eric Williams in Port of Spain in 1952 on 'Four Poets of the Greater Antilles' had introduced him to the work of Nicolás Guillén (Cuba), Jacques Roumain and Jean Brierre (Haiti), Luis Pales Matos (Puerto Rico); this is when La Rose remembers first hearing of the poetry of Aimé Césaire of Martinique.[6]

Alongside his developing interest in popular culture, La Rose had been actively involved in politics since he was 18. Soon after leaving school, he joined a Marxist study group in Port of Spain. In 1948 a section of the Marxist Study Class movement joined with remnants of the Marxist-oriented Negro Welfare Cultural and Social Association to form a new political party, the Workers Freedom Movement (WFM). La Rose became its General Secretary, and was active in building a youth movement within the party. Meanwhile the Trinidad and Tobago Youth Council, formed earlier in the 1940s – Pearl Connor was one of its founders – was involved in the early steelband movement, which culminated in the triumph of the Trinidad All Steel Percussion Orchestra (TASPO) at the Festival of Britain in 1951. In the early 1950s, the youth movement of the WFM joined the Youth Council. La Rose produced a fortnightly radio programme, 'Voice of Youth', in which he was able to promote his interest in music and literature, and especially steelband and calypso, and at the same time to help move the Youth Council towards support for independence and socialism in Trinidad.

La Rose was at this time equally active in the trade union movement; he was an executive member of the Federated Workers Trade Union. As a WFM representative, he held meetings throughout the oil belt of southern Trinidad, presenting oil workers with information on the oil industry. In 1952 radical trade unionists joined with the WFM to form the West Indian Independence Party, with La Rose as General Secretary. The new party was, in La Rose's view, 'the most dangerous ideological and political opposition the colonial authorities had encountered since the 1930s. They were determined to crush it'.[7] La Rose and the WIIP were defeated in the 1956 election, and he was forced into exile. As La Rose now sees his activism of the 1940s and 1950s, he was 'seeking a political end to colonialism, and I came to it through culture'.[8] His eventual choice of work in publishing gave validity to his position. In Trinidad he had also had continual experience of the creative interaction of a group of like-minded people: the Phoenix Literary and Debating Society in Arima, which he helped to revive; the Whitehall Players Group; a small writers' group; the Marxist group to which he was introduced by Neville Guiseppi. And always he remembers hearing about the 1930s and 1940s literary groups, among which the Beacon group was already something of a legend.

When, in London in the early 1960s, La Rose first met Wilson Harris, he suggested that there were enough writers and artists in Britain to have an organisation for the exchange of views:

> I had seen the need for an organisation of writers and artists, around the time that I began to think of publishing . . . . Here was a kind of Mecca for the Caribbean writer. So I thought that there was no organisation, there was no means of interaction which was taking place among those writers. And that the work of West Indian writing had required a certain amount of concentration about what it was that people were attempting to do in either the novel or in the short story or the poem. And to some extent in painting, for those were the things that interested me most – and drama. And the only one person I spoke to about this was Wilson Harris, at an earlier stage.

Harris recalls nothing definite that La Rose said about this, but states: 'I know that he was deeply interested in any kind of dialogue with and between Caribbean writers, and probably did speak of this association.'

La Rose's reason for seeking out Brathwaite in 1966 was for help in contacting Elsa Goveia, Professor of West Indian History at the UWI Mona campus in Jamaica, from which Brathwaite was on study leave. She would, thought La Rose, be just the person to write an introduction to his republication of JJ Thomas. Brathwaite meanwhile had been keen to meet La Rose, whose poems he had greatly admired when he was shown them, in typescript, by George Beckford and Norman Girvan of the New World Group at Mona. When Brathwaite, at their first meeting, put forward his ideas for some sort of group of Caribbean writers, La Rose agreed immediately.

Edward Kamau Brathwaite

Edward Kamau Brathwaite

After two years, 1963–5, in the History Department of the UWI at Mona, Brathwaite had been advised to take a postgraduate degree, as he explains, 'to equip myself, or retool myself, for teaching at the University of the West Indies'. For there had been a ten-year gap in his career as an academic historian, since he graduated in history at Cambridge in 1953.

Brathwaite had stayed on in Cambridge for a further year to take a Diploma in Education, and then applied for a wide range of jobs abroad. It was, he claims, pure chance which led to his being offered and accepting a post in the educational service of what was then the West African colony of the Gold Coast, now Ghana. 'So eventually, quite by accident, I went to the place where I should have gone all along, the place I should have known about all along, but didn't because of my education.'[9] In 1960 he took 'long leave', his first return home since leaving for Cambridge in 1950. In Barbados he met Doris Monica Wellcome, holidaying there from Guyana, and soon afterwards married her in Guyana. So when he returned to Ghana in 1960, Doris – a graduate in home economics (Leicester) and tropical nutrition (London) – came too, taking a post as teacher in a secondary school at Cape Coast. Brathwaite was now with the Ministry of Education's Textbooks and Syllabus Section at Saltpond, near Cape Coast. Here he started a Children's Theatre, for which he wrote and produced not only the plays subsequently published – *Four Plays for Primary Schools* and *Odale's Choice* – but also the unpublished *A Pageant of Ghana* and *Edina*. Doris was an able assistant in these productions; she had been active in drama in Guyana, first while a student at Bishop's High School, then with the Theatre Guild.

Brathwaite's long stay in Ghana was deeply influential on his future work. He witnessed the ferment of the run-up to and achievement of Independence in 1957 under Kwame Nkrumah. He was immersed in the rural community life and traditional culture of a part of West Africa from which the forbears of many

West Indians had been taken as slaves. Firsthand experience of community living made him aware of the limitations of the individual working alone, and the advantages of corporate thought and creativity. Firsthand knowledge of West African culture – from family customs to the music of the drum – equipped him to recognise continuing elements of this culture in the Caribbean. He became aware of the possibilities of oral poetry. By the time he and his family left Ghana he had, he reckons, 'lost a lot of that false colonial luggage which I had come up with, and I also began to get a true sense of community and culture. And my poetry really starts, I would think, from that experience of living and working in Ghana'.[10]

The Brathwaites came home to the Caribbean in mid-1962, to St Lucia. Edward Kamau was the island's Resident Tutor for the UWI Extra-Mural Department; Doris worked as a part-time tutor in mathematics and home economics, and helped with the department's drama productions. Brathwaite's post, in the distinctive cultural context of St Lucia, provided him with abundant scope for his interests and concerns, his enthusiasm and energy. He worked with the artists Dunstan St Omer and Harry Simmons and the playwright Roderick Walcott, with radio producers, actors, teachers and civil servants, to develop an Extra-Mural programme with wide outreach and creative potential. Simmons, in addition to painting and teaching art, was also an archaeologist and anthropologist, carrying out research into the folk culture of St Lucia. His work was of special interest to Brathwaite, who saw such culture as an extension of what he had observed and experienced in West Africa. Brathwaite took full advantage of the opportunities of radio for carrying out the Extra-Mural programme, using all the hours allocated to it on the Windward Islands Broadcasting Service, transmitting live Extra-Mural lectures and follow-up studio discussions, and many special programmes.

In June 1963 the Extra-Mural Department published *Iouanaloa: Recent Writing from St Lucia*, a 90-page book edited by Brathwaite as Resident Tutor, and signifying his interests and orientation. Its title, the old Carib name for St Lucia meaning 'the place of the iguana', is followed by extensive 'Notes on the Folklore in St Lucia' by Simmons. The usual governmental, university and Extra-Mural Department messages, addresses, history and so on – the publication originated as a souvenir of University Week – are eclipsed by twice as many pages of writing on art, drama, literature, calypso, and radio. They include a review by Doris Brathwaite of VS Naipaul's *The Middle Passage*, which is sensitive, intelligent, spirited and expressed with sense and clarity: evidence of the gifts, not always so fully articulated, which she brought to their highly creative partnership.

Brathwaite's own article in *Iouanaloa*, on 'The use of radio in a developing society', with criticism of the St Lucian government's limited use of broadcasting opportunities, and indications of the full use made by the Extra-Mural Department, its potential already proven, prompted the Brathwaites' departure from St Lucia after only a year. Brathwaite had already been invited to join the UWI Department of History at Mona, on a year's secondment; although reluctant to abandon his programme in St Lucia and re-enter an academic environment, he welcomed the facilities and contacts which Jamaica offered. He spent most of the first year there getting to grips with teaching history and working on his poetry. Louis James, teaching in the Department of English at Mona, 1962-5, has distinct, significant memories of Brathwaite at the time:

> I would work very early in the morning in the Arts block, and the only other person working in the early hours was Eddie Brathwaite . . . . I would hear the tapping and, if I got a bit bored with my work, I'd go up and we would share a coffee in his room . . . . I remember seeing a number of the poems that were to be incorporated into *Rights of Passage* lying round, and he would read them.

James also remembers the very good relationship which Brathwaite had with the students, and how responsive they were to hearing his poetry. James encouraged his students to write. West Indian writing was not yet taught at the university nor included on the syllabus, but Gordon Rohlehr, a student in the Mona English Department from 1961 to 1964, states that, 'people who taught English at UWI encouraged me to see the verbal rebellion of West Indian writers.'[11] Brathwaite, engaged in such 'verbal rebellion', seems not to have impressed James's colleagues. James recalls: 'He was very much an outsider in terms of the English Department. I asked other teachers what his standing was and they weren't at all encouraging.'

In the summer of 1964, Brathwaite wrote the first draft of *Rights of Passage*, at Runaway Bay on the north coast, and now says, 'I knew right away that it called for oral resonance, I just had to read it out onto tape almost at once and all the drafts after the first one were influenced by the sound on tape.'[12] Some of Brathwaite's colleagues on campus, and visiting West Indians – he recalls Derek Walcott, Errol Hill, Fred Cartey, CLR James – responded with lively interest to what they read and above all to what they heard. The New World Group people listened to the one and a half hour-long recording of Brathwaite's reading of the entire poem. In the summer of 1965, shortly before leaving for Britain, at one of the Group's Sunday morning seminars on Caribbean culture, on West Indian poetry, Brathwaite recalls, 'I kinda settled the argument that "dialect" in poetry could be used seriously . . . with a speaking of "Wings of a Dove" with Rex Nettleford shouting out above the surprised but excited audience, "beyond the boom boom".'[13] It was at this time that George Beckford and Norman Girvan showed Brathwaite the poems which La Rose had submitted to *New World Quarterly*, because, writes Brathwaite, 'this quite remarkable collection clicked with what the guys knew I too was trying for'.[14] Louis James and his family had already left Mona for the University of Kent. By the time the Brathwaites left for the University of Sussex in late September 1965, Brathwaite had had a short, but intense, regrounding in Caribbean cultural activity and possibilities, and had his first major poem ready for a publisher and an audience.

Brathwaite's work in literature, unlike his work in history, had been continuous and unbroken since his Cambridge days, as is evident from *Bim* alone. He was one of the magazine's most regular contributors, as well as, from 1965 onwards, an assistant editor. The only other Caribbean periodicals to carry his work during his years in Ghana, St Lucia and Jamaica, were *Caribbean Quarterly* in 1956 and 1958, and *Kyk-over-al* in 1960. That he had meanwhile kept up with new publications by West Indian writers is evident in his regular literary criticism and reviews in *Bim*. As he says: 'I knew their work intimately but had not seen any of them.' It is said that 'for Brathwaite, more than for any other West Indian writer, *Bim* has been continuously a sounding-board and a platform'.[15] A platform, yes; but a sounding-board only in so far as it gave him space to try out his ideas. Neither fellow contributors to the magazine, nor its readers, provide much feedback, especially to a contributor at such a distance; there was little sense of community amongst *Bim*'s contributors. Nor had Brathwaite been able to benefit fully from the London-based circle of writers contributing to *Caribbean Voices*, for he usually had to get a late train back to Cambridge.

Given the amount and quality of work by Caribbean writers in the ten years that he had been away, Brathwaite expected them and their work to be far more in evidence in Britain. He and Doris moved to London from Sussex in mid-1966; then 'I realised why I wasn't hearing or meeting these people. Because every one, although in London, was so scattered'. And it was soon after arriving in London that, as he remembers, the ideas began to come: 'Most of the people who are regarded as "the exiles" were still in London at that time. The return to the Caribbean of some of them hadn't taken place. So my idea was that I'd like to meet other people who were writing and so on, and why is it that we cannot get together?'

John La Rose was among the London-based writers whom Brathwaite wanted to meet, so he welcomed La Rose's approach to him. As La Rose recalls, he and Sarah White spent an evening with Edward Kamau and Doris Brathwaite, at their Mecklenburgh Square flat; Sarah White, John La Rose's partner and co-founder of New Beacon, was then a doctoral student at Imperial College, London University. After telling Brathwaite about his proposed publications, La Rose recalls how 'we came to talking about the idea of this kind of organisation which I had previously raised with Wilson [Harris]. We both agreed that there was a need for this kind of organisation.' Brathwaite's memories are similar:

> We started speaking about this thing; and it so happened we had similar ideas . . . . The concept was that we wanted first of all to have the writers meet together so we could talk . . . . But it started to grow from there. Because John said, 'Well, we can't do anything without Andrew Salkey'.

La Rose further recalls:

> We agreed that he [Brathwaite] would speak to Andrew, and I would speak to Wilson and others, because I knew Wilson and I thought that he would be an important person to be part of this . . . . It was really quite fateful in many respects, because we agreed so easily. And we have always agreed pretty easily, really, in terms of what we have been able to do and accomplish together.

Both men knew that Andrew Salkey was regarded as the key person for West Indian intellectuals in London, as a published novelist, poet and anthologiser, through his work at the BBC, and because of his particular personality. They knew, too, that he had valuable links with the British literary and arts establishment.

Andrew Salkey

Andrew Salkey

Salkey had, by 1966, reached his unique position through an amazingly active freelance life, and through the creative use he made of all his contacts. He was never employed as BBC staff: all his broadcasting work was freelance. From his own early contributions to and readings of other writers' work on *Caribbean Voices*, in the mid-1950s, he went on to do regular interviews and features for the Caribbean Service. But the bulk of his BBC work was for the Pacific Service, the African Service, and for the General Overseas Service which later became the World Service; he contributed not specifically as a Caribbean, but as a London-based radio journalist. The contacts he made and the company he kept were cosmopolitan and world-wide.

In addition to his BBC work, Salkey was highly productive as a writer and an editor. A long poem which he had started writing in 1952, and provisionally called 'Jamaica Symphony', was awarded the Thomas Helmore prize – as 'Jamaica' – in 1955. It was published as the book *Jamaica* in 1973. His first novel, *A Quality of Violence*, won him a Guggenheim Award in 1960. Set in rural Jamaica at the time of the great drought of 1900, it tells how the people of the parish of St Thomas-in-the-East turn to pocomania when their Christian prayers fail to bring rain, and how the violence involved in its rituals recur at all levels of the community. His second novel, *Escape to an Autumn Pavement* seems a contrast in every way. It tells the story of a young Jamaican, Johnny Sobert, who has escaped from the claustrophobic middle-class society of Kingston and his own dominating mother to London, in the 1950s, only to find himself confused and bewildered about his own racial, social and sexual identity. The two books may be seen as two faces of one experience, the first an attempt to assess the self-destructive aridity within an island culture, the second an exploration of an islander's escape to the fabled lure of metropolitan society.

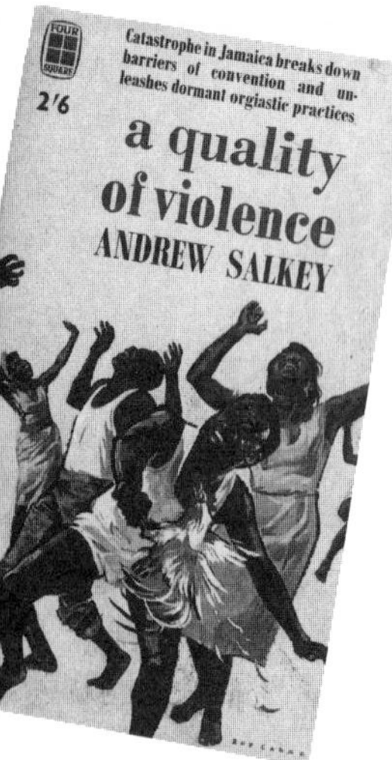

2/6
Catastrophe in Jamaica breaks down barriers of convention and unleashes dormant orgiastic practices
a quality of violence
ANDREW SALKEY

***Cover of Four Square paperback edition of Salkey's first novel,* A Quality of Violence**

In the early 1960s, Salkey wrote a series of novels for children, centred round the major natural disasters to which the Caribbean is prone: *Hurricane*, *Earthquake*, *Drought*. In addition, Salkey collected writing by fellow Caribbean writers: *West Indian Stories*, *Stories from the Caribbean*, and the Caribbean Section of *Young Commonwealth Poetry* (1965). These anthologies were in part the result of and in part led to, his unparallelled range of friendships with other West Indian writers; some only through correspondence – Salkey is known for his unfailing, prompt replies to everything that is sent to him – others face to face. Salkey cherished and nurtured several of the friendships which began through *Caribbean Voices*, and comments:

> I was the one that most of them got on with. I also made sure that I was of service to the friendships. For instance, there was always a little gap between people who liked Edgar Mittelholzer and those who did not . . . . Edgar was the main focus for admiration and in a sense some measure of detestation. He was the professional amongst us, the man who had authored very many novels and so on, the dedicated writer.

Michael Anthony recalls how, through *Caribbean Voices*, he and Andrew Salkey formed 'a very, very close friendship'.

Salkey particularly enjoyed 'serving these friendships'. It was he who introduced VS Naipaul to his future publishers, Andre Deutsch, as Naipaul has publicly acknowledged.[16] Salkey had met Diana Athill of Deutsch at the Sugar Hill Club in Duke Street, Mayfair, where he worked part-time as a waiter in his student days. Salkey's friendship with Charles Monteith of Fabers, which began through editing *West Indian Stories*, led to his being asked to comment on the manuscript of *Palace of the Peacock*, which Wilson Harris had submitted to them. Six readers had made neither head nor tail of it, and advised rejection. When Salkey read it, as he recalls 'I was simply blown away. So much so that I had the effrontery to say to Charles: "If you and your firm can take a chance on William Golding, certainly you can take a chance on Wilson Harris."' Salkey describes himself as having been 'a good sort of donkey person. I love the introducer role. It's easy: you get on the phone, or you write a letter, or you grab somebody's shoulder at a party and you say, "By the way, you know so and so?"' He also nourished the friendships with writers, literally, through the ready hospitality which he and his English wife, Pat, provided at their Bayswater flat.

Salkey's friendships and sense of community were not confined to literature and the arts. From his early days in London he met and talked with people who had come from all parts of the Caribbean in search of work – through the BBC and a variety of part-time jobs, and through simply living in London: 'Brothers and sisters who were factory workers, who worked at Lyons, who worked on the buses and the trains, nurses who worked in hospitals, chamber maids who worked in various hotels.' He remembers joining, when he first arrived, the 'tail end of Harold Moody's movement [the League of Coloured Peoples]'. He also recalls meetings and marches of the Movement for Colonial Freedom. For in addition to being a student at London University, he had set himself what he calls 'an alternative learning plan':

> I got a British Museum reading card, and I went to the Public Record Office nearby. And I really started learning about me and home and the history, because I damn' well wanted to talk to Jamaicans about Jamaica in the long poem that I was hoping to write. And therefore for the first time I began to realise myself as a colonial and us as a colony, and our history, and the way that we were forever at somebody else's beck and call. Our economy wasn't ours. Even our language wasn't really ours. We had to, at least I had to, relearn a great deal.

His political consciousness also goes back, he reckons, to the early 1950s, 'to the early days of George Lamming'; it acquired a formal Marxist structure while he was then a student; it was given further training and a practical context through the *West Indian Gazette*, to which he contributed, and through his friendship with Claudia Jones. He describes her as having been 'a marvellous teacher of people like myself'. He particularly remembers learning, through her experience in the USA, that Marxism and racism were not exclusive. Salkey was also amongst those who felt 'galvanised as persons in political struggle' by Martin Luther King's visit to London in December 1964; he recorded three interviews with him, for the Caribbean, the African and the General Overseas Service of the BBC. When CARD was founded, in 1965, he joined it, briefly, but he did not join any of the Black Power organisations active in Britain during the late 1960s. He 'fancied that no one group had it all, and I figured that I'd serve nearly all and be useful to all'. His core affiliation was to the political activism based at the Students Centre.

Andrew Salkey regarded John La Rose as his political friend. He had heard about La Rose first as a young activist in Trinidad, and read the reports which La Rose sent to the *West Indian Gazette*. In London, they found themselves at the same political demonstrations and marches: against the US invasion of the Dominican Republic, against the Vietnam War. They used to meet, Salkey recalls, on Tottenham Court Road, and talk, 'equally about poetry and politics', and about La Rose's publishing dream: 'In the early days John used to say, "We've got to do something for the permanent record, and publishing is one of the real ways of committing that act. . . . We've got to learn publishing."' Salkey and Brathwaite knew each other as writers: first, through *Caribbean Voices*, then, in *Bim*, where Brathwaite reviewed Salkey's *A Quality of Violence*. Brathwaite claimed 'peculiar distinction' for the book, from its contrast of style and theme; he commended its tone and spirit, its 'minute precision of detail, its sense of social and moral values'; he made comparisons with the fiction of Jane Austen and Vidia Naipaul; and he predicted that Salkey's exploration on all levels 'alone augurs well for the future of the novel in the West Indies'.[17] When they met again in London in 1965/6, what Salkey regarded as 'an extraordinarily insightful review' contributed, Brathwaite believes, to an instant rapport.

Initiatives for a Writers' and Artists' Group

Salkey remembers Brathwaite coming to see him at home, and putting to him the idea of forming a group of West Indian writers. But its premise, as Salkey recalls it, differed slightly from the initial idea shared by La Rose and Brathwaite:

> 'It doesn't seem to me,' he [Brathwaite] said, 'that West Indian writers are being noticed any more. The '50s, yes, they were then noticed. We don't hear from them, they are not in the bookshops, I don't see anybody giving talks in London, and so on. How about it, Andrew?' And I said, 'Whatever we can do first of all to get noticed among ourselves as West Indians in Britain, and for others to notice us, that's fine.' That is how the CAM idea was introduced to me. Naturally I swung behind it.

Brathwaite then arranged a meeting for the three of them at his flat; he remembers that Salkey was from the outset supportive though cautious about the idea. They had tried writers' groups before and they did not work: 'the writer's job was to concentrate on himself' – what was the point of any sort of organisation? But Salkey was encouraged to have a try, particularly as, at that stage, says Brathwaite, 'John and I felt we didn't want an organisation, we just wanted a format which would bring people together'. Salkey admits to being himself a person who likes community, in contrast to other writers whom he describes as 'supreme individuals . . .quite capable of standing on their own': George Lamming, Sam Selvon, VS Naipaul, Wilson Harris. He may have been reluctant to approach them about the idea in its early stages. Brathwaite recalls 'that at the very beginning none of the major Caribbean writers – apart from Andrew Salkey – were involved with CAM'.

After these preliminary talks with La Rose and Salkey, Brathwaite seems to have wasted no time in taking initiatives to get things going. His first two letters are to people whom he thought would be useful in specific ways – to Bryan King and to Edward Lucie-Smith: both born in the West Indies, both long-time resident and well-placed in Britain, both white. These letters show that the group whose formation Brathwaite, La Rose and Salkey had discussed was to be of writers and artists, and of critics; as La Rose puts it, 'people who, though not writers or artists themselves, were seriously interested in writing, art and culture'. They show that the group which Brathwaite at any rate had in mind was to be a structured organisation, beyond a simple format within which writers and artists could meet and interact with each other. Both letters refer to the formation of such a group as his own idea, which indeed, in this form, it entirely was. To Bryan King Brathwaite wrote:

> I had an idea today and am passing it on to you right away because I'd like your help and advice with it.
>
> The more I stay here in England, the more it seems to me that our writers and artists are missing a wonderful opportunity to communicate with themselves and with British and Commonwealth artists around them. What I'd like to start going (and it has no doubt been attempted before) is some sort of WI [West Indian] artists' and writers' group concerned with discussing WI art and literature. This would take the form of critical symposia, the discussion of recently published material and readings of work in progress: not only by established artists, but by students and others who feel they have something to say. I would not, however, like to see this confined to West Indians. There should be a link-up with C'wealth and British writers and artists: it is time they really got to know what we are doing and what we are worth; and time too that we had a chance of discussing their work with them. Some attempt should also be made to meet and discuss the work of French and Spanish-speaking West Indians. Here I think the staff of those university departments that deal with this sort of thing could help. I'd also like to see publishers, BBC types and British critics in on this. It seems to me that the WI contribution, after the little flare-up in the 50s, is being woefully neglected.

> I've already spoken to a few people, both WI and English, and they are interested. The first thing, I think, is to find a place where we can meet. Do you think it would be possible to use the WI Students Centre? I remember your telling me that it was being rather neglected these days. Here is a chance perhaps to do something about it. What do you think? If you like the idea, would you be willing to be in on this? Would you be willing, for instance, to approach the Students Centre with this idea, with a view to allowing me the use of a room there for this purpose? I'd like to start off about the 15th of January next year.[18]

Already the concept is of West Indian writers and artists talking not only among themselves but with British and Commonwealth artists; of extending the group beyond practising writers and artists to students and others; of including French- and Spanish-speaking West Indians; of inviting British publishers, critics and so on. And already the Students Centre is seen as the ideal place to hold meetings. Brathwaite's letter to Lucie-Smith puts forward similar ideas, widened specifically to include African writers and artists – James Ngugi (now Ngũgĩ wa Thiong'o) is named as 'doing a doctoral thesis on West Indian writing' – and goes on to hope that proceedings could be taped so as to build up an archive of material, 'and (who knows) even be able to set up a magazine which would reflect the work of the group'.[19] All these are ideas which were realised when CAM came into being.

The specific help required from King was over the use of the Centre: King had been Chairman of Governors since 1963, and indeed involved in its formation. He replied without delay, accepting and backing Brathwaite's proposals without question: 'Of course you have my fullest sympathy and all the support I can give . . .. I am asking the Warden to circulate your letter to the Board and to give you the fullest possible support.'[20] King recommends that Brathwaite and one or two more of the group should apply for Associate Membership, and let the rest be guests, initially anyway. The idea of bringing in 'the Africans' comes from King, with a promise to put an African poet at Cambridge in touch. King recommends inviting Edward Lucie-Smith, Andrew Salkey, John Press of the British Council, Tony Haynes of Bookers; he anticipates full support from the Students Centre Board to come from 'Parbaton, a singer and a lawyer, from, I think, BG [British Guiana], representing the House Committee on the Board and grappling with intractible inertia as best he can'. Clearly King's confidence in Brathwaite was absolute, to prompt so frank and so supportive a reply.

Brathwaite's specific requests of Edward Lucie-Smith suggest that he might well have approached him without King's prompting: 'How best shall we set up the group? What about finance?

Contacts? Programmes?' Lucie-Smith, born in Jamaica in 1933, had lived in Britain since 1946. Unusually he worked in the fields of both literature and art. By 1966 he had published two collections of poems, a book on art and an anthology of Elizabethan verse. In his own words, at that time he worked, 'as a journalist, mostly art criticism, as a broadcaster, and worked in a London advertising agency'.[21] He was clearly someone with just the scope, contacts and experience to be useful to the group as Brathwaite conceived it: 'I regarded Edward Lucie-Smith as an important West Indian in London who was also a member of the British establishment.' Brathwaite's letter ends by inviting Lucie-Smith to a meeting on 19 December, at 8.15 pm. No other letters of invitation have been kept. Were all asked for similar advice? Or were they simply telephoned, and Lucie-Smith singled out for a special approach?

Lucie-Smith's reply was helpful, but guarded:

> About the idea of a West Indian Group. Yes, basically a good one. I've, frankly, had my bellyful of organising groups after running one for eight or nine years – so don't count on me too much. However, if you'll let me remain somewhat in the background, I'll certainly help where I can. I think the West Indian Students Centre would be an excellent place to meet.
>
> Advice, rapidly: make those who want to come subscribe, however little (people don't value what they get for free). Use the money to circulate the membership – we used to circulate all poems to be discussed beforehand, in the group I ran. It's more difficult to do this with prose, of course, but it does help to keep in postal touch with people.
>
> Set the group up (ie create some kind of corporate identity) and then apply to the Arts Council Literature Panel for a grant.... As I know the Arts Council well, I'll do my very best for you in that quarter.[22]

Louis James

He declined the invitation for 19 December: 'I'm desperately over-committed and must do some writing that night.' Meanwhile Brathwaite had been over to the Centre to meet the Warden and have a look round, and decided that the library there 'seems a rather nice and convenient place'.[23]

The meeting on 19 December was to be, wrote Brathwaite, 'at my place': 47(B) Mecklenburgh Square, a basement flat in a London University hall of residence, near King's Cross. He and Doris Brathwaite hosted the meeting with John La Rose and Andrew Salkey. Of those whom Brathwaite himself had invited or hoped would be invited only Louis James, Antony Haynes and Orlando Patterson actually came. James was now teaching in the English Department of the new University of Kent at Canterbury; *The Islands in Between*, his collection (the very first) of critical

Orlando Patterson

essays on West Indian literature, prepared while he was in Jamaica, was shortly to be published. He had already brought out a seminal book on Victorian popular novels, *Fiction for the Working Man: 1830–1850*. Haynes was working for Bookers in London. Patterson was teaching at LSE; *The Sociology of Slavery*, based on his doctoral thesis, and his second novel, *An Absence of Ruins*, were about to be published.

Evan Jones, the other writer at the meeting, had been invited by Andrew Salkey: they had a long connection, from *Caribbean Voices* and from Jamaica in the 1940s. Jones says, 'Andrew – who was very active – was a great personal friend of mine, and I would have hated missing out on Andrew.' By 1966, Jones was a successful freelance writer of plays for BBC radio and television, and of scripts for films. His breakthrough into film had come in 1961 with the script for Joseph Losey, the distinguished American director's film, *The Damned*. Jones had followed it with scripts for such wellknown films as *Eve* (1962), *King and Country* (1964) and *Modesty Blaise* (1965). He had, as he explains, moved away from Caribbean writing at that time and was working in international film. Sam Selvon, whom Brathwaite had hoped would be there, was not. Nor was Frank Bowling, the only artist whose name was mentioned before the meeting – Bowling had left London for New York earlier in 1966. Aubrey Williams was not present, although Brathwaite's 1968 article on CAM includes him, probably because Williams was always regarded as a founder member of CAM, along with those who were in fact at the 19 December meeting.[24]

Only Brathwaite's contemporary account of this founding meeting of what became CAM survives. He, Evan Jones and Antony Haynes, have distinct memories of it. For the others who were there, it was one of several very early meetings of which memories tend to coalesce. Brathwaite's letters written shortly afterwards to Lucie-Smith and to Kenneth Ramchand – the Trinidadian postgraduate student at Edinburgh University, working on the West Indian novel, whom he hoped to interest in the group – add further detail:

> Everyone v. keen, but a division as to whether to take up my idea as outlined to you; or confine things for the moment to a small group which will 'hammer out the objectives'. Patterson, supported by Evan Jones, felt we should have a more positive direction than the one I outlined; proposed a 'dialogue' on 'the WI aesthetic'. This begins on January 6 at Patterson's place; everybody at the moment falling for the cosy, sitting-room atmosphere.[25]

Evan Jones remembers that he 'felt in sympathy with what was being discussed, but I also thought: "What am I doing here?"' His reaction is at variance with Brathwaite's subsequent public comment: 'It was clear from the outset that this was something that these artists had been hoping and waiting for.'[26] Jones explains: 'I have always been a loner, and a collection of writers seems to me to be a contradiction in terms.' Antony Haynes remembers feeling that he was rather negative about the proposed enterprise: 'I thought they were very ambitious and I wondered where they would get to and how they were going to focus themselves and what they were going to achieve.' Neither Jones nor Haynes attended the meeting on 6 January, nor, as far as they recall, any later CAM meetings or conferences. But both gave CAM generously of their expertise: Jones, by taking part in a symposium on theatre and a session on film; Haynes, by rounding up contributions to fund the two residential conferences.

Early, private CAM meetings

The circle of people who attended the meeting on 6 January was considerably enlarged. Held at Orlando and Nerys Patterson's flat, 83 Anson Road, London N7, it included, in addition to the Brathwaites, Andrew Salkey, John La Rose, Sarah White and Louis James – Gordon Rohlehr, Guyanese postgraduate student at Birmingham University working on Joseph Conrad, and James Ngugi, Kenyan postgraduate student at Leeds University working on George Lamming, and already a published novelist. Aubrey Williams was most probably also there, and a young, unpublished writer, the Trinidadian Faustin Charles.

The meeting took the form which Patterson had suggested, 'dialogue on the WI aesthetic', and he himself opened it. He was known to be a brilliant sociologist. Equally he was known as author of an immensely successful first novel, *The Children of Sisyphus* (1964), recommended to its publisher by CLR James, and winner of First Prize at the Dakar Festival of Negro Arts in 1966. He was also a frequent contributor to the *Times Literary Supplement* – where he had recently published an article on Negritude – and to the *New Left Review*, of whose Editorial Board he was a member.

The Children of Sisyphus is concerned with a group of the most deprived and destitute of Jamaica's urban poor, those living in the 'dungle' and 'Back-o-wall' Kingston, and focuses on its Rastafarians; the year is 1959, when many Rastafarians believed that repatriation to Africa was imminent. Patterson's closely documented study of West Indian poverty was drawn from his sociological fieldwork of the early 1960s; this is combined with what Bridget Jones describes as an attempt 'to give this condition universal significance'.[27] For Patterson draws on the retelling by Albert Camus of the fable of Sisyphus for his formulation of life as a heroic struggle by the individual to endure his fate.

Sisyphus was enthusiastically received on publication, as a breakthrough in Caribbean social realism, as the first fictional attempt to look seriously at the urban slum-dwellers and the Rastafarian community of Jamaica. The nihilism which provides the philosophical framework for Patterson's novel was criticised by some of his contemporaries; others considered its reliance on a doctrine inherited from French existentialism, and the sociological documentation and analysis, to be obtrusive.

But Patterson had already written a second novel, and intended to continue writing fiction. He was eager for dialogue with fellow West Indian writers about the aesthetic which should determine West Indian creative work and criticism, and for a chance to justify his own concept and practice of fiction as a sociologist. He and Brathwaite had first met at Mona in 1964, when he was back in Jamaica doing research for his LSE thesis; it was the year of publication of *Sisyphus* and, he recalls: 'We came to know each other fairly well; we talked a lot about West Indian writing.'

Patterson's paper which led off the dialogue (the only part successfully recorded and therefore transcribed) was entitled, 'Is there a West Indian Aesthetic?', for, he explained, in seeking to find 'the aesthetic standards by which we are to judge Caribbean arts', it is necessary first to question whether the concept of 'aesthetic', based as it is on Western European Christian art, is appropriate to the Caribbean. 'We must begin', proposed Patterson, 'with recognition of the basic facts of our cultural background', and this he found very difficult: 'West Indian society strikes me as one which is in many ways traditionless. One doesn't have a basis for retaliation against the colonial experience in an indigenous culture as occurs in the case of the African or Asian.' Quoting Frantz Fanon, 'all one has, has been learned from the colonial experience', Patterson stated his belief that one has, 'if one is to be real to oneself...to deny in many respects a part of one's own existence...to begin by wiping the slate clean'. He was dissatisfied with attempts made so far. Negritude, 'essentially a West Indian movement', provided no alternative, despite its positive usefulness for understanding West Indian historical development, and despite the evident survivals of African culture in the Caribbean, most importantly in Haiti. But as a way forward for Caribbean writers, as a useful explanation of 'the present style of living, the present attitudes' in West Indian society, he judged Negritude to be a dead end.

What then, asked Patterson, do we have, 'since we cannot retreat into the bosom of a suppressed indigenous culture?' He rejected as irrelevant the attitude summarised by the Jamaican national motto, 'Out of many, one people', as a 'facile, middle-class view', and likewise the concept of commonly held West Indian characteristics as 'a lot of bourgeois romanticism'. In

Patterson's view, the Caribbean artist should explore the problems of West Indian society, thus requiring the novelist to be also 'a kind of sociologist'. The sociologist-artist should then 'assume the role of arousing national, social and cultural consciousness, and explore the possible direction along which our social bias should develop'. Such a role for the artist necessitates a particular sort of art: 'I think all our art has to be didactic, and clearly so; I don't think we should conceal our intentions.' In conclusion, Patterson posed what he considered to be the urgent problem of form, particularly of the novel, citing his own doubts about the quality of Michael Anthony's novels, and expressing too his personal inability to judge West Indian painting.

Patterson brought together many of the current concerns of West Indian artists and intellectuals. But his view of these concerns, and his prescriptions, were very much his own. His dismissive attitude towards African cultural remains, his denial of an indigenous Caribbean culture, his rigid concept of tradition, above all his negative view of what could be achieved: these were fiercely challenged at subsequent CAM meetings.

Further discussion followed from a letter from Kenneth Ramchand, which Brathwaite read aloud. For Ramchand had replied immediately to the letter about plans for the group and an account of the preliminary meeting sent him by Brathwaite in late December, with stringent criticism of the group's basic rationale. He saw little point in 'a group of intellectuals meeting in London to discuss West Indian affairs'. His own priority concern was 'to get back to the WI in a favourable position and try to make WI . . . literature popular. This seems to me a logical development out of the *Bim* and *Kyk-over-al* stage. If we must have a cultural elite, it must be an elite diffusing sweetness and light to and drawing sweetness and light from the people'.[28] Ramchand did not see how such a group could help to rectify West Indians being 'rather left out of things' in Britain, nor to make contacts with other Commonwealth writers – an approach which he had become disillusioned with. But he welcomed the proposed links with French and Spanish West Indians as natural allies in a potential Caribbean political unit, considering 'our main task as West Indians . . . to do something to check the political and cultural separatism of the islands in the former Federation'. He would like to see such a group working out 'in what way we, as a group of "intellectual" exiles in London, interested in the Arts, relate to our society'. Ramchand put forward projects which the group might investigate, for instance, discussion of single novels: 'Let us relate our "aesthetic" to examples from our arts.' Several projects related to 'the African presence', but none to his own ancestry, for, he said,

> The Indians of India we can ignore. Few West Indians deriving from that Continent have sentimentalised it though recent political misunderstandings between negroes and Indians have caused retreats into Indian-ness, and older Indians act as a kind of brake on creolisation. I think time will be enough to bring a proper perspective.

CAM seems open to criticism for its failure to explore the Indo-Caribbean traditions, to rehabilitate the Indian presence alongside that of the African, in the Caribbean consciousness. But for Ramchand at least the exclusion was deliberate and reasoned. Finally he supported the idea of such a group, and offered to take part in a session.

At this first session one practical decision was achieved: the matter of a name for the group. Brathwaite has preserved his scribbled notes of the progress of suggestions: from CLAWS – the Caribbean London Artists and Writers Sousou (cooperative), CAS – the Caribbean Artists Society, to CAM, underlined; which was, as Doris Brathwaite remembered, the suggestion of Nerys Patterson.

Discussion closed at around 3.00 am – an hour earlier than the previous meeting. Louis James, writing to Brathwaite afterwards, was enthusiastic but critical: 'Excellent discussion with some brilliant moments, especially from Orlando, Andrew and Gordon R. Just the thing to bust the field wide open. First class first session. Worried because so often on the point of a good specific point, the discussion veered off.'[29] He put forward a number of suggestions, very tentatively – Brathwaite might be thinking of such points himself and they might, in any case, be 'the deadening didactic impulses of an oven-baked academic; all this may be on quite the wrong lines. Do pull to bits. I'd like to know what Andrew and Patto [Patterson] think too'. The suggestions are in fact fundamental and comprehensive: a more structured form of session, including a 'loosely-held closing time'; a cyclostyled account of each talk; enclosing his own notes on Patterson's talk, to be given or, ideally, posted to members before the next session, along with a short bibliography; an overall programme of topics for future sessions, of which he enclosed ten suggestions; building an archive of Caribbean art; producing a periodical or a booklet, and seeking Arts Council support for both; investigating properly headed notepaper. James in fact picked up and built on just the sort of aspects which Brathwaite was interested in.

Louis James was brought up and educated in Zambia (then Northern Rhodesia); his first academic post after Oxford was in the Extra-Mural Department at Hull, where he introduced African literature. So he shared with Brathwaite first-hand knowledge of Africa, and the scope and challenge of extra-mural university work. Both were far-sighted, energetic and innovative young university lecturers – James was in the process of setting up the first course on West Indian literature at the University of Kent. James believes that they had talked over the sort of organisation which became CAM long before the preliminary meeting in December:

> Even back in Jamaica, I remember talking with Eddie [Brathwaite] about the direction in which a Caribbean artists' movement might go. There was a need for bringing together, in particular, those who left the Caribbean to come to London or go to New York. . . . I remember being very impressed earlier on by what happened in the formation of Ghana by movements in London.

Of all the founder members, James was closest to Brathwaite in his overall concept of what CAM might be and do. He was also one of the most ready to help in practical ways. But his suggestions in this letter seem too comprehensive, have a touch of overkill, particularly the proposed list of topics which smack of the university lecture series, and hint a non-Caribbean focus. For close as James was to Brathwaite, and welcome as the others made him, he never forgot that he was not himself from the Caribbean. His letter ends: 'It is a tremendous privilege to be in this Movement and I am deeply grateful to you all for letting me be "in" on it.'

Gordon Rohlehr was dissatisfied with the group's first session, for similar reasons. Writing afterwards to Brathwaite, he asked:

> Did you notice how constantly urbanity was defeating thought at the last meeting of CAM? How some members could simultaneously admit and practise a polite evasiveness? Three-quarters of what was said was already known, was agreed to by everyone who then proceeded to say the same thing in his own words.[30]

In consequence, Rohlehr was asked to address the second of CAM's public sessions, and to develop points he had made about language in Sam Selvon's fiction. Brathwaite himself was sharply critical of and disappointed with the content of Patterson's paper, finding 'aesthetic' inadequately defined, and his point of view so negative that there was little to discuss.[31] At the next session, instead of reading *Rights of Passage* – his first long poem, shortly to be published – he proposed to present his 'own picture of a possible approach to the subject [of a West Indian aesthetic]'.

This second programmed session of the new CAM on 3 February 1967, was again smallish, informal, and held at the Pattersons' flat. Unlike Patterson's paper, Brathwaite's was not specially prepared for CAM. It was taken from a long article, the first part of which was about to appear in *Bim*[32] and seemed to Brathwaite to provide answers to much of what Patterson had posed as 'problems'. Although Brathwaite was ten years older than Patterson, he was at that time less wellknown or established as artist and academic. No book of his poetry had yet been published, he was still working for his doctorate. But he had been writing and publishing West Indian literary criticism regularly for over a decade and was, in the words of Gordon Rohlehr, 'one of the first West Indian critics of any importance and consistency'.[33] 'Jazz and the West Indian Novel' was the latest of a series of articles, first published in *Bim*, starting, in 'Sir Galahad and the Islands' (1957) with the fiction of migration, and since then keeping step with new work and current trends. His latest article drew equally on his own search for a radically new poetic form.

Brathwaite's thesis was that a correspondence may be found between jazz and contemporary Caribbean culture; that distinctively jazz elements can be identified in calypso and ska, in West Indian poetry and the novel; and that these jazz elements constitute the direction of a West Indian aesthetic. 'The West Indian writer is just beginning to enter his own cultural New Orleans. . . . It is in the first place mainly a negro experience, but it is also a folk experience; and it has a relevance to the "modern" predicament as we understand it today.' Brathwaite quoted George Lamming and Derek Walcott on the value of words to the West Indian writer, and correlated them with the jazz musician's notes. He quoted passages from recent West Indian and African fiction – Lamming, Sam Selvon, Gabriel Okara – as evidence of 'word, image and rhythm . . . the basic elements of what, within the terms of my definition, would go to make up a jazz aesthetic in the Caribbean novel'. Then he pointed to another essential element in jazz: 'What determines the shape and direction of a jazz performance is the nature of its improvisation.' Improvisation is to be found in many aspects of West Indian culture: in the oral tradition of its folk literature, in calypso, in Anancy stories, in speeches at 'tea meetings'. But 'the West Indian novel has so far made less conscious use of these possibilities than one might expect'. Brathwaite identified elements of improvisation, of 'jazz phrasing', in TS Eliot's *Burnt Norton*, and in the 'train scene' in George Lamming's *The Emigrants*:

> The 'theme' here is the train's journey. The improvisation is in the rhythm, the shifts of tone and rhythm, the repetitions, the apparently spontaneous variations of thought, point of view, and comment that make the journey 'happen'. . . . Here, at the end of the journey (the 'performance'), the ensemble re-asserts itself, though still expressing the individual group dilemma ('*But if a man see one single good break goin*') which jazz on the whole has resolved so successfully.

He challenged the West Indian writer to further improvisation if he was to achieve a jazz novel, 'to "improvise" not only with words and rhythm and images and motifs, but with the core of the novel itself – characterisation'. Two West Indian novels – Andrew Salkey's *A Quality of Violence* and Roger Mais's *Brother Man* – alone, in his view, demonstrated improvisation through character. 'Here, I hope, we shall at last be at the heart of the West Indian jazz novel.'

Brathwaite's talk to CAM seems rather loose in structure and at times open to question; in extracting and stringing together passages from the three articles, much is lost. But the span of Brathwaite's cultural examples and the thrust of his argument are, in the ex-colonial West Indian literary context, revolutionary. Jazz had been a serious interest since he was a sixth-former. Brathwaite's incorporation in *Rights of Passage* of specific features of jazz music such as 'repetition and refrain, improvisation', 'dissonance and discord', 'lyricism and flatness' enabled him to recognise its elements in the work of other writers.[34] His assumptions – that calypso and ska were of equivalent significance and interest to poetry and the novel; that the oral tradition provided a model for West Indian literature, particularly in its essential aspect of performance; that writing should be based on speech rhythms; that the 'folk' experience is central – suggested an indigenous aesthetic for West Indian creativity and criticism. Brathwaite's close acquaintance with the range of Afro-American folk culture, from spirituals, gospel and work songs to sermons, and equally with their transformation into blues and jazz, enabled him to position in jazz a viable West Indian aesthetic. If writers of the Harlem Renaissance and after could use the principles and motifs of jazz in creating fiction and poetry based on their own folk tradition, why should West Indian writers not attempt a similar strategy? But such an aesthetic was founded on a basic assumption which Patterson rejected. Conceding that 'not all West Indian artists are negro', Brathwaite still held that, 'to make "sense" they have to write about their society, which is predominantly negro'. Brathwaite, brought up in Barbados, working now in Jamaica, after nine years of living and working in West Africa, assumed a predominance of African culture in West Indian society which many of his contemporaries could not share. This resulted in antagonism and division in ways which continue to reverberate, 20 years on.

Alongside these programmed, private CAM sessions in early January and early February 1967, there were other occasions, at the Brathwaites' flat, to which particular people were invited. There are no records but several memories of occasions attended by artists who became key members of CAM. Brathwaite recalls how 'at that first meeting in my flat in December, we had immediately thought of Aubrey Williams. . . . I hadn't met Aubrey, I hadn't heard of him, nothing like that. And when he arrived on the spot, it was just an explosion, wonderful.' Aubrey Williams himself did not remember the particular occasion when he met the early CAM people, simply that either John La Rose or (most probably) Andrew Salkey brought him along and that Louis James was also there. The painter and art teacher Karl Craig (known to his friends, and in CAM, as Jerry; now formally known as Karl 'Jerry' Craig), and his wife Christine, then a drama student, were also invited to meet CAM's founder members, on a different occasion. Jerry Craig recalls that they were invited through Andrew Salkey:

> We talked about what we would do, and the identification of the Caribbean in England, how we could make them know more about us and our forms of art and expression. We talked about the various aspects of Caribbean art, but discussion was very heavily oriented on the writer and the poet.

Aubrey Williams's experience and stature as an artist and his articulate views, together with Jerry Craig's experience and practical organising ability, complemented the strong literary side of CAM.

The Jeannetta Cochrane (now the Cochrane) Theatre reopened in March 1992, providing a permanent home for Yvonne Brewster's Talawa Theatre Company

CAM's first public reading

Another informal early session at the Brathwaites' flat was to have especially far-reaching consequences. John La Rose and Sarah White were there and, as La Rose recalls:

> When we got to their flat, Eddie was already beginning to play a taped recording of himself reading *Rights of Passage*. I was amazed at the beauty and power of his reading. I had never known anyone read so well. Having heard the entire recording of the reading, I immediately proposed to him that New Beacon should put on a public reading. Sarah agreed.

La Rose and White decided to put the reading on at the Jeannetta Cochrane Theatre – a small building next to the Central School of Art near Holborn which had, since 1965, been the home of the London Traverse Theatre Company. Jim Haynes, a young American, started the original Traverse Theatre Club in 1962 in Edinburgh, where he owned a paperback bookshop. The Club became the first permanent home of Edinburgh's 'fringe theatre'. Less successful than the Traverse as a cultural and social centre, the Jeannetta Cochrane nonetheless continued its tradition of presenting new plays by living playwrights, along with 'jazz, underground films and happenings'.[35] La Rose and White knew Haynes and saw nearly all the plays at his theatre. Before reading there, Brathwaite already envisaged its future possibilities for CAM, writing: 'If this comes off well, we hope that the Jeannetta Cochrane will become available to us not only for readings such as this, but for more elaborate things like play-readings and eventually, perhaps, for the full-scale production of West Indian plays.'[36] But in the summer of 1967 Haynes moved on to found the Arts Lab in Drury Lane.

Brathwaite's public reading of *Rights of Passage* was presented by the London Traverse Theatre Company and New Beacon Publications at the Jeannetta Cochrane Theatre on 3 March 1967 at 10.15 pm. It seemed to Brathwaite a daunting ordeal. Writing shortly before it to Randolph Stow, the Australian poet, he said, 'Good to know, too, that you'll be in for the reading; though I must say that the prospect of the long lonely night of March 3 quite appalls me. But it's the test, I suppose, of the spoken word. Hope I'll be accurate enough to hold them (the audience, I mean).'[37] The audience from all accounts, and in many memories, was held indeed. The reading was a major Caribbean cultural event, a first, a breakthrough in many ways.

Cover of Brathwaite's first book of poetry, **Rights of Passage**

Rights of Passage was the first published Caribbean poem which attempted epic length and scope:[38] a narrative concerned with the West Indian's journey from his home country to London and New York and back to the Caribbean. It was publicised – on the book jacket and in the programme of the reading – as being Part 1 of a trilogy; publication of Part 2, *Masks*, was promised for the following year. *Rights of Passage* was also the first major poem to articulate the experience and condition of the West Indian immigrant in Britain. Several novels and plays had done so, and isolated short poems. But in *Rights of Passage* a sequence of related poems narrate the West Indian journey, and they are counterpointed with historical backgound, giving the immigrant experience a new self-awareness, depth and poignancy. In rhythm and language also *Rights of Passage* broke new ground for Caribbean poetry. The variety of form is dazzling – from the terse, broken couplets of 'All God's chillun' to the six-line-long flowing stanzas of 'South'. The rhythm has freed itself from the iambic pentameters which had pervaded Caribbean poetry for so long. Instead, there are rhythms which echo jazz, blues and calypso, and which approximate to the varied speech patterns of Caribbean people. The language likewise reflects the complete continuum of Caribbean speech, cutting between international standard English, Caribbean English, and creole, with appropriateness and fluency.

Publication by Oxford University Press was also a breakthrough, especially for so ambitious and large-scale a poem. Derek Walcott alone of Caribbean poets had been published by a major British house: *In a Green Night* (1962) and *The Castaway* (1965) by

Jonathan Cape. Jon Stallworthy, editor of the prestigious OUP poetry list and himself a published poet, recalls his first sight of Brathwaite's work:

> The typescript came in and I was immediately struck by it. What one always looked for, hoped for, was a new and unmistakeably authentic voice. . . . Eddie's did not sound like anyone that I had read before. The first things I remember were these very short little lines running into each other, which was very unlike what the Movement Poets were doing then. And I could hear through it a clear spoken voice.

Stallworthy recognised poetry written to be heard aloud. Sarah White recalls the impact of hearing *Rights of Passage* read by Brathwaite in a London context: 'It was a tremendous reading. I think people found it very exciting because they'd never heard anybody like Eddie, and it was a *tour de force* because British poets as a whole don't read as well as that, don't have that same tradition.' The reading came at a time when public readings of poetry were increasingly in vogue. The first International Festival of Poetry had taken place in the Royal Albert Hall in June 1965, four hours of readings to 7000 people. The only Caribbean poet billed to appear was Pablo Armando Fernandez of Cuba. British Caribbean poets resident in Britain had read individual poems at cultural events and at political meetings. Their first corporate public reading was in September 1965, as part of the Commonwealth Arts Festival's *Verse and Voice* – a festival of poetry, poems and ballads of the Commonwealth, held at the Royal Court Theatre in Sloane Square. On 27 September West Indian poets shared an evening titled 'Transatlantic' with Canadian poets, and stole the show. George Lamming presented and read alongside Errol John, Pauline Henriquez, John Figueroa, Evan Jones, Edward Kamau Brathwaite (just arrived from Jamaica); they read poems by Derek Walcott, EM Roach, FA Collymore, Mervyn Morris, and by themselves. Louise Bennett took part, not as a poet, but with West Indian folksongs. Each sequence of poems was presented continuously. The poets/readers were together on the stage throughout, grouped and seated informally. In all, the West Indian part of the evening was a highly effective stage performance. John La Rose had been in the audience. He was confident that Brathwaite's reading of *Rights of Passage* should similarly be produced on stage, so that the poet's placing and movements complemented and enhanced his actual reading. The reading was a performance.

For New Beacon to present, and Brathwaite to undertake, a one-person poetry reading was another first, another breakthrough. No other Caribbean poet had held an audience in Britain with a solo reading of his poetry. Andrew Salkey retains a vivid memory of the reading and of its importance for West Indians in Britain at that time:

> I can't tell you what that reading did for me and for the audience. And for us culturally in England. It was absolutely electrifying, a beautiful voice, Eddie has, a remarkable resonance. And it's a narrative kind of poetry-reading voice, it hasn't got that thinness of the abstract metaphor and so on.

For Pearl Connor, the Jeannetta Cochrane Theatre as a venue was as significant a breakthrough as the poetry reading itself: 'We hadn't presented any one of our writers, in the sense of poet, in that way before. It was really a first at that level then. It was a public theatre, a big place in a prominent position. People responded very well to it.'

OUP took no part in the reading which effectively launched its publication and its poet. But New Beacon had invited a number of people prominent in the London arts world to the reading, such as Douglas Cleverdon, BBC radio producer of Dylan Thomas's poem, *Under Milk Wood*. New Beacon also made sure that the book of *Rights of Passage* was available at the reading by obtaining copies from OUP on a sale or return basis. The new publishing house also took advantage of the occasion to display and sell its own first publications: La Rose's book of poems, *Foundations*, and *Marcus Garvey 1887–1940*, a monograph by Adolph Edwards, then a law student, written for presentation to a study group that met at the home of CLR and Selma James. Brathwaite's reading gave New Beacon its first experience of selling other books besides its own publications. It also made New Beacon more widely known.

The reading was also good publicity for CAM. Page 4 of the programme, headed 'The Caribbean Artists Movement, C.A.M.', promised a follow-up to the reading in a symposium on West Indian Writing in a week's time, at the West Indian Students Centre. It also announced CAM's plan for a series of lectures starting the following month, on *Arts and Artists from the West Indies*. It invited those interested to complete a slip on a sheet of paper inserted in the programme. This seems to have been a practical idea of Louis James's. He had written to Brathwaite beforehand:

> I would like Andrew or yr.self to say a few words about CAM at the evening, and a pile of leaflets adumbrating our aims, achievements so far, and a tear-off section indicating (1) interest; (2) desire to be a paid-up member. I am willing to sit at a desk and make up the books in the foyer. I would also cyclostyle leaflets, if you haven't already had this done.[39]

No record of completed slips exists. But a letter from Brathwaite to Gordon Rohlehr immediately after the reading mentions some of the people who were there and likely to be joining CAM:

> Thanks to John's enterprise last Friday, CAM, I think, has taken a great step forward. Lucie-Smith and Ronald Bryden are interested; so now are Wilson Harris and Sam Selvon (both of whom attended the reading) and Michael Anthony and Ronald Moody, the sculptor. Gerald Moore has joined and a lecturer from Canterbury; and we've got quite a few interesting people on the mailing list incl. Bloke Modisane. Beryl McBurnie and Pearl Connor were also at the reading; and Dwight Whylie, Randolph Stow (the Australian poet) and Calvin Hernton (an American poet) were at the reading and were among the 30-odd cats at a session at my place afterwards. I'm also to see the Arts Council big-wigs next week to discuss how they can help us. So you see, we're slowly getting somewhere. Colin Rickards has already given us some publicity in the WI Thompson-group papers; the ULU [University of London Union] newspaper *Sennet* is coming out with something; and a man from the *Sunday Times* 'Atticus' is also interested.[40]

Some of those who came to the reading already knew about CAM or had attended its private meetings. For Don and Betty Wilson, the reading confirmed the switch from their own study group to CAM:

> After that the three or four of us who had been the core of our discussion group got absorbed into CAM. There was no question, once you went to Eddie's reading, that an exciting event had taken place, something you wanted to be associated with and were very thrilled about.

So it was the performance of innovative creative work by one of CAM's founders, made possible and flanked by the enterprise and energy of his fellow founder-members, that completed the beginning stage of CAM, and heralded its real start: the first public meeting, at the West Indian Students Centre, on Friday 10 March 1967.

3 CAM Goes Public
March - July 1967

CAM's first public meeting at the Students Centre on Friday 10 March, a week after Edward Kamau Brathwaite's reading, set the style and pattern of meetings which took place regularly each month for the next three years, and more intermittently for a further two years. They were the backbone of a CAM programme of varied events which included talks and symposia, readings and performances, art exhibitions and films. Around the programme, there developed a range of activities which put CAM's objectives into practice: a newsletter, bookselling, and a network of useful contacts. Almost all of this programme was set in motion during CAM's first six months.

CAM meetings: public and private

When CAM went public, on 10 March 1967, anybody interested could hear views and join in a debate which hitherto had been aired only amongst members, at home. The cyclostyled programme for Brathwaite's reading of *Rights of Passage* the week before had advertised CAM's first public session thus: 'There will not be time – obviously – to discuss this poem and its implications this evening; but CAM has organised a symposium on "West Indian Writing" which follows naturally, we think, from any thinking about this poem.'[1] Sixteen West Indian writers and critics were named as taking part, with Edward Lucie-Smith as chairman. On the night five writers and critics formed the panel and delivered the 5-minute set pieces which they had been asked to prepare: Michael Anthony, Wilson Harris, Orlando Patterson, Louis James, Kenneth Ramchand. Andrew Salkey chaired the session; Lucie-Smith had accepted but at the last moment was unable to come. So all three writers on the panel, and the chairman, were novelists; of the two literary critics, one specialised in the West Indian novel. Although the chairman pointed out poets and dramatists and artists in the audience and invited them to speak – Edward Kamau Brathwaite, Evan Jones, John La Rose; Karl 'Jerry' Craig, Ronald Moody – prose fiction formed the focus of the session, now called 'New Directions of West Indian Writing'. These were almost all confined to new directions in the novel, despite the symposium's planned take-off from Brathwaite's reading, which so startlingly demonstrated new directions in poetry. But the novel was still, in 1967, the major West Indian literary form; and the three novelists on this CAM panel spoke about three distinctly different approaches to it.

Cover of **The Waiting Room,** *1967*

The Waiting Room
a novel by
WILSON HARRIS

During the 1950s, when he still lived and worked in Guyana, Wilson Harris had begun to immerse himself in the writing of fiction. The main purpose of his move to Britain in 1959 was to explore and develop his concept of fiction. Fabers accepted each of the manuscripts which he regularly submitted, so that by 1967 seven of his novels had been published. By 1967, too, Harris had spoken to audiences in Britain about his views on fiction and his approach to writing it – most notably to the West Indian Students Union, at the Students Centre, in May 1964, on 'Tradition and the West Indian Novel', published as a booklet by WISU the following year.[2] Here he expounded and explained what he was attempting in his novels. His concept of fiction was, he claimed, radically different from that of the 19th century European 'novel of persuasion', whose characters had to be 'consolidated' – the tradition in which West Indian novelists had so far been writing. He himself was engaged in a 'radical new art of fiction', in which he sought to visualise a fulfilment of character, and in which character and plot were subservient to images and language.

Harris now spoke to CAM about language, of his concern as a novelist with what he called the 'plight of the word'. His starting point was Brathwaite's reading of *Rights of Passage*. Use of the voice or a drum to accentuate its rhythms was, he agreed, exciting.

Wilson Harris

But as one who 'is deeply concerned with the novel', Harris felt he must stress that words had, over the centuries, acquired a certain kind of usage, and thus become 'encrusted with associations'. The difficulty of using voice or music with words was that, 'one may be adding to that burden of persuasion. And part of the crisis in the novel is in fact to implode, or explode internally, that kind of encrustation, that kind of accretion that has grown upon words'. Harris gave an example of how, in exploring a particular word, forgotten associations may be discovered, new feelings, sounds and 'visualisations in depth' may arise. Such a process was, he said,

> extremely concrete, because one is working with words in terms of a total consciousness. There is no persuasion, there is no voice, there is no drum. The whole historical accretion which has grown on that word and which has become part of one's prison – begins to break up in this implosion. . . . And therefore part of the task of the creative writer is to implode these words that you take for granted.

He found, he said, no attempt to break out of this kind of trap in 'the so-called West Indian novel; there is no new direction, you see'.

Michael Anthony

When Michael Anthony, 11 years younger than Harris, came to Britain in 1954, as an 'ordinary immigrant', he was determined to succeed in writing. His educational background, and his experience of working and writing in Trinidad, were very different from Harris's in Guyana. His three novels which had been published by the time of the CAM symposium were apparently written in the mainstream European tradition – good stories, with clearly defined and well-developed characters. They are set in the Trinidad of the author's childhood and youth, and are concerned with young people growing up in Trinidadian rural and urban society.

This was the first time that Michael Anthony had spoken about his work in the company of fellow West Indian writers, and to a student audience. He remembers feeling quite overwhelmed. He defined his concept of the novelist's role with deliberate simplicity. In the summary which he wrote afterwards, at Brathwaite's request:

Cover of **The Games Were Coming**, *1967*

> My contention was simply that the primary function of the writer was to write, and in our intellectualism we must be careful not to lose sight of the wood for the trees. I also said that EM Forster in *Aspects of the Novel* decided that the novel tells a story, and that the West Indian writer without encumbering himself unduly, can get on with the business of telling a story. Whatever story he tells . . . is bound to be the reflection of his experience and environment, which in turn was shaped out of his history.[3]

Orlando Patterson described, as at the private CAM meeting in January, the West Indian's inheritance of despair and imitation;

the futility of a search for a cultural heritage. He seemed provoked to an extreme declaration of his position by the statements of the two novelists alongside him, and by the memory of Brathwaite's challenge to novelists at the February meeting. The novel was to him, he said, 'simply a mode of expression, using prose . . . an amorphous, polemical form, whose technique is determined by the substance and content'. He refused to accept that 'radical' could be applied to technique or method. With regard to content, the marked contrast in approach of his fellow novelists on the panel to his own, and particularly Michael Anthony's expressedly neutral, innocent approach to depicting society led him to declare:

> One can never be neutral . . . [and] . . . take the position [that] art . . . is in any way divorced from reality. . . . To use an image which Sartre uses, in a sense, writing a novel is like firing a gun – a bullet comes out and it lands somewhere. Now to take a position that you're neutral is simply like shooting with your eyes closed and not caring where the bullet hits. . . . Not to commit yourself is itself a form of commitment. . . . The important thing about the West Indian is that to commit yourself is to be radical. To recognise the situation for what it is . . . to realise that one must change it.

Harris made a further significant contribution. He supported Michael Anthony's stated position, stressing the need to determine what tradition informs a writer. Anthony worked in a tradition which emerged from the 19th century conventional novel. But because of the difficulties peculiar to the West Indies, stated by Patterson, it was important to recognise archetypal traditions running underground. His own work was in this tradition. Harris stressed the importance of critical scholars examining not only the structure and language of West Indian literary work, but also the kind of tradition which informed it.

The two critics on the panel spoke on what they saw as 'new directions' in West Indian writing from their distinct positions. Kenneth Ramchand spoke in particular about Michael Anthony's novels, which he championed against 'West Indian readers' neglect' and reviewers' 'illiteracy'; also the writing of certain white West Indians, with what he dubbed – in a phrase from Frantz Fanon – their 'terrified consciousness'. This writing, too, he considered, should be given more serious regard. Louis James began his short opening paper on 'The Creative Potential of Isolation' with an account of West Indian culture as one built up by the destruction of a succession of civilisations, including indigenous cultures; he went on to claim that the resulting sense of tension and deprivation,

> can be to the highest degree creative, and in fact lies behind the West Indian literary renaissance which is one of the most exciting movements in literature in English of the last decades. . . . The lack

> of one precise, dictated literary tradition leads the West Indian into a creative exploration of new possibilities for his artistic expression.

He cited Wilson Harris and Edward Brathwaite as writers exploring such possibilities, together with VS Naipaul, George Lamming and Derek Walcott.

After discussion of 'the new directions' articulated by the novelists and critics on the panel, between themselves and with the audience, Brathwaite was invited to contribute. He picked up points made by previous speakers, stressing the importance of recognising that different writers come from different traditions, and, above all, that any impression given that CAM was negative was far from the case. He then set out how he saw his own 'new direction' as a poet:

> As far I am concerned, my . . . expression of West Indian society is, I think, a very positive one. I don't find that the indigenous forms which we have in the West Indies should be despised. . . . Our problem is that we have been trained over 300 years to despise these indigenous forms. . . . I think our indigenous forms are perhaps as vital as any other. . . . And this is what I'm trying to do in my poetry. . . . I lived in Africa for ten years and . . . having returned to the West Indies I was able to see the West Indies through West African-type eyes. And what surprised me was that the culture, the tradition in the West Indies was more living than I'd been taught to expect.

John La Rose also made a thoughtful contribution to the discussion at this, CAM's first public session. Observing that the period of easy optimism in West Indian literature was finished, he said: 'CAM, and what we are doing here, is an indication of the kind of crisis and impasse that West Indian literature faces' – a crisis also apparent in the current questioning of what had been the received tradition. He stressed the need for 'the rehabilitation of the African experience'. He spoke of the ways in which contemporary French and Spanish West Indian writers were concerned with the same problems as had been raised at this CAM session. 'I feel,' he concluded, 'that publishing has to bring the closeness of this kind of experience to a general Caribbean audience and to a general world audience.'

For those on the panel, and for those in the audience, this meeting of writers and readers was unique and unforgettable. Michael Anthony recalls:

> That occasion was certainly the first time that I had talked to a group like the CAM group. . . . The people on the panel with me, were writers for whom I had a very great admiration. . . . And then of course most of these West Indian students were people of some erudition, and I remember feeling really overwhelmed to be in that company. . . . One hardly met West Indian writers in England.

Christopher Laird, a student and avid reader, comments: 'It made a great impression, that first meeting: meeting these people. And they were so varied in their styles and the depth of their explanations, specially Wilson and Michael.' Writing after the meeting to Michael Anthony, Brathwaite was very positive: 'I've already had a few comments from people who felt that, for them, the most important "happening" on Friday was your statement of position. Even more importantly, people who have not read your books wish to do so now.'[4]

The topic for CAM's second public session had been agreed by Gordon Rohlehr with Brathwaite after Orlando Patterson's paper to CAM in January. 'I will try,' he wrote to Brathwaite, 'to comment on the use of creole in Sparrow's calypsos and Louise Bennett's dialect verse, and suggest that the medium of creole is in fact amenable to some of the subtlest effects of mind and irony. . . . Selvon's achievement in *The Lonely Londoners* and some of his short stories will form the final part of my paper.'[5] Brathwaite suggested as a title, 'Selvon, the Calypso and the Creolisation of Experience', and referred to the talk as being on 'Creole Responses'.[6] Belief in the 'creole' and the importance of 'creolisation' was the core of the positive approach to West Indian society and culture which they shared. But Rohlehr's actual paper included no comparative study of the use of creole by Bennett, Sparrow and Selvon. He titled it 'Sparrow and the Language of Calypso', and, introducing it, explained: 'I found that when I got down to Sparrow's calypsos, the range was so wide and the subject so vast that I had to limit it to Sparrow alone.' He drew on Sparrow's book, *One hundred and twenty calypsos to remember*, published in Port of Spain in 1963, and on some of his more recent records.

Based in Birmingham, and in the final stages of writing his PhD thesis, Rohlehr had attended neither of the intervening CAM sessions, and had not taken part in their debates on contemporary West Indian fiction. Instead, he singled out and illuminated a complete seam of indigenous Caribbean culture in the popular art form of the masses of Trinidad, and highlighted the lyrics of its supreme master, Sparrow. Although Rohlehr was from Guyana, he was familiar with Trinidad and Jamaican popular music; he played in a steel band in Birmingham, and he shared with Brathwaite a passion for jazz. He opened his paper by stressing the significance of the 'creole' in Caribbean art and culture, describing calypso as the 'music of the masses of Trinidad . . . a lower class creole occupation', and carnival as a 'creole bacchanal'; 'both have little to do with the culture of the white boss'.[7] Sparrow, Calypso King, he pointed out, was not amongst the exiled West Indian writers in London, being 'of his world and supported by it'.

In examining the language of Sparrow's calypsos Rohlehr set out to show what Sparrow reflects of general attitudes within Trinidadian society; he also critically examined the intelligence behind calypso. Rohlehr used quotations to identify sociological attitudes in Sparrow's calypsos – from relationships between men and women to distrust and hatred of the police. At the same time he demonstrated that Sparrow's calypsos show an impressive range of literary qualities: 'beautifully organised narrative', 'subtle devices of irony and surprise', 'delicacy of understatement', 'mastery of tone of voice', 'the essential art of the dramatist'. Rohlehr made full use of his training in European literary criticism, comparing Sparrow's 'sanity' to that of Jane Austen, and admiring his 'Chaucerian effortlessness'. Finally, Rohlehr concerned himself with what he saw as the most significant quality of the language in Sparrow's calypsos – rhythm: 'There is a definite speaking voice behind the lyrics. One doesn't feel that language is being coerced into the rigidity of form, but that language is alive and fluid as it plays against the necessary strictness of the music.' Rohlehr went on to stress the significance of Sparrow's use of rhythm for West Indian writers:

> It seems to me that there is in the spoken language of Trinidad a potential for rhythmic organisation which our poets have not yet discovered, or if they have, have not yet exploited. . . . It may help the West Indian poet to realise the rhythmic potential of his ordinary use of English. For the calypsonian's language is pretty close to Standard English, yet his organisation of language is entirely different. . . . What I am thinking of here is not merely an attempt to reproduce vernacular, but to appropriate the *metrical* forms of calypso for use in poetry. I feel that just as the calypsonian is able to use speech rhythms in his songs, the poet, working from the opposite direction, may be able to use calypso rhythms in his verse, and *still preserve* the sense of being true to the speaking voice.

The apparently extravagant nature of some of Rohlehr's claims drew a lively response from the audience. John La Rose, chairing the session, deliberately invited this. 'We want to have as free an interchange between the audience and speaker as we can possibly permit.' Questions and comments provoked Rohlehr into further clarification. Afterwards Brathwaite invited Don Wilson and George Odlum to put their questions in writing; he published them in the next CAM *Newsletter* and, later, Rohlehr's replies.[8]

Brathwaite himself took up the challenge thrown by Rohlehr to West Indian poets. Their dialogue was carried on initially in correspondence, then reproduced in the CAM *Newsletter*, later in *Caribbean Quarterly*, and is of particular interest.[9] Taking up Rohlehr on his generalisations about the 'West Indian poet',

Brathwaite named several – including Derek Walcott, Wordsworth McAndrew, Dennis Scott – as having successfully used West Indian speech rhythms, and, he added, 'of course *Rights of Passage* is committed to this approach right down the line. . . . In ignoring what in fact has been attempted, and failing to link these attempts with Sparrow's achievement and present them for further discussion, you lost a chance . . . to help elucidate the work of the artists involved.' Rohlehr admitted that he had not had time for this at the meeting, and now developed his argument in more detail: 'I felt that because Sparrow's musical language is so close to that of speech, there must be something in the speech itself which hearkens towards music. . . . We can create the metrical equivalent of heroic verse by a consciousness of the extreme variety of our speech rhythms and our musical rhythms.' He praised the poem 'Calypso' in *Rights of Passage* as 'the best example I know of the rhythms of calypso being exploited by a West Indian poet to heighten the rhythmic potential of speech'. Brathwaite, concluding the exchange, agreed that the poets had not yet made enough of West Indian speech rhythms. 'More,' he wrote, 'will be done as "dialect" becomes validated by critics such as yourself.' He stressed, too, the importance of the performance aspect of calypso, and how it should be seen as part of the wider oral folk tradition in the West Indies.

Rohlehr's topic and thesis made important links not only with Brathwaite's work, but also with that of La Rose: his long-standing interest in kaiso, calypso and carnival – La Rose had, with Attila the Hun (Raymond Quevedo) written a pioneering study of calypso in 1956/7;[10] his republishing of JJ Thomas's work on creole; the use in his own poetry of creole as part of the West Indian speech continuum.

Rohlehr's paper was a landmark in West Indian literary criticism. By applying the same criteria to the sung lyrics of a popular calypsonian as to the poems of literary writers, he attempted for the first time to break down the separation between the oral and written traditions. By looking at Sparrow's attitudes to society, he drew attention to expression of the experience of the 'masses' by their own spokesman. He touched on, but had no time to develop, the role of the calypso in society as revolutionary protest. His paper and the subsequent debate strengthened Brathwaite's attempts to counter the negative approach to Caribbean culture put forward by Patterson. Moreover, this paper launched a highly creative critic-writer relationship between Rohlehr and Brathwaite. Rohlehr showed informed and relevant West Indian understanding of Brathwaite's new directions in poetry. A new sort of poetry required a new sort of criticism, and found it in the work of Rohlehr.

For the audience, this was an outstanding meeting. Yvonne Sobers, a Jamaica-born young teacher, remembers it as 'the meeting that had most impact. Gordon Rohlehr's talk, "Sparrow and the Language of Calypso", was absolutely fantastic. [He spoke] in a serious and academic way and in a highly entertaining way.' For Andrew Salkey:

> That was sparkling, that was head-wrenching. We never heard that kind of conspectus on our culture. . . . If the culture had been derided by alien commentators, been ignored by our teachers, had been vilified by officialdom, there was Gordon telling us, convincing us that we mattered. Our drawings at schools mattered. The songs in the street mattered. There was Gordon telling us that there was tremendous vitality in the festivals that we put on. In our ordinary everyday utterances, there was poetry.

Susan Craig, from Trinidad, reading sociology at Edinburgh University, was also in the audience for this CAM session. She claims that Rohlehr's talk transformed her whole way of seeing calypso and the sensibility of ordinary folk.

The series of formal public meetings at the Centre was the visible face of CAM, open to everyone. It was backed by and dependent on a continuing network of less formal, private meetings at CAM members' homes, open to a more select group. Some were programmed sessions, to which paid-up CAM members were invited and sent a printed notice beforehand, such as:

> A Members Only Meeting at Orlando Patterson's flat, 83 Anson Road, N 7 (Tufnell Park tube): on Friday 21 April at 8.00 pm. There will be a little Sherry and John La Rose and Faustin Charles will read some of their recent poetry. Hope you'll be able to come along.

Faustin Charles

As Faustin Charles recalls, there was 'quite a fair number of people at the reading, surprisingly, for a poetry reading'. It was a new experience for him to read his poetry to a West Indian audience and then have it discussed afterwards.

John La Rose demonstrated his range of style and breadth of concerns of his book, *Foundations*, in the selection which he read and the comments which he made. Four of La Rose's poems were read twice and discussed in detail; the small, specially invited audience questioned him closely about their intention and meaning. What was said by La Rose himself, and by his fellow practising poets Edward Kamau Brathwaite, Faustin Charles, Peter Figueroa, and by critics/teachers Wally Look Lai and Don Wilson was frank and revealing.[11]

John La Rose prefaced his reading of 'Fantasy in Space' with, 'This is intended to be recited to a background of a folksong, calypso, steelband – I particularly have one in mind done by the

HARROW CAMPUS LIBRARIES
UNIVERSITY OF WESTMINSTER
Watford Rd, Northwick Park
Harrow, Middlesex HA1 3TP

Invader Steel Band.' There were, he said, various layers of meaning which he was attempting to convey. Brathwaite accepted 'a form of rootlessness' as 'the basic intention', and went on to comment on the 'mixture of Standard English and dialect', whose passages each related to something different. But La Rose asserted:

> The 'dialect' is directly concerned with the Standard English because, you see, the 'dialect' is within both. I think it is a continuous form of West Indian speech, both things are closely combined. I attempt therefore to combine both things simultaneously.

Lengthy discussion of La Rose's poem, 'The Faded Vision', was divided between those who felt (Faustin Charles) that it was 'difficult to analyse a poet's sensibility like this', and others who regarded it as important to 'get to the meaning' and then assess how successful the poet was in conveying this meaning. Wally Look Lai warned against the danger of making a sharp distinction between form and content. Brathwaite confessed that he found it a very difficult poem to understand, and that the poem had not, he felt, communicated an obvious meaning. 'Did you,' he asked La Rose, 'set out to write this way? If you wrote it again, do you think it would be clearer or would it become more dense?' La Rose said he could not know, but maintained: 'I know I want to say it like I said it.' After La Rose had read 'The Passing Show', also concerned with words and the writer, Brathwaite asked: 'How much stress, John, do you put on image and metaphor when you write? . . . To me the important thing is image and metaphor.' La Rose replied: 'I am essentially concerned with the abstract thought.' Brathwaite stressed to the audience that the three poems read and discussed were not a complete reflection of what was in this book, and that some poems were the opposite of abstraction. Peter Figueroa chose to read La Rose's 'Their Bullring'; the poem drew a warm response from the audience for its immediacy and rhythmic movement.

Then Brathwaite invited Faustin Charles to read, urging him to talk a little about his poetry first – 'It's always a good idea.' To Brathwaite's question as to whether Trinidad affected his poetry, Charles replied that it related to the whole Caribbean. His poems were introduced with very short sentences, and ran continuously, not provoking the discussion which La Rose's poems had. Brathwaite commented: 'We all felt the direct communication of the first three.' La Rose's 'Their Bullring' and Charles's 'Haunted Caudillos' were printed in the CAM *Newsletter*, No. 2.

A more informal, selective members' meeting was held, also in April, when Brathwaite, La Rose, Salkey and Wilson Harris met and talked with Aubrey Williams in his studio: half of the

Aubrey Williams in his studio in the 1960s

ground-floor flat where he and his wife, Eve, lived in Greencroft Gardens, West Hampstead. Williams was, by 1967, a mature and internationally known artist. In the best Guyanese tradition, he was widely read and broadly-based in his intelligence and outlook; he was also very articulate. At this meeting with fellow CAM founder members (there is reference to an earlier visit to his studio by Brathwaite and Salkey at least), all of whom were writers, he explained his work, its process and philosophy, through the canvases on the walls and stacked around his studio, and from colour slides. Also, the writers explored links between what Williams and they themselves were attempting in their work.

Williams attempted to show, through his paintings, how his work had developed from being figurative to abstract; the European and tropical influences; the all-pervasive Amerindian influence, and his use of American Indian myth and motif – from the Maya in Mexico and the Inca in Peru, to Carib, Warrau and Arawak Indian designs from the Guyana interior. He answered the writers' somewhat floundering questions with patience and clarity: Brathwaite's plea that he should 'build up and break down a painting. . . . We want to know about your creative process', and the request, 'tell us something about your paintings', to which Williams replied: 'I am trying to tell you about my paintings all the time.' His exchanges with Wilson Harris, whose background and approach seemed in many ways to be similar, are of particular interest. Williams deferred to him, saying, for example, that 'our dear brother and compatriot here' could explain the meaning of *timehri* better than he. Harris in turn said he found Williams's images 'authentic within that sort of landscape that I know intimately', and considered that, in the West Indian context, Williams was 'reversing a tradition' of the conventional, photograph-type painting. Painter and writers shared a common regard for the importance of myth and a concern to keep it alive in Caribbean artistic work. But the Jamaican, Barbadian and Trinidadian amongst them were made acutely aware of the absence and lack of continuity of myth in all but the mainland countries of the region: except, Brathwaite reminded them, in Haiti, where African myth lives on. Williams was prompted to make comments which seem central to his approach to painting:

> I have value for the painter who has come out of figuration, one who has come out of an investigation of the known world. Because his work must be imbued with the human predicament or else it's just a piece of decoration. . . . All the time I'm trying for visual strengths, forms that disturb. They intensify your looking, seeing, feeling power.

Brathwaite asked: 'Why don't you base your thing more firmly on the folk?' Williams, agreeing with a suggestion that he lacked 'a lieutenant', replied: 'No matter how renaissance a man is, he can't do everything at top performance. And anything that is not done at top performance is not good, won't last.' Throughout Williams was brimming with awareness and energy and confidence about all that needed to be done: public frescoes of the Amerindian myths, a historical visual record – though that was not in his line, but for 'the young in the whole Caribbean to do'. When Salkey started a sentence, 'There are so many things that are closed up already, explored and tapped, but in our area . . . ' Williams completed it, 'the sky's the limit'.

An informal meeting of the CAM committee at Orlando Patterson's flat in May 1967 was attended by the Cuban writers Pablo Armando Fernandez and Edmundo Desnoes. They came for ideas as to which West Indian writers and artists should be invited to the forthcoming First Cultural Congress of Havana. Salkey recalls:

> Because the two Cuban friends only knew me, they were watching and listening deeply. I have a feeling that, like most invitations sent out of Cuba, they didn't want to make mistakes. They wanted to see where the orientation of these CAM people lay. . . . So out of that the list for the Cultural Congress was drawn. It wasn't specially set up at all. People came as they ordinarily did to a meeting of CAM, and then the two guests were brought along by me.

In the foreword to his *Havana Journal* Salkey lists as present at this 'impromptu committee session of the Caribbean Artists' Movement' Orlando and Nerys Patterson, George Lamming, Edward Brathwaite, John La Rose, Aubrey Williams.

The third CAM public meeting, on 5 May, again on literature, aimed to take up where the March symposium had left off. A member of the audience had said that five minutes per speaker was not enough, and that the themes raised required fuller direction. Two of the novelists, Michael Anthony and Orlando Patterson, had just published new novels; they were invited to speak again at the May meeting in greater depth about their new work, and with other writers and critics. But in early April Michael Anthony was seriously ill and could not come. So Brathwaite invited Kenneth Ramchand to give a paper on Anthony's work. Ramchand agreed, although not with the focus on Anthony's new novel, *Green Days by The River*: 'We think very highly of Michael's work in the Edinburgh school and I would like to use *The Year in San Fernando* as a way of showing Anthony's outstanding qualities as an evocative novelist, his purity as a teller of stories, and his freedom from the chauvinism of so many of his contemporaries.'[12]

John Hearne

John Hearne, Gerald Moore and Kenneth Ramchand agreed to engage in a 'colloquy' with Patterson about his new novel, *An Absence of Ruins*. This short, spare, work of fiction tells of the return home to Jamaica of Alexander Blackman, a young sociologist, 'charting with uncompromising rigour the mental dilemmas of an alienated West Indian intellectual'.[13] John Hearne, born in Jamaica in 1926, had won a considerable reputation as a novelist ten years earlier. Between 1955 and 1961 he had published five novels, with Faber and Faber. Unlike most of his novelist contemporaries, he wrote them all in his Caribbean home country. All five are set in Jamaica, among his own social circle, the coloured middle class. Hearne's perspectives of and focus on this small, privileged section of West Indian society, and his apparent concern with the individual, with personal rather than political commitment, have provoked harsh criticism from some of his contemporaries; this had not been articulated at the time of CAM, and more recently, with a longer view, his particular concerns have been recognised as giving importance to his work. From 1966/7 he was visiting Professor of Commonwealth Literature at the University of Leeds, 'a "writer in residence" position awarded annually to outstanding Commonwealth writers'.[14] Gerald Moore had recently joined the School of African and Asian studies at the then new University of Sussex; an Englishman, he had taught at universities in West and East Africa in the 1950s and 1960s, and had published critical work on African writers. He was teaching Caribbean literature for the first time, as part of an innovative, interdisciplinary course on Caribbean culture. His book, *The*

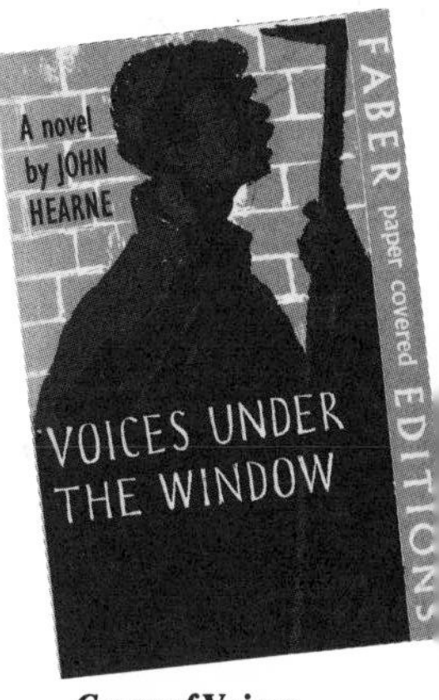

Cover of* Voices under the Window. *1955

Chosen Tongue: English Writing in the Tropical World, which includes critical studies of Caribbean writers, was in preparation.

The May meeting fell into two distinct parts. In the first, chaired by Brathwaite, Kenneth Ramchand gave a paper, entitled 'Childhood in the West Indian Novel: Michael Anthony and Camara Laye'. In it, Ramchand undertook a detailed comparison between Anthony's fictional account of a boy growing up in Trinidad and Laye's autobiographical recollections of his childhood and youth in Upper Guinea, in *L'Enfant Noir*: in its English translations *The African Child* or *The Dark Child*. Ramchand justified such a comparison at the start: 'I'm quite convinced that *The Year in San Fernando* is a much better work than this highly celebrated autobiographical account.' In his paper Ramchand also undertook to distinguish between novels of childhood and novels which use children as characters; he intended to show how *The Year in San Fernando* is a novel of childhood, 'in which the author deals exclusively through the consciousness of the young boy'. Ramchand juxtaposed what he considered to be comparable aspects of Anthony's and Laye's work, using quotations to demonstrate the contrast in treatment. Whereas, for example, Laye interrupts his recollections to tell the reader about a particular custom or aspect of his traditional society, Anthony, 'insinuates rather than tells. . . . Never once does the mature man impose an adult's perception on his adolescent narrating character'.

Ramchand's championing of Anthony's novels was fired not only by some unappreciative reviews which they had received, but also by attitudes which had been expressed at CAM's March symposium. He sought to defend Anthony against critics who accused him of being too simple and naive, or who seemed to miss the significance of Anthony's oblique ways of treating such issues as race, class and politics. A proper response to Anthony's work required, claimed Ramchand, a new sort of criticism: 'Criticism has to find new words to express the way in which a simple passage like this can evoke in the reader a sense of actual participation in the emotions that are being described.' And it required a new attitude from the reader: 'I don't feel that we as readers or critics should set up a system of values by which the best novels are the ones that deal with race and colour and politics.' The comparison of Anthony's book with Laye's seemed somewhat overstretched, but Ramchand's paper enabled him to share with members of the audience his discerning appreciation of Anthony's text, and to draw attention to its qualities.

The second half of the meeting, 'Colloquy on *Sisyphus* and *Ruins*' [*The Children of Sisyphus* and *An Absence of Ruins*], chaired by Gerald Moore, was introduced by Patterson. He did not, he said, intend to talk about his books, but about 'the relationship between the artist, the novelist and the sociologist'. The West Indian literary tradition, like the Anglo-Saxon one on which it was based, had, he claimed, a suspicion of sociology, mainly due to bourgeois ideology with its strong emphasis on individualism. Such an autonomous concept of the individual held that people are responsible for what they are, whereas, explained Patterson, the sociological view is that man must be seen in society; and such a view holds radical implications for literature. In Patterson's opinion the sociologist must become an artist, and the artist a sociologist, and he had himself adopted this reconciliation: 'For me, the artist and the sociologist are one.' It explained, he said, publication in the same month of his novel and his book on the sociology of slavery: the result not of 'intellectual schizophrenia' but of a similar process 'whereby one seeks to understand'. This view has, he believed, implications for literary criticism and literary practice. As a sociologist/artist himself, he found it impossible not to take an extra step: 'I feel that as a sociologist it is part of my job to evaluate the society I have analysed and to suggest ways in which it can be improved. . . . One must make a stand. By the very nature of one's activity one is committed to improving the world.'

Gerald Moore opened the 'colloquy' by engaging Patterson in dialogue about his two novels. Patterson was drawn to assert that in *An Absence of Ruins* he was concerned with 'West Indian alienation . . . also with the problem of identity per se', that it was 'an attempt at wiping the slate clean' so that he could move on – 'which is what I'm doing in my third novel'. Then John Hearne came in: lightly, informally at first, showing himself familiar with Patterson's existentialist frame of reference, then with sharp, hard-hitting criticism. He described *Sisyphus* as 'strong Jamaican social realism with a sort of philosophy tacked on' which, by its abrupt transition, 'denies the relevance of the social situation which you have so intensely evoked'. Patterson responded by accusing Hearne of imposing an interpretation which was rooted in the Anglo-Saxon literary tradition, and defended his tendency to write on different levels: what did it matter if it was against certain literary traditions? Then Hearne moved into a full attack on Patterson's work as a novelist:

***Cover of* An Absence of Ruins**

> When I read *Sisyphus* a year ago, and *Absence of Ruins* in the last couple of weeks, I wondered, seriously, whether the writer of these two books had any concept at all of the purpose of fiction. Listening to the author give his analysis of his basis for approaching life through fiction, I'm pretty sure he does not. We had about 1500 words from Patterson tonight on his concept of the novel, in which he managed by a singular exercise, never to mention the fictional approach to life. . . . There was a curious lack of importance

> attached to fiction as a way of seeing. Neither *Sisyphus* nor *Absence of Ruins* seems to me a novel in the sense that Kenneth Ramchand was talking about a writer like Michael Anthony. . . . Patterson's specifically stated philosophical approach to the novel seems to me completely sterile. . . . I can judge from internal evidence . . . of a boredom with the passage of life, with which the novel is concerned. . . . My belief is that both these books would have been much better written as a discussion between the Blackmans of this world, put on a verandah, where they have this sort of discussion, with merely the incidental passing of drinks and lighting of cigarettes which gives a certain simulacrum of life going on.

Towards the end, the chairman tried to intervene in order to avoid, as he put it, 'a head-on clash'. But Hearne seemed set on completing his case of demolition. His final judgement on the two novels was: 'sociological delineation which is extremely valuable. I would prefer to see it in case studies.'

Patterson was not thrown by the comprehensiveness and ferocity of the attack. Hearne was arguing, he claimed, from a dogmatic assertion of what he considered to be 'the novel', and seemed to be suggesting only one tradition which, since the 1930s, had been much questioned; Patterson challenged Hearne to state what he considered the novel to be. Side-stepping a 'systematic enquiry . . . we could be here all evening', Hearne claimed that 'a primary indication of a novel is a manipulation of time, which is not consciously perceived by the reader', recommending that Patterson use the form followed by Thomas Love Peacock in *Gryll Grange*: 'There we would really get an examination of West Indian society in the sort of depth of which he is capable.'

At this point Hearne went out to get a drink. Some of the audience, recalls Don Wilson, assumed that he had left in a huff. When he returned, glass in hand, braced for the next round, the formal part of the session had closed. Meanwhile Gerald Moore drew Patterson further on his portrayal, in *Ruins*, of a character who attempts to live outside history, questioning whether such a character was in fact 'material for a novel'. This led Patterson to assert: 'I'm taking certain themes from West Indian society to their logical conclusions. . . . I think it is an absurd position that one finds oneself in as a colonial.' One or two others then entered the discussion, including Ramchand who quoted from *Ruins* – 'I like to pin these things down to the text wherever possible' – to show what a difficult experience Patterson was attempting to write about. But then it was time to close.

There was almost no public debate, as planned. Brathwaite had written to Hearne beforehand: 'The idea will be for a small panel to enter into conversation with the writer in the hot seat and then gradually open up the discussion to the audience.' Kenneth Ramchand had planned to air his own strong views about Orlando

Patterson as a novelist. He wrote to Brathwaite beforehand: 'I will go to my grave swearing that Patterson is a sociologist and not a novelist and the twain have not met in any fruitful way in his work *as yet*. I look forward to putting questions to him too.'[15] But he had little chance. No one had a chance to turn the tables and challenge Hearne as a novelist, as might have been expected and was, presumably, part of the point of having him in on the colloquy.

But the quality of the colloquy itself more than compensated for the lack of wider discussion. Rounding off the session, Brathwaite said: 'Where else but in CAM, if I may use a little propaganda, can you have an artist not only explaining in great detail what he feels, but also have a fellow writer, fearlessly and honestly, giving a contrary view?'

It made a great impression on several people in the audience. Salkey remembers one novelist turning on another: 'There was something edgy and accusatory about John's jabs. . . . Some very harsh things were said. I think that even though Orlando seemed at the time well disposed to the jabs, it certainly hurt.' The young Donald Hinds was awed to observe two famous novelists in open combat: 'I was standing at the back, I can visualise that meeting. It was very lively. And I thought, God, these are the giants, I can't say a thing.' As Don Wilson recalls:

> That was quite an occasion. . . . It was all very cosy up to that point. There had been a fair amount of patting people on the back at the beginning of CAM. We were all enthusiastic and excited and nobody had said anything different from the orthodoxy and enthusiasm of the times. And then John Hearne came and delivered himself of about five minutes reaction to what was being said, with particular reference to *Ruins*. He left everybody flabbergasted.

In a letter to John Hearne after the session Brathwaite characterised it as: 'Not only usefully critical but *creative* as well. You made it quite clear that a group such as CAM has a useful function to perform if it can get West Indians and other artists together not to slap each other on the shoulders, but to confront each other with what they hold to be the truth of their art and discipline.'[16] And Hearne felt he had made his comments in the right spirit: 'Patterson is such high calibre that it was worthwhile considering his work seriously for a serious audience.'[17] No comparably outspoken public criticism by one author of another's work ever again took place at a CAM meeting, to many peoples' regret.

After these three literature sessions, at which writers and critics were more than ready to speak, it was the artists' turn, who traditionally received far fewer opportunities to expound their views about their work. CAM was again a pioneer in inviting West Indian artists to speak. Their art forms could seem enviably free of the encrusted words, rhythms and other literary devices from which fellow writers were attempting to break away. An artists' symposium was planned for June, and Aubrey Williams, Ronald Moody, Frank Bowling, Karl 'Jerry' Craig, Art Derry, Althea McNish and Errol Lloyd were invited to take part. All except Bowling and Derry did so. Its organisers believed that Sir Roland Penrose had agreed to be chairman. Penrose, an English painter and writer on art, was wellknown as a promoter of contemporary art in Britain; he had co-founded, with Herbert Read, the Institute of Contemporary Art (ICA) in 1947, and organised several major exhibitions for the Arts Council. When Brathwaite wrote to him to confirm the details, Penrose replied: 'I am rather appalled to find that you expect me to take the Chair at the Caribbean Artists' Symposium. I did not realise in my short 'phone conversation with Mr Andrew Salkey that I had committed myself so definitely.'[18] He would not be in London on 2 June at 7.30, so could not take part in what he called a 'highly interesting and admirable activity'. Gerald Moore was asked instead – as Brathwaite recalls, 'one of CAM's staunchest members'.[19]

Brathwaite, planning the session, had wondered whether an exhibition of work by these artists could be mounted at the Centre; he proposed it to Bryan King as a 'joint CAM/Centre effort'.[20] King welcomed the idea, but realistically saw it as something for the future. Instead, slides and film of work were shown. Brathwaite had announced 'A Symposium of West Indian Artists' at the end of CAM's May meeting, describing it as 'the first time we have been able to get West Indian painters together. . . . This is going to be an extraordinary night, I assure you.' The artists involved certainly felt it to be so. Aubrey Williams said: 'I can't remember when last I felt so proud as I do tonight, catching a glimpse of Caribbean art.' Karl 'Jerry' Craig explained: 'It has come as just as much of a shock to me as to Aubrey Williams. Because, unknown to most of you, I suppose, this is the first time that we have ever been together as artists. I happen to have known only two of the artists here before we came together.' But the five artists were from such a spread of generations and backgrounds, at such different stages of achievement, they were engaged in such varied forms of art and held such different concepts and aims, that it proved impossible to identify and debate any common ground.

Karl 'Jerry' Craig and Althea McNish were in their late twenties. Craig was Senior Lecturer, Arts and Crafts, at the Avery Hill College of Education, McNish was an international textile designer, selling to such prestigious firms as Liberty's and Tootal. Ronald Moody was in his late sixties, at the peak of his achievement and reputation as a sculptor. Errol Lloyd, in his early twenties, was just beginning. His ability and interest in sculpture

Althea McNish in her studio, 1966, with 'Pomegranate', exhibited with CAM in 1968, in the background

became known amongst West Indians in London, and by 1967 he had been invited to undertake busts of CLR James, Gary Sobers and Sir Alexander Bustamante; he had also done some portrait painting. Aubrey Williams's work had already been introduced to CAM.

Both Craig and McNish spoke of the ways in which the tropical vegetation and light of their Caribbean environment, known from childhood, continued to be the main inspiration for their work. Both, too, acknowledged European influences, especially of Italy. Craig, after a return visit to Jamaica, had become, he said, deeply interested in plant and animal life, and involved in images of growth. For McNish the range 'of things that excite and inspire me, the places that I go to and different scenes' were unashamedly eclectic. She showed how agate became a motif for a headscarf or dress length; how flowers from her London garden were used on a fabric for a show flat at the Ideal Home Exhibition; how stained glass for a church in Yorkshire was used in a textile design. A Mexican mask and corn goddess were included in the range, but with no special meaning attached, indeed she referred to them as 'another of my more primitive things'.

Lloyd modestly introduced himself as a painter and sculptor 'very much in the embryonic stage' in explanation of the 'conventional' manner of his work so far; of his painting as 'very much homework', in explanation of his figurative style. His painting, like his sculpture, was all of people. 'I'm very interested in faces.' One he saw as a 'comment on old age and poverty', another, 'a black girl . . . to show the beauty and texture of the skin'. He explained how, in his sculptures, he had tried to be true to what he regarded as the person's essential quality and character.

Moody spoke quietly and hesitatingly. He admitted to finding it very difficult to talk about his work and could, he said, give only a general idea of the direction in which he was going. The influences responsible for his work were not from Italy or Europe, but from Egypt and the East:

> I was not greatly moved by the works of the Renaissance. The beauty I saw and the craft . . . but what really moved me was . . . the sort of inner feeling of movement and stillness of Egyptian and Eastern art. . . . This led me to realise that the important thing for me, at any rate, was the *imagination*: in the sense that all our institutions and way of living turn upon an inner source.

He contrasted such a central role for the imagination with the materialism of the technogically advanced nations of the West, which, he felt, led to division and to strife.

> And this seems to me something that we in the West Indies will have to make up our minds about: because if we follow the 'analytical' method . . . we are going to end up with the same trouble, the same difficulties, and end up in the same kind of mess. Therefore it comes always back to the person, the man: the importance of having emotion and intellect in some kind of balance.

Later, in reply to a question, he repeated the heart of his advice to the West Indian artist: 'I think the important thing is that he is seeking to find himself . . . [and] trying to avoid the errors of Europe.' Here, as in all Moody's statements, there is evidence of his firsthand experience of World War Two in France, and of its bitter personal consequences.

Aubrey Williams was generous about his overall impression of the work shown by his fellow West Indian artists, which to him seemed to demonstrate 'a great respect for humanity and man's acquaintance with his environment'. He was outspoken about the reaction of the audience, from which he had expected more intimate questions about the work and whom he told: 'Go home and think.' He was articulate about his work and hopes for Caribbean art generally:

> In art, I have always felt a wild hunger to express the rather unique, human state in the New World, in the Caribbean. I find there an amalgam of a lot that has gone on before in mankind, in the whole world. It seems to have met there, after Columbus, and we are just in on the brink of its development. The forces meeting in the Caribbean and all around the archipelago will eventually, I feel, change this world . . . not in the sense of a big civilisation in one spot, but as the result of the total of man's experience and groping for the development of his consciousness.

Williams claimed to find 'claw-like forms' in the work shown: 'It seems to be a sort of Caribbean signature theme. . . . If you look at the work of the artists here tonight, you will find this strange, very tense, slightly violent shape coming in somewhere. It has haunted me all my life and I don't understand it.' Craig agreed that it was a subconscious thing which had come out. For Salkey, concerned with 'the possibility of a definition towards a common Caribbean image', the claw was not a 'total image of violence' but looked like 'something left after a destruction'.

The session was as valuable for showing the very different directions which Caribbean artists were exploring, and for stimulating other peoples' understanding of their work, as for uncovering common ground. Artists were demonstrably less used to, less able to, talk about their work than writers. The audience was pretty much at sea. But questions and answers indicated some of CAM's future directions. Craig was challenged on the absence of political motivation in his work. Lloyd, replying to a question about how he saw his responsibility to society, said: 'You can't entirely ignore your environment. If you live in England it is very difficult to deal with West Indian problems all your life. . . . Personally, if I could paint in the way that Sparrow sings calypso, I'd be very happy.'

Brathwaite arranged what he called, inviting Louis James, a 'follow-up small group session' on 23 June, which would, he hoped 'be a useful interchange between writers and artists'.[21] He also invited two younger Caribbean artists, Kaywal Ramkissoon and Keith Simon.

The informal sessions which carried on after public sessions were high points of the CAM experience for all who came to them. And a far wider section of CAM did come, even more than to the formal 'small group' sessions. John La Rose recalls how these gatherings used to take place, after CAM meetings, in different peoples' homes, and that they were known as 'warishi nights', Aubrey Williams's term for 'unburdening'; 'warishi' is the Amerindian name for a crude type of haversack. Younger writers such as Faustin Charles particularly valued these and other small CAM sessions for the easy access to established writers, and the encouragement and stimulus which resulted. Some gatherings were not advertised, not even to paid-up CAM members. They risked becoming exclusive and cliquey; at the same time, they were essential to the dynamic inner core of CAM.

The first series of CAM's public sessions was rounded off on 7 July, with a lecture by CLR James. His pioneering work as novelist, critic and historian, in formulating and presenting a Caribbean point of view, had made him a natural hero-figure for CAM. *Black Jacobins* in particular was a key text for the CAM generation. Brathwaite, writing to confirm La Rose's verbal invitation, expressed CAM's feelings towards him: 'It's a great honour for us to have you and there is no need for me to say that we are all looking forward very much to this occasion.'[22] He enclosed a statement of the aims and objectives of CAM and copies of the first two issues of its *Newsletter*, and invited James and his wife, Selma, to become Honorary Members of CAM. James's response was positive and encouraging: 'Let me wish your organisation all success and please be assured that anything that I can do to help in any way I shall be only too pleased to undertake. I am glad to accept your honorary membership.'[23] Bryan King agreed to chair the meeting: he and Frank Collymore had been invited at the same time to be Honorary Members.

James spoke on 'What the West Indies have contributed to Western Civilisation'. As he commented beforehand, 'The subject is so wide that no title can do justice to it.' His paper set out to show some of the ways in which the contribution of West Indians has been integral to the development of European and Western civilisation. He identified and described four such categories of contribution which, he stressed at the start, were not simply those of 'distinguished people'.[24]

First, the political contribution. So far this had, James reckoned, been a contribution more to Western civilisation than to West Indian polity, but he found evidence 'that we have the capabilities, the qualifications sometime or other to develop a West Indian society which will be one of the most remarkable in the modern world'. This contribution began with the French Revolution, 'one of the greatest events in the history of European civilisation, in the history of the world'. Because the British failed to suppress the 1791 slave revolts in Haiti, they were unable to attack the French Revolution. The resolution which abolished slavery in the French territories was passed by the French *Chambre des Deputés* in 1794 because one of the three representatives from Saint Domingue, Bellay, a former slave, spoke up and asked for it. The abolition of the slave trade which followed was the direct result of Haitian Independence in 1804; and the successive independence of South American countries also resulted from that event. A further political contribution was to the 20th century independence of African states, through the work of George Padmore and the International African Institute, seven of whose ten members, including Padmore and James, were West Indians, and through Marcus Garvey and his movement, the Universal Negro Improvement Association. After World War One such men 'made the African question a part of the consciousness and political perspectives and development of Western civilisation'.

Second, the literary contribution. James considered himself unqualified to talk about art, but of literature, 'I can speak with confidence and hope to astonish you'. His examples, all of French writers – because he could not, he said, read Spanish – were indeed impressive, though some of their West Indian connections were far-fetched. It was, as someone pointed out afterwards, Alexandre Dumas' father, not the great Romantic novelist himself, who lived in the West Indies, to which James replied, 'I expected this.' Other examples, especially St-John Perse and Aimé Césaire, were more apparently valid.

James discussed the influence of Anglophone West Indian writers separately, along with cricketers, between 1939 and 1967 as the third sphere of contribution stating: 'I do not know of any body of novelists in any country anywhere that can definitely be said to exceed the work of our body of novelists. Thank God,' he continued, 'for Vidia Naipaul and George Lamming and the rest of them.' He singled out Wilson Harris for a fuller statement. Harris had, he claimed, gone further in philosophical appeal in literature than any writer whom he knew: 'He's saved by one thing. He is writing about the Caribbean. And once you write about the Caribbean and you have your eyes open, the social structure, the conflict of classes, the need for social regeneration cannot be excluded.' Had James perhaps been in the audience for the two recent CAM sessions on Caribbean fiction?

Finally, James looked at the impact which he felt confident would be made by West Indians 'from 1967 onwards'. Here he spoke of his own work in historical research, finding links like those outlined in his paper. 'We have no history in the past. We have nothing we can look back to as our own. And therefore West Indians who come to Europe, one of the first things that they do is to get some historical conception.' He closed with an expression of supreme confidence in the future contribution of West Indians to Western civilisation, with one proviso: 'That they recognise that however much they study abroad, the basis of their future work must be at home.'

Questions afterwards were all related to literary topics and drew James to speak incisively on the effects of exile on West Indian writers; on the contrast between France and Britain in their reception of and response to West Indian writers; how he found in the work of Michael Anthony and Earl Lovelace 'an absence of the European literary tradition which permeates the work of Lamming, Naipaul, Walcott'. The tone of his assertions, the claims themselves, some of the examples, may sound exaggerated and over-confident. But they were validated by his statement of what he was about: this work of finding links, of creating a historical framework, of letting West Indians know about and be proud of their contributions. Again and again he would interject phrases such as: 'not a thing that should be forgotten', 'the Caribbean people have got to educate the Caribbean people'.

CLR James was an excellent choice for closing CAM's first series of public meetings; with his long years of study and political activism; his informed interest in and dedication to West Indian society and its arts, sport and culture; his concern to build a historical consciousness, a West Indian society; his emphasis on home as the West Indies, where the work was to be done and the society to be built. All this was to be taken further by Elsa Goveia, the opening speaker at the first session of CAM's second series, at the First Conference.

CAM members' appreciation of the talk, and the importance they attached to it, is reflected in the fact that it was reproduced, in an edited form, in three subsequent issues of the *Newsletter*. It resulted in an especially lively 'warishi night'. Brathwaite wrote to Wilfred Cartey – Trinidad-born critic and poet, then a member of the English faculty at Columbia University and about to be visiting Professor at the University of Ghana – that 'the evening after CLR James was stimulating. We could have gone on for hours.'[25]

John La Rose and WK (Pony) Hynam at the Students Centre

Venues for CAM

The regular use by CAM of the Students Centre for its monthly public sessions was welcomed by and greatly benefited both. When Brathwaite approached Bryan King, the chairman of its Board of Governors, in late 1966, the Centre had been going for 11 years and was, King told Brathwaite, 'being rather neglected'.[26] A regular programme devised by, and featuring, leading Caribbean intellectuals and artists must have been attractive indeed to those concerned with the Centre's life. At the same time, the arts focus and academic impetus would ensure approval from the West Indian governments. After King put CAM's proposals to the Board of Governors in late March 1967, he wrote to Brathwaite: 'We would like to be very closely associated with CAM and would like, for an initial period at any rate, to have CAM's activities identified with the Centre's activities as far as possible.'[27] Honorary membership was offered to Brathwaite, as 'president' (the Centre's term), and honorary assistant membership to those whose names he wished to put forward. Brathwaite substituted the role of 'organising secretary' for himself, and replied to the warden, WK Hynam, that the CAM committee wished to submit also the following names:

Dr Louis James: critic and lecturer in English Literature at the University of Kent at Canterbury
Evan Jones: poet, playwright and film scriptwriter
John La Rose: poet and publisher
Aubrey Williams: painter[28]

Andrew Salkey was shortly afterwards appointed to the Board of Governors of the Centre. The committee proposed that individual members of CAM should apply for honorary assistant membership of the Centre, until funds permitted CAM to apply for a group subscription.

From the start, students and others using the Centre regularly attended or infiltrated CAM sessions. Louis James remembers: 'There was a very strange mixture in that there were people coming in from the bar, with their Red Stripe beer and so on. Often people were so interested in what they heard that they would then stay and make comments afterwards.' CAM sessions provided students at the Centre with something new. Brinsley Samaroo points out: 'This kind of intellectual activity was not conducted at the Students Centre previous to CAM. As academics, there was nothing to engage our minds. When CAM introduced this, it added a new dimension to the relevance of the Centre.' CAM brought new ingredients to the Centre's programme of activities, new interests and a new focus for many of its members. In turn, the Centre provided CAM with a new element in its audience – students and activists from the 'ordinary immigrant' community.

Although no exhibition of work by the five artists taking part in the June symposium proved possible, smaller collections of work by CAM artists soon began to be shown at other venues. On Sunday 25 June 1967, 'Activists for the Theatre Royal, Stratford, E15' held what, according to the notice, 'promises to be a smashing afternoon'. It was directed by Bari Jonson, who had had a strong connection with this theatre since playing Samson in its very successful production of Wole Soyinka's play, *The Road*, in 1965. A number of CAM members took part. The two and a half hour programme included 'Satirical Sketches by Agit Prop', 'Original Poetry read by Adrian Mitchell, John La Rose and Peter Figueroa', Louise Bennett's poetry read by Oliver Clarke (Jonson remembers this as outstanding and that Clarke also read one of his own poems), dancing by the West Indian and Indonesian Dance Group, songs with guitarists and folk singers. Early comers were invited 'to view new art and sculpture being presented by the Caribbean Artists Movement'; Karl 'Jerry' Craig and Art Derry are known to have exhibited. The following month a more substantial CAM exhibition was held, again at the Theatre Royal Stratford, with work by Aubrey Williams, Karl 'Jerry' Craig, Ronald Moody, Errol Lloyd and Althea McNish – the artists of the recent symposium.

Also in June Clifton Campbell, now a young professional painter, had put on a special exhibition for the CAM committee at his King's Road studio. He was then employed in the scenic design and painting department of the Old Vic, and had previously worked at the Royal Opera House, Covent Garden. During 1967 two of his paintings were exhibited in the London Group Exhibition at the Royal Institute Galleries, and a one-man show of his work was held at the University of Birmingham.

CAM was formed and took off in London: partly because leading Caribbean writers and artists had settled there, and several postgraduates were studying there; partly because of the Students Centre. Early on, hopes were expressed and attempts made to encourage branches wherever out-of-London CAM members found themselves. But the only provincial branch which was in fact formed, and which flourished – at Nottingham, from 1968 – did so through its own initiative. A branch in Birmingham must have been proposed to Gordon Rohlehr when Brathwaite first told him about CAM in early January 1967. Rohlehr's reply was definite and realistic:

> I really would not be able to form a branch of CAM in Birmingham. As it is, I am months behind in writing my thesis, and would do what I normally do when things become tough, study something else as if in deliberate invitation of chaos. Moreover the West Indian student body in B'ham consists mainly of engineers and technologists, and it is more difficult to raise a group such as the forum in London. This city is not so inspiring.[29]

In Edinburgh, Kenneth Ramchand, fired by what he heard and saw of CAM in the first half of 1967, and missing 'discussing with fellow countrymen',[30] made contact with the West Indian Association and with its student secretary, Douglas McFarlane, and together they tried to get a branch going. To Brathwaite Ramchand wrote:

> There are moves now to open up a branch of CAM in Edinburgh. I have suggested that we go ahead and form CAM here and then write to you saying we wish to be regarded as a branch of CAM. The West Indian Association will pay one pound to London CAM and each CAM member here will pay five shillings to be kept in Edinburgh. The West Indian Association here will subsidise Edinburgh CAM from time to time. Could you send introductory material about CAM to: Douglas McFarlane, c/o Men's Union.[31]

A practical and promising initiative. Brathwaite replied to McFarlane rightaway, expressing delight and encouragement, sending all the CAM material to date, and asking for news of their plans, 'so we can splash it in our next newsletter'.[32] But nothing more was heard of the branch.

CAM Newsletter and Book Service

From the very beginning, Brathwaite's concept of CAM included recording, and if possible publishing, the proceedings of CAM meetings. In his introductory letter to Ramchand, in late December 1966, he wrote: 'We'd also like to tape record all our talks, readings and discussions; and if things go well, we might even be able to feed this material into a magazine of our own.'[33] Publication of a periodical was an aspect of the group's activity which Louis James also pressed for. The first publicity sheet about CAM, prepared by Brathwaite and tucked into the programme of his public reading of *Rights of Passage* in March 1967 stated: 'It is hoped eventually to start a magazine, one of whose objects will be the linking of artistic endeavour in the West Indies with that going on in Britain: thus bridging the gap between "the exile" and his origins.' Meanwhile, until a journal could be realised, CAM produced a newsletter. Its aim was to provide a record of what was said, discussed or read at CAM meetings: for those who attended, and those who could not, especially those in the Caribbean. It invited critical comment, for although each CAM talk was followed by lively discussion, this was difficult to transcribe. Don Wilson recalls how his critical response to Gordon Rohlehr's talk on 'Sparrow and the Language of Calypso' came to be written and included: 'I had got up at the meeting and made some comments on what Gordon had said. Of course Eddie's eye was always for possible people who might contribute, and encouraging them to contribute. I remember writing a two-page comment as a result of this.'

The first newsletters appeared regularly: every two months, on stencilled foolscap sheets, stapled together. Correspondence reveals the work involved. A tape recorder, mostly Brathwaite's own – a specially-purchased, heavy Akai reel-to-reel machine – had to be transported to each meeting, usually by Doris Brathwaite on her motorbike. Doris also operated it; as Brathwaite advised, 'Doris is the expert on this'.[34] Tapes were transcribed laboriously on a manual typewriter, without the benefit of a transcription machine; whenever possible, the text was checked with the speaker before publication. Brathwaite, who set the newsletter style, and was its editor for numbers 1–5, did most of the initial transcription work himself, and Louis James the rest; Brathwaite solicited and collated news items, and drew on voluntary secretarial help for stencil cutting and running off. *Newsletter* Nos. 1, 2, & 3, of April – July 1967 contain a report, extracts or a complete transcript of all CAM's public meetings of the first six months, together with poems, and some critical comment, biographical notes and so on. The other regular ingredient was 'news', at first a simple list of recent and forthcoming publications. But as early as *Newsletter* No. 3, 'CAM News' also covered art exhibitions, plays, films, radio and television programmes, recordings, talks and lectures, by CAM and Caribbean writers and artists; the prizes and awards won by them; news of their travels between the Caribbean and Britain, North America and Africa. They indicate

***CAM's first* Newsletter**

the profusion and variety of Caribbean cultural work then in progress, and the mobility of its practitioners.

Writing to Rohlehr after CAM's first public meeting at the Centre, Brathwaite commented:

> What I *didn't* mention (and I regret this very much) is La Rose's New Beacon contribution; and the kind of enterprise he showed after the Cochrane reading. After all a literature isn't only its writers; but its readers as well. Attempts to attract, inform and enlarge a West Indian reading public are as important as anything else.[35]

John La Rose had founded New Beacon as a publishing enterprise. It was already in operation by the time that CAM began, and constantly reminded CAM of the possibility and desirability of independent publishing. Wilson Harris's memories of first meeting La Rose in London in the early 1960's are of his publishing ideas: 'I remember that he was interested in publishing a critical series, or several critical books, which would engage with the Caribbean perspective.' A collection of Wilson Harris's own critical essays, *Tradition, The Writer And Society*, was published by New Beacon in 1967, as its third title. All of New Beacon's early titles carry striking covers designed by La Rose's fellow Trinidadian, Art Derry, who recalled: 'He never told me what he wanted. He said he'd leave it to me. He said that he wanted a plain cover. So I did it in black and white.' In CAM, La Rose was known both as poet and publisher, and took part in public and private sessions in these roles.

New Beacon's bookselling began as a service to CAM's authors and readers, and was soon known as a Book Service. After displaying and selling copies of *Rights of Passage* at Brathwaite's reading, New Beacon found it natural to do the same with new books by speakers at CAM's first series of public sessions: Michael Anthony's *Green Days By The River*, Orlando Patterson's *An Absence of Ruins*. For La Rose, bookselling at the Centre was a natural extension of what he had begun with publishing. New Beacon's bookselling, like its publishing, added immeasurably to what CAM was able to achieve.

At the time of CAM's first public sessions, March to July 1967, Brathwaite too was exploring ways in which CAM could extend the reading public of Caribbean literature. Through frequenting Dillon's Bookshop in Malet Street – five minutes' walk from his flat in Mecklenburgh Square, and only a slight diversion from the way to the British Museum Reading Room – he got to know Gillian Shears, in charge of the African Book Section, and encouraged her to stock Caribbean literature, and place special orders of books to be discussed at CAM meetings. She wrote to him, in mid-April: 'I've arranged to have fifteen copies of Orlando's novel on sale. It will be in the African Section, as I have had a word with bearded Ted, who runs the literature department, and he thinks (as we all do) that West Indian literature sells better upstairs (ie with me!)'[36] By the following month Brathwaite was encouraging sales of Caribbean literature by other means. In simultaneous, and similar, letters to what were then the leading British publishers of Caribbean literature – Deutsch, Evans, Faber, Heinemann, Hutchinson, and Longmans – he gave an outline of CAM, asked to be placed on their mailing list for 'review/publicity/advance copies of forthcoming books by West Indian authors, in all categories', promised them copies of 'reviews, talks, discussions' involving their authors. In a few letters he referred to copies of West Indian books 'having already been sold through the Book Service we've set up.'[37] Later he wrote to Longmans that 'CAM's discussion sessions, backed up by its Book Service, helps to sell your books'.[38]

By the end of May, both approaches were showing some success. Gillian Shears, now a CAM member, had opened a West Indian Section at Dillons, and put on a special display of the new Anthony and Patterson titles to coincide with the CAM symposium. Brathwaite informed Rohlehr that 'John La Rose has also started his Book Service'.[39] Meanwhile *Newsletter* Nos. 1–6, of March/April 1967 to January/March 1968, contained detailed listings of recent and forthcoming publications. Publishers' advance publicity leaflets of new Caribbean titles were at times mailed with the *Newsletter*.

Public events, July 1967

Shortly after CLR James spoke to CAM, on 7 July, Stokely Carmichael (now Kwame Ture) visited London. Carmichael, born in Trinidad, had been active in the Student Non-violent Coordinating Committee (SNCC) of the Civil Rights Movement, first as a student at Howard University, Washington DC, then, since graduation in 1964, as a full-time SNCC worker. Since June 1966 he had been associated with the slogan 'black power', which quickly attracted a large following amongst Afro-Americans; he had also co-authored a book, *Black Power*, published in 1967.

In London, Carmichael attended meetings of CARD and of the West Indian Standing Conference, spoke at rallies in Notting Hill and Brixton, and was interviewed on the BBC. He had been invited as one of the main speakers at the Congress on the Dialectics of Liberation, held at the Round House, Chalk Farm, in North London, 15–30 July 1967 – an international gathering instigated by four psychiatrists, with the aim of linking 'the internalised violence said to be characteristic of psychotic illness with the mentality which fuelled the US war in Vietnam'.[40] Carmichael, regarded by one of the Congress organisers as 'an activist in the most real sense of that term',[41] was invited as part of Congress policy to 'bridge the gap between theory and practice. . . . At the Congress we were concerned with new ways in which intellectuals might act to change the world, ways in which we might move beyond the "intellectual masturbation" of which Stokely Carmichael accuses us.'

In his talk to the Congress, as printed in its book of papers, titled simply 'Black Power', Carmichael stressed the need for black people to control the economic, political and social institutions in their communities. He urged the development of 'black consciousness' through pride in and knowledge of their African heritage. Violent means might, he implied, be necessary to enable black people to win their liberation from colonial structures. Although he spoke from the context of the United States, he drew parallels with the condition of black people in Britain, and these rang true with his audience. Moreover he made references to his upbringing in the West Indies and to the 'white power' which he had encountered:

> I had to read Rudyard Kipling's 'The White Man's Burden'. I thought the best thing the white man could do for me was to leave me alone, but Rudyard Kipling told them to come and save me because I was half savage, half child. It was very white of him. What has happened is that the West has used force to impose its culture on the Third World wherever it has been.[42]

He also spoke of the 'black power' which he had wished he had:

> All I used to read about London when I was small was the beauty of London, and how peacefully everybody lived, and how nice life was – at my expense. And I used to say, 'I sure would like to get to London and burn it down to the ground'. But that's violence.[43]

Carmichael quoted from the Martinique-born writer, Frantz Fanon, whom he referred to as 'one of my patron saints'. In short, he spoke as a fellow West Indian.

A handwritten, cyclostyled notice of a talk by Carmichael at the Round House at 4.30pm on Sunday 23 July was circulated amongst West Indians in London:

BLACK EYES
BLACK VOICES
BLACK POWER
HEAR
STOKELY CARMICHAEL

This seems to have been Carmichael's final speech at the Round House, titled 'Black Power', 'Address to the Black Community'.[44]

Carmichael also addressed a select gathering of West Indian community activists, invited by John La Rose, at McDonald Stanley's All Nations Club in Hackney. Earlier on the same day

Carmichael had met with CLR James and the young Trinidadian lawyer, Cris Le Maitre, at La Rose's flat in Hornsey Lane. CLR James had already heard him speak at the Sir George Williams University in Canada, in March. 'Now,' he commented, in August 1967, 'he [Carmichael] speaks with a scope and a depth and range of political understanding that astonishes me.'[45] For most West Indians, Carmichael's visit to London provided their first chance to hear about the then new, explosive concept of 'black power'. For CAM members, Carmichael's Round House speech was most memorable. Brathwaite wrote three years later, from Jamaica, how Stokely Carmichael,

> enunciated a way of seeing the black West Indies that seemed to many to make sense of the entire history of slavery and colonial suppression, of the African diaspora in the New World. . . . He produced images of shared communal values. A black International was possible. West Indians, denied heroes by their imposed education, responded.[46]

The British Labour Government responded to Stokely Carmichael by banning him from Britain, three days after his Round House speech. Race riots in two areas of the USA during that month of July had been given 'wide coverage and . . . prominent display by the British press';[47] Carmichael's 'fiery political rhetoric'[48] could, it was feared, exacerbate already tense race relations in Britain. In Brathwaite's view, certainly in terms of CAM – its concerns, audience and direction – Carmichael's visit was a decisive staging post: 'Links of sympathy, perhaps for the first time, were set up between labouring immigrant, artist/intellectual and student.'[49]

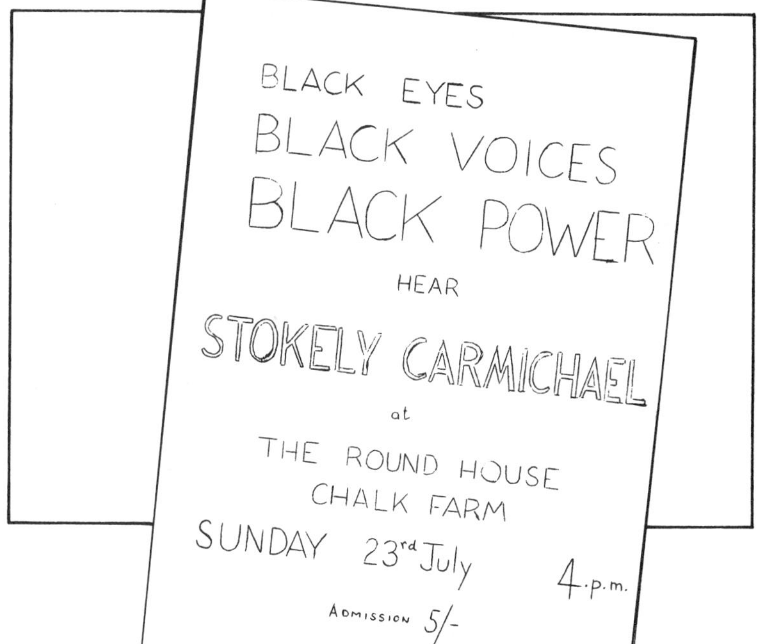

4 A Wider Audience
September-December 1967

'The Caribbean Artists Movement', reported the Barbados *Sunday Advocate* in late September 1967, 'started in December last year by a small group of West Indian writers . . . has been making a considerable impact on the West Indian artistic and student community here in London through public lectures, discussions, art shows, book exhibitions and poetry readings. Now it appears to have made a breakthrough towards a yet wider audience.'[1] The 'breakthrough' was the residential conference with which CAM started its second series of public sessions. Held at the University of Kent, Canterbury, it brought a wider audience to CAM than the crowded public sessions at the Students Centre, or the intimate small group meetings in members' homes. Reports of the conference, and the *Newsletter* which covered it, took news of CAM and its conference far afield and, together with members returning home, introduced CAM to an audience in the Caribbean itself. After the conference, the second series continued with three conference follow-up public sessions which reminded CAM of a wider potential audience within Britain – not simply that of the 'artistic and student community', but also that of the 'ordinary immigrant' now described – in the US terminology which accompanied Black Power – as being in 'the ghetto'.

CAM's First Conference

Louis James suggested the University of Kent as a possible venue for a conference. Brathwaite eagerly responded to the weekend dates which were free, 15–18 September, and urged Louis James to attend the small group session on 23 June, 'because we could take the opportunity to discuss the whole thing in concert'.[2] A few days later, plans began to take shape: Brathwaite confirmed CAM's booking to the University of Kent, and sent out the preliminary circular to all CAM members. The conference was called a 'weekend summit conference', and members were invited to 'detailed and continuous discussion on several aspects of West Indian artistic expression in comfortable, attractive surroundings'. They were promised 'Talks and seminars led by West Indian and Commonwealth artists and critics in literature, drama, painting, sculpture and music; play and poetry readings and an exhibition of West Indian art, designed as a follow-up to the recent successful symposium held at the Students Centre.'[3]

Brathwaite meanwhile was working hard at persuading people to attend. He spread the net wide, believing that people in the British arts establishment would be, or should be, interested in the arts of the Caribbean. He wrote personally to invite all publishers with Caribbean connections; all the West Indian High Commissioners; Henry Swanzy of the BBC (whom Brathwaite also asked to accept honorary membership of CAM) and Edward Lucie-Smith; editors of leading British newspapers – *The Observer* and *The Sunday Times*; the London offices of *The Jamaica Gleaner* and *The Guyana Chronicle*, and JS Barker of Thomson Newspapers; the editors of *The Critical Quarterly*, *The London Magazine*, *The New Statesman*; the Arts Council and the British Council. For he pursued his initial concept of the conference as a 'summit', and his belief in CAM as forming a bridge between Caribbean and British writers and artists:

> Publishers, because we were not satisfied with how publishers were defining Caribbean literature; the English critics, because reviews had ceased appearing in the British press ever since George Lamming's *The Pleasures of Exile* apparently upset certain members of the English establishment. . . . We wanted also other writers to come in. . . . The idea was that the conference would provide an open forum for the Caribbean to meet the rest of the world. . . . We had dreams of a summit conference between the West Indies and everybody else interested in literature at that time in Britain.

His letters to *The Observer* and *The Sunday Times* indicate how confident he and his fellow CAM committee felt about the importance of the event: 'Something of an historic occasion. . . . There have been *Présence Africaine* things in Paris and Rome, but nothing of this kind before in Britain.'[4]

From this wide casting of nets, only the British publishers responded in force: James Currey, of Heinemann Educational Books (HEB), in charge of the African Writers Series and soon to start its companion Caribbean Writers Series; Frank Pike of Fabers, editor of Wilson Harris and Garth St Omer, in a firm which already had a substantial and distinguished Caribbean list; Bill Lennox of Macmillan and Anne Walmsley of Longman, both building up lists of school and general Caribbean books. Perhaps publishers, of all those invited, saw a useful practical outcome of such an event.

The absence of other British establishment arts people at the conference was not in the event regretted. So many people – 80 to

90 in all – and such a range of people came to it, contributed so fully and gained so much, that it was regarded as hugely successful. Brathwaite, looking back, comments:

> It didn't get as far as the summit effect with the Establishment. . . . But it didn't matter, because what happened was that West Indians themselves discovered that they had so much to say to each other at this time of crossroads, we realised that it might not really have been a good idea to have attempted both things at the same time.

The majority of those who came were West Indians and included, alongside the writers and artists and actors, critics and university teachers: students of drama and medicine, literature and history; school teachers and librarians; an architect and a barrister; a physiotherapist and a laboratory technician; several housewives. In addition to this range of West Indians, and the British publishers, there were academics from several Commonwealth countries – Ghana, Nigeria, Canada, Australia, and Britain itself.

The West Indians especially seemed to appreciate the chance to be all together, in one place, for the length of the conference. From the moment they piled into a specially chartered bus, at Victoria Coach Station, a West Indian atmosphere was created, a camaraderie as the bus sped through the familiar yet deeply alien suburbs of south London. Anthony (Tony) Phillips, a lecturer in the history department of UWI at Cave Hill, Barbados, recalls: 'There was singing and everything and making jokes and picong [ridiculing things] – as the Trinidadians say.' The University of Kent, its open campus set imposingly on a hill outside Canterbury, the cathedral framed in the main window of the dining room of Eliot College, where the CAM conference was held: all this could have seemed equally alien to the participants, and its deeply English character could have jarred. But the university was new; it had opened, with Eliot its first college, only two years before, in October 1965. The staff made every effort to be welcoming to this crowd of West Indians, thanks to Louis James, as go-between: 'We managed to get the first session down in the Junior Common Room and we lit a fire and had a barbecue, which would never have happened here before or since. . . . We were able to get long bar extensions.' Some sessions were held in a lecture theatre; others, less formally, in the JCR. Still more informally, small groups met in the bar, in passages and corners, in students' rooms.

Speakers and sessions

Several speakers at the first conference had already addressed a CAM audience: CLR James and Michael Anthony, Kenneth Ramchand, Louis James, and Aubrey Williams. What they said, and what was discussed, followed on from talk and debate at earlier sessions. Speaking to CAM for the first time were George Lamming, novelist, and Clifton Campbell, painter. So, too were Bari Jonson, Horace James, Lloyd Reckord, actors and theatre directors, who took part in a session on the Performing Arts, an area of the arts not yet discussed in CAM. But the outstanding newcomer was Elsa Goveia, whose keynote speech at the start of the conference set Caribbean arts in context and directly challenged the commitment of its artists. Almost every subsequent speaker at the conference quoted or referred to what Goveia had said.

Elsa Goveia

Elsa Goveia seemed to CAM founder members the obvious choice as opening speaker. She had joined the UCWI/UWI teaching staff at Mona in 1950, with a first class degree in history from London University and two years at the Institute of Historical Research. At UWI she pioneered degree courses in West Indian history, and became the first Professor of West Indian history. Her teaching was supported by exemplary research in the history and historiography of the region. She was thus a major influence on a whole generation of students. In September 1967 she had just arrived in Britain for a year's study leave in order to work on a four-volume history of the Caribbean, being prepared by staff members of UWI. At Mona she had been Brathwaite's inspiration and mentor, the only one in the history department to show sympathy and support for his joint history/literature interests, and for his research into Caribbean creole society. La Rose knew and admired her research and writing.

Goveia spoke at this first CAM conference, as a historian to artists, on 'The Socio-Cultural Framework of the Caribbean'. Taking colonialism and consequent dependency as the common West Indian factor, she looked first at language as exemplifying cultural dependency and opportunity. Writers who use the Standard English of the metropolitan country find a larger audience outside than inside the Caribbean. But language in the West Indies 'is a double-edged sword. It is European on the one hand, and it is West Indian Creole on the other'.[5] A similar dichotomy is to be found in cultural patterns, in social behaviour, and in religion. In all these areas, peoples' class determines which pattern predominates in their lives: 'There is the metropolitan pattern which is particularly strong among the upper classes, and . . . there is a creole culture which is born in the West Indies and which contains non-European forms in large numbers.' Goveia considered this contrast in culture, based on class, a divisive rather than a unifying factor in West Indian society. What integrates the society is commonly-held attitudes to race, in particular, 'the acceptance of the inferiority of negroes to whites'. These attitudes, inherited from the slave system, have resulted in a social structure in which colour still largely determines class. But universal suffrage and independence pose a paradox. While the West Indian social system ensures continued dominance by the light-skinned minority over the black majority, the new political system depends on the support of the black masses. This, said Goveia, is the contemporary social and cultural framework in which Caribbean artists have to operate: one in which there is constant conflict between the 'very strong, very entrenched interest in racial inequality' and the new political system.

Goveia suggested that artists had a vested interest in ensuring that the current system of classification by race and wealth be abandoned – how else could an artist expect to find a way of living in his own society? West Indian writers and artists, deeply influenced by the political changes of the 1940s and 1950s, had already started to do this: by using Creole, by writing stories about the West Indies, by painting black West Indian people as not inferior. One of the conditions under which they consented to stay in the West Indies was that its society should change fundamentally. She challenged West Indian artists and intellectuals in CAM to make a choice 'between the conflicting elements of which our society is composed at present, between the inferiority/superiority ranking according to race and wealth and the equality which is implied by the slogan of one man one vote'. Their art and writing, their teaching in schools and universities, depended on it:

> Until we have made this choice we are not going to be in a position to be really creative as individuals because our energies are going to be absorbed by the terrible job of working from two completely different sets of premises. . . . Until we make a decision about the way in which we want the future to be built it is not going to be possible to find enough creative energy in the West Indies to produce the new culture which we need.

Goveia pointed to recent elements of integration in the cultural field such as the appreciation of calypsos and the new prestige given to folk songs and dances, and urged that more such work should be consciously done, 'as a choice about the way in which we want West Indian society and West Indian culture to grow'.

Such an analysis, such a strong challenge, provoked discussion in which many of the leading West Indian artists and intellectuals in the audience took part. Discussion revolved around questions of the sort of art which the committed artist should produce (CLR James, Knolly La Fortune); which art forms were most effective (Bari Jonson); how the artist communicates and to whom (George Lamming); how the masses may be educated and democratised and become articulate (Douglas Hall). CLR James referred to Goveia's ideas as 'explosive' and George Lamming suggested that her challenge involved the possibility of physical intervention. Eric

Huntley alone made a link with 'a very topical trend, the question of Black Power and its relevance to the West Indies', and spoke of the way in which, despite political democratisation in Guyana, its society had come 'quite near to tearing itself apart' – a reference to the 1962–3 crisis, which involved rioting and fighting between Indo- and Afro-Guyanese.

Goveia's talk had great impact, both on those who heard it at the time, and on those who read it later. Rex Nettleford read the transcript in CAM's *Newsletter*: in *Caribbean Quarterly*, of which he is editor, he stressed that Goveia, an academic historian, spoke with 'no reservation about the centrality of the arts to Caribbean development'.[6] Andrew Salkey, in his personal notes on the conference, summarised her talk thus: 'She talked about the desired and desirable Cultural Resistance, the socio-cultural revolution and the necessary attention to be paid to folk wisdom, the people's cultural needs, and the artist's responsibility.' Her extempore, non-academic style impressed Lloyd Reckord: 'She gave this information and she didn't sound at all pompous. So that an ordinary layman like myself found that I was swallowing it hook, line and sinker, and without any pain.'

Elsa Goveia had prefaced her challenge to artists and writers with a specific example, asserting that some West Indian painters 'tend to think in terms of abstract art rather than in terms of painting which can be socially influential'. The two painters who spoke later in the day – Aubrey Williams and Clifton Campbell – both worked in styles which were predominantly abstract, and were concerned to defend it as no less socially committed than figurative painting.

Aubrey Williams's opening statement related directly to the breadth of Goveia's analysis and challenge. He was, he confessed, 'very disturbed, intellectually' by her view that the creative arts were at the forefront of social change in the Caribbean. Taking up her point about the writer's problem of communication with a mass audience which was largely illiterate, Williams proposed that 'the visual arts, being the simplest and the most direct, should be a little ahead of literature'.[7] But this role for the visual arts does not necessitate a particular style. Williams was worried by a 'prevalent conception that good art, working art, must speak, it must be narrative'. He pointed out that the arts of past civilisations were to a great extent non-figurative, and gave examples from traditional decorative arts. But he was unwilling to be categorised as an abstract artist, saying: 'I don't even think of my paintings as being abstract. I can't really see abstraction. . . . I am not very sure that I understand the meaning of the word.'

Williams went on to defend the visual arts against another much-abused term, 'modern art', holding that Caribbean artists should be able to develop their own style, free from labels. As at earlier CAM sessions, he described the relation of his own paintings to the pre-Columbian civilisations of the New World, but now went on to state his belief that such work could be automatically appreciated by people of the Caribbean and Guyana since they share an environment which appears,

> naturally 'abstract', . . . not [yet] rearranged too much by the hand of man. We are losing it fast, but we are lucky to have our roots still in the earth of the Caribbean. . . . It is a very strong landscape and the primitive art that came out of this landscape remains unique. We should be proud of our non-figuration.

He asked, in terms familiar to his mainly literary audience, for freedom for the artist to explore his own style: 'If our painters must grope and search and forge ahead, we do not as yet know the language they should speak. We will have to grow into this language.' Williams made a plea to fellow members of CAM to become more involved with the output of visual artists, for more interchange between all the arts in the Caribbean. With more interchange, he affirmed, 'the dialogue with the people would then be automatic'.

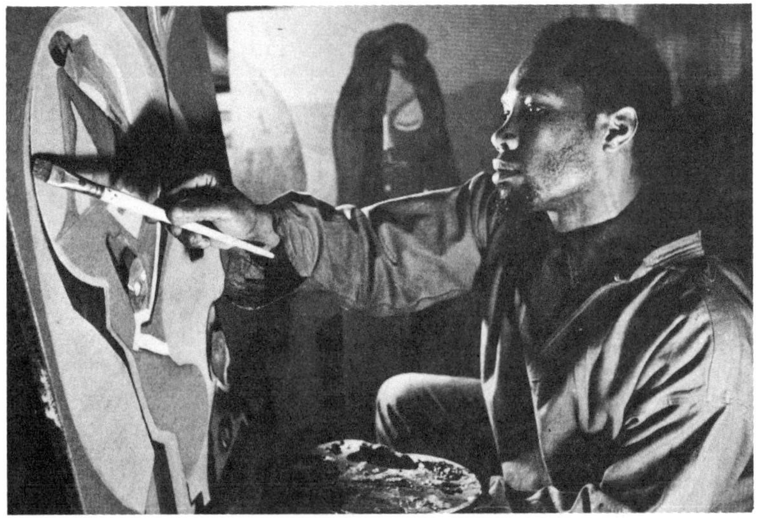

Clifton Campbell at work in the 1960s

Clifton Campbell had not spoken to a CAM public audience before, only to the CAM committee in his studio. He felt diffident in talking publicly about his work and prefaced his part of the session quite frankly with: 'I haven't got much to say. I'm going to run through some slides and if there are any questions after my slides, then you can ask what you feel like. But I must present my work first.' But the CAM audience did not give him a chance, constantly questioning and commenting on the slides, and indeed demonstrating Aubrey Williams's earlier complaint about the Caribbean intellectuals' lack of understanding of the visual arts. 'What do you wish the onlooker to see most of all, do you have a focal point in your painting?' asked one; 'I didn't think the political allegory of the painting worked at all,' commented another. Campbell countered desperately: 'Most of the West Indians might think that I'm being rude if I said my painting speaks for itself.' Finally, Aubrey Williams intervened: 'After watching my colleague being pilloried by intellectuals, I must conclude that the level of visual art appreciation among intellectuals is very, very low. Visual painting is a very valid language, it's just as valid as the words used by a writer.'

Later points made even by CLR James and Kenneth Ramchand confirmed Williams's comment; their familiarity with literature in no way seemed to have prepared them or qualified them to speak sensibly about visual arts. Campbell was articulate, and very honest, about his work as an artist in relation to society. He would, he said, return to Jamaica if the society really wanted him, and if a job were to be offered him there. Meanwhile he was in England, and had to fit into the surroundings and environment that he was in. And, he concluded, 'I believe that I'm doing something for the West Indies.' Williams found himself having to expound further his doubts about 'narrative painting', which, as 'hand-me-down missionary art', was in danger of becoming 'tourist representational art'. He gave details of a campaign for 'grassroots work' in the arts in the West Indies. But he felt confident that a start had been made: 'I think that, though late, we've got the vehicle now, at least in England we've got CAM.'

The next session was shared by two writers. CLR James spoke on 'Discovering Literature in Trinidad: the 1930s', Michael Anthony on 'Growing Up with Writing: A Particular Experience'. Each gave a vivid personal account of the place of literature in his life as a young man in Trinidad. There was a marked contrast in the context of the two accounts: the 1920s and the 1940s, urban and rural, a middle-class, bookish background and a working-class illiterate home. But both accounts confirmed Elsa Goveia's analysis: both men grew up black, both would have found few opportunities if they had stayed in Trinidad, both came to England to work and to write.

CLR James stated squarely at the start that the origins of his work and his thoughts were to be found in Western European literature, history and thought. From his home background – his father was a school teacher in a small town, friendly with the local priest and parson – he grew up with 'a sense of intellectual and moral responsibility to the community'.[8] As a young man in Port of Spain he and his contemporaries studied 'the best that there was in literature in order to transmit it to the people'. Like many of his contemporaries, inside and outside Trinidad – George Padmore, Aimé Césaire – he became a Marxist and was educated by Marxism. Many of them also became writers. Unlike his white contemporaries: 'If we wanted to write and do something, we had to go abroad. We couldn't make it at home.' He and his contemporaries had European training, but they also grew up with the inheritance of JJ Thomas and Marcus Garvey, and of a particularly West Indian type of mind. Because their literary tradition was European, they wrote 'in the definite tradition of English literature. For us in the thirties, there was no literature otherwise'. So too, claimed James, did those who began writing after 1945 – of which 'the most notable one is Mr Wilson Harris'. James went on to hail Earl Lovelace and Michael Anthony as examples of 'a new type of West Indian writer':

> They are not writing with all the echoes and traditions of English literature in their minds . . . they are native writers, in the sense that their prose and the things that they are dealing with spring from below, and are not seen through a European-educated literary sieve, as some of the finest writing in the West Indies up to today has been.

James referred to St-John Perse and Aimé Césaire as Caribbean writers who had broken away earlier from the European tradition, but, he commented, 'you don't get out of a linguistic tradition so easily'. It was, James concluded, the fact that West Indian writers have the same language as the British and a civilisation based on the British, that was at the back of their success in Britain. Their work was accepted as part of English literature, like that of the American and Irish writers who had dominated English literature throughout the century. 'We are part of the civilisation, we can come here and live here.'

James's paper began and ended with the experience and success of writers who, like himself, had been brought up in the European literary tradition and whose work was accepted as part of it; he exemplified Goveia's example of the exiled intellectual and writer. At the same time he recognised, and was excited by, writers of a younger generation who seemed, at any rate in part, to be working in a native tradition, and had chosen to break with metropolitan culture.

When Michael Anthony spoke, he was aware of the contrast of his story, and how it carried on, in the 1940s, where James had left off. There was nothing literary in his background, at home or at school. In Mayaro, his coastal village, 'culture did not mean anything'.[9] His first encounter with writing about the West Indies, at primary school in the 1930s – while CLR James and the Beacon

Group were active in Port of Spain – was Charles Kingsley, which led him to wonder whether he could not think of his own words and images to describe his environment. Instead of grammar school in Port of Spain, he went on to technical school in San Fernando, and then took a job as an iron founder at Point-a-Pierre. Meanwhile, by the early 1950s, the *Trinidad Guardian* had started to encourage West Indian writing; its acceptance, in 1951, of Anthony's first poem gave him, he said, confidence and made him determined to be a writer. But although almost everything he sent in from 1952-3 was published, he felt disheartened that there were no other openings for the Trinidadian writer: 'I think you write to communicate.' Although Anthony claimed not to have come to England in 1953 in order to write, and that he would have continued writing in Trinidad despite the lack of openings, he confessed that it was handy to have publishers around, and he welcomed the broader horizons of living in Britain. Yes, the place of the West Indian artist was in the West Indies, but only when it had developed sufficiently to offer him a fair living; he did not expect this to be in the near future, not even in his lifetime.

Anthony went on to relate how vital had been his association with *Caribbean Voices*, and to acknowledge the practical help given him first by VS Naipaul, later by Andrew Salkey. It was with the close of the BBC programme, in 1958, that Anthony began to write novels. Now, almost ten years later, he felt he had reached the end of his present path. His three published novels all drew wholly on his Trinidad background but, he went on, 'I don't know how long one can depend on recollections.' Not only had he himself changed, but Trinidad had changed, in the 14 years since he left. If he were to go on writing he must, he felt, return to the scene of his material: 'I am unable to get on with my writing now because I feel as though I am falsifying certain things, dialogue for instance. When you are writing dialogue you have to really hear it.' Novels set in England were not an alternative for him: because he had not made emotional contact with it; also, because he might be expected to write 'race' novels, which were not in his nature and which anyway he felt often did more harm than good. Since he must continue writing, he had no choice but to leave England.

This was at last the full statement about his writing which Anthony had been prevented by illness from giving earlier to a CAM audience. In the context of the conference, following directly after CLR James, it had maximum impact. His own account of his background, of his exile, and of his writing, showed him as exemplifying the new sort of Caribbean writer, advocated by Goveia, recognised by CLR James. Even so, the audience gave Anthony a hard time, unable to accept why he felt he could not write about England as almost all his fellow novelists 'in exile' had done, unable to understand his doubts about 'race novels'. CLR James intervened, memorably, in Anthony's defence, with characteristic timing and authority: 'The artist must write what he wants to write when he wants to write it, no matter how much you tell him what he ought to write.'[10] Even so, Anthony had to spell out that he was a supporter of anti-racial discrimination legislation and that he was not against raising the issue of race, and to repeat, 'The novel of protest is not my sort of novel . . . I want to tell a story and tell it well.' James used Anthony's response to elaborate on the ways in which the work of Anthony and Lovelace 'comes naturally from what is taking place on the ground and is an immediate response' – although the naturalness and ease of their response was, he claimed, thanks to the tradition of literary work and communication that had already been established by earlier writers.

In addition to the talks and readings by eminent Caribbean writers, two sessions were addressed by literary critics: in line with CAM's expressed concern that a new, appropriate criticism should accompany new forms of writing. Kenneth Ramchand and Louis James had both contributed to earlier CAM sessions. Ramchand was given a prime spot in the conference programme, on the first morning, directly after Goveia. Alone of all the speakers he had not prepared a special paper, and spoke about writers and aspects of West Indian literature which seemed not directly relevant to the current burning concerns of CAM's writers and readers. This, Ramchand explains, was deliberate; he felt that the writers and issues about which he spoke were being neglected in the interests of current topicality.

Ramchand's paper, 'The Early Phase of West Indian Writing', was drawn from his PhD thesis, just completed, on the West Indian novel. He used material from its early chapters to talk briefly about Herbert de Lisser and Tom Redcam – the first published novelists and the first to use a black character as central – and about the Trinidad writers of the 1930s. But, Ramchand pointed out, picking up on Goveia and anticipating CLR James, de Lisser and Redcam were white and therefore had a more privileged place in West Indian society. The now familiar course of exile for the black West Indian writer was pioneered by Claude McKay, who went from Jamaica to the USA in the early 1920s, and became a key figure in the Harlem Renaissance. Ramchand proceeded to read directly from a later chapter of his thesis, 'The Road to *Banana Bottom*', where he argues that although McKay felt he must express himself in racial and political terms, he was essentially a man who was trying to find a place for himself in the world.

Ramchand interspersed material from his thesis with comments which attempted to relate to CAM's concerns: how the novels of West Indian writers were still, as in the early phase, published first in Britain; how the Trinidad writers of the 1930s, 'worked in a model of social realism and compassionate protest which is a persistent feature of West Indian writing. . . . These were precursors building up a tradition, using dialect, social protest, introducing the negro as a central character.' He could, he said, see Malcolm X making use of the first chapter of McKay's autobiography, *A Long Way from Home*. He described the Harlem Renaissance as 'the American Negro version of Negritude'; he stated that in McKay's *Banana Bottom* 'you will find jazz in the West Indian novel'. Such interjections seem to show Ramchand on the one hand uncertain of the level of knowledge and understanding of his audience, and on the other, attempting to relate to CAM's earlier debates, but in too superficial and fragmented a way for his criticisms, of what he felt to be certain ideologising tendencies, to be clear. Nonetheless the range of Ramchand's pioneering research and the quality of his exposition and analysis were very impressive. It confirmed his reputation as the leading West Indian critic of fiction. It also led to publication of his thesis as a book by Fabers; Frank Pike approached Ramchand there and then about it.

Louis James spoke at the first session on Sunday morning, on 'Caribbean Poetry in English: Some Problems'. In the version subsequently published in *Savacou* 2, his argument and examples run thus. Despite the quantity of verse written in the English-speaking Caribbean, only two poets – Derek Walcott and Edward Brathwaite – approach the stature of the major West Indian novelists writing in English. This may be due to certain problems which face the Caribbean poet. First, a problem of 'voice'. In the West Indies there are North American and European poetic traditions, and the popular traditions of the Anancy story, folk-song and calypso, but as yet no strong West Indian poetic tradition. Furthermore, the poet is faced with a range of 'voices', from Standard English to dialect. Whereas a novelist can include the whole range, a poet, using a more concentrated form of writing, may be confined to one 'voice'. So two ways seem open to the poet: either he masters the European cultural tradition so thoroughly that he can then do with it what he will – as Derek Walcott does; or he makes use of the dialect tradition, which has always been present but was until recently rejected by West Indian intellectuals. Now, with recognition of the importance of Louise Bennett, and with publication of Edward Brathwaite's *Rights of Passage*, 'the dialect tradition has also emerged, as a seriously accepted poetic medium'.[11] The use of dialect can heal the split between the popular culture and the voice of the poet, opening the way for cultural expression in dialect in the mainstream of Caribbean literature. An important feature of poetry in dialect is that 'it gives us a *person*, and has to be read aloud for its full effect'. Louis James quotes Brathwaite to demonstrate the point, and proposes that the approaches of Walcott, Bennett and Brathwaite show the possibilities of 'voice' open to the Caribbean poet.

The second problem, suggests Louis James, is one of attitudes. He regrets the minor place of poetry in modern society and proposes that 'in an area like the Caribbean . . . literature is likely to have political significance'. Because English-speaking poets of the Caribbean have been less politically-minded than their French counterparts, their major poems seem to lack such attitudes. The 'transforming vision' of Walcott and Brathwaite works primarily to transform language: Walcott, by 'the burning up of cliches and muddled thinking about the Caribbean situation', Brathwaite, by 'the clarifying of ordinary words and speech cadences – the rhythms, too, of popular music'. The third and final problem is of objects. Because the Anglo-Saxon tradition of poetry has been concerned with the physical environment which conditions personality and experience, early Caribbean poets seemed concerned to show awareness of their tropical environment, but not to go beyond surface observation. Louis James shows how Wilson Harris and Derek Walcott are rare in going deeper, and proposes that in his poem 'The Castaway' Walcott overcomes all three potential problems.

A comparison of Louis James's paper as published in *Savacou* with the contemporary recording shows how substantially he altered and adjusted it in the light of what he learnt when it was presented. His conference talk, picking up Elsa Goveia's point about the divide between Standard English and the creole, discussed at length the problem of the West Indian poet's choice of language. He may, Louis James suggested, be caught between a creole which expresses emotions, and Standard English which may be very much more complex and subtle: in which he may find he can say more, but in which he will 'cut himself off from certain roots of emotion, from his pattern of speech rhythms, a part of himself'. Louis James went on to spell out what he saw as the limitations of creole:

> Sentence structure is rigid, and it relies very much on intonation. The various inflexions of English syntax are greatly simplified in creole. . . . At the same time the finer points, the subtleties are seen to go; and . . . because it is so direct and charged with emotion, it seems to me to lack the metaphysical dimension.

He cited one poem, 'Uncle Time' by Dennis Scott, as an example of how dialect could be extended to contain a metaphysical dimension, claiming to know of no other poet 'that makes quite this extension of experience by means of dialect'. He went on to praise the ways in which Derek Walcott, 'a poet of the highest international genius' – handled Standard English. He spoke of 'this new flexibility and excitement in *Rights of Passage*'. Yet 'South' was the poem which he asked to be read aloud as an example of Brathwaite's use of language, and then dubbed 'a weaker passage . . . rather too literary in the English style'; he did not mention the creole poem 'The Dust'.

Discussion following Louis James's paper showed how far off course it was judged to be. Gordon Rohlehr asked about the influence of calypso on poetry, which had not been mentioned. CLR James went further: 'No real analysis can be made of West Indian poetry which does not take into consideration what Sparrow is doing.' John La Rose said that the popular poems of the calypso constituted the fundamental tradition in the southern Caribbean which underpinned and made almost non-existent the other formal tradition. Someone else asked, understandably, for a clear distinction between 'creole' and 'dialect'. Brathwaite, the only poet present whose work was discussed in the paper, came in very strong against the views expressed there:

> I cannot accept this concept of West Indian poetry at all. I think that unless you make a study of the rhythmic tensions, the vocabulary of West Indian poetry, you cannot make a viable statement about the achievement and objectives of West Indian poetry. Dialect as such is not enough. It's the rhythmic impetus of the dialect, and it is the study of the rhythms, so that when you say that . . . the normal creole expression is physical and not metaphysical, I think that it is the concreteness which transcends into the metaphysical. . . . There is an entirely different West Indian tradition which must be observed, and if I may again say it, that poem of mine, 'The Dust', is an attempt to express through concrete terms, a metaphysic.

Louis James defended himself as best he could. To Rohlehr: that he knew he should not have left out calypso and the performing arts, how he had included a section on their importance in his introduction to the forthcoming book, *The Islands in Between*. To Brathwaite: 'This might be all-night haze, but I think I was trying very hard to say what you are trying to say.'

Louis James's paper had clearly been prepared and presented against great odds. Not only was he fully stretched as programme organiser and host of the conference, also, at the last moment, he had to give his paper in the spot reserved for George Lamming, who was still sleeping. And yet, as the only non-West Indian to speak at the conference, giving a paper on poetry – the literary form in which a leading CAM member was consciously charting new directions, and following a paper, and CAM *Newsletter* debate, in which a convincing case had been made for calypso as poetry – the omissions and emphases in Louis James's paper inevitably met with a harsh response.

George Lamming's membership of CAM had been eagerly sought from the start as the most respected novelist 'of exile' of the 1950s. He was down on the conference programme as a speaker, but he explained at the start that he did not intend to give a talk, instead he would – echoing Clifton Campbell the previous evening – present slides from his as yet unfinished novel, *Natives of My Person*. He prefaced his reading of a series of extracts with a few brief comments: on his work generally – the recurrent theme of a journey, the continuity between his four published novels; on this particular novel – intended to be short and meticulously plotted, based on the element of suspense. Such concern for the device of plot was, he said, new in his rendering of fiction.

Lamming read passages from the first four chapters of his novel, setting the context for each. Seven years had passed since publication of *Season of Adventure*, and the chance to hear passages from a new novel, in progress, read by Lamming himself, was eagerly anticipated and warmly welcomed: evidenced in the recorded applause, and in Brathwaite's subsequent comment: 'Throughout Lamming's remarkable lecture-reading there appeared again and again that general deep concern for the continuing democratisation of West Indian society.'[12]

Before the conference, Marina Maxwell, an arts and humanities graduate from Mona now studying drama and working for a master's degree in London, wrote to Brathwaite with lively, wide-ranging ideas for the programme. They came too late for all to be included, but the essential ones were, and heralded another breakthrough for CAM:

> Hear too that you are doing 'Poco' to the dancers. Great! And best of luck! Will any Latin American poetry be read? Neruda, Paz, Carrera Andrade, etc. And music from Latin America, Haiti, Cuba. Interaction time. Hope the novelists will not be swamping everything and there'll be time for discussion on the future of the theatre which has such mobility and impact and we ain't start work on it yet.[13]

In the final session, a symposium on 'Performing in Britain and the West Indies', three successful professional actors and theatre directors – Bari Jonson and Lloyd Reckord of Jamaica, Horace James of Trinidad – performed and spoke. No details exist of what was said. Brathwaite afterwards described the discussion as 'very lively' and as giving additional relevance to Goveia's and Lamming's 'concern for the continuing democratisation of West Indian society'. La Rose recalls talk about the West Indian actor's lack of acceptance in British theatre, and of the need to accept that theatre can take place in a variety of settings and is not confined to

Symposium on The Performing Arts in the Caribbean at the First Conference, (l to r) Lloyd Reckord, Horace James, Bari Jonson

the 'proscenium arch'. Bari Jonson recalls that he did a section from his one-man show, *Ex-Africa*, which included Caribbean folk songs – a calypso by Lord Kitchener, a Jamaican mento by Andrew Salkey – and dialect poems by Shake Keane and Brathwaite. Patricia (Patsy) Patterson, over from Jamaica for a year to study textbook publishing, went to see *Ex-Africa* in consequence, and reckons that the conference generally made her aware of the importance of the performing arts. Significantly, this was the only session in which the context of Caribbean arts was both the West Indies and Britain. It led directly to another, more extended symposium as part of CAM's follow-up to the conference, in November.

Between the talk sessions there were readings of prose and poetry. Doris Harper Wills performed a dramatised Guyanese folktale, 'The Samaan Tree', George Lamming read part of Penelope's Diary from *Of Age and Innocence* and poems by Martin Carter; Edward Kamau Brathwaite, Peter Figueroa and Knolly La Fortune, Kwabena Amoako (Ghana) and Calvin Hernton (USA), read or performed their poems. Marina Maxwell read poetry from Cuba, and CLR James read Aimé Césaire and St-John Perse, in translation. All demonstrated the continuing strength of the oral tradition.

Conference exhibitions

Caribbean art, and books, were on display throughout the conference. Several large canvases by Aubrey Williams, which had recently been shown in the Guyana pavilion of Expo 67 in Canada, hung in the corridors and Common Room of Eliot College, alongside smaller paintings by Clifton Campbell and Art Derry, and sculpted heads by Errol Lloyd. A small wood-carving by

Ronald Moody, a contemplative head, was placed amongst the books assembled for sale by New Beacon, in a separate room.

For the first time New Beacon was displaying and selling not just its own publications and books by CAM speakers, but also books by a wide range of writers from the whole Caribbean region. Gordon Rohlehr remembers buying novels by Denis Williams, Jean Rhys, Earl Lovelace; Anne Walmsley bought Alejo Carpentier's *The Lost Steps* and JM Cohen's anthology, *Writers in the New Cuba*. Sarah White claims that the experience of assembling titles for the first conference set New Beacon off as booksellers. Books unsold after the conference formed the basis of its stock. This bookroom at CAM's first conference was in effect the first New Beacon bookshop. The opportunity to see, and buy, the books on display pushed horizons wider for many conference participants. Brathwaite's letter of thanks to La Rose called it,

> a very careful, loving exhibition of books that added a new dimension to the conference. It fully justified our belief in *self-help*, in tunnelling under the established structures towards a new order of our own. No commercial bookshop could have created your kind of display and demonstrated Caribbean literary achievement in the way you did. For this we will always be beholden to you and Sarah who, although not there, was very much present in spirit and dedication.[14]

The conference was regarded as a great success, a breakthrough in Caribbean cultural development. It launched CAM as a serious arts organisation, with an active concern for the role of art and culture in the new West Indian society. Writing afterwards to Sir Lionel Luckhoo, Guyana's High Commissioner, the only West Indian High Commissioner to respond to CAM's invitation, Brathwaite wrote: 'The standard of lecturing and discussion was an experience in itself; everything just seemed to get better and better. . . . It was, I think, one of the most significant West Indian/Guyanese cultural events that have taken place here in Britain.'[15] But despite all Brathwaite's attempts to have the conference reported in the British press, *The Daily Telegraph* alone carried a short account of it, which included: 'Calypsos were heard in the cloisters and the dependence of the West Indian writers on English Literature was debated.'[16] The report made much of Louis James v Edward Brathwaite over dialect poetry. So Brathwaite wrote to the editor to correct what he called the paper's 'inadequate and misleading article', summarising the main themes at the conference and concluding, 'its influence in the future will be felt'.[17] The letter was not published. But articles by Brathwaite on the conference were carried in the *Barbados Advocate* and in several other newspapers of the Thomson Caribbean group, in the *Dominica Star* (Editor Phyllis Allfrey) and in

The West Indies Chronicle; also by conference participants in *Bim* (Anne Walmsley) and *Enquiry* (Vishnudat Singh). Lucille Mathurin Mair – at UWI Mona since 1957 as lecturer in the Department of History and Warden of Mary Seacole Hall – had attended the conference while on leave in Britain. She spread news on campus of its success, praising particularly the quality of the contributions and the organisation.[18] She recalls: 'We were all very excited about CAM, seeing it as the beginning of a sense of a Caribbean culture.'

'Our problem now,' wrote Brathwaite to Don Wilson, recently returned to Jamaica, 'is how to recover from the success of the conference. We've planned three follow-up sessions.'[19] Gordon Rohlehr considered that CAM should now attempt to tackle some of the points raised in greater depth, and recalls: 'There was still a lot of punditry going on, a lot of too general talk taking place.' And amidst the post-conference euphoria, John La Rose wrote Brathwaite a sombre, farsighted letter which drew on his Caribbean experience:

> I have lived through two such phenomena: the PPP in Guyana in '53, and Williams – his educational mass movement ('University of Woodford Square'), his party and the avalanche of peoples' lives. I heard Bill [Eric] Williams in one of his less self-important moods state on a public platform, 'We struck a chord'. I spoke with Cheddi [Jagan] on a platform in Broad Street at what must have been one of the biggest mass meetings in Barbados in 1952. We had previously met with Grantley at his office. People including Grantley were 'expecting'. We confront a multiplicity of hopes with our action and here we are. On this level CAM is a movement. A very real one. Not a structure. We too have struck a chord. With such things, in my experience, people take out of it what they are looking for and bring what they must give. Then the communion is over. Structure remains long after the communion is done. And it lives; and we inherit it; and it passes on. The vital spark of life and spontaneity, I have discovered, in my own life, is not long-lasting. Glowing embers remain and we mistake it for fire. I mention this only that we would know what to expect.[20]

Conference follow-up sessions

Public sessions for October to December were planned directly after the conference. Topics and speakers were suggested by Brathwaite to Louis James in late September, after being agreed by La Rose and Salkey. Advertised as 'Kent Conference Follow-Up Sessions', the topics showed CAM eager to explore three areas where Elsa Goveia's challenge seemed applicable: the communications media, theatre, and poetry. Because such areas allowed forms which did not depend on literacy, they were capable of addressing and involving the 'black masses'. Questions of language and tradition were now discussed in the context of a wider audience, actual and potential.

The session on 13 October, a symposium on 'Communications Media in and to the West Indies' arose, said Brathwaite when he invited George Lamming to take part, 'directly out of the point raised by you during discussion of Elsa Goveia's lecture . . . about control of the media, the use of radio etc.'.[21] He tried to arrange for a panel which could speak from the inside about radio, newspapers and publishing, by inviting and briefing carefully a range of professionals. JS Barker of Thomson newspapers and Alan Ross, editor of *The London Magazine*, declined, so that the press was not represented. But radio was expertly covered by Jeremy Verity, and publishing by Diana Athill of Andre Deutsch (in a letter, read aloud, as she was out of London for the session), Jon Stallworthy of OUP, James Currey of Heinemann, and John La Rose of New Beacon.

George Lamming spoke now not as a novelist but as a Caribbean intellectual, concerned with the role of the mass media in developing a culturally independent and democratic society in the Caribbean. His interest was in radio broadcasting, which he regarded as the most urgent and important medium of communication in the West Indies because it reached all sections of society. Its potential power particularly at the mass level was, he considered, largely wasted. Radio's essential function was, as he put it, to offer the lives of people back to them, by helping them to define themselves and what they imagined their future to be. In contrast, the reality of broadcasting in the West Indies was that it assumed no responsibility for the community; that only a fraction of its programme content concerned local affairs. This was because West Indian governments had largely given broadcasting over to the private sector. He proposed instead that there be a National Board for Radio in a particular territory, responsible only to Parliament, which should be responsible for the definition of policy and the organisation of services. Furthermore he had, he said, ideas for a policy for the region which would facilitate cultural regional exchange. Lamming's evident concern and idealism had little patience with the current realities of radio broadcasting and consequent constraints.

Jeremy Verity, who spoke next, was astringently realistic, while sharing Lamming's broad social concerns. Now a successful radio broadcaster, Verity came from a background of Jamaican middle-class nationalist culture. His father, Robert Verity, had started the Junior Centre at the Institute of Jamaica, and was part of Edna Manley's circle. He himself was trained in broadcasting in Jamaica, but found it too commercially-dominated to provide sufficient scope. So he came to England and worked for the BBC, where he was now a producer on the Caribbean Service. Part of the BBC External Services at Bush House, it broadcast regularly and directly to the Caribbean. Verity put forward the essential realities of broadcasting: that no West Indian government could afford to dispense altogether with commercial sponsors; how a 'broadcasting directorate', responsible to government as suggested by Lamming, had been tried but had broken down; that the average West Indian broadcaster reflected his primary responsibility – to the sponsor, not to the community; why no West Indian regional broadcasting existed. He agreed with Lamming that Caribbean broadcasters, in the West Indies and through the BBC, were avoiding their responsibilities by considering only the middle class in their audience, not 'the majority working class'. Verity blamed the continuing West Indian regard for British middle-class values and culture, evident, for example, in the discouragement of the use of dialect on radio; also, the absence of audience involvement and feedback. Although Verity had not taken part in a CAM session before, he showed himself in tune with its thinking, especially as sharpened and focused by Goveia at the conference. His practically informed inside knowledge of radio was welcomed by the CAM audience, whose main experience was in literature and books. CLR James spoke of the exemplary use of radio by Dr Eric Williams, whose series of lectures, 1957–9, was, he said, 'the most popular programme on the radio', and on which Williams sought personal feedback.

Brathwaite, chairing the symposium, opened the second half, on book publishing, with the views of Diana Athill of Andre Deutsch, whose list included Eric Williams, VS Naipaul, Jean Rhys, and Michael Anthony. Athill, its senior editor, had been with the firm from its beginning in the 1950s. With an upper-middle-class home background and an Oxford degree in English, she might seem to exemplify the best sort of traditional British publisher: widely read and travelled, liberal in outlook, alive and sympathetic to other cultures and traditions. As a writer herself, she brought special editorial understanding and skills to her publishing work. The underlying doubts of the CAM audience were that, despite all this, such an editor would inevitably be steeped in European cultural values. Brathwaite had asked her 'to give the point of view of a British publisher very much involved with the presentation of West Indian material of all sorts'.[22] Now he read aloud her reply. She disclaimed anything special in her firm's attitude towards West Indian writing: if they liked a manuscript, they treated it as any other book, regardless of where it came from. Indeed, for creative writing,

> I'm even against bringing West Indian-ness into consideration. It's how well the man writes that I care about: how vivid and honest his

> writing, how effective his construction, how moving or amusing (as the case may be) he is. Since people write best about what they have experienced most deeply, this means that a *good* West Indian novel or poem is *likely* to be concerned with some aspect of specifically West Indian experience, and therefore a particularly West Indian view of things does get promulgated. But I can't say that the promulgation of that view is our first aim, in this publishing firm. Our first aim is publishing books which we think good.[23]

Brathwaite questioned the criterion used by Deutsch of what is 'good'; the influence of a particular tradition; in particular, the attitude towards work in non-Standard English – and suggested that discussion start there. La Rose, characteristically, broadened the base of discussion. He showed how publishing and broadcasting were both part of the continuing colonial structure of West Indian society, in their financing and ownership: hence the cultural dependency of the society, and the validation of writing and criticism by publishing houses outside the West Indies. But, speaking for the one-year-old New Beacon Books: 'This idea of West Indianness means . . . breaking with the historical hiatus which each generation faces. . . . We are attempting to establish something quite new.' New Beacon was new not only in the selection of books it chose to publish, but also in its deliberate attempt to build a West Indian reading public.

Jon Stallworthy had little to contribute. Poetry editor of OUP and a poet himself, his only knowledge of the West Indies was through publishing Edward Brathwaite. He expressed amazement that Brathwaite could not be published in the West Indies. From experience of co-publishing Irish poets with a press in Dublin, he suggested that similar arrangements with West Indian publishers might be explored. James Currey of HEB, the last publisher to speak, was far more positive. He had, for a start, a broader international base. His father, RN Currey – South African poet, broadcaster and schoolmaster – worked for the BBC alongside Henry Swanzy; George Lamming and other writers from *Caribbean Voices* used to visit his home. Currey worked in publishing first in South Africa. He had attended the CAM conference and now contributed realistic points: that a publisher's reaction to a manuscript in dialect would depend on the potential market – Standard English after all had a large international readership; that the criterion for publishing a West Indian text was bound to be different for a British publisher. A CWS was possible, Currey claimed, because of interest in Caribbean writing from British and American universities in Caribbean writing. La Rose compared this with the situation in the Caribbean, at UWI and particularly in schools: 'The West Indian writer is not being used in the educational system. He is excluded deliberately from that system.'

Despite Brathwaite's careful briefing of all participants, and his own chairing of the session, it was not generally rated a good session. Brathwaite described it in a letter to Don Wilson as 'rather lack-lustre, I think, though it needn't and shouldn't have been.'[24]

The next follow-up session – a 'Symposium on West Indian Theatre' – on 10 November, was anything but lack-lustre: vivid, lively, noisy, with a range of theatrical speakers and a fully participating audience. Of the speakers, Lloyd Reckord had already taken part in a similar symposium at the conference, and Marina Maxwell in the readings; Evan Jones was a CAM founder member. But the other speakers were new to CAM, and two came direct from a new dramatic production: Ram John Holder, playwright and lead actor and Celia Robinson, producer of

Ram John Holder

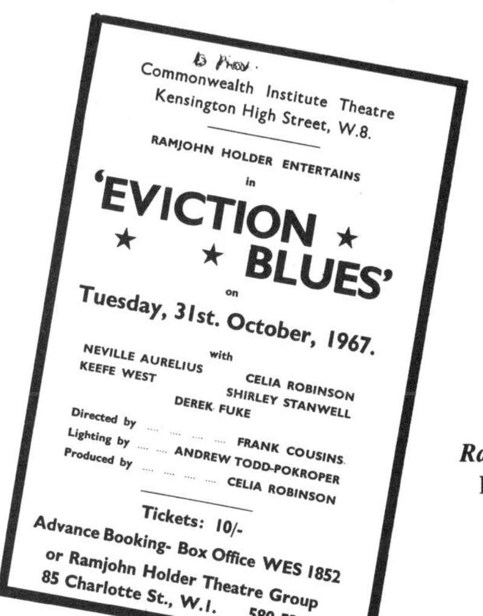

Handbill for Ramjohn Holder's **Eviction Blues**

Holder's *Eviction Blues*. This was one of two plays which had been staged at a week of Festival Events in Notting Hill in mid-October. The other, Langston Hughes's *Shakespeare in Harlem*, in which Holder took the part of the Harlem preacher-hustler, was preceded by readings by Evan Jones and John La Rose. Courtney Tulloch, a Jamaican journalist and co-editor of the community newspaper *The Hustler*, hailed *Eviction Blues* as the first attempt at real theatre in Notting Hill, which 'showed how a little bit of theatre in the ghetto can turn people on'.[25] Holder's play was given a one-off performance at the Commonwealth Institute Theatre, Kensington High Street, on 31 October and, at the time of the CAM symposium on 10 November, was poised for a transfer to the West End. Brathwaite tried to arrange for a performance for CAM at the Students Centre; in a letter to Holder he proposed that CAM would charge admission and pay Holder a fee, and continued: 'It seems to be a good opportunity for writers, painters etc to see what is going on in theatre here, right now; and for you to listen to the reaction of colleagues.'[26] This performance, scheduled for early 1968, never came off; such an audience was not a priority for the play's author and producer. But at least they took part in CAM's symposium, and brought to CAM for the first time firsthand experience of presenting Caribbean art to an audience of the 'black masses' in Britain.

Jeremy Verity, as chairman, set out a clear structure for the symposium. It would look at theatre in the West Indies; theatre in Britain in which West Indians took part, for a British audience; West Indian theatre primarily directed at West Indians living in Britain – 'something which has only started to emerge in the last three to four years'. Verity's introduction and CAM's notice billing the speakers, showed the different background and experience of each participant:

> Ram John Holder: Guyanese actor, singer and playwright
> Frank Thomasson: English producer, founder of the Theatre Guild of Guyana
> Lloyd Reckord: Jamaican actor, producer and playwright
> Evan Jones: Jamaican poet, playwright and film script writer
> Celia Robinson: Trinidadian singer, actress and producer
> Stanley French: St Lucian playwright
> Marina Maxwell: Trinidadian singer, dancer, actress and producer

Robinson, fresh from producing *Eviction Blues*, was asked to speak first, and then Holder, its author. Robinson gave the play's history: written when Rachmanism was rife, but describing 'life in the ghetto that is still going on today, the sort of thing that people try to forget'. It was put on at very short notice for the Notting Hill Festival; 'people who never ever would buy a ticket for a theatre seat, they were there and they were with us all the way.' Holder followed with a claim that his play heralded a new era of West Indian theatre: 'Now the time has come for us to move into themes that relate to us . . . to our problems . . . to our people, because . . . our people are the proletariat of the world.' Courtney Tulloch came in from the audience in full support, with: 'Where it's at, right now, is for black people to begin to be conscious of their own culture and there's only one way of doing that, and that is to get in touch with the ghettos, where the people are.' Lloyd Reckord, long-time theatre professional in Jamaica and in Britain, welcomed this suggestion, and built it onto Goveia's challenge at the CAM Conference:

> It is most gratifying to find that suddenly a younger set are saying, look, we don't care about the money, we don't care about playing

> on the West End or on Broadway or for TV. . . . [Our attitude] should be, I want to write a play about my society because I think it has to do something towards changing this society.

But Pearl Connor protested that this was nothing new. Those whose involvement in theatre in Britain went back, like hers, for 19 years, had, she said, been 'plugging away with original West Indian material, trying to present an image of our people as they were, with the hardships and all the things they were feeling'. She was provoked, not only by assumptions expressed by Holder and Robinson that they were describing a completely new development in West Indian theatre – Holder had acknowledged Edric and Pearl Connors' Negro Theatre Workshop as a 'wonderful and important starting point' – but by what seemed to her an uncritical enthusiasm for *Eviction Blues*. This indeed was the main issue of contention. Some held the audience to be the judge of a play's quality: 'If Ram John's play inside of the ghetto turns people on and they think it's beautiful, then by God it is beautiful', and that the intellectuals' assumed right to judge was irrelevant. Others cautioned against such a loose attitude. Pearl Connor said: 'We must have a critical faculty about ourselves. We can't just be submerged in self-love for our own peoples' sake, we must give them a standard. . . . Let us present this thing properly.'

For the next topic, theatre in the West Indies, Frank Thomasson described the formation, in 1957, of the Theatre Guild of Guyana and its progress since. He described its aims and achievements and claimed it to be a truly national theatre which had made a contribution to the identity of Guyana. But Ram John Holder implied its limited orientation by mentioning a cultural group called Itabo in Guyana, in which he had been involved; whereas they were burnt out in the riots of the early 1960s, the Theatre Guild was left alone. Another expatriate who had been associated with the Theatre Guild in Guyana recalled how Derek Walcott brought his Basement Theatre there: all West Indian actors, all the plays West Indian and in dialect, a good standard of acting – and yet it played to an empty house. 'The audience which we had built up was used to going to see Westernised plays, or English and American plays.' Lloyd Reckord described similar experiences in Jamaica when locally written plays were put on. With so few opportunities, not surprisingly all the promising young actors left the country. And yet after a few years in Britain, they realised that its opportunities in theatre could not satisfy them.

Stanley French was asked whether, as a playwright writing for groups in the West Indies, he found himself limited because of the lack of professional expertise. But French had as yet, he explained, no experience of getting his plays produced in St Lucia; he was working with groups in Britain where he had indeed found this to be the case. Certain plays were well suited to amateur actors: 'We did one play in town which was a great success'. Others required professionals or very competent amateurs, who were generally unavailable. Evan Jones, known to be a successful professional playwright and screenwriter in Britain – he had scored a further success with *Funeral in Berlin* (1967) – was asked how he saw his responsibilities as a West Indian writing for the stage and cinema. Jones spoke coolly and realistically:

> I think it is vainglorious to say that I feel I should carry any banners, because I don't. I try to make a living. . . . I'm very proud of the fact that I am a West Indian doing well. And if any opportunity comes up for me to write for West Indians in England, either on TV or film, I do so. But I am constricted by what will be bought and by the quality of actors and actresses that have made reputations.

Finally, Marina Maxwell was invited to present her ideas on how West Indian theatre should develop. She quoted the challenge to artists in Elsa Goveia's conference speech, and stressed the need for all West Indian theatre people to make a choice about the kind of theatre with which they worked. This, she believed, should not be 'theatre produced by intellectuals on top and given to the people'. Instead, Maxwell urged that they should look at cultural forms which already existed: steel band, calypso, carnival. 'This is the sort of material we have to be working with.' The theatre which she wanted to develop was 'documentary theatre', defined as:

> Experimental theatre that leads to revolutionary material, and let us free ourselves too from having to create characters who develop in a nice little way. . . . If we are going into problems that are so profound, so universal, so particular, so abstract, so big, we should free ourselves of any idea of form and walk in there and create our own form.

Such theatre could only be developed in the West Indies; whatever happened with the performing arts in Britain was, in her view, secondary. But Maxwell put forward practical suggestions of what CAM might do in Britain: appoint a CAM committee on the performing arts; put on one major production per year; provide a framework and an organisation for the projection of the theatre artists in Britain.

Despite the noise and confusion, the interruptions and confrontations, this was an especially valuable CAM session, Theatre, after all, is an art form potentially far more 'popular' and relevant to the 'ghetto' than the novel or poetry, certainly more so than is literature in the European tradition. The session's dynamic came from the speakers' many-sided involvement in theatre, in the West Indies and in Britain. For the first time CAM was directly asked to consider the demands of the 'ordinary immigrant' in the 'ghetto'. This, too, was the first session in which Marina Maxwell had a chance to express her views about a new sort of theatre which would be central to Caribbean culture, and would act as a revolutionary force for bringing about a changed social order.

The speakers and audience for this CAM session on theatre reflected the new and changed attitudes amongst West Indians in Britain following Stokely Carmichael's visit in July 1967. His speeches had radicalised the position of many blacks in Britain, and had had tremendous impact on the burgeoning black youth movement. The Barbados-born teacher and schools inspector, Winston Best, has described 1967 as 'an important landmark and indeed a watershed in my involvement with the black community', and described it as 'a period of protest, of Black Powerism, and of assertivenesss of the black person as s/he struggled to make his/her presence felt and recognised throughout the white world'.[27] Carmichael's presence and speeches in Britain also bolstered the attitudes of West Indians who had experienced discrimination in the USA; Ram John Holder had already studied and worked in the USA before coming to Britain. But regular CAM members felt uncertain about the new audience and new character of the session. Oliver Clarke, not there himself, had heard of it as 'a visitation from the militant sphere of the community at the meeting on Friday'.[28] Ken Corsbie, a drama student, wrote to Doris Brathwaite – they had acted together in Guyana in the 1950s: 'No, not discouraged by the CAM meeting. A little shocked that even under these conditions there seemed to be so much anarchist behaviour leading to almost political and personal denouncements, with very little to hold on to in the end.'[29] Brathwaite described it to Louis James, not present, as 'black power boys an' ting from de Ghetto boy!'[30] Writing to thank Verity for his 'skillful and restrained chairmanship', Brathwaite commented: 'I thought it was an interesting and stimulating session; though like you I was just not at all happy about the bad-mannered element that crept in.'[31] Given the location of CAM public meetings, the open access to all frequenters of the Centre, the mood amongst West Indians in London following Stokely Carmichael's visit, their concern with theatre – such an element seems, in retrospect, not surprising or out of place. Not before time, CAM was being challenged by outsiders, or at least by other points of view.

The final session of 1967, when Brathwaite spoke on 'An Area of Experience: West Indian Poetry', again followed directly from the conference. It was CAM's third public session on poetry and at last, nine months after his landmark reading, a chance for Brathwaite himself to expound his 'new directions'. His own poetry was not however the main focus of the paper, but rather, in his words after Louis James's paper at the conference, the 'entirely different West Indian tradition which must be observed'.

Brathwaite's thesis was that West Indians are strangers to their own community and environment, evident in the divided allegiance between Africa and Europe, between the Caribbean and Europe, in their imagination. Because of the problems caused by such alienation, particularly in their expectations of West Indian society, they face an urgent need for choice. Brathwaite used the same key paragraph from Elsa Goveia's conference paper which Marina Maxwell had quoted. He defined the choice for Caribbean artists and intellectuals as coming to terms with aspects of themselves and their environment, their colour and its meaning, their history and the fact of slavery, and with their folk culture.

From a quick survey of the contributions of leading Caribbean writers, artists and intellectuals, Brathwaite concluded that none carried a social creole ideology, such as was represented in his work. Nor had West Indian sociologists provided a dynamic which would show him where to go from here. But an American sociologist, Robert Redfield, working in the Yucatan of Mexico, had proposed a theoretical framework which could be applied to West Indian society. It seemed to provide the necessary dynamic for such an ideology: the theory of the Little Tradition (LT) and the Great Tradition (GT).

According to Redfield's theory the rulers in society – the aristocracy, politicians, soldiers, priests – are part of the GT, and the ruled – the peasants and labourers – belong to the LT. Artists and intellectuals act as go-betweens, agents of integration. Because of the unique nature of West Indian society, a colonised society, the centre of its GT is not within the West Indies but in Europe, and therefore its carriers are European and white. In this society, the intellectual go-betweens have a particularly important role. And yet, because they are educated into the GT, often in Europe, they impose the GT and the folk, or LT, is neglected. When they come to Britain, they want to be integrated into British society. If they return to the West Indies, they find they are expected to ally themselves with those of the GT. But, claimed Brathwaite, West Indian writers are in a different position from other West Indian intellectuals:

> They have on the whole in their writing been concerned with describing the folk society. They have been concerned with the people who speak dialect, the backyard, the lower class . . . their writing is subversive. They are writing about, they are trying to establish, trying to articulate the needs and demands of an entirely different tradition, that is the LT.

The task of West Indian writers, he continued, if they are to bring about change in their society, is to evolve their own GT. In this process of change the teacher will be an important go-between, and the UWI will play a crucial role; it will have to be concerned with West Indian studies and established as a West Indian institution: 'Then everything else will follow.' So their concern must be to free their LT so that their whole new society may be based on it.

Brathwaite described this all-important LT, which he also referred to in turn as the 'little society' and the 'folk culture', as consisting of the 'uneducated, illiterate masses, whose souls are therefore unspoilt'. They are conscious of Africa – and he qualified these masses, unashamedly, as those of the 'negro segment, because I think the greater understanding I have of my own segment, the easier it is for me to understand the others; there is nothing to do with separation'. Their social structure is based on the extended family, which is on the whole polygamous. Their cultural life revolves around certain focal points and activities, such as markets, and religious and political meetings. This LT, from which the new GT is to develop, should be aware of Africa as its super GT. It should also be aware of slavery; West Indian writers should make an attempt to retrace their steps and see what happened for themselves. Brathwaite's account of the LT culminated in his defence of the poet's use of 'dialect', in its widest sense:

> By dialect we don't just mean taking off a word, a little syllable at the end of a word, but it is the thought process behind it. My poem 'Ananse', although it is not in dialect, to me the use of Ananse, the attempt to reincarnate the spider back into the original creative god that he was, is a form of dialect.

Brathwaite read 'Ananse' and 'Grandfather', also not in 'dialect', from *Islands*, the as yet unpublished third volume of his trilogy, at the start and centre of his paper and 'The Dust', in creole, from *Rights of Passage* at the end. His paper showed the centrality of 'dialect', of a social creole ideology, to Brathwaite's work as historian, teacher and writer. His explanation of the GT and LT formed an easily grasped distinction between the metropolitan tradition of the elite and the folk tradition of the masses which carried on from Goveia's paper, and showed how a poet's choice could work out in practice. Also, it justified the role of artist/intellectual as a go-between or mediator between the two traditions.

Finally, Brathwaite spoke about CAM: of what he had learnt through it about democratic practice and power-sharing. This, he said, explained CAM's structure, the way it operated, and its

New Beacon bookstall at a CAM public session at the Students Centre, (l to r) Sarah White, John La Rose, Doris Harper Wills, Edward Kamau Brathwaite, Andrew Salkey

attitude to members. 'We're accepting everybody because it is the only way we can find out what is going on.' Brathwaite acknowledged the presence of Andrew Salkey and John La Rose at the session, on his right and left. Both helped to field questions in the subsequent discussion. Andrew Salkey spoke despairingly of any signs that educationalists in Jamaica were 'moving anywhere near the people'. John La Rose spoke dismissively of the university: 'So far as I understand it, a university is a source of maintainance of a certain kind of tradition.' But he warmly supported Brathwaite's thesis. 'There are the traditions which are already there which can replace Humpty Dumpty: it's that we are not aware, or we are not making ourselves aware. . . . It's the imposition of the Great Tradition whereby you absorb it to the extent of not wanting to teach your child that.' And La Rose supported most positively Brathwaite's belief in the need to go back and retrace where they had come from. It was, he said, what at one of CAM's 'warishi' nights had been called 'a theory of unmaking, and it is to some extent reversing an entire historical process. You go back to where you were to resume where you want to go to, to build something new.' Brathwaite expressed particular regret that Louis James was not present: 'Now he isn't here so perhaps he'll never know what I think.' Nor was the talk transcribed and published in the *Newsletter*. But those who attended the session remembered and held to this articulation of Brathwaite's central and determining ideology.

CAM after the conference

Continuing cooperation between CAM and the Students Centre after the conference had been ensured by the success of CAM's monthly sessions from March to July. In September 1967 Alain Rickards of the House Committee wrote to 'some of the more prominent members of CAM asking when they would be available for a series of discussions at the Centre, and for their suggestions'.[32] The monthly programme issued by the Centre and the West Indian Students Union now included each CAM meeting. In December 1967, Hynam, the warden, wrote to Brathwaite: 'The [Board's] members were very impressed with what you are trying to do and asked me to give you every facility here at the Centre, which you already know you can count on.'[33]

From October 1967, New Beacon's bookselling at the Centre became a regular and important feature not only of CAM sessions but of WISU and other events there. Brathwaite recalls how 'before a CAM meeting there was a lot of milling around at the tables, and buying and chatting, and it became a focus in itself.' Locksley Comrie, a student and a member of the WISU Committee, remembers New Beacon's stall at many Students Centre meetings:

> John would subsidise all our meetings through his books, and he would make our meetings more, in a sense, functional. Because after we talked about the subjects, the books would be outside there and we would pick up very very cheap books, pamphlets, and up-to-date books about what was happening in the Caribbean, in America, and even what was happening in London that you weren't familiar with.

For John La Rose himself, bookselling at the Centre was a natural extension of New Beacon's work, as he puts it, 'trying to introduce all those people to the new work being published'.

CAM's art exhibition at the Centre, planned for the autumn, was again postponed: Karl 'Jerry' Craig did not yet feel ready to stage a fullscale show. But the Centre's Board of Governors requested from CAM a few paintings for a reception on 12 December, for donors to the Centre's renovation and redecoration fund. The Centre's Appeal stated that 'the Centre hopes to be a showcase of West Indian arts and crafts'.[34] Craig agreed to arrange it, and selected work by Clifton Campbell, Art Derry and Aubrey Williams.

CAM made every attempt to build on the success of its first conference by publishing its papers; by applying for financial help; by urging and assisting CAM branches to be formed elsewhere, especially in the Caribbean. The *Newsletter* which appeared in October 1967, No 4, August-September, contained a report on the conference by Brathwaite; the complete text of Elsa Goveia's talk;

two of the poems spoken by Kwabena Amoako, a Ghanaian student; further CAM comment on Rohlehr's calypso paper – extracts from an exchange of letters between Brathwaite and Rohlehr. The conference papers were indeed considered by the CAM committee to be of such high quality and wide interest that they deserved publication as a book. The talks, discussions and readings had been recorded by the University of Kent's audio-visual unit, and most of the talks transcribed by the university's secretarial staff. Louis James put a proposal to James Currey of Heinemann for a two-part book – edited papers from CAM meetings, followed by those of the conference. He and Brathwaite would be joint editors, as they knew the range of material available, and Andrew Salkey would write an introduction. Currey, whom they met in October, may not have been encouraging, despite James's assertion, 'I think it would be a worthwhile venture. I believe interest in West Indian literature is going to enjoy a second forward impetus in the next few years.'[35] James and Brathwaite continued to work on the proposed material, but by early 1968 references are to New Beacon as publisher. The conference papers, with a few substitutes and additions, finally came out as *Savacou* 2, September 1970.

Meanwhile the conference tapes, like all the session tapes, were regarded as an extremely valuable part of CAM's work. Brathwaite, La Rose and Salkey, guarded them with the greatest possible care. Vishnudat Singh, a postgraduate student in English, described 'the library of tape recordings by artists and critics . . . an invaluable source of reference for West Indian critics'.[36] Louis James was interested in their usefulness for the University of Kent's West Indian literature courses. He persuaded the university to provide CAM with cheap tapes and to copy them free of charge. His anxiety to help CAM as much as possible with their transcription resulted in his being blamed when the recording of the session on the Performing Arts went missing.

When CAM was first formed, Edward Lucie-Smith and Louis James both urged Brathwaite to seek Arts Council funding, as the only available substantial, longterm means of financial backing. After the conference Brathwaite wrote to Eric Walter White: Assistant Secretary and Literature Director of the Arts Council and Secretary of the Poetry Book Society which had made *Rights of Passage* one of its 1967 recommendations – and Sarah White's father. As a result, CAM was advised to put in an application; the Arts Council seemed ready to help on specific CAM events and activities. No such application was ever made, but the possibility of the prestige and security of such a grant added to CAM's confidence after the conference.

During the summer of 1967, several active CAM members returned home to the Caribbean. Brathwaite at least had high hopes that CAM branches would be formed around them. In August he wrote to a Spanish artist who wanted to make contacts with artists in the Caribbean: 'Quite a few CAM people have just returned to Jamaica, so it's Jamaica which will have the first Caribbean CAM. Orlando Patterson, c/o Department of Sociology, UWI; and Dermot Hussey, c/o RJR [Radio Jamaica Rediffusion], are the people to contact.'[37] In a letter requesting funds for the First Conference: 'There are signs, too, that links will soon be formed between CAM (UK) and artists and audiences in the West Indies – a most vital and necessary development.'[38] Links were formed through a few individuals and institutions taking out group membership, and thereby receiving the *Newsletter*. By November 1967 the Institute of Jamaica, the Barbados Arts Council and public libraries were members; the poet and critic Mervyn Morris, a lecturer in the Department of English and then Warden of Taylor Hall at Mona, was an early member; he recalls receiving the first issues of the *Newsletter*. The writer Phyllis Shand Allfrey, who met the CAM Committee in London in August 1967, wrote subsequently in her paper, *The Star of Dominica*: 'Incidentally I would advise any artist (whether in words or paint or design) to join CAM. It costs only a £1 a year and will keep young West Indian intellectuals informed on trends among the brilliant exiles as well as giving them fresh thoughts from the homelands.'[39] But actual branches of CAM, as had been formed in London, were not so easily established. Brathwaite wrote anxiously to Don Wilson, 'Does it look as if a CAM group will appear in Jamaica? Have not had a word from Orlando/Nerys.'[40]

A WIDER AUDIENCE

Non-CAM events in which CAM members took part during this period indicate some of their interests and the opportunities open to them. John La Rose spoke at the Students Centre in September on the crisis in Anguilla; CLR James at the Friends House, Euston Road, on the 50th Anniversary of the Russian Revolution, chaired by Richard Small, in November, and at the Students Centre on 'The History of the West Indies' in December. Brathwaite gave a repeat of his talk on 'The West Indian Jazz Novel' at the Africa Centre in December. Bari Jonson gave his one-man show, *Ex-Africa*, at the ICA in October; Horace James's production of *La Petite Musicale* with the Trinidad Folksingers was presented at the Commonwealth Institute Theatre in December. Ronald Moody's work was on show at the Portrait Sculptors' Exhibition in November. Many CAM members and much of CAM's new audience took part in a huge anti-Vietnam protest rally in Trafalgar Square in October, at which Obi Egbuna spoke about Black Power. It was

Egbuna, a Biafran playwright and poet, who had formed the first avowed Black Power group in Britain in August 1967, following Stokely Carmichael's visit – the Universal Coloured Peoples' Association.

In September, after the conference and before the first of the follow-up public sessions, two CAM private or 'small-group' sessions took place: both readings from newly published work. Lindsay Barrett (now Esoghene), of Jamaica, read from *A Song For Mumu* (1967). This his first and – until recently – only novel followed private publication the previous year of *The State of Black Desire* – three poems and three essays. Edward Kamau Brathwaite read *Masks*, the second long poem of his trilogy, complete, in his flat, on 27 September. Other similar meetings certainly took place.

Small-group sessions were also held for the discussion of CAM business. Brathwaite summoned CAM's founder members to one on 12 December: 'An' we need *all* de boys present at this meetin' since is a very important one.'[41] Special letters of invitation were also sent to Kenneth Ramchand, and to Christopher Laird, a Trinidadian student and poet. The main items for discussion were:

The Constitution of CAM, for which Oliver Clarke had ideas
The Secretaryship of CAM, since Edward Brathwaite was to be in Jamaica for two months from 3 January
The Conference Papers

Ronald Moody's 'Sheila Henry', exhibited at the Woodstock Gallery, November 1968

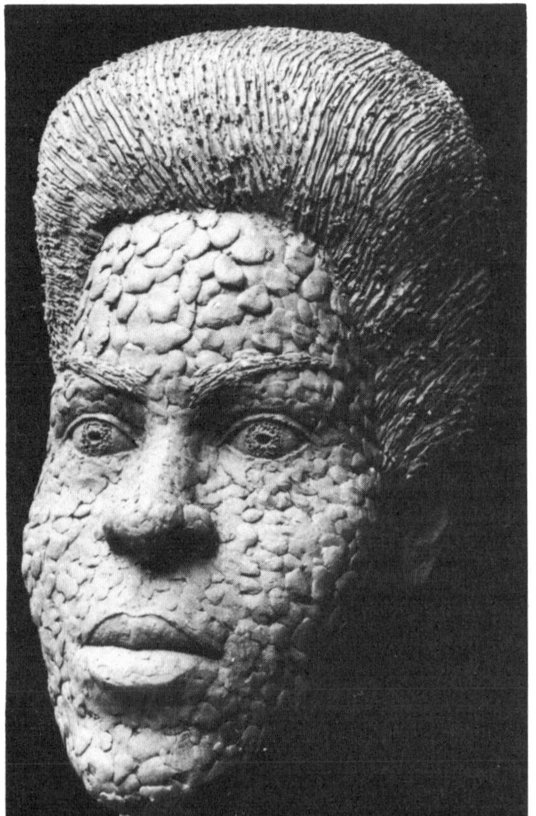

Generally, Brathwaite told Ramchand and Laird, its purpose was 'to discuss, plan and spew out ideas for Phase II'.[42] Some plans had already been laid. Louis James had raised the question of a second conference for 1968, and of where it should be held; Brathwaite had invited speakers for the first few months' public sessions of the New Year. But Brathwaite was on the point of leaving Britain for two months' research work in Jamaica. With the imminent absence of CAM's founder member and abundantly active secretary – on the one hand, and the enlarged, eager and challenging audience for CAM on the other, December 1967 decisively marked the end of CAM's first phase.

5 A Broader Context
January - August 1968

CAM in Britain, January – March

Organisation

Brathwaite sent off a final burst of letters before his departure for Jamaica on 12 January 1968. They reveal new arrangements for CAM's administration and outstanding matters to be resolved. From 1 January, Marina Maxwell was CAM secretary, with Brathwaite continuing to serve as a member of the CAM committee. The responsibilities informally assumed by other members of the committee continued, with more significance now that Maxwell was Secretary. Brathwaite explained the new committee arrangements and set them out in a letter on 10 January, although he had 'decided not to publish in Newsletter as it is quite informal; these are the people appointed by the CAM Committee to help Marina in certain areas'.[1] Most of the 'appointments' simply confirmed responsibilities already being carried out: Andrew Salkey – literature; Bari Jonson – performing arts; Jerry Craig – arts; John La Rose – publications; Louis James – newsletter, 'though', added Brathwaite, 'I shall probably continue with this for a little while longer.'

In naming Jonson for the performing arts, there was recognition of theatre alongside literature and art as an area of concern and activity, a representative if not yet a separate CAM committee on theatre as urged at the November symposium. Brathwaite justified the appointment of Roy Henry for 'recordings' thus: 'Roy Henry is not yet a member of CAM – see why I'm loathe to publish? – but has promised to join. He is apparently an expert in the gramophone record production trade. The idea is that he will help us move towards getting WI voices reading on record.' Such recordings, arising naturally from CAM's emphasis on and practice of spoken poetry, had been proposed by Louis James to Brathwaite after the First Conference; he had offered to write to Argo (the Decca subsidiary which specialised in literature) to urge them to publish Brathwaite's readings of his work, and to suggest a CAM album of West Indian poets reading. Argo's eventual issuing of all Brathwaite's trilogy was, however, mainly thanks to Decca's Peter Orr, formerly of the British Council, which sponsored the recorded readings. No CAM album was issued. Roy Henry became a CAM member and attended the Second Conference, listed as 'concert singer', but seems not to have attended committee meetings, or to have been active on CAM's behalf.

The final appointment listed by Brathwaite was the most significant: 'Richard Small – ghetto'. Brathwaite went on to explain: 'It is felt that we have, so far, no contact with the "real immigrant" communities. Richard's job to find ways and means of remedying this.' Richard Small had been an active member of CAM since it first started to hold public meetings at the Students Centre in March 1967. His involvement with the Centre and WISU had begun when he was a law student, 1961 to 1964. He had been elected to the committee of WISU in his second year and president in his third; this was during a period of intense debate as to whether the Centre should continue to cater exclusively for students or also be open to the broader West Indian community. During this period he had also become involved with the West Indian Standing Conference, the coordinating body of a number of West Indian immigrant community groups and organisations which held its meetings at the Centre. After completion of his LLB degree he continued his involvement with the West Indian Standing Conference and with other activities at the Centre. But a role for Small within CAM as described by Brathwaite was never publicised. Small indeed himself has no memory of being asked to take it on, nor of attending committee meetings in this capacity.

When, three months later, in *Newsletter* No. 6, the responsibilities of individual CAM members were publicised under a heading 'CAM Organisation', Horace James's name also appeared alongside 'performing arts', and Oliver Clarke was listed as treasurer. There was no mention of Roy Henry or Richard Small. John La Rose has no memory of their being 'appointed'; he points out that, because of the nature of CAM's organisation, decisions were often made by informal consultation.

Matters relating to the Students Centre were amongst those which Brathwaite handed over to Maxwell. The Centre's January programme had announced: 'Strict control over entrance. Nonmembers will only be admitted when accompanied by a member, or when their names have been given to the person on duty as expected guests.'[2] But CAM meetings were advertised as public meetings. The ruling seems to have reflected the continuing tension within the Centre over its openness to 'ordinary immigrants' as well as to students. CAM's recent Theatre Symposium had attracted a wide, noisy audience. But CAM alone could hardly be a seen as a threat to the Centre, and it was important that the public nature of its monthly meetings be safeguarded. Also, Brathwaite urged confirmation that the first Friday of each month would continue to be reserved for CAM. He left instructions with

Maxwell over taping meetings: the Centre's own facilities were inadequate, but either Doris Brathwaite would handle it, or John La Rose and Sarah White would bring their tape recorder along with books for the New Beacon stall. Brathwaite suggested items for the next committee meeting: unsatisfactory correspondence with the Jamaica and Trinidad High Commissions; publication of the conference papers; the tapes; *Newsletter* No. 5. Although Maxwell seems to have been a comparative newcomer to CAM – certainly not one of the founding group and not making her presence felt publicly, at least, until the First Conference – Brathwaite expressed complete confidence in his successor: 'Very glad that you have taken over as Secretary. Things are going to go from good to better. All the boys *have* to help you.'[3]

Marina Maxwell herself was full of enthusiasm. She convened a committee meeting in late January adding, 'So much work ahead. CAM must swing out for 68.'[4] One of the ways in which she and other members tried to implement this was by investigating a London, non-university venue for the Second Conference, to be held later in the year.

Directly after the First Conference, Louis James had put forward ideas for a venue for the second. He wrote to Brathwaite: 'We would be delighted to have you and are building up interested staff all the time; Leeds or Sussex would also be glad to be hosts.'[5] All were universities. By February, other ideas were afoot. To hold another campus conference, out of London, would mean excluding the urban West Indian students and immigrants. The new CAM committee tried hard to find a suitable London venue: Marina Maxwell and Oliver Clarke wrote to a dozen or more university, hospital, and other possible institutions. But none that was suitable would be vacant when they wanted it. Meanwhile Louis James submitted a short paper, setting out clearly the pros and cons of a London venue. It would be more widely accessible, especially to those of limited financial means; on the other hand, it could not be properly residential, and would lack the opportunity for extended talk, and the concentration, afforded by all participants being together in one place. Also, James gave a realistic warning of the organisational work involved, and the need – if the conference were to be held in London – to plan for this. He did not push for a second conference at Kent, but without a venue or organisational network and facilities in London, it eventually had to be there.

Meanwhile a weekend school on West Indian literature was put on by Nottingham University's Department of Adult Education, from 6–7 January 1968, and resulted in a branch of CAM being established in Nottingham. Robert Reinders, an American historian teaching at Nottingham University with a special interest in

Claude McKay, had approached the Jamaican High Commission in September 1967 for help with setting up the school. Reg Phillips, Deputy High Commissioner, passed on information about CAM sent by Brathwaite, with whom he put Reinders in touch. As a result, Louis James and Kenneth Ramchand went as course tutors. Twenty people, West Indians and British, attended. The Adult Education Centre was very impressed and decided to sponsor a lecture-reading by a West Indian author. But the more significant consequence was that students of the school decided to form a Nottingham 'Chapter of CAM', with Reinders and a student, Milton Crosdale, as its organisers.

Louis James reported back enthusiastically to the CAM committee. In a letter to Brathwaite he described 'a live group that united both academically qualified people and those whose vision was unqualified by any "intellectualisation" (I use "unqualified" in both senses, nothing patronising: they had a unique contribution to make).'[6] To Marina Maxwell he wrote:

> They would like information about aims and nature of CAM further to the fairly long talk I gave on it. Have we a CAM brochure? If not, suggest we formulate and cyclostyle/print copies as soon as possible and in the meantime you could write to the Nottingham people congratulating and encouraging them.[7]

In a memo on Nottingham which he presented to the late January committee meeting, he described the nascent branch and its potential, and urged a helpful response. But despite this, and several requests from Reinders for guidance on setting up a branch of CAM and of its relation to London CAM, Maxwell did not respond.

Thanks to a reply from Doris Brathwaite, Reinders wrote to Edward Kamau on his return in late March, and received an immediate reply. They would like to welcome the Nottingham group into their circle. Brathwaite had spoken with the committee now and agreed on a 'federal relationship': Nottingham should have its own organisation, keep its own funds and no doubt put out its own newsletter. All CAM London requested was a £1 group subscription per year. He apologised for the delay: 'The cats say they were waiting for me to get back.'[8] Officers of the Nottingham branch corresponded regularly with the CAM committee, expressing their pride at having a share in the movement, asking for speakers to address their meetings, setting out the names of their officers – Milton Crosdale, Vice-Chairman, Lavonnie A White, Secretary – and details of their monthly meetings, sending a £1 group membership fee, arranging for two folk singers to perform at the Second Conference. Peter Figueroa remembers speaking to the new Nottingham branch, on 19 April, on 'The West Indian

Writer in Britain'; it continued to invite speakers throughout 1968 and 1969.

Speakers and sessions

Speakers for early 1968 CAM public sessions in London had been booked by Brathwaite the previous autumn. He invited VS Naipaul to speak on 5 January, as writer to writer, with a mix of confidence and deference – recalling their acquaintance through *Caribbean Voices* in the early 1950s, greetings passed on via Derek Walcott, and modestly referring to himself, Brathwaite, as 'still doing a little writing'. Brathwaite continued, 'I've also got this Caribbean Artists Movement started', that a CAM handout and programme were enclosed, and added 'we're wondering if you'd care to come and talk to CAM early next year.'[9] Naipaul's reply, a week later, was not just a definite 'no', it seemed ambiguous in its response to Brathwaite's own work and to that of other Caribbean writers.[10] Naipaul had, he said, already thought of writing to Brathwaite to say how pleased he was to read of his recent Arts Council award, how clearly he remembered Brathwaite's work from *Caribbean Voices*, and how pleased again that he had decided to publish with OUP. But the *Guardian* report had misspelt Brathwaite's name as 'Braithwaite' – a common error, and one to which Edward Kamau was especially sensitive since it confused him with the Guyanese novelist, ER Braithwaite. Naipaul seemed to dwell on and develop the confusion caused by the misspelling. As to the CAM invitation, which he described as addressing Brathwaite's Caribbean friends, he declined on the grounds that he was bad at talking connectedly and might not be in the country at the time suggested.

Brathwaite took the reply badly, and still recalls it with bitterness, despite Salkey's reponse: 'The VSN matter is very gentle, very moving, sincere even. I haven't seen this side of the coolie man for years. Beautiful. The nicest rejection in years, actually.'[11] Salkey's use of 'coolie' was a term of affection for a friend and in no way pejorative.

Other approaches met with a positive response. Academics were signed up for the February and March 1968 meetings. Jean Franco, University of London, spoke on 2 February, on 'Spanish and French West Indian Literature Today'. She had been in Latin America at the time of the CAM Conference and was sorry to have missed it. Brathwaite proposed the title, adding: 'We all want to hear something about Césaire and Guillén etc, but we should also like to know how things have gone on (are going on) from there.'[12] Franco, Reader in Spanish-American literature at London University, was author of *The Modern Culture of Latin America: Society and the Artist* (1967), a pioneering study of the social character of Latin American art and literature, from 1888 to the present. By the time she came to speak to CAM her talk had additional topicality. John La Rose and Andrew Salkey had just returned from the Havana Cultural Congress, and were fully informed on the latest cultural developments in Cuba and Latin America.

Franco's approach to the CAM audience was open and enquiring. She knew, she said, very little of what was going on in the literature of the English-speaking Caribbean, and was eager to know if its writers shared the preoccupations of those in the French and Spanish-speaking islands. By way of introduction she outlined what were held to be the three main problems of Latin American writers: first, of 'commitment'; second, the writer's relation to Third World culture and to the metropolitan cultures of Spain and France; third, the search for roots, usually expressed in questions about the Indian in South America. Although the context of such problems was Latin America as a whole, Franco examined attempts to solve them in the French and Spanish-speaking Caribbean: by the exiled writers, living in Paris or London, who had 'little or no native tradition and therefore turn to English and French culture for appropriate techniques to help them with their own writing';[13] by the emergence of Afro-Cubanism in the Spanish-speaking Caribbean during the 1920s, which anticipated Negritude in the French-speaking Caribbean during the 1930s.

Franco looked in detail at particular French and Spanish-speaking Caribbean islands: Martinique and Cuba, Haiti and Puerto Rico. Whereas French 19th century culture was one of the most brilliant in Europe, and French colonial policy until 1939 encouraged the integration of Martinicans into metropolitan culture and society, Spanish contemporary culture was regarded as 'backward' and provided no model or guidance. The all-powerful influence of French culture in Martinique was indeed responsible for its writers turning to Africa, if largely as a mythical continent, and for formulating the ideology of Negritude. The surrealist movement, started in France, lived on as a dynamic force in Caribbean writing long after it had died in Europe. Aimé Césaire's poem, *Cahier d'un retour au pays natal*, first published, unnoticed, in 1939, was possible because of these two movements.[14] Meanwhile Afro-Cubanism in Cuba had found a voice in the poet Nicolás Guillén, a mulatto, who declared his heritage was of both races; and surrealist techniques had been used by the novelist Alejo Carpentier, a white Cuban. As for Cuba since the 1960s:

> A fantastic outburst of energy in Cuba recently. New sectors of the population have been educated and begun to write; there are new opportunities given to writers to publish, and a period of censorship

> and restriction has been followed by the most permissive revolution anywhere in the world. There is no attempt now to dictate what the writer should say, or to demand social realism.

The situation in Haiti was a bitter contrast; its vigorous Haitian French culture, rooted in its folklore, and its brilliant literature had been all but extinguished since Papa Doc Duvalier came to power in the 1950s. And Franco referred to the culture of Puerto Rico as 'schizophrenic...probably the only place in Spanish America where people have gone to look for roots in Spain in reaction against the Anglo-Saxon and North American culture'.

Discussion, like Jean Franco's introduction, tended to stray from the Caribbean into Latin America generally. John La Rose in particular demonstrated familiarity with the literature and socio-historical background of the whole region, and talked as an equal with Franco, whose book he clearly knew well. They, and others, considered topics such as where a Latin American writer was to find a sense of community; how the American Indian, his language and his culture, was regarded by Latin American writers. But the majority of questions asked and points raised attempted to relate English-speaking Caribbean culture to what was happening in the other islands; how people of the Southern Caribbean already had a sense of Caribbeanness such as Carpentier exemplified (La Rose). Knolly La Fortune, whose *Legend of Ti-Marie*, a Trinidadian folk-tale retold, was being published that year, made a key point about the writer and native tradition: that this need not be literary, and that the writer can draw on this oral tradition even though it seems dormant. One of several informed, articulate women in the audience took his point further: 'These so-called masses in the Caribbean that the writers attempt to patronise in fact have a language of their own and are developing a culture of their own, and this culture is not necessarily illiterate.' Marina Maxwell and another woman argued closely as to whether or not the more 'dynamic, revolutionary atmosphere' to which Latin American writers were accustomed meant that since the English-speaking Caribbean was only now 'getting to this revolutionary point' its writing was lagging some 40 years behind.

This brought the discussion to central questions such as those of tradition, of the definition of 'commitment', of the danger of using the classification of a pro-revolutionary writer as 'progressive' as a criterion of literary judgment. The weakness of the discussion was the absence of specific examples from writing in the English-speaking Caribbean, despite Franco's requests for it. Points and arguments tended to be particular with regard to Latin American literature only. Brathwaite's *Rights of Passage* alone was mentioned, as exemplifying the English-speaking literary use of the African oral tradition, to which Cuba's new Afro-Cubanism was approximating. When more details of the explosion of new writing in Cuba had been given, La Rose suggested that with 'neo-Negritude' Cuba was closer to developments in the English-speaking and French-speaking Caribbean.

Robert Reinders, the speaker at CAM's public meeting on 1 March, had himself suggested the topic, drawn from his own field of research: 'The Origins of Jazz: the Franco-American Culture of the New Orleans Free Negroes'. Brathwaite may have seen the potential for valuable historical material on the musical form which he claimed as a West Indian aesthetic and which was so significant a determinant of his new directions in poetic form and rhythm. If so, he would have been disappointed. Reinders approached the topic only as a historian.

New Orleans was identified by Reinders as the only place in the United States which has ties with Cuba and Haiti and their African populations: almost 2000 free negroes came from San Domingo, via Cuba, in the early 19th century. So there are to be found in New Orleans cultural remains such as voodoo [sic: vodun more widely used in CAM] and Yoruba gods, African musical and dance traditions. Between 1830 and 1860 negroes formed approximately one-fifth of the total New Orleans population. They were prominent as craftsmen, such as stone carvers, as writers, and as musicians. They were heirs to the French culture of New Orleans, and adapted work by French intellectuals. The free negroes composed, played and taught classical music, not popular, Africa-based negro music. Their writers' poetic models were French: indeed, the playwright Victor Sejour – the greatest Louisiana playwright of the 19th century – was a key part of French cultural life in France in the Second Empire. CLR James, added Reinders, might mention him when next he listed Caribbean contributors to western civilisation. After the American Civil War, many of the free negroes of New Orleans dispersed and their culture, along with the whole French culture of New Orleans, largely disappeared, swamped by Anglo-Saxon culture. Reinders concluded: 'It seems to me that it is rather appropriate that I mention them [the free negroes of New Orleans] here, it's as if New Orleans is part of the Caribbean. Maybe you yourselves can define these people and give them some sort of place in history.'

Only when directly questioned did Reinders talk on the connection between this 19th century New Orleans culture and the origins of jazz. So-called Dixieland music evolved from music played by bands at funerals; a dirge on the way to the cemetery, a fast number on the way back. Jazz musicians such as Louis Armstrong came not from the creole, light-skinnned New Orleans descendants of the free negroes, but from fully negro people with a rural tradition. Similarly the persistence of work-songs really had no connection with the free negroes of New Orleans, but came out of slave society. 'The slaves were more original than these free negro intellectuals who operated as other Frenchmen . . . they were the ones that really maintained the African influence in music.' Only with jazz musicians from the New Orleans creole community could a connection be made: eg Jelly Roll Morton, who writes in his autobiography of the important role that opera played in his creole community. Persistent questions about the origins of jazz and of the blues caused Reinders to confess to being a musical illiterate. The title of his talk had posed the possibility of a connection between the origins of jazz and New Orleans creole society. This was not substantiated, and Reinders did not seem fully equipped to explore it. But he described a little-known extension of Caribbean cultural history, a 'people who had a history and then suddenly had it taken away from them'. And John La Rose saw it being of interest and relevance to the West Indies: 'Because the tradition of the calypso, as a "little tradition", say, of all free negroes, in a different way – is a tradition from the black mass of society which remains there and which the free negroes take up in search of identity.' La Rose thus made valuable connections with earlier CAM speakers – Elsa Goveia on the tradition of the black masses, Brathwaite and the 'little tradition', and Knolly La Fortune and the 'dormant tradition'.

Alongside its public meetings, CAM continued to be active with art exhibitions and book displays. Karl 'Jerry' Craig arranged exhibitions early in 1968 at the Digby Stuart College (teacher training) in South London and for the West Indian Society at the LSE, in February and March. CAM artists Campbell, Craig, Lloyd, McNish, Williams, were, for the LSE show, joined by Winston Benn, Carlisle Chang, and Peter Minshall from Trinidad and by Edmund Gill from Barbados. Benn and Gill went on to show at later CAM exhibitions. New Beacon Books set up book displays at both venues.

Outside events

No reference appears in recorded discussion at the February and March public sessions, or in early 1968 correspondence, of significant outside events, which were to escalate and to challenge CAM's direction later in the year. On 1 March Britain's Labour government, led by Harold Wilson, passed the Commonwealth Immigrants Act 1968. It was rushed through Parliament in three days of emergency debate, in order to restrict the entry into Britain of Kenyan Asians who held British passports. A clause in the Act ensured that 'patrials', white passport-holders from Britain's former colonies, could still enter freely. Its passing had been preceded by scare stories in the press and emotive speeches by politicans about the threat of large-scale Asian immigration into Britain. Enoch Powell's speech in Walsall, in February, in which he called for a virtual embargo on the entry of Kenyan Asians, was specially influential.

In the USA, Martin Luther King's campaign was becoming markedly more radical. On 23 February, the 100th anniversary of the birth of WEB DuBois, King's keynote address reminded people that DuBois had been a communist in his last years, and asserted: 'Our irrational, obsessive anti-communism has led us into too many quagmires.'[15] By early 1968 'black power' had become the dominant ideological concept amongst the majority of Afro-American youth, and a significant number of its working and middle class. Contacts between American and British Black Power groups continued. Rap Brown, a Black Power activist in SNCC who often appeared on the same platform as Stokely Carmichael, spoke in London in March.

Meanwhile unrest in the whole student population was beginning to erupt in universities and colleges throughout Britain and on the Continent. A sit-in, in March, at LSE was the first of many partial or complete occupations by students demanding more representation, more participation, and more relevant curricula. On 17 March a massive demonstration against US involvement in Vietnam was held in Grosvenor Square, London, the most violent since the war began, and hundreds of demonstrators were arrested.

Party at the Havana Congress for CLR James's 67th birthday, (l to r) Aime Cesaire, interpreter, CLR James, Edmundo Desnoes

CAM people in the Caribbean:

Cuba

CAM's meeting in May 1967 with the two Cubans, Pablo Armando Fernandez and Edmundo Desnoes, resulted in several CAM members receiving invitations to the First Cultural Congress of Havana, 4-11 January 1968. Only CLR James, John La Rose and Andrew Salkey were able to attend. Brathwaite, Wilson Harris and Aubrey Williams, for one reason or another, could not be there. George Lamming and Orlando Patterson, then at the Mona campus of UWI in Jamaica, were expected in Havana but did not in fact appear. However the Jamaican historian, Robert Hill, then a postgraduate student in political science at Mona, was at the congress; he joined James, La Rose and Salkey as the small but prominent West Indian group.

The congress was 'a meeting of intellectuals from all the world to discuss problems of Asia, Africa and Latin America'.[16] Its theme was 'Colonialism and neo-colonialism in the cultural development of peoples'. The points of its agenda, which formed the topics of the five congress commissions, were:

1 Culture and national independence
2 The integral formation of man
3 Responsibility of intellectuals on problems of the underdeveloped world
4 Culture and mass media
5 Problems of artistic creation and problems of scientific and technical works

In addition to taking part in the commission of their choice, and attending the various official congress functions, delegates were given every chance to see for themselves the transformation in Cuban life and culture which had taken place in the nine years since the revolution. The three CAM members, like most delegates, reached Cuba a week before the congress began, and stayed on afterwards: La Rose until 14 January, Salkey until 21 January, and James until the end of the month.

Andrew Salkey's account of their time in Cuba, *Havana Journal*, records vividly what they saw and heard and took part in, and provides valuable asides. These show, for example, in what high esteem CLR James, referred to as 'Professor Jamms', was held at the Congress; his 67th birthday, which fell on 4 January, was marked by a special lunch for 40 guests, including Aimé Césaire and René Dépestre, and the SNCC delegation. They show how John La Rose's fluent Spanish, his wide reading in Latin American literature, and his political activism in the Eastern Caribbean, enabled him to understand what was taking place in Cuba and to view both the revolution and the congress with critical scepticism as well as with pride, admiration and approval. La

Rose, like James, had the confidence and experience to challenge congress assumptions. James startled Commission Three – in which all three CAM delegates took part – with the proposal that 'all intellectuals, those from the developed world and those from the underdeveloped, should be firmly discouraged and in fact abolished as a force';[17] La Rose, equally, by proposing that the term 'Latin America' be abolished where applied to a cultural definition of different peoples in the South American continent, Central America and the Caribbean. La Rose had earlier expressed to Salkey his worry about the 'non-existence' of the English-speaking West Indian intellectual and artist within Commission Three and the congress generally: 'It goes further than just a congress omission. . . . We don't figure at all. When the Third World is defined as 'Asia, Africa and Latin America', the West Indies doesn't really come into it. . . . We're supposed to have been taken care of elsewhere.'[18] It was La Rose who suggested a sub-committee to look into Eric Hobsbawm's special report on North American Foundations and the enticements of fellowships and 'other instruments of cultural penetration'. This was La Rose's second visit to Cuba. But it was Salkey's first visit not only to Cuba but to any Caribbean island other than Jamaica, hence the sharp freshness of his response.

Pedro Perez Sarduy, the Cuban poet and journalist, describes the Havana Congress as having been 'controversial', and recalls that he and his friends regarded it as 'ambitiously international in outlook, especially where Europe was concerned'.[19] He was one of a group of young Afro-Cuban writers, film-makers and socio-ethnological researchers who, as he puts it, 'looked to the Caribbean'. They were not invited to attend the congress, but had been given a chance to put forward their points of view at a special forum some weeks earlier. Sarduy remembers how, at the time of the congress, John La Rose and Andrew Salkey sought out his group 'because they were interested in our concerns', and how La Rose initiated the organisation of an 'informal' session in a down-town theatre, 'though this didn't sit too happily in official circles'. Prominent amongst those who attended this informal session, chaired by La Rose, were Aimé Césaire and CLR James and, amongst the young Cubans, Rogelio Martinez Furé and Nancy Morejón.

Frank Collymore, drawing by Karl Broodhagen

Jamaica

Edward Kamau Brathwaite spent from mid-January to mid-March 1968 in Jamaica. Since the purpose of his trip was research for his doctorate, he stayed in Spanish Town, where the Jamaica Archives are housed, and not on campus at Mona, some 12 miles away. But, as in London, he combined cultural observation and activity with his research.

Two significant events in the Caribbean arts took place at UWI, Mona, in February, both of which Brathwaite attended and reported in the CAM *Newsletter*. Frank Collymore, founder and editor of *Bim* and an Honorary Member of CAM, was awarded an honorary MA. And the Creative Arts Centre (CAC) was opened, with George Lamming as its first 'writer in residence'. Describing the facilities of the CAC, Brathwaite quoted its handout: 'We believe that a Creative Arts Centre, based on the university, will be one of the most stimulating institutions in our community.'[20] Fresh from a year of CAM in Britain, Brathwaite pointed to three danger areas in the CAC as it had been set up. First, that 'community' would not be interpreted generously enough; he urged that it include not only writers on campus such as Orlando Patterson, John Hearne, Mervyn Morris, Dennis Scott, Timothy Callender, Wayne Brown, but also writers 'in the wider community outside the University: Vic Reid, Peter Abrahams, Basil Lopez, Louise Bennett, Elaine Perkins, Norma Fay Hamilton, Lloyd Reckord and several Rastafarian writers'.[21] Second, that the CAC might become too involved in the local Jamaican community, and not represent the whole Caribbean. Third, that it might be limited to the English-speaking Caribbean; he suggested that the Roger Mais week at the CAC be followed by presentations of Aimé Césaire, Haitian painters or Cuban dance.

Most of Brathwaite's observations were concerned with the state of theatre in the English-speaking Caribbean, which he judged had 'not yet started to make sense'. By theatre, he went on,

> I mean the whole activity of the art of the stage: the plays themselves, the techniques involved in presenting them, the audience to which they are directed. It is a community art. In the West Indies, without a sense of community, we cannot have that theatre which is perhaps the fullest expression of it.

George Lamming, drawing by Denis Williams

The Jamaica Playhouse was putting on Broadway successes, the Barbados National Theatre Workshop, plays by Anouilh, Strindberg, Pinter and Ionesco. But Brathwaite saluted Trinidad's Basement Theatre, 'based upon Derek Walcott's own considerable achievements as a playwright', and likewise Theatre 77 – newly formed by Yvonne Jones (now Brewster) and Trevor Rhone – at the Barn Theatre, Kingston, Jamaica. There he saw *It's Not my Fault, Baby* (based on an idea by Trevor Rhone, with script by Rhone, Daryl Crosskill and Sonia Mills), but felt that the script and the acting obscured its relevant and contemporary points. Brathwaite's critical faculties had been sharpened by discussion of theatre at CAM's two recent symposiums, and by expressed notions of community theatre; now he showed himself open to and prepared for the new experiment in theatre which would involve him on his return to Jamaica later in the year.

A staged reading of Brathwaite's *Rights of Passage* had been produced by Noel Vaz – co-administrator, with John Hearne, of the CAC – as a pre-opening event, in November 1967. Vaz's production note in the programme said: 'This is an attempt to "stage" a poetry reading, against a background of types of jazz.' Reviews and personal reports sent over to Brathwaite confirmed the view which he expressed in a letter to Salkey: 'Mistake, I think, is to try imposing music on the poetry. . . . The poetry makes its own music. But,' he added, 'it's nice to know that the boys liked *Rights* enough to go to all that trouble.'[22] Brathwaite himself gave a reading of *Masks* at Taylor Hall, UWI, early in 1968; he referred to it in a letter to Gordon Rohlehr as 'a sort of test-out for CAM in our parts'.[23] Mervyn Morris, warden of Taylor Hall from 1966 to 1970, remembers the reading as very effective and impressive, much enjoyed by a wide audience.

Also, in 'News from the Caribbean', a separate section in CAM *Newsletter* No. 6, Brathwaite greeted and listed the contents of the first two issues of the new *Jamaica Journal*; announced the launch, by St Lucia's Extra-Mural Department, of a Drama and Dance Group; and reported his week of lectures and poetry readings in Barbados, at the invitation of its Arts Council, on his way from Jamaica to London in mid-March.

Brathwaite also found time during his visit to write a long, comprehensive article on CAM for *The Jamaica Gleaner*.[24] It describes how and why CAM came to be formed, who was involved, what it had achieved. The concept of CAM expressed was his own, but noticeably modified by the views of fellow members and by the experience of CAM in operation. He claimed for CAM one purpose not articulated before: 'The isolation of West Indian writers from each other and from the society in which they lived . . . could do nothing to contribute to perhaps the most important problem of our times – the problem of the future of race relations in Britain.' The increasing pressures on the immigrant community, and the racist statements by politicians such as Enoch Powell, had been impressed on Brathwaite in Britain, especially through the 'ghetto' pressure group within CAM.

Meanwhile in January 1968 a young Guyanese historian had joined the history department at Mona, at its invitation. Walter Rodney had graduated there, with a first-class degree, five years earlier, had been awarded a doctorate by London University in 1966 for his thesis, *A History of the Upper Guinea Coast, 1545–1800*, and had then taught for a year at the University of Dar-es-Salaam, Tanzania. At Mona he launched a new course in African history, and was soon to have a strong influence on history and politics students, some of whom acted as his 'lieutenants' on campus. Also, soon after his return, he started giving open lectures on African history on the UWI campus, on Sunday mornings. Soon, too, he was speaking, sometimes by invitation, sometimes on his own initiative, on the subject to groups of people – from middle-class clubs to Rastafarians – in Kingston and other parts of Jamaica.

Brathwaite's reports of, and letters from, Jamaica between January and March 1968 make no mention of Rodney. Rodney seems at first to have kept very quiet on campus. Brathwaite was busy with the Jamaica Archives in Spanish Town; he scarcely visited campus, and the Department of History not at all – when he needed to consult with Elsa Goveia, he went to her home. But there are striking and significant parallels between what had been advocated in CAM and what Rodney was doing. Like the new demands of CAM in London, like Brathwaite's criticism of the new CAC, 'the community' to which Rodney spoke was as much outside as inside the university. Rodney was engaged in just the sort of activity which Elsa Goveia challenged the CAM conference audience to pursue in September 1967: as a black intellectual, he attempted to get in touch with, and work with, the black masses. Rodney seemed also to be practising what Brathwaite had advocated, in his December 1967 talk to CAM: the teacher's role as that of go-between, drawing on the masses' consciousness of Africa.

Rodney's activities were to have explosive, far-reaching effects in Jamaica and throughout the Caribbean. By the time the Brathwaites returned in October, these activities had been drastically cut short, but they and other CAM people in Jamaica were able to build on them.

CAM in Britain, April – May

Newsletter No. 6, January/March 1968, showed CAM in the context of Britain and the Caribbean for the first time. Brathwaite's Caribbean Report and News was published alongside a transcript of Jean Franco's February talk, 'Caribbean Writing in French and Spanish'. There was also an announcement of further changes in CAM's organisation. First, in the key post: 'Marina Maxwell, who acted as CAM Secretary from January, returned to Jamaica in March. Edward Brathwaite has, for the time being, resumed as Secretary.' Second, in listing, for the first time, members of the committee and their respective responsibilities. In handing over the secretaryship to Maxwell only three months earlier, Brathwaite had understood that she would be staying on in London for a while. He had hoped that she would continue as CAM secretary after his return to London in late March, leaving him free to write his thesis, due to be submitted in August.

To Don Wilson and Gordon Rohlehr, already returned to the Caribbean, he confided his disappointment about CAM's current organisation and his worries about its future. 'CAM is struggling to survive at the moment', he wrote to Wilson, explaining that Maxwell's departure 'leaves me the difficult choice of sacrificing the chance of doing the kind of thesis I should like to do (or doing the thesis at all) or continuing to run CAM until it's time for me to leave'.[25] He described CAM to Rohlehr as 'in plenty trouble':

> Responsibility has been decentralised as you once suggested, but apart from Jerry Craig (art), I don't think anyone else is really pulling their weight. . . . What CAM needs is a full-time secretary – paid if possible – to consolidate things. Failing this, someone who is prepared to sacrifice his own time, as I did, at great cost to self, work and writing. Neither Andrew nor John, the obvious take-over men, were prepared to do this. And there is also a flank attack from envious gooks at the Centre who don't want to see us succeed. But I'm still hopeful. Tomorrow or the next day, the right man or woman might turn up before it's too late. If only Louis were in London, he, I am sure, would do it; though CAM would then be criticised for relying on an Englishman.[26]

La Rose claims that he did not regard CAM as 'being in plenty trouble', for he himself continued to hold the concept of CAM expressed in his letter to Brathwaite after the First Conference. Nor did he fear a 'flank attack from envious gooks at the Centre'; he accepted as inevitable that there would be a critical response to CAM's middle-class character and focus on the arts from the Centre's increasingly radicalised and politicised student members.

Brathwaite was due to resume his post in the Department of History at Mona in October. As long as he was in London, it seemed out of the question for anyone else to run CAM – together with Doris Brathwaite, increasingly recognised as co-secretary of CAM. So Brathwaite took back the files, picked up all the threads, and somehow, alongside the final stage of writing his thesis, brought renewed energy, ideas and vitality to CAM in the crucial summer of 1968. There was liaison with the fledgling branch in Nottingham, also announced in *Newsletter* No. 6. There was the current series of public sessions at the Centre to reorganise and run. The first Friday in April had been earmarked for a Poetry Symposium back in October, and at least two people had been invited to take part: Gordon Brotherston, of Essex University, a specialist in Latin American and American Indian literature; Rosey Pool, editor of the anthology, *Beyond the Blues*.[27] But the committee decided that a report on the Havana Congress was urgent and should take precedence. 'After this', Brathwaite wrote to Rohlehr, 'I am proposing that we revert to the small group format. There is a great deal to talk about and think about; and I don't think we are achieving that in the public lectures.'[28] There was too much to report and discuss in one session on Cuba; another was planned for early May, and resulted in Douglas Hall speaking at the June session. The July session was a special evening of readings in memory of Martin Luther King, assassinated in early April.

Also, there were arrangements to be made for the Second Conference. After the failure of the interim committee to find a venue in London, in early May Brathwaite asked Louis James to take up the available weekend dates at the University of Kent, 31 August – 2 September, and he sent off letters to at least ten possible speakers. Then there was the forthcoming book of papers from the First Conference, the contents of which Brathwaite and Louis James, as joint editors, had now finalised. And there was always the *Newsletter* to prepare and bring out every three to four months. Although Louis James was now named as the sole committee member responsible for it, Brathwaite was still involved, particularly with the CAM News section. Meanwhile students and visitors to the Centre increasingly put pressure on CAM to form links with the black immigrant community, through repeated challenges to CAM during its 1968 public sessions.

Public sessions

CAM's two public sessions on the Havana Congress, on 5 April and 3 May, were memorable occasions for CAM and the Students Centre. Since its 1959 revolution, Cuba had been found of particular relevance and interest to radical intellectuals in the English-speaking Caribbean. Richard Small recalls:

> I was in Jamaica at the time of the triumph of the revolution. . . . We were tuned into the Havana radio describing the entry of Fidel

> into Havana. . . . We had the records of his Havana Declaration. That was part of our political education. It had a tremendous impact amongst those people who were thinking in terms of where the Caribbean had to go.

Oscar Abrams from Guyana recalls: 'We were all interested in Cuba, because Cuba had brought a new dimension into our lives . . . the most exciting thing in that region, in our time.' Now the CAM and Centre audience were to hear senior CAM members giving a firsthand account of revolutionary Cuba and its pioneering congress.

The lounge at the Centre was packed for both sessions; discussion, particularly at the second, was lively and constructive. CLR James, John La Rose, Andrew Salkey, 'three outstanding West Indians, political, novelist, poet', were billed to report on the congress and to 'speak on the Cuba they saw'.[29] A fourth delegate, Irving Teitelbaum, British human rights lawyer, spoke at the second, with Salkey; James and La Rose spoke at the first. Each speaker talked about a different aspect of Cuba and the congress, each consciously and demonstrably from his own national and ideological position, each view coloured by personal work and experience.

CLR James reported, 'as a Marxist and a socialist', on the ways in which he had found Cuba's governing Marxist party, led by Fidel Castro, to be building a socialist society, and putting into practice 'new-look' Marxist theory. Cuba was consciously attempting to build socialism and communism simultaneously, thus breaking with original Marxist theory which believed that the first should precede the second. James claimed that Cuba had taken steps taken by no other state in building a socialist society. While Cuba's government recognised the help of Russia, it saw a different future for itself from that of Eastern Europe. The USA had attempted to prevent Cuba from succeeding. But no further invasion was possible; James predicted that in another ten years Cuba 'will be absolutely a model of what the USA is not' and was meanwhile 'doing extremely well'. It had solved the unemployment problem and halted the flow of wealth to the USA. The Cuban peasant's earnings had risen steeply; 80% of new building was in the rural areas. James had himself been convinced that the Cuban people were not bothered by food rationing and had enough to eat. Through a special programme at the Isle of Pines, thousands of young people were being specially trained in the building of a new society, in the building of new people. James concluded: 'The things they are saying and the way they are tackling it shows us that here, at any rate, fundamental Marxism is taking a step forward which it hasn't made for the last 30 years.'

John La Rose reported on the Cultural Congress itself, and on a specific aspect of Cuban life. He was frankly critical of certain aspects of the congress. Although it had been planned to deal with the problems of Africa, Asia and the Americas, the distribution of delegates was far from representative. Of the 471 intellectuals, writers, artists and scientists attending, 70 delegates were from France and 22 from Britain; there were only 2 from India, none at all from China. He also criticised the organisation: delegates had been invited beforehand to submit papers to all five of the commissions, which proved unrealistic and unwieldy. The Presiding Committee of Commission Three had been selected by the Congress Co-ordinating Committee, and was neither elected nor ratified by the commission; yet all delegates had been in Cuba for up to a week before the congress began. All such weaknesses, La Rose concluded, could be put down to Cuba's swift transition to socialism; as CLR James put it, there had been 'no interlude of democracy'. La Rose reported in detail on Commission Three, and of its very relevant discussion of the role of the intellectual in developing countries, in which the traditional and political intellectuals had distinct and different functions.

The specific aspect of Cuban life on which La Rose reported was the 'neo-Negritude movement' – in the arts, painting, sculpture, film, novel, poetry: a recognition of African art and its validation. Unlike Negrismo of the 1920s, all the artists and ethnographers of the current movement were themselves Afro-Cubans; La Rose regarded this as 'a certain kind of affirmation of interior life of the Africans inside Cuban society' which was, in his view, very important for that society.

One member of the audience wanted to know about the wider implications of Cuba's revolution. Was social revolution in the whole of the Caribbean and Latin America necessary for Cuba's survival? James replied in terms more of its influence, and its far-reaching effects. But most questions were concerned with Cuba's black population: had conditions improved for them under Castro? (Michael Anthony). What were race relations like in Cuba? Andrew Salkey spoke of undercurrents of racial antagonism, how his mulatto guide had expressed fear of violence from Cuba's black population. CLR James was defensive: although few black Cubans were apparent among teachers and intellectuals, the problem was being faced. La Rose spoke of the 'tremendous sensitivity on the part of black people to their situation inside Cuba', how the neo-Negritude movement showed black intellectuals 'seeking to express the interior life of the African sensibility inside the revolution'.

For CLR James the significance of Cuba was as an apparently successful attempt at building a new socialist society on Marxist-Leninist theory, and he was almost uncritical in his praise. Only when pressed on the distinctiveness of Cuba's revolution did he mention that its population was Caribbean, whose people spoke a modern language, open to the impact of contemporary world events, and that it was an essentially colonial society. While John La Rose's support for the Cuban Revolution in its own, and in Caribbean terms, was understood, on this occasion he expressed his clear interest in the black mass of the population and concern that its culture, the world of its intellectuals, should be fully accepted in the new society.

Cover, **Havana Journal,** *1971*

Andrew Salkey and John La Rose at the Havana Congress

Andrew Salkey's response to Cuba was above all that of a fellow Caribbean. Brought up in Jamaica, 'to think of Jamaica only', he was amazed and delighted to discover this 'real first-class neighbour'. His other, related, discovery was that Cuba was essentially West Indian rather than communist. The month's stay in Cuba affected Salkey profoundly in personal terms: being in Cuba, in the company of CLR James and John La Rose, he became, as he put it, 'acquainted with myself', and especially of his Jamaicanness; he became aware of the ways in which Spanish colonialism had differed from British; he had, he felt, grown up. What impressed him most about revolutionary Cuban society was the breadth and quality of freedom enjoyed at all levels, the extent to which its intellectuals had incorporated the spirit of their inheritance into their intellectual life. He quoted at length a statement by a young Cuban intellectual which seemed to exemplify this, and to reaffirm the Caribbean/West Indian stamp on everything Cuban.

The personal reaction to Cuba of Irving Teitelbaum was inevitably different because he went as a European. On a previous visit as a 'well-meaning liberal'- representing Amnesty International – he had been filled with enthusiasm for 'a society where people had hope and dignity and were working together for things which I believed were good and they believed were good'. On this his second visit, he realised that there was nothing he could give to Cuba, but plenty which it could give to him. He was, he said, particularly impressed by the Cubans' feeling that they had lost a brother in Che Guevara, by their real, personal love for Fidel Castro, by the way in which people and leaders were working together. He itemised the points of progress in Cuban society over the past nine years, all in the face of aggression from the USA and arguments with Russia.

Each of these two CAM sessions took place immediately after a public event, the significance of which threw everything that was said about Cuba into sharper focus, and propelled subsequent discussion – particularly after the second session – into as fully participatory and constructive a CAM public session as was ever held. On 4 April, Martin Luther King had been shot in Memphis, Tennessee. On 20 April, Enoch Powell had told a Conservative-party meeting in Birmingham that 'rivers of blood' would flow in Britain's streets unless black Commonwealth immigration policy were drastically tightened and repatriation enforced. Brathwaite, who chaired both sessions, asked for a minute's silence at the start of the first session. Opening the second, he suggested the same, 'to mark the passing of the British liberal conscience'. In a long, carefully prepared preamble, Brathwaite spoke for and to CAM in the words of Elsa Goveia's challenge, but now in solidarity with all West Indians in Britain, not as a visiting intellectual and poet.

> It is no longer a matter of being committed or not being committed. We have not any CHOICE. I think the time has come for us West Indians in this country to recognise that we are strangers in this world and that the time has come to find out *where* our brothers are.[30]

Powell's speech implied no distinction between educated, middle-class West Indians and the black masses: all were made to feel unwelcome in Britain. Brathwaite urged CAM writers and artists to cease thinking of political action as distinct and separate from intellectual and creative action: 'The two men must be part of the same man . . . part of the same plan.'

Contributions to both sessions referred to these critical contemporary events. On 5 April, CLR James placed Martin Luther King's assassination in the sequence of those of John F Kennedy and Malcolm X, and expressed fears that Stokely Carmichael would be the next victim. On 3 May, Salkey referred to 'the state of embattlement in the place in which we live. One is thrown on one's own reserves more and more every day.' Teitelbaum blamed 'liberal intellectuals' like himself. They had put their energies into demonstrating against US involvement in Vietnam, or in support of Cuba, but had ignored or not particularly cared about things happening in Britain: 'Now that Enoch Powell has made things which were not respectable before he spoke respectable in this country, I think we find ourselves in a state of complete unpreparedness, to the extent that we may have rendered ourselves irrelevant.'

What the speakers reported about Cuba's revolutionary society, the role of intellectuals within it, and about the new Afro-Cuban 'neo-Negritude' movement in Cuba's cultural life, led to detailed discussion at the second session of two fundamentally important questions. Why had the English-speaking Caribbean countries not yet attempted a revolution in any way similar to Cuba's? What could CAM's artists and writers learn from Cuba's revolutionary burst of creativity and the activity of Cuba's intellectuals?

Douglas Hall, Professor of History at Mona, over on study leave, was in the audience; he was called on by the chairman to explain the historical reasons for Cuba's revolution. Earlier revolutions had, said Hall, been attempted in the 19th century against Spain, a weak colonial power, and in the early 20th century, because of major US intervention. Then there was the tradition of revolutionary action in Latin America, albeit by the creole middle class whose European outlook replaced Spanish colonialism. Such revolutions were political; only Mexico, in 1910, and now Cuba, had attempted social revolution. Haiti's revolution had not developed, because the leaders separated themselves from the people, unlike 'the democratic authority that apparently is now developing in Cuba'. John La Rose joined in at several points: agreeing with Hall's analysis, adding more examples, and referring to his own very active part in the political life of the West Indies in the 1950s and its awareness of the need to destroy the hold of the USA. Turning to the British West Indies, Hall explained how Emancipation precluded any real social revolution, since the colour-based class structure, set up under slavery, remained unchanged. Black ex-slaves became the black working class, still at the bottom. Only now were long-established criteria being broken down, yet new criteria had not yet been created, possibly because West Indians were so accustomed to looking abroad for guidance. 'As long as we keep asking this we will never have a revolution.' Cuba's importance, Hall affirmed, was that it was 'concerned with creativity'. But the world is generally not concerned with creativity at all. The 'revolutionary thing' was present in the West Indies, but had not yet come out. With regard to the widespread current talk amongst West Indians about being a black, about Black Power, Hall affirmed: 'What is happening in Cuba, which is West Indian, and which is a social revolution of a fundamental kind, is of much more value and importance to us in the West Indies than what is happening in the USA.'

Discussion moved, prompted by the chairman, to questions of creativity. Had the West Indian artist, Brathwaite asked, failed to create a sense of creativity in his community? Salkey cited the recently published poetry of Brathwaite and La Rose, and 'their influence on West Indian readers', as proof that they at least had not failed, adding a very personal note:

> The large failure, I would imagine, is . . . in not physically moving back to the area that needs your physical presence. I know this sounds like lip-service from a man who has spent 16 years away from his island, but believe you me, I keenly feel this betrayal.

For one member of the audience their fault lay in continuing to use the '"White media". The black majority don't read . . . the black man in the ghetto won't go to buy a book of poetry'. He challenged writers to get whatever they were saying across to the ordinary people, to try to relate to themselves, giving as an example blue-beat, the latest Jamaican popular musical form.

Discussion then shifted back to Afro-Cubanism, as evidence of the 'persistence and reinterpretation of the African presence in Caribbean society'. La Rose cited the Cuban movement to stress the difficulties of West Indian writers and artists and their apparent failure in communicating with the black masses, for, he said, 'We, the artists, the black and brown middle classes in our society, are within the received tradition' – referring back to Goveia, and, more recently, to Brathwaite. Calypso and so on were, until recently, frowned upon. Yet what was regarded as 'the black mass of nonentity . . . has been the most creative section of our community'.

Another speaker from the floor pressed a similar challenge:

> To me and to many Trindadians our creative artists are the calypso singers and they speak a language that the ordinary man in the street understands. . . . I believe that our writers have not as yet been able to come through to the masses. They write for the middle and upper class whose outlook is definitely outside the West Indies. . . . I would like to find out therefore whether you feel you radicals are not coming to the masses in the same way the calypso composers do, and how you think you can come to us.

An objection by Ivan Van Sertima, quoting Dostoevsky, that it is not necessary to speak in a language available to the vast masses to be a creative writer was ignored. La Rose and Brathwaite carefully attempted to counter the Trinidadian's challenge. La Rose, calling dialect 'our intimate language . . . to some extent my first language', spoke of how it had been looked down on. The dichotomy between Standard English and dialect, the need for a movement between the two, 'a very difficult task with regard to the reorganisation of our society' had been and continued to be, he said, discussed in CAM. For an attempt to realise this movement, to arrive at a synthesis, he advised the questioner to read *Rights of Passage*. 'Never heard of it', came the reply. This led Brathwaite to explain that, although written on a page, the poem was intended to be spoken to people. At his readings – and to those of 1967 in London had now been added those in Jamaica and Barbados in early 1968 –

> I find a rapport between myself and the audience, the poem gains a much greater importance when it is heard. But it is only one form of communication. I quite agree that the spoken word, the oral tradition in our literature, in our language, in our culture, has been neglected. One way West Indian artists can begin to communicate with their people is to communicate in the way that the calypsonian does, that the man with the ska does: to use the rhythm, to use the dialect, and to make it a communal experience. It can no longer be an individual, solitary activity.

La Rose reinforced this statement, and Brathwaite's opening statement about commitment, by linking both to the Cuban revolution and the Cultural Congress. A 'new kind of intellectual made the revolution; the traditional intellectual was passed by and only came to life after it'.

In this second Cuba session, partly thanks to Brathwaite as chairman, the problems and achievements of Cuba's socialist revolution brought into question a comparable restructuring of society, a change in cultural practice, in the West Indies. Brathwaite thanked the CAM audience 'for expanding this thing into all sorts of interesting areas'. The continuing reminders of the 'black masses' and the 'ghetto', of popular cultural forms, balanced the traditional intellectual and academic voices, however radical and would-be revolutionary. Brathwaite's final words were to remind the audience of CAM's forthcoming Second Conference as 'the place, above all others, where we can thrash out this sort of thing, and I hope . . . ' He was interrupted by, 'I say in Brixton', and replied: 'Brixton will come, but Brixton needs a hall and a certain amount of organisation.' But calls for Brixton did not go away.

First CAM art exhibition

Later in May, the long-planned CAM art exhibition was at last mounted at the Centre. More than 40 pieces of work were shown, by ten Caribbean artists: paintings by Winston Benn, Clifton Campbell, Karl 'Jerry' Craig, Art Derry, Errol Lloyd, and Aubrey Williams, also by Ronald Savory, newly arrived from Guyana; fabrics and plastic panels in laminate by Althea McNish; sculpture by Errol Lloyd and Ronald Moody. Sculpture by the Guyanese veteran Karl Broodhagen, long resident in Barbados but passing through London, was also shown at the last moment, but not listed. Almost all the work was for sale, and several pieces were sold. Comments in the visitors' book indicate the range of spectators:

> 'An interesting presentation with a few outstanding pieces' (R. Playogg)
> 'Colourful, but good' (Anthony McKinney)
> 'Quite impressive, inspiration to young artists' (H. Sealey)
> 'Very interesting: more room for wild life scenes' (N.J. Smith)
> 'A representative collection of fine West Indian craftsmanship' (Christopher Leech)

Art Derry's 'Shango' and 'Arawak' and Karl Craig's 'Boats on a shoreline' were singled out for comment by three visitors. Sir Lawrence Lindo, High Commissioner for Jamaica, opened the show – to the chagrin of some CAM members. Craig, who had invited him, recalls:

> I got such a flack and uproar. Marina Maxwell had really crucified me, and a lot of other people jumped on me about this. How could I ever dream of having this man come to open the Centre, blah blah, and all this. And I said, because of the exposure it would give us. My point was that we wished our art to be seen, and what was the point of having an exhibition if it was just for the CAM members. That we wanted to bring in all the Caribbean people, and not just an element of it. . . . We also needed the English to recognise that we were not just people jumping out of Half Way Tree.

It touched off a debate which was to reverberate increasingly within CAM: whether to be separate or to integrate and risk compromise. Other CAM members defended Craig, including Dwight Whylie and Oliver Clarke. Brathwaite was wholly approving of the choice – of Lindo's words, and of the style of the occasion. Writing to the High Commissioner after the opening:

CAM Art Exhibition at the Students Centre, May 1968, above Sir Lawrence Lindo – High Commissioner for Jamaica – and Clifton Campbell, below Karl 'Jerry' Craig and Edward Kamau Brathwaite

> I've never heard the aims and purposes of CAM so well put forward and capsuled as you did for us yesterday. The whole occasion gave us tremendous encouragement – not least the cocktail party which you so generously provided. As you've said in your opening remarks, we have gone about matters under our own initiative and that is how it should be; but when our own people and the representatives of our own government, such as you, begin to take an interest, then life somehow begins to seem worthwhile (the artistic life, I mean here). *Everyone* enjoyed yesterday. It did us good and it will, I am sure, do the organisation good.[31]

To Craig, Brathwaite also dropped a line of thanks and congratulations: 'It was a CAM highlight.'[32]

The show was certainly a highlight for the artists. For all of them, it was the first time they had exhibited in a Caribbean art show of this size; for several, it was the first time they had shown, and sold, to a mainly West Indian audience. Winston Benn recalls:

> It was the first time that I had put my works among other West Indians. It felt totally different, really, because I knew my work was different from that of the indigenous population simply because of things like my themes and colours. Exhibiting with other West Indians was really a nervous sort of situation. There was much more competition. It's the way of Trinidad again, when you feel that if you were to come in, you've got to be good, because the other people were just as good or much better than you are. . . . I took those four paintings down [to the Students Centre] and I asked for my space. And I remember Errol Lloyd, and Brathwaite, he was hanging, then Aubrey. Errol Lloyd was finishing off a painting on the day – a portrait of a girl. Karl Craig, yes, I thought his work was really professional. And what happened this day at this exhibition, I asked, 'Where am I going to hang my paintings?' Somebody said, 'Well, you'd better find a screen'.

Benn recalls selling two paintings, one to a Jamaican; Art Derry, of selling all four of his paintings. Ronald Savory appreciated the exhibition as part of the CAM experience, which provoked at least one writer's response, and gave a higher profile to West Indian art:

> I was happy to be part of the exhibition because for the first time in my life my involvement was in a show when I didn't have to do any work other than to fetch my work to the West Indian Students Centre. Karl [Craig] tied up all the loose ends, kept contact and was on the ball. . . . I remember being at the exhibition and was happy at the criticism or remarks Wilson Harris made when he was viewing my painting, 'Composition on Timehri' – the value of which did not seep into my consciousness until years later when I got up the courage to read his stuff.[33]

The success of its Art Exhibition at the Centre gave CAM confidence to agree to exhibit at the House of Commons in the following September. Most importantly, it strengthened the interest of the Commonwealth Institute in putting on a major exhibition, *Caribbean Artists in Britain*, in 1971.

Meanwhile Clifton Campbell's paintings were also exhibited at West End galleries in the spring of 1968: at the FBA Galleries, Suffolk Street, in May, and in a one-man show at the Woodstock Gallery in April – which Ronald Moody commended to CAM members: 'I was struck by his bold, clear designs, his pleasing, though on occasions, harsh sense of colour. . . . The contemporary scene, social and political, with an emphasis on the changing post-colonial problems, absorbs him. However he never becomes a propagandist in the ordinary sense of the word.'[34]

CAM in Britain, June – August

Public sessions

On 7 June Douglas Hall spoke on 'Colonialism and Colour in the British West Indies': a topic which, as he wrote in his confirmatory letter to Doris Brathwaite, 'is wide enough to allow me to say almost anything'.[35] It seemed to promise an expansion of Hall's ad hoc contribution to the second Havana session; most regrettably, it was neither summarised nor recorded.

The July 5 session was CAM's response to the news of Martin Luther King's assassination. Titled 'An Evening Of Poetry And Prose From The Third World In Memory Of Martin Luther King', it was, as John La Rose recalls, CAM's first fully international event. Contributions had been invited from writers in Canada and the Caribbean: Dennis Scott, Orlando Patterson, George Lamming, Jan Carew, Derek Walcott, Mervyn Morris, John Hearne, Austin C Clarke all responded. Readers were listed as including Calvin Hernton and Ibrahim Ibn Ishmail (USA), Dennis Brutus (South Africa), George Awoonor-Williams (now Kofi Awoonor), and Kwabena Amoako (Ghana), CLR James, Faustin Charles, John La Rose, Pearl Connor (Trinidad), Andrew Salkey, Courtney Tulloch, James Berry, Peter Figueroa (Jamaica) and Edward Brathwaite (Barbados). A typescript report records the evening thus:

> Andrew Salkey announced, before the programme began, 'the pride-making news' that the Trench Town Comprehensive School in Kingston, Jamaica, will be renamed the Martin Luther King High School, and that Dr King will be considered posthumously for the Marcus Garvey prize, marking the International Human Rights Year 1968. The programme ranged from the lyrical contributions of James Berry, John La Rose and Faustin Charles, through the cryptic utterances of Kwabena Amoako and the measured traditional verse of Awoonor-Williams, to the satirical Black Power lines of Courtney Tulloch and the angry, very violent poetry, of Calvin Hernton. Pearl Connor read a selection of recent American verse inspired by Dr King's assassination, and Dennis Brutus read five poems he had written as a tribute to an earlier death – that of Chief Luthuli. CLR James read movingly from the Bible and from the Letters of Toussaint L'Ouverture. Ibraham Ibn Ishmail delivered a 'sermon poem' and the evening ended with a contribution, in Bajan dialect, by Edward Brathwaite, who also helped to arrange the programme.

Salkey wrote afterwards to Brathwaite:

> As usual, your help, your quiet advice and your outstanding contribution to our evening for Martin was so typical of your continuing dedicated leadership of CAM. I thank you, Edward, very much indeed. Your piece restored the reading and healed the terrible gash which preceded it. Bless you again for supporting our committee and for guiding it to yet another public success.[36]

Of the 'terrible gash' there is neither record nor memory. A vivid reminder that the evening took place at the Students Centre exists in a note amongst Salkey's papers which says, 'Before you pack up, will you announce our Dance to be held tomorrow evening. Say it in a way which will *guarantee* at least eighty per cent of tonight's audience turning up.'

Response to outside events

CAM sought to put on its own sessions at its own chosen venues. When it agreed to collaborate with other organisations, it insisted on its being on CAM's terms, and with CAM in control. An invitation from Michael Kustow, Director of the Institute of Contemporary Arts (ICA), reached Andrew Salkey in early May, at the suggestion of Adrian Mitchell – they had been fellow delegates, and became friends, at the Havana Congress. Kustow's letter seems to have been worded with care and sent with the best British liberal intentions:

> I want to present at the ICA at the end of June a Caribbean one-day [later, two-day] event. The purpose of this is both artistic, and to make a gesture against the post-Enoch Powell hysteria we're suffering. . . . In the first half we would have readings by the best Caribbean 'immigrant writers' in London . . . followed by a jamboree with music and dancing provided by the very best West Indian groups and performers we could find. . . . Adrian and I both thought that the organisation, contact of artists etc should rightly be in the hands of a coloured organiser. We don't know where to find him. And Adrian also thought you would be able to compile the best list of writers and performers for both parts of the evening.'[37]

If he agreed, Salkey was asked to ring Kustow and meet for a drink. But something clearly went wrong with the negotiations. The only record of CAM's response is in a letter from La Rose to Brathwaite the following month: 'By now you will have heard about the ICA debacle. Those cats don't have respect for black people. I hope they learn from this reaction of ours.'[38]

Speakers from the Students Centre audience at CAM public sessions reminded CAM regularly of the 'ghetto' and what it involved. Richard Small was flanked in particular by Locksley Comrie, a fellow Jamaican, but with a very different background; Comrie, from a working-class Kingston family, was studying engineering at the Brixton School of Building, on a Jamaica Government scholarship, 1964–69. He recalls his early experience of the Students Centre:

> The students using it were primarily studying law. You couldn't imagine engineering students going inside, participating in discussions at that time. We didn't know what they were talking about in the first place. And, secondly, we felt that we were running away from something and we didn't want to run back into that thing which we saw being perpetrated in the Students Centre: the High Commission officers selected the topics, the speakers, the time that we would talk and the time that we would leave the Students Centre.

From March 1967, each of CAM's Friday night sessions was advertised in the Centre's monthly programme, and drew in non-CAM members at the Centre – Comrie amongst them. Comrie dates his interest and involvement in the Centre from the start of CAM's sessions, drawn in by what he heard from outside: 'We heard drumbeats accompanying Eddie Brathwaite's poem, "The Making of the Drum", or something like that. That is what took us from the bar into the discussions.' He began to participate in CAM's 'more interesting, relevant topics'. Then, when he was elected discussion officer at the Centre: 'Not being prepared for that role, I got in touch with Andrew, John La Rose and Eddie Brathwaite. I said, "Listen, I got myself in trouble, please help me." So I would have discussion with them and they would guide me into the type of topics we would have.' By mid-1968, Comrie was sufficiently part of CAM to go on after a public session to the 'warishi' in the Brathwaites' flat, and recalls, 'We'd stay there for the night because we had no late subway or late bus, stayed there till next morning. And Eddie and his wife would entertain us with early morning breakfast. And that's how we got really involved with CAM.'

Enoch Powell's rhetoric and recommendations, together with the importance taken on by Black Power in the United States after Martin Luther King's assassination, combined to strengthen black consciousness and pride and, particularly amongst West Indian students and young people, to promote Black Power in Britain. The Black Panther Movement and the Black Unity and Freedom Party were prominent amongst consequent organisations. Generally, in the words of Gus John, 'British blacks [were] provided with models of resistance linked to a continuity of struggle'.[39]

Many young West Indians were also caught up in the spread of student revolt. After the historic May events in France, student unrest spread to many more British universities and colleges including Essex, Hull, Leeds, Surrey and London. Ansel Wong, a Trinidadian, then a third-year student in English at the University of Hull, belonged to the Radical Students Alliance and was involved in the university disruptions that occurred there. Hull was, he recalls, one of the first English universities to follow France with students occupying the university. Wong was one of the student senators elected to represent students at the Senate level. Throughout his student years he was also an active member of the federal body of West Indian Students, and therefore

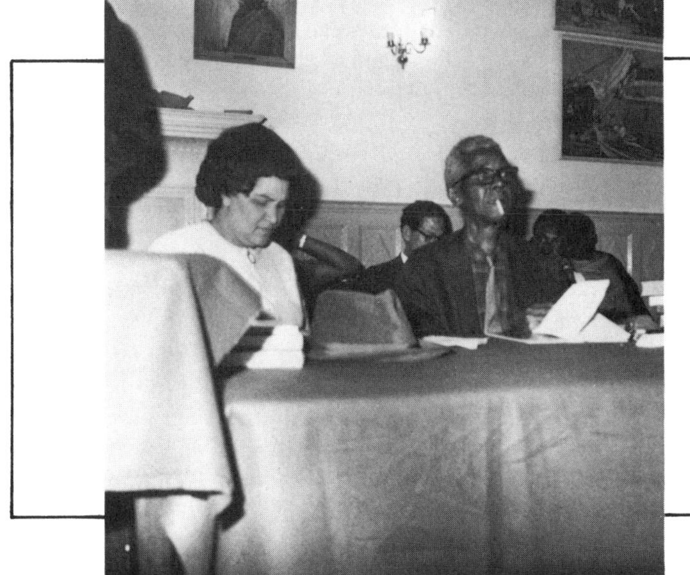

Poetry and prose evening for Martin Luther King, July 1968, Pearl Connor, Dennis Brutus, CLR James

frequented the Students Centre whenever he returned to London, each summer vacation. He recalls the rise of black consciousness and how, 'when I came to London, that [student] involvement deepened to look at issues in relation to race. Because in Hull, I had a much broader socialist perspective.' Wong, like Richard Small and Locksley Comrie, came across CAM through the Students Centre. But his involvement was less personal; as a member of WISU and chairman of the Centre's House Committee, he worked with CAM on the joint sponsorship and arrangement of events.

The interest of several student and immigrant groups in Black Power culminated in a seminar, mounted by WISU at the Centre from 16–18 August 1968, called 'The Realities of Black Power'. Locksley Comrie, who organised it, invited Brathwaite and John La Rose to read at it, alongside Calvin Hernton. Comrie wrote that he feared the proposed title would have to be changed to 'Human Rights and the Black Man', in order 'to please MANY BIG BROTHERS IN HIGH PLACES',[40] ie the High Commissions. But Andrew Salkey, he recalls, from his position on the Centre's Board of Governors, strongly urged Comrie not to change it. Ansel Wong was billed to speak on 'The development of Negro literature and its relevance to the revolution'. A panel discussion on 'The role of Black Writers in the Movement' was provisionally billed in place of Obi Egbuna's address – 'in the advent of a refusal for leave by HM Prisons'. Three talks on Saturday afternoon, the birthday of Marcus Garvey, show the extent to which concern for the 'ordinary immigrant', sharpened by recent developments, was central to the Centre's, if not yet to CAM's, programme:

> Cris le Maitre: 'Black organisations in Britain
> Carol McGavan: 'The road to awareness of being black in Britain'
> Jeff Crawford: 'The Development of WISC [the West Indian Standing Conference] in relation to the changing racial scene in Britain.'

A message from Mrs Amy Garvey, Marcus Garvey's widow, was read out; it was later published, as a pamphlet, with the help of Jessica and Eric Huntley – who were soon to start Bogle-L'Ouverture Publications. The seminar was opened with the unveiling, by the Tanzanian High Commissioner, of portraits of Marcus Garvey and George Padmore by Errol Lloyd.

Two weeks later CAM's Second Conference opened at the University of Kent at Canterbury. Brathwaite, La Rose and Salkey were the organisers. Small and Comrie were amongst the participants; they took every opportunity to challenge CAM on its role in relation to Britain's black immigrant community, and provoked a crisis within CAM's membership.

6 Confrontation and Crisis

The second conference, 31 August-2 September 1968

The programme for CAM's Second Conference was more ambitious than for the first and was planned farther ahead. It could be a fuller programme, for the weekend included Bank Holiday Monday. Rutherford College, not Eliot, was offered this year by the University of Kent, but its layout was almost identical and it would provide similar facilities. Brathwaite had got busy with plans and invitations soon after he resumed as CAM secretary in April 1968. The conference was to be the final CAM event in which he and Doris Brathwaite took part before they returned to Jamaica in October 1968.

A central theme was proposed, initially 'The West Indies at mid-Century', then 'Cultural Cross-Currents in the Caribbean'. Sessions were planned which would reflect the broader context for Caribbean arts now apparent in CAM: on French Caribbean poetry, West Indian drama, the West Indies and modernism, Afro-American poetry. Wellknown artists and scholars were invited to take part, from the Caribbean and from Britain: Aimé Césaire – to whom John La Rose personally sent a cable 'with best wishes on behalf of the writers, painters, critics and sculptors of CAM';[1] Alejo Carpentier and Léon Damas; Gordon K Lewis, Professor of Political Science at the University of Puerto Rico whose book, *The Growth of the Modern West Indies*, had just been published; Stuart Hall, now teaching at the Centre for Contemporary Cultural Studies, University of Birmingham. Some CAM members were asked to speak at specific sessions – Evan Jones, Edward Lucie-Smith; others were sent open invitations – Wilson Harris, Sam Selvon, Gerald Moore, also Elliott Bastien and Faustin Charles as people engaged in writing but not yet widely published. Bastien, also from Trinidad, was a student at Birmingham; he, like Kenneth Ramchand and Mervyn Morris, had contributed an essay to *Disappointed Guests* (1965), and one of his poems had been included in a CAM *Newsletter*. Brathwaite sent a pressing personal invitation to Henry Swanzy, honorary member of CAM; after *Caribbean Voices* Swanzy had worked for the BBC in Ghana, where he and Brathwaite often met.

But the conference programme had to be modified again and again as a result of speakers' limited times of availablilty, non-replies, and last minute non-appearance. Bobby Moore, lecturer in history, University of Guyana, was invited to speak on West Indians in the West Indies, in place of Gordon Lewis; his session was planned to open the conference, 'pitching it the right way, as it were', suggested Brathwaite, 'in the way that Elsa [Goveia] did last year'.[2] Stuart Hall was invited to speak on West Indians in Britain. But Hall could only come to the first day of the conference, so his became the opening talk, and the key talk – partly because there was after all no companion session on the West Indies. Ivan Van Sertima, who took Moore's place at the last moment, spoke more as literary critic than historian, and only about Guyana. The session on drama fell through. Evan Jones was unable to take part because he was out of the country, working on an Italian film; Errol Hill was not available. A performance by Knolly La Fortune's Folk Group had to be cancelled because of the costs involved. A session on French Caribbean literature did take place, on its masterpiece – Césaire's *Cahier*, addressed not by Césaire himself, but by Clive Wake, an academic, and a specialist in Francophone African literature. Edward Lucie-Smith had agreed to take part in a session on modernism, but no one was found to speak alongside him. Sam Selvon, who had replied that he would be 'happy to take part. Not for the whole thing', did not appear at all. Wilson Harris accepted CAM's invitation and delivered a carefully prepared paper, but no other published Caribbean writer addressed a main session. An artist and a poet billed to speak on the final programme, handed to conference participants, failed to appear: Patrick Betaudier, Trinidadian artist working in Paris, and Calvin Hernton, Afro-American poet at present in London. Ad hoc symposiums were substituted, with chairmen and panel members drawn from the conference participants. CAM's Second Conference moved on from what was originally planned; its focus became West Indian arts in Britain rather than the Caribbean, its programme became more widely participatory, less a succession of papers.

The preliminary conference notice expressed confidence in high attendance. 'After the success of our First Conference, you will hardly need any propaganda on this score from us. . . . As places will be limited to 100, we suggest you book now!' But only 70 registered, slightly fewer than the previous year. West Indians represented about two-thirds, British, French and Americans, one-third.[3] The white British proportion seemed larger, because it took a greater part: as main speakers, and in discussion. It contained fewer publishers – only Eric Dalton of Evans and Anne Walmsley of Longmans. But there were more people from the

British establishment and arts/media network than the year before: Felicity Bolton, parliamentary lobbyist and secretary of the British Caribbean Association; John Davidson, solicitor; Gillian Shears of Dillons Bookshop; Eric Walter White of the Arts Council, Edward Lucie-Smith and Henry Swanzy; Karina Williamson of the University of Oxford (formerly at Edinburgh), Gerald Moore of the University of Sussex and Clive Wake of the University of Kent. If Lucie-Smith was the only mainstream writer and critic present, there were at least at CAM's Second Conference far more broadly-based British people with whom Caribbean artists and intellectuals could have dialogue in an open forum. But the Caribbeans, and others, were very diverse. In addition to the core of CAM founder members (Edward Kamau and Doris Brathwaite, Andrew Salkey, John La Rose and Sarah White, Aubrey Williams, Louis James), and CAM Committee members (Oliver Clarke, Errol Lloyd), there were CAM 'regulars' from meetings and the First Conference: writers, critics and artists (Ronald Moody, Kenneth Ramchand), post-graduate students (Brinsley Samaroo, Vishnudat Singh); African writers (Kwabena Amoako, Cosmo Pieterse) as well as those who had encountered CAM at the Centre but for whom this was their first conference: James Berry (poet), Paul Dash and Edmund Gill (painters), Roy Henry (concert singer), Joyce Linton (writer and actress). Their professions ranged beyond the arts, and included a senior nursing officer, a railway clerk, secretary, engineering supervisor, shorthand typist/SRN. The journalist Naseem Khan also came to the second CAM conference through the Centre. Born in India, educated at a girls' public school in England, she was then running *The Hustler* with Courtney Tulloch.

There was also a distinct, highly visible contingent from the Students Centre: Richard Small, Locksley Comrie, and Lowell Marcus, a Jamaican law student. Small had attended the 1967 conference, but was virtually unnoticed. Joined now by Comrie, straight from the success of their weekend seminar on Black Power at the Students Centre, one or both spoke at every CAM conference session. At every opportunity they challenged what seemed to them the predominantly white, colonial outlook of CAM members, and their apparently elitist, high art stand. They urged CAM artists to work with the immigrant community, and to be open to its popular culture. Stuart Hall as lead and keynote speaker gave their views a certain validity from the start; Hall and Small shared a radical ideology, and saw the West Indian immigrant community in Britain as victim of imperialism and racism.

In 1968, as in 1967, at least seven books by CAM members were published; in 1968, for the first time, critical books appeared alongside new creative writing. All seven authors or editors took part in the 1968 conference; their books were all referred to, adding interest and urgency to the sessions. Wilson Harris's *Tumatumari*, the fourth novel in his second sequence, takes place within the consciousness of a woman, Prudence; her, and the book's, central experience is at Tumatumari Falls, in the interior of Guyana, whose Amerindian name means 'sleeping rocks'. The critic Michael Gilkes, fellow-Guyanese, writes of it:

> *Tumatumari* is, in a sense, an attempt to free the creative imagination from the prison of historical, 'dead' time – to 'repair' the damage done by that 'deep, amnesiac blow'. And Prudence, immersed in the 'well of the past' at Tumatumari Falls, suffering but held by the unmoving 'Eye' of the Waterfall, reaches through her helpless, deprived condition to a truer knowledge of the past. It is a process of *anamnesis*.[4]

Andrew Salkey's recent series of novels had been for children. With *The Late Emancipation of Jerry Stover* he returned to adult fiction, set in Jamaica. The novel tells the story, and suggests the emancipation, of Jerry Stover, young civil servant, son of a middle-class, school teacher mother, and one of the 'Termites' – his contemporary, cosmopolitan, hard-drinking Kingston friends – in the early 1950s. Edward Brathwaite's *Masks*, the second long poem of his trilogy, continues the poet's journey which began in *Rights of Passage*. *Masks* examines the nature of his loss in Africa, celebrating the qualities of African culture which have endured through their passage and change in the Caribbean; it describes his return to the seaport of Takoradi in an attempt to discover his ancestral birthplace, and to find out what cultural flaws existed in African society, and in himself, that might account for his enslavement. The search ends with a confrontation between the New World negro and his other self.

The Islands in Between: Essays on West Indian Literature, edited by Louis James, was the first critical book on this literature to be published. It contains essays on novelists Wilson Harris, John Hearne, George Lamming, Roger Mais, VS Naipaul, VS Reid, Andrew Salkey, and one poet, Derek Walcott, by critics, and a novelist – the majority West Indian – who had been colleagues, or were connected with UWI, in the mid-1960s. As a pioneering book, it was inevitably limited by depending on texts already published, and on critics who were available at the time it was prepared. Coming out when CAM had been in full swing for a year and a half, it was already out of date and, more crucially, out of step with the emphasis expressed in CAM on the oral tradition and the use of its rhythms and language in literature. The absence of essays on Sam Selvon and Edward Brathwaite seemed glaring omissions. But Louis James's long introduction, completed in August 1967 when the other contributions had long been assembled, provided a comprehensive survey of the field, which included the CAM experience and debate to date. Brathwaite is quoted, and discussed, in depth, alongside Walcott; calypso, dubbed here by James as 'essentially a Caribbean folk art' is thoroughly explored, and its possible influence on West Indian literature is stated;[5] 'dialect'/creole is described and its use in Caribbean literature discussed. CAM papers and views are quoted and extended. The jacket design is by Aubrey Williams.

Simultaneously, New Beacon brought out two collections of critical essays. *New Beacon Reviews*, edited by John La Rose, is far shorter, and focuses on Claude McKay, Wilson Harris, Eric Williams and Jean Rhys; its contributors include Robert Reinders, Elsa Goveia and Wally Look Lai. The short introduction, by La Rose, describes the collection as 'a statement of vision', which 'throws open new windows on the world, stressing a particularity

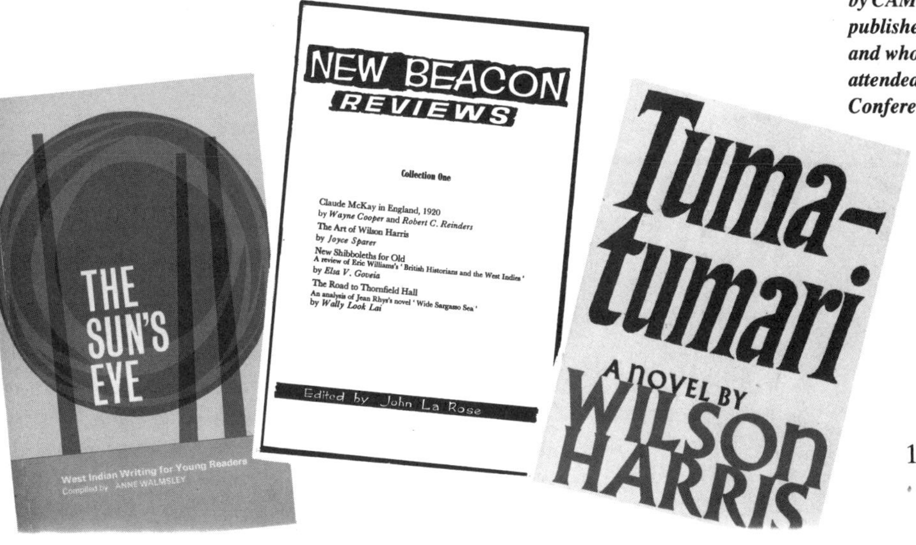

Covers of seven books by CAM members, published in 1968 and whose authors all attended the Second Conference

of vision, steeped in tensions, wrought in the living tissue of Caribbean contemporaneity'.[6] Ivan Van Sertima's *Caribbean Writers: Critical Essays*, consists of short pieces on eleven West Indian novelists, on French African poets, and on one Afro-American writer. Written as a series in 1963, on commission from the Central Office of Information for broadcasting, their publication was intended to contribute to 'a critical assessment which no longer accepts a validation from outside the society but provides its own; and in so doing challenges assumptions about Caribbean writing and subverts hallowed ideas about writing itself.'[7]

The anthology, *The Sun's Eye: West Indian Writing for Young Readers* began when its compiler, Anne Walmsley, taught English for three years to the junior forms of a Jamaican rural secondary school from 1960, and introduced West Indian alongside English literature to her students. The anthology juxtaposes prose and poetry, and includes 'West Indian forms of the English language' alongside Standard English. A special feature is the 'Notes about the Writers', for whose first-person, contextual approach she was indebted to Brathwaite; the note which he wrote to accompany his poem, 'The pawpaw', set the style for all the rest.

The main sessions

Stuart Hall was introduced by Andrew Salkey, chairman of the opening session, as Deputy Director in the Centre for Contemporary Cultural Studies, School of English, University of Birmingham; a former editor of the *New Left Review*, author with Paddy Whannel of *The Popular Arts* (1964). Unlike most of his West Indian student contemporaries, Stuart Hall had stayed on in Britain, achieving a distinguished role as a radical academic with a special interest in the sociology of culture. He described this, his first talk to CAM, on 'West Indians in Britain', as 'a very informal opener', and hoped that some of his remarks would be found controversial.

Hall reminded the CAM audience that the large numbers of West Indians who had, amongst other coloured immigrants, come to Britain over the previous decade, came to work, not to study, driven by economic necessity and by 'a kind of historic idealism'. They were completing the third leg of the triangular trade. Their meeting with the British in Britain brought special problems, to West Indians and British alike, problems which were the legacy of 300-400 years of history.

All coloured immigration created a problem area for the British and was 'the final demystification of some areas of darkness in the British consciousness'. Under direct, physical, day-to-day interchange with people of African and Asian descent, certain very carefully protected areas of the British experience had been exposed, and this at a time when British society itself was passing through a prolonged social, economic and political crisis. Until the recent large-scale immigration, few British people had faced up to the degree to which the history of the Empire was deeply entwined in British society with class, with the idea of history itself. Hall had, he said, found himself having to explain to West Indians what it felt like to be British.

For the West Indians, the problem of meeting the British in Britain was markedly different from that of Asians because of their history, and because of the nature of their immigration. Hall called their meeting that of 'intimate enemies', using the phrase with which William Styron, in *The Confessions of Nat Turner* (1967) describes 'house niggers' as distinct from 'field niggers'. West Indians know Europe intimately, from the inside. In coming to Britain, they are in a real sense coming home; British civilisation and culture is external to West Indians, but has at the same time been internalised by them. The central experience in the formation of the West Indian personality is not Africa but slavery, plantation life and colonialism.

Hall then pointed to ways in which West Indian social patterns are transformed by the experience of being an immigrant group; by ways in which immigration affects the West Indian personality. This profoundly traumatic experience would, he believed, be strengthened by some kind of political consciousness, very different from what they had needed in the West Indies. British society scarcely distinguished between West Indians and Asians, regarding them all as 'coloured immigrants'; therefore West Indian immigrants required a new definition of themselves. But the full impact of immigration on West Indians in Britain would not be known for some time:

> It is in the next generation, the generation of young boys and girls for whom the return to their historical past has for a second time . . . been cut off, whose way home is genuinely blocked; whose expectations and definitions of themselves as black has been formed and forged in the teeth of the immigrant experience. . . . For those younger people, the immigrant experience is a truly revolutionary experience, in personal, political, social, worldwide terms. . . . It is only the very deep breaking of links with that complex past which I think happens not in the first but in the second and third immigrant generations that we begin to see what the truly immigrated West Indian is actually like.

Almost all the points in Hall's talk were taken up in discussion: the comparative reluctance and ineffectiveness of West Indian political organisation compared with that of other immigrant groups; whether British 'demystification' was in fact taking place, given the racist opinions and the following of Enoch Powell; how

British class attitudes were confirmed, and the correlation exposed between race and class, because most West Indians arrived at the bottom of the British class structure. Hall's analogy of West Indians to 'house niggers' caused some confusion and controversy, and he had to repeat that he used the term simply as a metaphor of plantation colonialism. Discussion moved on, more constructively, to West Indian immigrant writing, and what the role of Caribbean writers and intellectuals should be. Hall's grounding in literature and his work with popular culture enabled him to speak with authority and farsightedness:

> The task of any intellectual and any writer in relation to that group of people in Britain now [is] preeminently to help them see, clarify, speak, understand and name the process that they're going through. . . . The language of that experience will be different significantly from the language of the West Indian novel and West Indian poetry to date, because it comes out of a new matrix. And it's crucial that this period does not go past without the language being forged. . . . What people in that situation want to know is, 'Who am I?' and 'How the hell do I get out of it?' and 'How do I bring about change?' and that really requires analysis, thought and, crucially, language.

Hall's definition of the West Indian intellectual's and writer's task in Britain encouraged Locksley Comrie to challenge CAM directly:

> What is the role of CAM?. . . . There is a certain compromising going on right now. . . . I think probably there should be more statements by Enoch Powell to get a fusion of the intellectuals and the grassroots. . . . What we should have done is taken this Conference to Brixton Town Hall. . . . Until we can really make our art functional and collective and committed we are not artists at all.

Brathwaite was defensive: 'All I can say is that Locksley hasn't read a damn thing we've been doing.' La Rose picked up Comrie's point and linked it with Hall's earlier hypothesis: 'The Afro-West Indian has had a kind of clarification of experience in the last decade in Britain that the West Indian at home, with the neocolonial regimes, has not had.' He called Stokely Carmichael's visit, the year before, a catalyst from which 'fantastic development' had already occurred. Hall agreed: the West Indian had been obliged to define himself in global terms, in terms of movements of black peoples throughout the world. A warning that the Afro-West Indian should not give himself false directions by following the Afro-American lead too closely (Aubrey Williams) was swept aside by Richard Small. Small, like Hall, applauded the way immigrants in Britain were now becoming conscious of themselves as black people in the world, in terms of the Third World and of

Black Power. He followed up Comrie's challenge to CAM: 'We have to talk about West Indians in Britain because that's where we are', but his concern seemed to be more with assisting in an international movement to overthrow racism, than with developing the creative consciousness of West Indian immigrants in Britain.

Stuart Hall made an eloquent case for the direction in which British-based CAM artists and intellectuals should be turning, but any possibility of constructive discussion was blocked by Comrie and Small. Their intervention seemed based more on Afro-American rhetoric than on firsthand experience; neither was an artist or involved in cultural activity.

The final talk at the conference was also concerned with West Indians in Britain, but from a different viewpoint. Henry Swanzy, editor of the BBC programme, *Caribbean Voices*, from 1946 to 1954, gave 'Some thoughts on West Indian Writing'. Andrew Salkey, again chairman, introduced Swanzy as one of the editors, along with AJ Seymour of Guyana and Frank Collymore of Barbados, who had worked 'very closely . . . with great care and great concern with the writers of my generation'. Swanzy was sharply aware of being not only out of date with West Indian writing; he also made clear, given the issues of the conference, how little right he felt he had to speak of the present situation.

Swanzy's overall view of West Indian writing, albeit from a distance, was that its development had been 'infinitely greater and richer' than even he, in the euphoria and company of the early 1950s, had expected; his viewpoint was that 'the corpus of writing in the Anglophone Caribbean . . . has been one of the distinctive fields of development in English letters since the War'. By way of introduction, he shared with the audience entries from his 1954 diary, which logged broadcasts of work or talks by, amongst other West Indians, Wilson Harris, Andrew Salkey, Edward Brathwaite, and Stuart Hall.[8] Swanzy quoted from a piece he had written on 'the general situation, I think this is in 1952, when there were about two or three novels which had been published, probably Mittelholzer and the first of Selvon and Lamming. . . . Obviously one knew who the stars were, but one was also interested in the people who were not stars . . . They were in many ways as important as the seed-bed of the future.' Swanzy read from the end of this piece:

> 'In Tobago, there's a poet EM Roach, who has the genuine, lyrical gift which he puts at the service of the peasant, with no sense of condescension. In Guyana, there is another poet, Wilson Harris, a land surveyor, who has an astonishing quality of imagination, almost of mysticism. . . . As the mind ranges, it begins indeed to wonder whether the lesser names beneath the peaks may not have

> the real heart of the matter in them, so far as the development of a true canon of self-understanding is concerned. There is the gentle story writer, RLC Aarons, with his sense of pity and the strange imagination of Inez Sibley, which can inject power into old legends . . . . There is a student, Evan Jones, with a wonderful "Ballad of the Banana Man", fresh and vigorous and true, and the East Indian, VS Naipaul,'

– and here Swanzy interjected, 'and I must say this shows how wrong in many ways one was. Because I said, "with his gentle humour". Certainly with humour, not altogether gentle'.

Despite his lack of close acquaintance with Caribbean literature for many years, and, moreover, because his current work was concerned with 'social and political matters in areas other than the Caribbean or Africa', he had a 'proletarian' standpoint which could, he felt, usefully raise questions about the direction of West Indian literature: was what was true in the early 1950s still so in the late 1960s? First he asked whether there was still the danger of its being a regional literature only and not providing 'a comment on the total, human predicament in the world. My impression remains that Caribbean writers are still casting about for a new centre and . . . still inhabit a narrow world of their own, with their main readership . . . in Britain and North America.' Then he asked whether the paradox still existed whereby writers expressing the life of the people – whether peasants or urban proletariat – conveyed it vividly and urgently, whereas those exploring middle-class, bourgeois themes seemed inhibited and used a flaccid, lifeless style.

This led Swanzy to question whether a hypothesis about the end of the Roman Empire, put forward by Arnold Toynbee in *The Study of History*, might not usefully be applied to West Indian literature and Britain. The British bourgeois tradition of literature was being challenged and renewed by the 'internal proletariat', ie working-class writers from provincial British cities, and equally by an 'external proletariat' of writers from Britain's former colonies. Swanzy confessed that the crucial question for people like himself, concerned primarily with the mainstream of British culture, was whether the internal and external proletariat – who had for so long been kept under, never before had a chance – could fuse. If not, what was the writer to do? Agreeing that writers should not accede to demands of commitment to a particular cause, or become propagandists for a certain type of political action, he cited Wilson Harris, 'whose remarkable archetypal images and wide-ranging ideas seem very often to be a precursor of the ideas of the latest wave and reaction in modern industrial societies . . . the sort of atomistic concern, basically, with the human individual'.

Discussion revolved first about commitment and/or versus communication, raised by Kenneth Ramchand, answered by Brathwaite in a key statement:

> The poetry itself springs from a desire to rehabilitate in my case the consciousness of certain sections of West Indians. And therefore the effort to write is going to be, first of all, my own technical ability, and secondly, the attempt to get over to them, to communicate to them, the way in which their images, their consciousness, should be shared.

A request (Hester Marsden Smedley) for there to be 'a lot more about' West Indian women writers and poets at next year's conference was greeted with applause and cries of 'hear, hear'. Finally, Locksley Comrie saluted Andrew Salkey's new novel as art which was 'really connected': 'Jerry Stover and the Rastafarians are merging together, and we want our writers to keep telling us what is going on. . . . We can use these things. We see so much happening in Jamaica to say and we're not saying it.' Salkey replied that most of this book had been written when he 'went home' in 1961 and was,

> born out of a very early disgust. It was awfully private and very personal. If it was social, it was in that it was related to one man's confusion and torment . . . my own. And then one sort of presumed that there was a vision coming up inside the person Salkey. And because I couldn't do it politically, I tried to do it artistically.

Henry Swanzy's 1968 diary about the conference records that the early part of his talk went down quite well, but that Toynbee's theory 'went flat. . . . In discussion, they took me at my word, a "Rip-van-Winkle, a Swanzy zombie"'.[9] The concern of Caribbean writers at the CAM conference was not with ways in which their literature might, along with provincial British proletarian writing, renew mainstream English literature, but with its role in Caribbean society, with its significance for Caribbean people.

If Henry Swanzy felt himself to be a 'zombie', out of date, out of place, and outside CAM's current concerns, the two other non-Caribbean main speakers also had reason to feel so. Clive Wake, of the French Department at the University of Kent, a South African by birth, had spent much of his teaching life in Africa. Speaking after Stuart Hall on the first day, on 'Aimé Césaire and the French Caribbean', he confessed: 'I've never been to the Caribbean, and the more I read Caribbean literature, the more I'm aware that I'm entering a world which is very different from the world that I know so well in Africa.' He promised, and gave, a systematic account of Césaire's poem, *Cahier d'un retour au pays natal*. Regarded as a major work of French literature, it was relatively unknown by English-speaking readers because it had only just been published in translation.[10]

Wake introduced the *Cahier* as a poem about Césaire's awakening to himself and to his origins, the beginning of a new outlook on life for himself and for his people, the awakening to his *négritude*; its double theme was the effect of the European coloniser on the West Indies, and the vision of something new which had to be created, through the restoration of the old beauty. Wake then gave a detailed exposition of the poem: summarising its content, commenting on its language, form and imagery, identifying its themes – all with appropriate quotations, in translation. From this it was evident that Césaire's experiences in Martinique, the ways which he had evolved and which he recommended for bringing about change, echoed recurrent points in the ongoing debate within CAM. On commitment to change: that the creative writer in the Caribbean must be committed to revolution in the state of his people. On attitudes to slavery: that West Indian people will not be able to rise above their present condition until they can exorcise the traumatic experience and the dreadful wound of slavery. Wake pointed out how, in the *Cahier*, 'the complete pessimism of previous expression is replaced by a sense of complete creative ability'. Similarly, Wake's discussion of Césaire's wrestling with appropriate form and language seemed relevant to the problems which some writers in CAM were attempting to resolve.

Louis James, as chairman, had opened the session by linking it with Stuart Hall's talk, suggesting that awareness of the wider Caribbean was involved in the English-speaking West Indian's discovery of his identity. Now he led off discussion by picking up those points from Wake's exposition which seemed to concern CAM. John La Rose related Césaire's use of language to the poetry of the English-speaking Caribbean. Given the power of creole speech, 'the most popular poetry we've had, which has . . . acted as a kind of break upon conventional poetry, is the poetry of the calypso'. James invited Brathwaite to comment on the relation between the *Cahier* and his trilogy; yes, he would like to make certain points, but at his own reading the next night. James asked about the impact of hearing the *Cahier* read aloud, and members of the audience referred to readings which they had heard: at Dakar in 1966, in a semi-dramatic reading; at UWI; in Guadeloupe, when many of the audience 'chipped in, joined in, unrehearsed'. A reading of the poem, in English translation, was promised for that evening.

This was, as La Rose remarked, the first time that an English-speaking West Indian audience had ever heard the poem discussed in detail. Clive Wake's sensitive, scholarly exposition combined with Louis James's attentive chairmanship made this a valuable and significant session.

The following day, Gerald Moore spoke on 'The West Indian Presence in Africa'. Introducing him, Salkey listed Moore's African experience and his publications on African literature, adding that he had 'now assumed certain literary responsibilities in the Caribbean where West Indian literature is concerned'. Moore was uncertain how to take the comment but opted for its being 'without overtone or undertone, because it has always seemed to me that one cannot in fact study African literature, or for that matter, African history or politics without taking the West Indies into account'. Moore opened with a comparison between the attitudes of West Indians and Africans to a 'Western city of exile', as reflected in their writing. He then moved on to his main topic: the impact of Africa on West Indian writers and intellectuals who had worked there. Noting the 'extensive West Indian literature recording the experience of Africa', he proceeded to give a detailed account of Denis Williams's *Other Leopards* (1963) which, he concluded, 'encloses a great deal of the West Indian experience of Africa'; then, of Edward Brathwaite's *Rights of Passage* and *Masks* which he called 'the most impressive and complete work yet produced in this literature of the black revenant'.

Despite being somewhat loose in structure, and over-weighted by lengthy synopses – Swanzy described them in his diary as 'remorseless' – Moore's talk prompted lively discussion. Kwabena Amoako made a statement: 'The poems in *Masks* do not only speak for the Caribbean immigrants, he [Brathwaite] speaks for us Africans, in a word, Ghanaians.' Then discussion developed from a question about the need for Afro-Americans and West Indian writers and artists to go back to Africa. Moore pointed out that it was nonsense for many West Indians to look for their origins in Africa, and that they were excluded if an African fount for West Indian culture were postulated. John La Rose agreed, but declared what was, he believed, of vital importance, and why: the rehabilitation of the African presence in West Indian society, because 'that presence has been denied or has been debased or has been a motive of self-contempt'.

James Berry, speaking at a CAM session for the first time and introducing himself 'as one of the writers myself', agreed: 'I very much sympathise with and understand this great need to associate once more with Africa. It's as if a very important part of oneself and one's own consciousness has been completely blocked off.' He recalled his schoolboy's view, like that of an English boy, of Africans as savages, so that he had wanted in no way to be associated with Africa. Yet when, years later, he saw African dancers perform at the Albert Hall during the Commonwealth Arts Festival in 1965, he felt himself caught up in what they were doing, an experience which he would never have had before his search for self-discovery, of going back to Africa. 'It is rather as if you had to return to a scene from which you had no choice [but] to be removed from it', he concluded, echoing – consciously or unconsciously – Brathwaite and La Rose in December 1967. Andrew Salkey denied that there was any kind of poetic search between himself and Africa. This encouraged Gerald Moore to deny any special significance in his choice of topic, which showed how far he was outside the thinking shared and expressed at CAM sessions. Richard Small contributed to the discussion only after it had moved to radio in Africa.

A session on West Indians in the Caribbean, planned to complement the opening session on West Indians in Britain, fell through because Bobby Moore, the scheduled speaker, was ill. Instead, at a day's notice, Ivan Van Sertima gave a paper based on his recent month's stay in Guyana, after nine years' absence. He called it 'The Void of History in the Caribbean'. Van Sertima opened by referring back to CAM's debate of early 1967. Then he had attacked Orlando Patterson's view of their home region as one without either history or an indigenous tradition. Now he agreed, expressing deep concern for 'the void of history in the Caribbean and its tragic consequences for our multiracial societies'. His definition of 'history' was 'a body of insights, an illumination, not just a mere accumulation of happenings. . . . A rediscovery of beginnings, of roots, of the springs of our sensibility'. History, in such terms, should 'draw together the strands of our complex heritage' and also 'take on the configuration of the grand myth' so that it becomes 'an imaginative reconstruction of our reality in these places which can illuminate the nature of our peculiar, multiracial, multicultural heritage in the New World'.

Van Sertima had found Guyana in a crisis which sprang, he claimed, from the Guyanese void of history, its 'ignorance of the ground of a native tradition'. He cited Guyanese peoples' ignorance of significant events in their Caribbean past, and their contempt for what they are – holding school syllabuses and texts largely responsible. Novels by VS Naipaul and Edgar Mittelholzer were more likely to be introduced by the Ministry of Education to the young because they were 'the most popular and the most cheap'; and it was the 'witty but castrating satire' of Naipaul, the 'spectacular but racially bigoted melodramas' of Mittelholzer which, more than any other imaginative writing, helped to foster and sustain Guyanese peoples' self-contempt.

A new climate would be very difficult to create, involving the introduction of literary work 'that endeavours to recreate our past and illuminate our complex traditions of blood and races in a more challenging and profoundly imaginative way'; that used non-derivative literary forms and structures, through which 'a new charter of sensibility may be drafted to illuminate and liberate us from the past'. Van Sertima claimed that only one Caribbean writer, from Guyana, had so far attempted work of this sort, which he described as:

> an all-inclusive drama . . . of consciousness, in which so many interior levels and rhythms of our existence are revealed that the positing of possibilities of fulfilment and transcendence over one's condition in the future rather than encripplement and overpowering by the past, emerges in the shattered human.

His unnamed reference to Wilson Harris would have been understood by most of the audience. Van Sertima stressed that there was not just one way; that the Caribbean native tradition was being explored and shaped in its literature in ways very different from 'the settled, more coherent tradition of Europe'.

In attempting to fill the void of history, there was a need for grand myth. But Van Sertima discounted Negritude as 'doubly false for Caribbean man', because it could bring to an end the Caribbean concept of multiculturalism. At the same time, the continuing African presence in Caribbean culture and society should be valued and investigated. While the region's writers and intellectuals recommended such investigations and the exploration of all Caribbean indigenous culture, at the same time they dismissed experimentation in language and form as an 'ivory tower exercise'. But this 'native tradition' did not exist in the forms in which it was often sought, such as the 'ruins' for which Orlando Patterson looked in vain. It could be tracked down only through works of the imagination, through 'an art of memory, an art that seeks to rediscover and illuminate the collective unconsciousness of our people'.

Edward Kamau and Doris Brathwaite engaged Van Sertima in discussion of the complexity of indigenous traditions in the Caribbean, and their diversity in Africa. Henry Swanzy questioned Van Sertima closely on his claim that Guyanese society was in crisis partly as a result of people reading books by Mittelholzer and Naipaul, and a battery of comments on Naipaul followed. Brathwaite: 'One of the most important novelists in the whole of the West Indies'; La Rose: 'Dangerous to underestimate Naipaul's influence'; Salkey: 'Stylistically pleasing and [has] enormous metropolitan approval'; Aubrey Williams: 'A brilliant novelist . . . not an artist because he has no magic.' John Ramsaran – Trinidadian, lecturer in English Literature at the University of Swansea, a newcomer to CAM, offered to speak about Naipaul from his insider background; he was brought up in a Hindu family, his father became a Christian. 'I think we are in too much of a hurry to condemn what we don't like about our society. . . . I have seen the complex society which is described in Naipaul, and I think that it is very much a true picture . . . a very percipient and artistic presentation of life.' Brathwaite asked Van Sertima to expand on the alternative tradition, until recently ignored, which he claimed to see emerging. But discussion of the Caribbean novel and its possibilities continued, with Van Sertima calling for fiction which was the opposite of the conventional novel, with a structure 'which evokes a totality'. John La Rose took this further: 'If we do not break our tête-à-tête with Europe, and this self-abasement to a certain kind of form which we have inherited through the language, we cannot explore all these possibilities.' Until this point no one had named Wilson Harris as the writer of fiction new in form and compass. Karina Williamson did so, comparing his novels with those of Orlando Patterson. Locksley Comrie said he was a fan of *The Children of Sisyphus* until he read *The Late Emancipation of Jerry Stover*, and he asked La Rose or Brathwaite to relate the connection with Harris's fiction. Salkey did so, subtly and with some personal anguish:

> I think it's awfully important that we first of all ask a man to free himself, to face up to himself, to place himself, and then to lose himself. Because that is exactly what is happening with Wilson, and not happening with Naipaul, or myself, or possibly George Lamming.

And Van Sertima, in conclusion, could only repeat that there is 'no one way out of the creative dilemma' and that as a creative writer one should 'seek to come close to the life inside of you'.

The session was concerned with the void in knowing and understanding Caribbean history, and with a new kind of fiction which would enable the void to be filled. It again turned on the task of Caribbean writers and intellectuals in a particular Caribbean community. But it assumed literary preeminence, magnified because Van Sertima echoed the thinking of the writer whom he most admired, so that his own exposition took on, at times, a Harris-like complexity.

Wilson Harris, implied by Ivan Van Sertima, cited by Henry Swanzy, as the exemplary Caribbean writer, was himself scheduled to speak on the final morning, on 'The Amerindian Presence in Guyana'. Kenneth Ramchand introduced the session; he was now a PhD, listed as 'literary critic' and a lecturer in Commonwealth Literature, University of Sussex.

Ramchand's introduction was a reading, with comments, of four extracts from Harris's novels, of episodes which contained confrontations between people of different races: one with an East Indian, one with a person of African origin, two with Amerindians. He prefaced the readings with a statement aimed at the

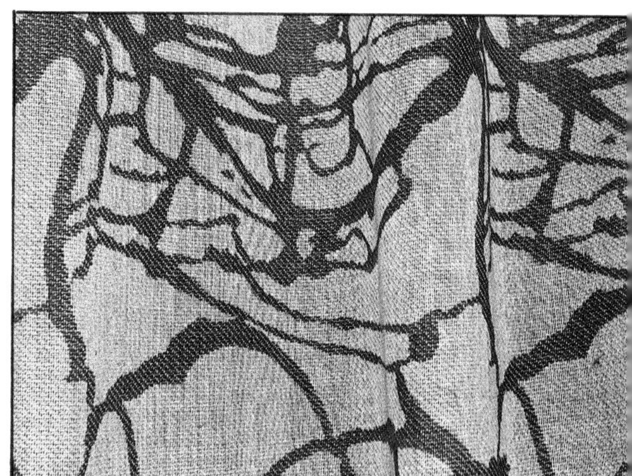

Althea McNish, ***Azul***, 1967

Althea NcNish,
Pomegranate, 1967

Karl 'Jerry' Craig,
Tropical Landscape, 1970

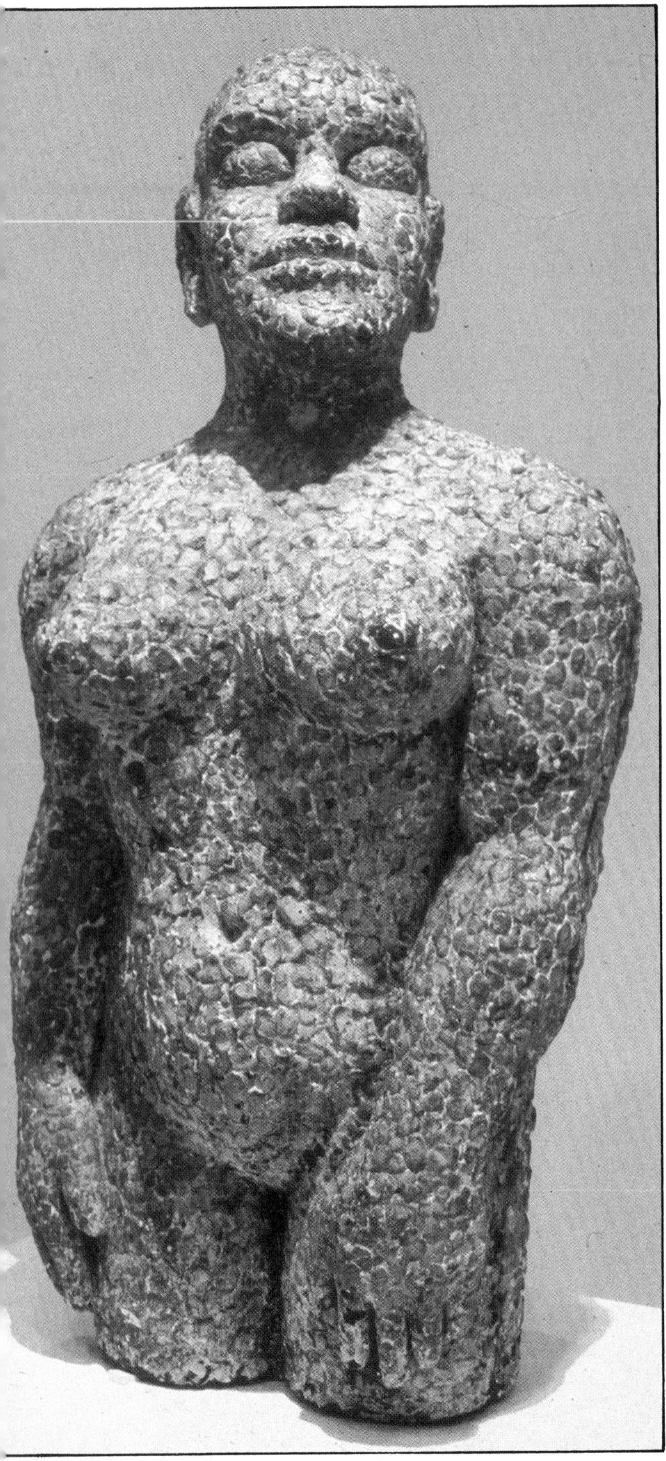

Ronald M
detail of ***Johanaan***

Ronald Moody,
The Mother, 1958

Ronald Moody,
Man . . . His Universe,
1969

Ronald Moody,
Orchid Bird, 1968

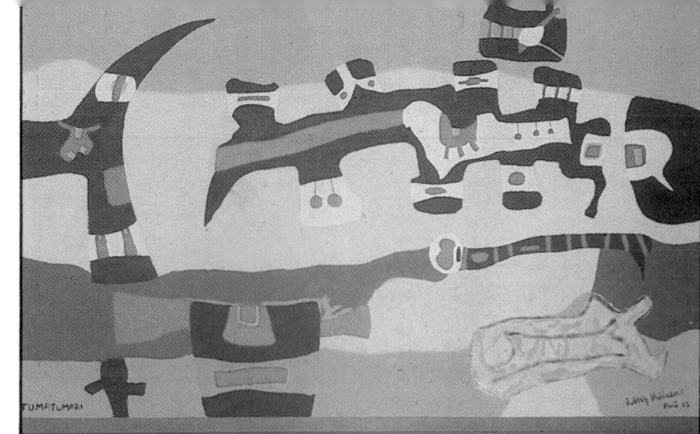

Aubrey Williams, mural, ***Tumatumari***, 1970

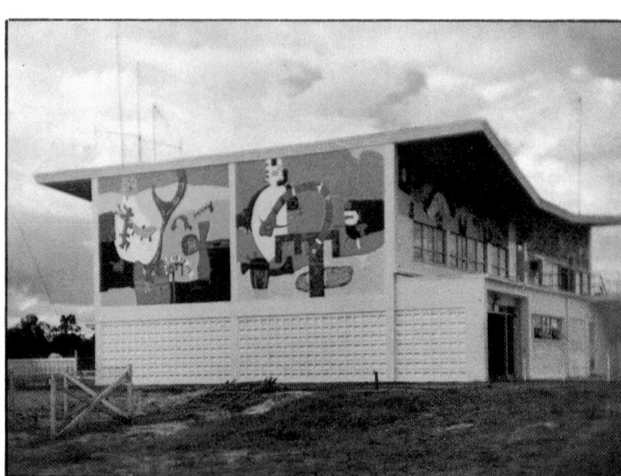

Aubrey Williams, murals at Timehri Airport, Guyana, 1970

Aubrey Williams, ***Warrau 2***, 1972

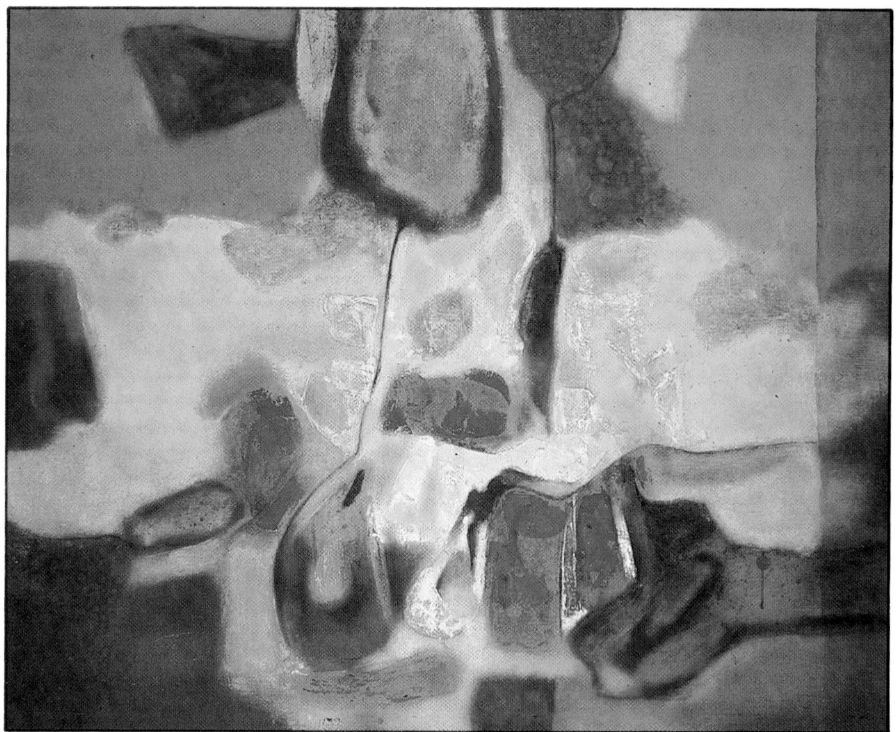

Aubrey Williams,
Visual Idea, 1963

Aubrey Williams,
Ning-Ning, 1969

Art Derry,
Manzanilla Moon, 1965

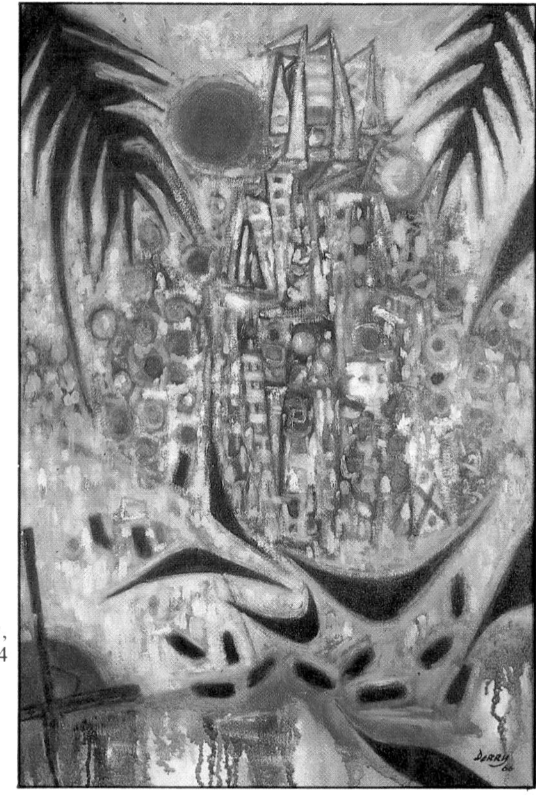

Art Derry,
Hosein Festival, 1964

Paul Dash, ***Figures Dancing in the Street***, 1965/6

Errol Lloyd, ***Waiting***, 1970

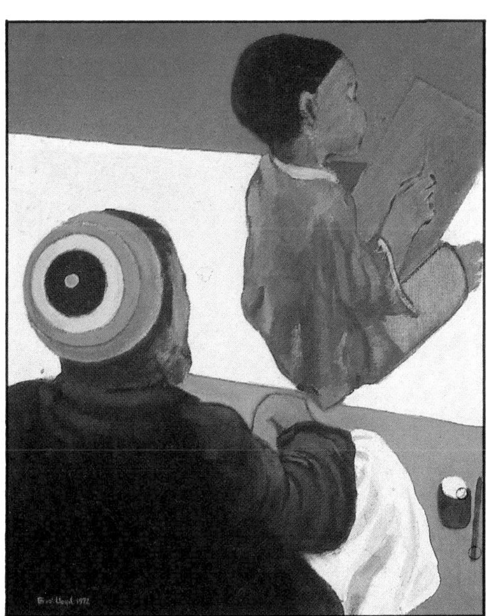

Errol Lloyd, ***The Lesson***, 1972

Errol Lloyd, ***Richard Small***, 1968

Winston Branch, ***Liberty was my Friend***, 1970

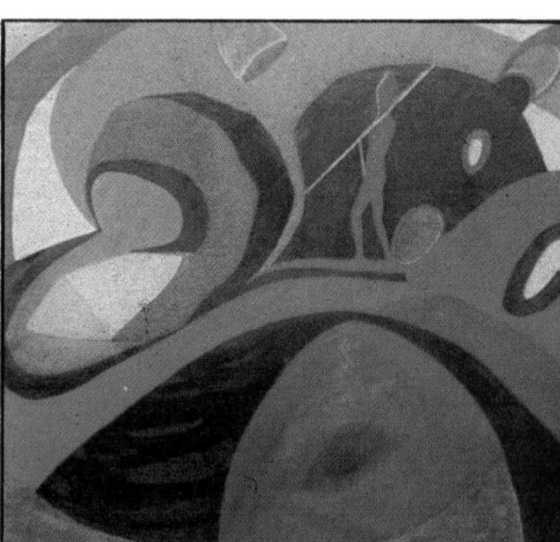

Clifton Campbell, ***The Man and the Tightrope***, 1964

Clifton Campbell, ***The Bird Watcher***, 1964

response of some West Indians to contemporary events: that to seek for their Indian or African heritage is a racial and political oversimplification, and provides no formula for problems 'that can only be settled when we conceive of ourselves as human beings in a world that is in crisis'. The passages which Ramchand read from *The Far Journey of Oudin*[11] and from *The Secret Ladder*[12] showed, he claimed, 'that in Harris's fiction it is not all that easy to settle upon a formula of what your roots are and who are the folk and what you belong to', and rejection of 'the one-sided thing of return to Mother India or Africa'. Whereas the Amerindian, 'a peripheral figure in Caribbean societies', seemed of little interest to West Indian writers, he came into his own only in Harris's fiction, 'as an image of the human being in the vast Caribbean landscape'. The passages which he read from *Palace of the Peacock*[13] and from *Heartland*[14] showed, in the first, the idea of man's unity; in the second, the dehistoricised Amerindian woman becoming the ancestral mother. Harris was not concerned, claimed Ramchand, with the simple definition of finding roots, or to paint a documentary picture of the Amerindian: 'he tries to envisage these characters as agents who help the reader and the characters in the novel to come to a new conception of themselves'.

Wilson Harris described his paper, which he read, as 'an attempt to point out that the function of character in the novel can no longer be sustained as a consolidation of features': a change foreshadowed in Herman Melville's *Moby Dick*, and in Malcolm Lowry's *Under the Volcano*, but not yet a breakthrough that was really felt or understood. This was not surprising since 'the function of character carries the difficult and obdurate concretisation of the past – as', Harris added, 'Dr Ramchand so beautifully illustrated'. Also, because, 'the translation or transmutation of this legacy of history remains a formidable problem'.

Harris then moved to the focus of his paper, the Amerindian, giving an account of his important role in Guyana under successive periods of colonisation by the Dutch, French, Spanish and British: a role which evaporated when slavery was abolished, by which time the Amerindian forces had vastly declined. Those Amerindians who have survived into the 20th century, 'possess all the symptoms of historylessness, rootlessness or, as I would put it, stigmata of the void'. But this need not be 'a totally disabling factor or feature. In fact, it may constitute a most fruitful obsession . . . with an art of compassion'. And, he went on, 'we must begin, I believe, to visualise the globe within a new corpus of sensibility, wherein the function of character within the interior of the novel will begin to displace the helpless and hopeless consolidation of powers.' He recounted an historic encounter between the English Governor of Guiana and the American Chieftain as an occasion when 'a new hunger and a new subsistence of memory comes into play'; both

> are implicated in the dust of history blowing, as it were, towards a new, terrifying, yet liberating immaterial conception, an art of fiction where the agents of time begin to subsist upon the real reverses the human spirit has endured, the real chasm of pain it has entered, rather than the apparent consolidation, victories and battles it has won.

Harris made reference to 'significant stratagems' undertaken by other Caribbean writers: by John Hearne, in *The Land of the Living*, and by Edward Brathwaite, in *Masks*, which 'sought to appoint African losses down the centuries in the Caribbean imagination'. He claimed that Hearne and Brathwaite had discovered, through their use of medieval and African art, that 'an art of memory which dislocates in some measure an idolatrous claim of realism by immersing us in a peculiar kind of ruined fabric, may help to free us from a consensus of bestiality, monolithic helplessness, monolithic violence.'

After quoting definitions of the novel by Anthony Burgess and Georg Lukács, Harris admitted his own interest in the 'weak person and the middle-of-the-road hero', where a breakthrough from what was to be found in the contemporary European novel might lie. He described the new artist whom he saw emerging, with potential for effecting change, but also open to danger:

> I must speak of the middle-of-the road hole within my iconic landscape – middle-of-the-landscape sculpture or waterfall or river or escarpment or jungle or rockface, down which a phenomenal erosion happened quite suddenly, precipitately, of conquered peoples. . . . With the mutilation and decline of the conquered tribe, a new Shaman or artist struggles to emerge, who finds himself moving along the knife-edge of change. He has been, as it were, cross-fertilised by victor and victim. And a powerful need arises to invoke the lost generations in a new creative, visionary light. It is a task which is profoundly personal and archetypal, and therefore accompanying an enormous potency for change, for vision into resources, runs the danger of self-enchantment or hubris.

In the creative translation of such cross-fertilisation may be invoked 'the emergence of a new and profound order of comparison within the novel . . . the new radical art of fiction'. He outlined what the exploration of such fiction involved for the author, whose role he defined thus:

> He is the complex ghost of his own landscape or history or work: to put it another way, his poem or novel, his subsistence of memory. In the final analysis, the reality of his existence as agent or clown, as a unity of strange powers, turns upon faith: faith in the powers and

> resources of the human person, at many levels of feeling, translation and enquiry, to invoke a presence with an absence.

And Harris quoted the final lines from Derek Walcott's poem, 'The Voyage Up River', dedicated to him, for 'the last, strangely defiant word'.[15]

Questions from the audience led Harris to make further key statements. LA Marcus quoted Harris's 1950 essay, 'Art and Criticism',[16] and asked how he saw 'the new architecture of the Third World'. Harris's reply began with a warning against the domination of static architecture and with scepticism about violence and protest; it ended with: 'Everything depends on the last line I wrote a week ago, which is altering all the time.' A challenge from Cosmo Pieterse, Namibian-born poet, that Harris was now abdicating a position he assumed at a symposium two days before, when he said he believed in words, provoked:

> The word possesses this translative medium, the word itself, precisely because one has to become involved in it at a certain distance from the object which one is recreating. . . . One approaches it and is baffled, is thrust back by it. You have no words for it. You have to start searching with words to find the equivalent of that kind of alien experience. In the end, the subsistence of memory is a profound act of consciousness, and the closest one could come to this is . . . through the word . . . so the word for me is absolutely supreme.

A statement of belief in commitment, wherein the political and the artistic person are linked, led Harris to refer to contemporary events in Biafra, in Czechoslovakia, to the terrifying related problems, and the role of the artist:

> For centuries there has been a peculiar function associated with the imagination, whether priest, poet, odd sort of man whatever he is. This man who tries, who is tested from all angles, who has correspondence with the devil and everything else, because he is profoundly immersed in the ruined fabric . . . he is compensating for losses. That kind of man has up to now expressed the only tradition of freedom that we know of.

A question about the ideal novel was answered with:

> I don't know what an ideal novel is. I mean, I am merely concerned with this immersion, you see, where one is in fact so deeply involved, both in the past and the present and the future, that one has no alternative but to accept the invisible thing which is pushing one behind it. So one translates this as best as one can.

This was an impressive and memorable session. Kenneth Ramchand's introduction was alchemised by his readings from Harris's fiction, and exploded by Harris's own paper. It is impossible to paraphrase Harris; the alternative, a series of quotations, is difficult to follow. Only in hearing or reading what he has to say in its entirety can meaning come through. Enough came through from this CAM session for several people in the audience to become attuned to the 'radical new art of fiction' which Harris expounded, and to be won over to the integrity of his role as a writer. After 20 years, for two participants at least – Naseem Khan and Judith Laird – hearing Wilson Harris was the most memorable feature of the conference.

The conference programme listed a symposium for its first evening, on 'New Directions in Caribbean Arts', following its stated policy of giving a hearing to young, unpublished or unexhibited, writers and artists. The line-up, as listed, was promising:

> Peter Figueroa (Jamaica): poet, research student at LSE
> Christopher Laird (Trinidad): artist
> John La Rose (Trinidad): poet, creator of New Beacon Publications Ltd
> Winston Branch (St Lucia): artist, Slade School of Art
> Knolly La Fortune (Trinidad): teacher and poet
> Audrey Payne (Guyana): writer

But Laird alone took part on the night; although La Rose and Payne attended the conference, Figueroa, Branch and La Fortune did not. Alongside Laird instead were Joyce M Linton (Jamaica); writer/actress/civil servant, and Karina Williamson (England), housewife and tutor.

Opening the symposium John Ramsaran – chairman, as planned – asked: 'What is the CAM really out to do?' He referred to the disagreement voiced after Stuart Hall's talk that morning, and stated his own view: 'More than anything else, I think any movement that is going to live must break new ground; we can't be forever in the old mould, we mustn't be tied down by convention.' His subsequent comment that the region's 'cross-section of cultures, of peoples, of languages, of origins' were evolving into 'what we like to call a West Indian culture' seemed reminiscent of sentiments of the 1940s and 1950s. But Ramsaran had left Trinidad 20 years before. He was struck now, at a CAM conference, by what he called 'this great dialogue between all the people of the Caribbean', which had been entirely lacking when he lived in the Caribbean.

The aim of the symposium was to 'find out what other people are doing who have not actually yet got into the limelight, but we hope they will soon'. Ramsaran introduced Joyce Linton as a writer of short stories, 'a tradition in the West Indies neglected at present', and then questioned her as to why she liked writing short stories and what sort she wrote. Linton's replies included: 'I don't particularly like controversial subjects. I prefer emotional themes . . . I steer clear of politics, but I like religious themes. . . . I prefer universal themes. . . . I prefer the average individual.' Karina Williamson, as fellow panel member, attempted to relate the short story to West Indian prose fiction, but as an Englishwoman was frankly diffident: 'I'm asking questions rather than giving answers because I'm such an outsider.' Henry Swanzy and Andrew Salkey contributed practical points from their working experience. But no discussion developed about the form and language of the short story, nor as to why it was, if indeed it was, neglected. The tone and direction of discussion had been set by Linton who seemed to be writing for the narrow, clearly-defined requirements of a particular magazine.

Christopher Laird, in vivid contrast, was, said Ramsaran, still searching for the medium in which he should work, for 'a new medium to fulfil his own needs' – though it soon became clear, when Laird himself spoke, that he was equally aware of the needs of his audience. In practice as much a poet as an artist, he described how inadequate he found 'making scratches with ink on white paper': in the English language, using the Roman alphabet, using a traditional, age-old implement. It was 'up to the artist to try and catch up with technology', a new area which he could himself control. The book was 'coming to be a tired-out sort of clumsy implement'; therefore the artist should also be aware of being able to express himself using film, new recording techniques and so on. Laird found the possibilities for poetry particularly exciting:

> Using oral poetry instead of just printed poetry, you come a little closer again to actual experience, because you start to break down still further the alphabetical image, the image of the words. . . . The means of reproducing sound these days is so far advanced that it can be used at many levels and in many different ways, and there's a whole new area by which poetry can be expressed.

The new medium which he was exploring for his own work was 'poetry with painting and words'. Ramsaran, glancing at an example, drew comparisons with work by George Herbert and William Blake. A traditional Western frame of reference continued to be held by Swanzy and Williamson, with reminders of the danger of limiting 'the area of verbal connotation', of cutting out 'ambiguity and resonance'. They provoked Laird to a clearer statement of his own direction: 'I find that the West Indian language is mainly an oral one. . . . It's very hard to be really creative in the metres of our language, in writing it. It doesn't express half of what it is when we are speaking it.'

Then Wilson Harris intervened, from the audience, with: 'I really think there is a connection between the painting and the poem.' Referring to Frances Yates's *The Art of Memory* (1966) he explained: 'There is the kind of writing where the writer is intensely involved in things that are seen. Each phase of his work discloses new things which he never saw before and in fact he is drawn on and on.' And therefore, he continued, 'the link between the painting and the poem is a question of getting inside the fact of the painting'. He concluded:

> The word is part of the fact of one's experience, it's part of that primordial landscape which takes all sorts of shapes and forms so that one is actually involved in a living experience and once the word functions like that there is nothing which, in my view, can limit the word. So that . . . in fact the word is an ally of the painting.

He spoke as one 'steeped in the Caribbean' of his experience in the interior, when he would see a certain kind of landscape for which he had no words then, and for which it might take 20 years to begin to discover the words.

Laird, reassured on the relation between poem and painting, returned to the difficulty which he personally found in expressing himself, as a West Indian, in written English. Wilson Harris asked how long he had lived in the West Indies, and went on: 'I have lived there for a long time, I've travelled deeply, and I don't particularly find that.' This encouraged Laird to develop further his personal quest:

> I am not as West Indian as you are, maybe . . . I have to settle my way, looking back, just as much as most West Indians seem to be trying to find themselves, their history, and their traditions in regard to Africa, India and wherever. I have to find my tradition as regards England, Europe.

Yet again he returned to oral poetry, this time in relation to the illiterate West Indian, stating that, in his belief, the best poetry being produced for the West Indies was the calypso. This led, at last, to a question about music. Were West Indians involved in any other form of music than the calypso? 'You feel that there is this potential for some kind of tremendous music to go on somewhere.' Locksley Comrie took the opportunity to tell CAM about 'a new art-form in Jamaica', blue-beat, or rock-steady. This used 'the language of what we call the "rude boys" . . . they are rebelling against the existing order'. Through their songs, not understood by the Jamaican establishment, they could get their message across from one district to another.

The third panel member, Karina Williamson, who was introduced as working on a biography of Roger Mais, appeared somewhat embarrassed and defensive about her role: 'I can't pretend this is a contribution to Caribbean arts, I do see my function as parasitic.' She had, she said, been very unwilling to take on the biography, and only agreed because no Jamaican appeared willing to do it – though she felt that 'someone outside might see things that a Jamaican or West Indian might not'. Rather than saying what she had found out, she put questions about Mais to the audience: 'Why alone of his generation does Mais not write about the West Indian predicament? . . . Why is there no race and colour problem, no Federation problem, no provincialism problem, no urban v rural society?' Henry Swanzy, Jerry Craig, Andrew Salkey, John La Rose, gave answers, contributed personal memories and views on Mais. Salkey's, as a fellow Jamaican novelist and close friend, were of special value. Mais was, he said, a revolutionary before his time, struck down for daring to speak out against British imperialism. He dared write about people whom others didn't; there would have been no *Sisyphus* without Mais; he had great sympathy, and saw the sharp divisions in Jamaican society. But Karina Williamson's attempts to engage in close critical discussion on Mais came to nothing; she seemed to assume that the audience had more detailed knowledge of Mais's work than was the case. Meanwhile, records Swanzy in his diary: 'In the deep well of the room, Black Power supporters talked loudly among themselves, and one fixed Messrs King and White, beside me on the long settee, with a penetrating stare.'[17]

Only Christopher Laird's contribution, the one original panel member, explored and provoked others to speak about new directions in Caribbean arts. And what Laird said was taken up later in the conference. Discussing new forms for Caribbean writing, in Van Sertima's session the next day, John La Rose made connections with what Laird had said, and with what Césaire was attempting in the *Cahier*.

A second symposium, 'The Artist in the Caribbean', on Sunday afternoon, was substituted for the scheduled talk by Patrick Betaudier. It drew on four of the artists attending the conference: Karl 'Jerry' Craig, who introduced and chaired it; Errol Lloyd, Ronald Moody, and – the only newcomer to a CAM session – Edmund Gill. But, Craig pointed out, none of them knew much about working as an artist in the Caribbean, since they had all lived in Britain for some time. Instead they would discuss 'the lack of representation of the artist in Britain in comparison with the writer', and how the writer seemed to 'have got a lot further' in Europe and America than the West Indian painter.

Craig himself, in his double role, took every opportunity to expand on what he considered were the problems hindering this 'lack of representation', problems whose roots were, he considered, in the West Indies. Some arose through art education, still limited by examination syllabus requirements to representational art, still dominated by expatriate teachers, or in the hands of artists more interested in 'selling paintings for a living than in art education'. Other problems arose from the very limited, unimaginative commissions and purchases of Caribbean art for public buildings. West Indian artists working in Britain were faced with other problems. Because they were far removed from the 'atmosphere and imagery of the West Indies', when 'all that remains is the feeling for design and the sense of colour', they tended to work more in abstraction. He blamed the under-representation of work by West Indians in Britain in part on their lack of exposure in exhibitions; also on their under-use as illustrators of books by West Indian writers.

Craig envisaged CAM as playing a major role in overcoming such under-representation: by arranging more exhibitions – for individual artists, when the whole range of their work could be shown, as well as more group shows; by enabling Caribbean artists and writers to get to know each others' work. Before the founding of CAM, he had read little Caribbean writing; he spoke of the 'great inspiration' which he had now found, particularly in the work of Wilson Harris and Edward Brathwaite. Until CAM, he knew only two other Caribbean painters. CAM had awakened in him 'something which for years I didn't even know I had' and had given him a sense of self-confidence. Throughout Craig made references to his recent visit to Jamaica, in 1966, and to his planned return to work there the following year.

Of the other three panel members, Errol Lloyd spoke most, and with far greater confidence than when he had taken part in the first CAM Artists' Symposium, at the Centre, in June 1967. The artist's problems which concerned him were different from Craig's at almost every point. He came in, significantly, after John La Rose had intervened in order to question the West Indian artist's problems at a deeper level, and to relate them to those of the novelist. Referring back to a point made by Aubrey Williams at the Ivan Van Sertima session that morning, La Rose urged that Caribbean artists, like novelists, should not simply return to a tradition, but should go beyond it: 'The painters and writers who, like everyone else, have been so derivative in that to some extent they are modifying a received tradition rather than daring to create something which comes from a deeper, inner experience.'

Lloyd, continuing the comparison with literature, spoke of how, in Jamaica, art had only begun to express what was native to Jamaica with Edna Manley's sculpture and the nationalist movement of the 1940s. The problem, in his view, was 'that we have no real tradition in art at all'. This accounted for the artist's expression being more 'advanced than the people for whom he is supposed to be painting', and hence what to him was one of the main drawbacks in art: that 'it doesn't matter so much to the people'. Artists were, in his view, too caught up in the mainstream of European art and consequently there were gaps between the artist and the people. The artist had started with the representational and moved onto the abstract, but the public had not been following him through these stages because of the lack of real tradition in art. It was not a question of the artist being under any obligation to communicate, but of artists and the people not moving in step.

Lloyd's focus was on Caribbean artists and people in Britain. To James Berry's regret that 'we'll never be able to see the pathos in our faces, the anguish of our times, communicated to us', and request that a Caribbean artist's work should contain 'something that will communicate to us the tremendous feelings of people here in London', Lloyd replied: 'I think what is going to happen is that these people who are themselves experiencing all these things will one day produce the artist.' He resented a suggestion (Eric Dalton, of Evans) that a painter needed a patron to get started, and went on to question Craig's basic assumption that it was necessary for an artist to 'arrive'. Errol Lloyd's point of view, expressed piecemeal, in reply to questions and in comment, was consistent, deeply felt and evidently evolving.

Edmund Gill spoke briefly and simply of his view of art as self-expression, which was for him compulsive: 'I paint because I have to.' The experience of immigration to England had made it impossible to continue: 'Living in this country for 12 years, I was dead, emotionally, as a West Indian. I could not function as an Englishman and therefore I could not express myself as a West Indian and I stopped painting.' Since exhibiting with and then joining CAM, he had started to paint again.

Ronald Moody spoke briefly but, as always, most memorably, prompted by what La Rose, then Lloyd, said about the artist and tradition:

> Each one of us has to . . . delve within himself and really begin to find out what he is. . . . I definitely was never influenced very much by European art, my influences came from Egypt, India and Africa. And gradually a kind of inner fight had to take place, throwing away so much that I had learnt at school . . . and getting down to what I really felt I could do. And this was a very, very difficult kind of long pilgrimage. I think that is the fundamental thing that the West Indian is faced with. And I think there will be a variety of styles even then because they come from so many sources.

As a much-needed conference session on art, the symposium was less substantial than its counterpart at the Centre because it was ad hoc, had fewer panelists, and lacked an independent chairman. But the session enabled younger artists to express their views, and allowed early debate about art and West Indians in Britain. It also resulted in more commissions by British publishers to Caribbean artists for cover designs and illustrations of West Indian books.

Poetry in performance, books on display, art in exhibition

Readings and performances also took place in the Common Room, far into the early hours of Sunday and Monday. Each programme had two parts. On Saturday night/Sunday morning, there were readings from Césaire's *Cahier*, in French by Daniel Moreau, in English translation, from the Présence Africaine edition, by John La Rose; then songs, with guitar accompaniment, by CAM Nottingham members, from the West Indian folk song 'Yellow Bird' to Bob Dylan's 'Blowin' in the Wind'. On Sunday night/Monday morning, La Rose read from a long Mali poem on creation; then Brathwaite gave an hour's continuous reading from *Rights of Passage*, *Masks* and the typescript of the as-yet unpublished *Islands*, a selection on the theme of 'The Journey', on arrival and understanding.

For the Second Conference the New Beacon display was much enlarged, with John La Rose and Sarah White in attendance. French and Spanish Caribbean books were much in evidence, including the Présence Africaine edition of Césaire's *Cahier*. Henry Swanzy recalls buying Fanon's *The Wretched of the Earth* (1967). Anne Walmsley's contemporary notes on the 'book room' list 'poetry, history, fiction, French, Caribbean and Cuban literature, school texts, Caribbean and African magazines'.

The art on display was considerably more varied than at the First Conference. 'We thought,' wrote Craig to Brathwaite in mid-1968, 'that the younger artists should dominate the show this year at Kent. Have been trying in vain to contact Frank Bowling.' Bowling continued to evade CAM, for he had stayed on in the USA after first going there in 1966. Craig gave Errol Lloyd full details of the names and addresses of CAM artists and responsibility for organising the show, and recalls: 'Errol was a tremendous support and help. He was good at the gathering of information, getting in touch with the younger artists, getting work organised.' Lloyd travelled to Canterbury in a van with the paintings. Again there were paintings by Campbell, Williams and Craig, sculpture by Moody and Lloyd.

But this year there were also paintings by two young Barbadians, Paul Dash and Edmund Gill, and pottery by Madge Rivers, a Jamaican woman living in Nottingham. Dash, in his final year as a student at the Chelsea School of Art, had been greeted by John La Rose when his work was shown as part of a Royal Commonwealth Society exhibition. La Rose told him about CAM, asked if he'd like to join, and introduced him to Errol Lloyd. Gill had himself contacted CAM after his work was shown at the LSE West

Indian Society's show in February. He commented, when returning his CAM application form to Marina Maxwell, 'I look forward to taking part in any future activities of the group. This has given me the incentive to paint seriously again.'[18] In May he wrote to Brathwaite, saying he would be glad to contribute some of his work if an art exhibition was planned for the next conference. Madge Rivers had been amongst the group at Nottingham which formed a CAM branch, and Robert Reinders wrote to Louis James: 'Mrs Rivers, the lady with the small daughter and married to a tall, bearded Englishman, is a potter. Do you think it would be worthwhile for her to exhibit a work or two for the conference?'[19]

The younger artists' work came to be included in the second CAM conference exhibition by a variety of routes. If their selection was apparently haphazard, at least the CAM organisation picked up and made good use of their interest. By the time CAM had been operating on a public platform for 18 months, several younger artists had been given the chance of showing their work alongide that of established, professional artists in a Caribbean grouping, to a mainly Caribbean audience.

CAM's 'business' meeting

Intervention by Locksley Comrie and Richard Small at the Artists Symposium had been minimal: there were no suggestions of a CAM art exhibition, or art classes, in Brixton. Comrie simply urged CAM to make more use of the Students Centre, to take more part in its activities, and mentioned the new Black Community Centre for which they were raising money. But he and Comrie and, to a lesser extent, Lowell Marcus, had kept up pressure on CAM throughout the conference to reconsider its direction and concerns. Because of their insistent voice, raised at every session, the CAM Committee agreed to hear and respond to their views. A special meeting was called at 11.15 pm on the final evening for what was announced as a quarter of an hour's 'business'; it was in fact a two-hour session of sharp criticism, considered defence, and heartfelt debate.[20]

John La Rose chaired the meeting. Opening it, he explained that it had been called because of the apparent need for direct communication and discussion of ideas about CAM. Some members had expressed the desire to plunge into public activity, but the essence of CAM was 'interpenetration between artists'. It should accommodate private and public activity. CAM's dynamism came from the fact that it was structureless as an organisation.

Locksley Comrie spoke next. After a preamble expressing amazement that the biography of Roger Mais was being written by an Englishwoman, and urging that 'we must write our own history, have our own heroes', he launched into a direct attack on CAM. It should move out from the Students Centre to Ladbroke Grove and Brixton, and bring to the people 'what they're missing', for example, plays on Marcus Garvey and George Padmore. Also, CAM should be protesting against the banning of Black Power writing in Jamaica, and what he saw as the setting up of a police state there: 'Where are the protest writers?' He saw the opportunity for CAM 'to do a lot more', if it would 'get off its intellectual backside'.

Richard Small followed. He summarised what he saw as CAM's progress and achievements so far, concluding, 'discussion has clicked'. But, he went on, 'Now what? A new move must be made.' He was not urging a CAM revolution, because of respect for its open structure, but 'suggesting a new conception of art and culture which we as a people need'. He pointed out how in the USA, artistic expression ran parallel with political struggle. The black community in Britain was moving; if CAM did not move with it, 'it will be drowned'. CAM should be discussing not just the relation of the West Indian artist to society in the West Indies, but to the black community in Britain; the relation started here could be of value when CAM members return. Groups were being formed in Britain to fight housing discrimination, police brutality and so on; art should come alongside. He specifically urged CAM to take literature in performance to Brixton: Brathwaite's reading of *Rights of Passage*, Bari Jonson's *Ex-Africa*, would act as 'a spark to set off expression in the black community'. The current concept of art in the West Indies and in Britain as something formal was false, and the way in which culture was presented must be broken down, so that people could interrupt, contribute during performance. Small's final, overall plea was for the West Indian artist in Britain to 'become spiritually part of the black community'.

Brathwaite replied. He acknowledged no conflict and reaffirmed CAM's loose structure. When CAM first went public, so as to 'communicate with people who needed to read and see', the Students Centre was 'the only common ground'. The next stage might well be to go to Brixton and so on. It was up to individual members to go and do these things; they constitute CAM – there is no 'CAM' body to ask. Small agreed there was no conflict: he was seeking, and welcomed, such clarification. If individual CAM members would indeed think of their function wherever they were, and would go to places where black people live in London, then 'some of the sort of discussion we have will be altered very fundamentally'. Andrew Salkey cited the Nottingham branch as an example of CAM flourishing in a place where black people live.

Then Wilson Harris spoke, at length; he must, he said, warn of the danger that he saw if CAM followed such advice. He drew a parallel with the coming to power in Guyana of the PPP, which had felt the same compulsion to become part of a deprived group. For some, this was 'a liberating force on the imagination', for example, Martin Carter. But the tragedy was that whatever seeds were there at the time were lost, and the result was a ghetto community. If CAM was to function at all it must somehow or other undermine the ghetto. Harris acknowledged the comfort of being in a fortress. But, he maintained, if there is anything genuine about art, the artist must stand out, he cannot conform to a group. The fundamental reality is the human person. Harris had seen the tragic consequences of the PPP intellectuals' and writers' alignment in Guyana; they had to become public men, and there was consequent stultification of their creativity. The ghetto became entrenched; no self-contemplative artist was working there now. 'Let Brixton buy our books. But if CAM is to function in terms of real responsibility, it must painfully reject becoming part of the black or the white community. This is not the way.'

Small hastened to defend his stand. He had not suggested that artists and writers should identify with a particular group, he was 'just as concerned that artists should not feel politically pressured'. All he was urging was another step in communication; buying books was not enough. Interjections by Felicity Bolton and Eric Dalton about the communication difficulties of British artists were answered by Doris Brathwaite: 'There is a special urgency for the West Indian to communicate.' Lowell Marcus contributed an uncompromising Black Power position: 'I talk to black men, of art for the black man.'

Edward Kamau Brathwaite expressed the possibility of a new stage in CAM. While artists themselves were in control of CAM, they were in sympathy with Wilson Harris and would avoid any direct commitment. But as CAM became larger and involved more non-artists, it would change and take CAM out. If, he said, we remain where we are, CAM is in danger of becoming an inbred group. La Rose too tried to keep CAM together, stating that CAM needed both the writers and artists, and the public. Oliver Clarke pointed out that few organisers of the West Indian community were present at the conference; that CAM was set up as a 'battery which would recharge all races', as a cultural organisation; that middlemen were needed to take West Indian art to the public. This prompted Ivan Van Sertima to plead: don't split up the races of the West Indies – and Locksley Comrie to deny having Black Power interests. Doris Brathwaite brought CAM back to a practical next step: 'Just ask the artists to go and speak, and they'll go,' which Andrew Salkey confirmed: 'Yes, we are on tap.'

Wilson Harris added a little to his statement the following morning, before giving his paper:

> I want to emphasise what appears to me to be the role of the creative imagination whether as painter, poet, artist, priest, scientist, craftsman. Down the centuries, one finds here something invaluable in human terms, which has always been threatened by pressures to conform to a monolithic convention or a monolithic tribalism. . . . I myself believe that the imagination has a curiously sacred function in terms of a commodity which transcends common sense.

Richard Small, after hearing Wilson Harris's paper, admitted later that he could not disagree with him. 'It's the kind of exploration that the individual artist needs.' Harris's participation in CAM was of its essence, but did not continue after the Second Conference.

CAM's 'business' meeting had concluded with a proposal, by Richard Small, that the CAM conference send a cable to the Jamaican government in protest at its banning of Black Power literature. Small's draft resolution, and an amended version by Gerald Moore, proposed by Bryan King, were discussed and voted on at the close of the conference the next day. A majority vote of 40 (8 against, 5 abstentions) passed the following:

> The Second Conference of the Caribbean Artists Movement held at the University of Kent at Canterbury, 31st August, 1st and 2nd September 1968, expresses its opposition in principle to all limitations on the free expression of ideas, and specifically condemns the action of the Jamaican government in banning the writings of Malcolm X, Stokely Carmichael and Elijah Mohammed. The Conference calls on the Government to renounce this prohibition order.

Snapshots taken at the Second Conference showing Margaret and Wilson Harris, Kenneth Ramchand, Errol Lloyd, Doris and Edward Kamau Brathwaite, Andrew Salkey

This amended resolution had added the general principle of free expression to Small's original draft. It had dropped a clause in Small's original draft which elaborated on the particular value of Black Power literature: 'These three men and their writings represent part of the most important development in the liberation of the minds of the people of Africa, Afro-America and the Caribbean.' Swanzy recalls that Doris Brathwaite in particular wanted to restore this passage from the original draft.

Andrew Salkey closed the conference: first, with comprehensive thanks, including, 'For last night's late session on CAM, which was absolutely marvellous and very, very pathfinding, I want to thank Locksley Comrie, Richard Small, Doris Brathwaite and the audience.' The names mentioned seem to indicate Salkey's own alignment. Second, with a farewell:

> Heartfelt thanks to Edward and Doris Brathwaite for their enormous work in CAM, for starting the damn' thing and getting us moving, you see. And for their influence on our Committee, and on the members, and the members' friends, and on British society. We'll miss Edward and Doris very much indeed. They're going back home. We wish you success and some kind of happiness at the University.

Audrey Payne, presenting a piece of pottery by Madge Rivers to the Brathwaites, said: 'We hope the Jamaican branch will interrelate with us.'

Because the Second Conference papers were never published, not even in the CAM *Newsletter*, the talks given by the main speakers did not reach the wider audience of previous, or some subsequent, CAM sessions, and so were prevented from forming as strong a part of the on-going debate in CAM as they deserved. Brathwaite has commented on the high level of public discussion at the conference. Even the very selective contributions reproduced here indicate its liveliness, its breadth, its cross-references, its awareness of the significance of contemporary events.

This conference is generally most remembered for the confrontation of Students Centre Black Power activists with CAM's artists and founder members. West Indian newspapers, in London and Trinidad, made the most of it. *The Hustler* quoted as key comments the duty of members to contribute to the 'international movement in the Third World towards the global overthrow of Racism'. *The Trinidad Guardian*, under a headline, 'Black Power splits Caribbean artists', gave an account of the attack and predicted CAM's rapid disintegration.[21]

Artists who attended the Second Conference recall particularly the 'big split', articulated by Harris on the one hand, Small and Comrie on the other, and the challenge to where they themselves stood. Christopher Laird felt more in sympathy with what Harris said: 'But at the same time, conscious of being white, I was a bit worried about why I had that stand.' Jerry Craig was strongly supportive of Harris's line; the direction advocated by Small and Comrie was, he felt, 'what killed CAM as a continuing movement'. Ivan Van Sertima says that his intervention was provoked by the extreme way in which Small and Comrie expressed themselves.

Richard Small attempts now to clarify his position. His main concern was that CAM should be aware of, and its artists assist in, the discovery by West Indian immigrants in Britain of their cultural identity:

> It is *that* that I believed that I sensed CAM did not have its finger on, why I felt that it was necessary for it to change direction . . . the tremendous political, cultural and artistic possibilities that existed in the immigrant community which CAM was cutting itself off from. . . . I saw one of the functions of the artists and intellectuals as helping in the freeing of the minds and concepts of the black people, building that confidence and expressing it, exploring it and showing the possibilities.

La Rose sees Small as having been trapped in an ambiguous position, believing both in the freedom of the artist and of the need to politicise CAM. 'But I myself', says La Rose 'had no ambiguity. I regarded CAM as an artistic and intellectual movement, not a political movement. I knew that politics and art could not work together. Artists must have freedom. If artists are to be serious, they will always be awkward and challenging.'

Brathwaite stresses now, as he did at the time, that there was no CAM body, only individual members. 'We never expected consensus of artistic thought or practice, though we constantly tried to define what we had in common. CAM had no central thinking.'[22] By pointing to, criticising and attacking what they chose to identify as CAM attitudes and practice, Small and Comrie put CAM into a position of corporate answerability which was false to its character. Most seriously, it caused individual artists and writers to feel that CAM was becoming politicised, and that they could no longer be part of such a movement.

With the Brathwaites gone, and CAM thus threatened, its future in Britain after the Second Conference seemed highly uncertain.

7 Grounding in the Caribbean

October 1968 - December 1970

If at the end of the Second Conference CAM's future in Britain seemed highly uncertain, the prospects for forming CAM in the Caribbean seemed very bright. Not only were the Brathwaites returning to Jamaica, with almost two years of experience as CAM secretaries, but several active early members had already gone back. All were living conveniently close to each other in Kingston, almost all teaching at the Mona campus of UWI. Orlando Patterson had returned in 1967, to a post in sociology. Don and Betty Wilson returned in March 1968, Don to a post in the then Department (now School) of Education, Betty to teach French and English at St Peter and Paul, now Campion College. Marina Maxwell followed early in April, combining a teaching job at the College of Arts, Science and Technology with research at the UWI Institute of Social and Economic Research. Edward Kamau and Doris Brathwaite returned in early October; after a successful PhD viva at the University of Sussex, Brathwaite resumed his post in the Department of History. Kenneth Ramchand arrived shortly afterwards and took up a post in the Department of English. Since April, Gordon Rohlehr had been teaching in the equivalent department at the St Augustine campus of UWI in Trinidad. CAM members seemed to assume that a branch would be welcomed in Jamaica, and probably also in other West Indian countries.

The context for CAM: Jamaica

October 1968 was the Brathwaites' second return home to the Caribbean. In 1963, after nine years in Ghana, Brathwaite had, as he writes,

> . . . returned to find Jack
> Kennedy invading Cuba
> Black riots in Aruba
> And Trinidad.[1]

Now he walked straight into the greatest upheaval in Jamaican society since Independence, he himself says, since Emancipation.

Rumbles of trouble had been heard at CAM's Second Conference, in late August and early September 1968. The Jamaican government's ban on the writings of international Black Power leaders threatened more widespread censorship. Brathwaite braced himself for what might be in store. When, after the conference, the text of its resolution to the Jamaican government was prepared by the CAM committee for dispatch, the question arose as to who should sign it. Brathwaite, returning the text to Salkey, wrote:

> The other day you phoned to say that John, I think, felt that my name should not be used as a signatory. I do not, and cannot agree, to this. If a *single* name only is to be used, I would without hesitation vote for your name. But if, as I think, it should be a *Committee* signature, then my name *must* be there. I know the fear is that there might be recriminations against me. If so, what? I would welcome them. I cannot say one thing in my writing, and act another way in my life. I am going back to the West Indies because I believe that that's where the real battle *has* to be fought.[2]

In the event, Salkey seems to have been the main signatory, for he received the Prime Minister's routine reply, dated 27 September.

On Tuesday 15 October Dr Walter Rodney, returning to Jamaica from a Congress of Black Writers at McGill University, Montreal, was served with an Expulsion Order when his plane reached Kingston airport. Students at UWI, Mona, responded to the news with a protest march, starting early on the morning of Wednesday 16. Their leader was Ralph Gonzalez, from St Vincent. Riot police soon appeared; they tear-gassed and batoned the marchers, but neither arrested them nor stopped the march. Members of the public joined the march, in sympathy with the

Walter Rodney 16 October 1968, refused entry to Jamaica

students and their cause; Rodney's lectures on and off campus had drawn devoted audiences. When the march reached down-town Kingston, it split and got out of hand; long-suppressed discontent amongst the most deprived sections of the people resulted in widespread destruction of property and looting.

On Thursday 17 October, police and military personnel surrounded the UWI campus; students and staff set up machinery for writing and distributing publications in order to let their version of events be widely known. They also called an emergency faculty meeting in Mary Seacole Hall, with Douglas Hall – Dean of the Faculty of Arts and Professor of History – as chairman. The meeting coincided with a live television broadcast by the Prime Minister, Hugh Shearer, speaking to the House of Representatives, and claiming that Walter Rodney and other non-Jamaicans at UWI were plotting a violent revolution. Those at the meeting listened to and watched Shearer's broadcast, in which hostility to UWI was very apparent. On Friday 18, the first UWI publications covering the crisis were distributed: an unofficial issue of *Scope*, the students' newspaper, published by the Guild of Undergraduates, and mimeographed 'bulletins' from the Free University Press. That night five of the six entrances to the campus were sealed off. Student solidarity, heightened by the siege, was further reinforced by hearing from a law lecturer that recent government action – not students' – was illegal. But on Sunday 20, the Vice-Chancellor, Philip Sherlock, banned all further unofficial student meetings on campus and rebuked the Free University Press for its activities. On Monday 21, a lead story in the Jamaican *Daily Gleaner* implied that radicals from outside the university, and Eastern Caribbean students, especially Ralph Gonzalez, were inciting the students not to resume classes. That afternoon, Sherlock ordered all classes to resume in two days' time. Students were forced to comply, despite the Staff-Student Policy Committee having reached consensus on conditions for resumption of classes.

No authenticated evidence against Walter Rodney was ever produced. His lectures on African history at UWI and, most significantly, to middle-class and workers' groups, to large crowds of Rastafarians – in Kingston and surrounding rural parishes – were perceived by the Jamaican government to be subversive because, in the words of Dr Norman Girvan, two months later, they 'gave to black people a sense of past achievement and therefore of future purpose'.[3] In Richard Small's view, Rodney's lectures challenged '400 years of the colonial viewpoint and the colonial relationship on which the present society is based'.[4] The government's apparent aim was to counter and suppress an emerging consciousness of Black Power which had been fuelled by

Rodney's lectures. The collusion of the *Daily Gleaner* and of the UWI administration was essential to government strategy. Courageous student activism and rare staff-student solidarity was rendered irrelevant and shown to be powerless.

The Brathwaites had just reached Jamaica when the momentous week's events began. They joined in the UWI students' protest march, and Brathwaite wrote about it fully, soon afterwards, to Andrew Salkey, enclosing a copy of *Scope Special*, the first, widely circulated, UWI students' publication on the events. Salkey's long, immediate reply included: 'We respect and admire what all of you did on the home scene; it must have been hellishly difficult.'[5] The 'Rodney Affair', as it came to be known, was the first confrontation between the black government and its black majority population. Brathwaite returned to UWI as it attempted open, active protest against the government for the first time. His efforts at founding CAM (Jamaica); all his and other members' CAM-related or CAM-inspired work was affected by this upheaval and its consequences. Their activities after 1968 took place in the context of a defiant and irrepressible articulation of Black Power. There was a thirst for knowledge about Africa, an acceptance of African links. Features of the Rastafarian movement, which had been gathering strength in Jamaica throughout the 1960s, became widely accepted. All this was accompanied by a widespread 'implosion' of experimentation with new art forms,[6] by hitherto submerged sections of the community such as the Rastafarians, the 'yout', and women.

With UWI reluctantly back at work, Brathwaite lost little time in attempting to set up CAM (Jamaica). He called a meeting of all those who he thought would be interested. Sam Selvon was visiting the campus at the time, and provided a focus. A letter to Salkey, soon afterwards, described what Brathwaite called the 'fiasco' of his 'Sam Selvon exploratory CAM evening':

> Doomed to fail from the start, I know. But typical of what we're up against as you will remember from your last stint here. Amongst those present were the following, revolving poles apart:
>
> | | |
> |---|---|
> | J Hearne | Bobby Hill |
> | Cecil Gray | Marina Maxwell |
> | M Morris | Orlando Patterson |
>
> Need I go further. We just split apart on the personalities alone. But never mind; there'll be CAM here; though I'm sure (and hope) not in the form imagined by either of the protagonists. Bobby wants a mini-Montreal downtown; Marina wants to have nothing to do with the arts centre and the establishment; Mervyn Morris wants to start small and literary; [Norma] Hamilton wants to have the regge [sic] boys in; John Hearne wants [?? Salkey cut stamp off reverse of airletter form]; Orlando wants something like 'the London situation'.[7]

In retrospect, Brathwaite sees that the context – in place and in time – posed special problems:

> It was a university rather than a Jamaica thing; some people felt that it was going to be too academic. And then it was at the time of the Rodney crisis, the business of Black Power, student power, sufferers, radicalism. So that the venue of CAM . . . became an element of polarisation. Some people said it had to be off campus, and then they split again . . . Ghetto or Red Hills.

Other CAM members say in retrospect that they were not surprised that it failed to take off in Jamaica. Don Wilson comments: 'It wasn't the same thing as it had been in England . . . [where] we were creating a West Indian environment that we felt proud of . . . whereas in Jamaica, well, we are here.' The agenda had by then, he points out, moved to 'political and social problems' away from 'the idea of West Indian cultural identity'. Mervyn Morris saw no particular need for a CAM in Jamaica: 'The kinds of activity, the meetings and discussions which tended to be part of what CAM did: those things have always happened, particularly on the Mona campus.' Lloyd Reckord saw no personal incentive to join a CAM in Jamaica: 'When you get back home, you tend to get very involved in your little neck of the woods.' Clifton Campbell's return to Jamaica in mid-1968 as a successful London artist – he had left as a schoolboy – was a bitter disappointment. He had looked forward at least to finding again community friendship and opportunities through CAM: 'I thought that when we came back here, we'd be in touch with each other and we'd have the sort of thing that we used to do in England, like meet at certain times, and share ideas, and so forth. But everything died.' He blamed Brathwaite. But Brathwaite had decided, after the 'fiasco' of the exploratory meeting, that CAM could not exist among what seemed the potential membership: 'I realised that it would ruin the whole spirit of CAM . . . if I attempted to work under those conditions. So I allowed that thing to fizzle out. We had no more meetings.'

CAM/New World seminars

Since her return in April, Marina Maxwell had been eager for the Brathwaites' arrival and for the chance to work with them as CAM in Jamaica. Writing to Brathwaite in mid-1968, she said that the New World Group had proposed a seminar on the arts, and asked her to plan it. New World, founded by Lloyd Best, a Trinidadian economist, in Georgetown, Guyana, in 1963, moved with him and grew when he was a Research Fellow of the Institute of Social and Economic Research at Mona from 1964-68. New World was, like CAM, pan-Caribbean in its membership and concerns. Its members included many of the brightest young intellectuals of the region, several of whom also belonged to CAM. It was concerned with radical change in Caribbean society. But it was different from CAM in significant ways. New World had been founded, and operated, within the Caribbean alone; its members were mainly economists and political or social scientists; its aims were clearly defined and the change for which it worked was specific:

> New World is a movement which aims to transform the mode of living and thinking in the region. The movement rejects uncritical acceptance of dogmas and ideologies imported from outside and bases its ideas for the future of the area on an unfettered analysis of the experience and existing conditions of the region.[8]

Maxwell was, she wrote, counting on the Brathwaites' help and saw such collaboration with New World as an opening for CAM in Jamaica:

> Need help, need you, need CAM: it's a jump-off point for CAM here. These cats are *waiting* for it. They *know* they need it, I feel, and are beginning to bend a bit. Even Rex [Nettleford] feels the pressure. . . . It's the time for the *surrealist point* to be fought and start a beginning.[9]

She asked for the CAM membership list, so that she could make links between CAM and the New World Group: 'It's a place to start with, I think, and garbly and academic as they often are, several New World people like G Beck [George Beckford] and Norman [Girvan] are very sound.' She wanted to know exactly when the Brathwaites would reach Jamaica, and to make CAM plans for the end of September or early October. Would Brathwaite read *Masks*, and give papers he had given to CAM in London to the seminar? Maxwell stressed that Brathwaite's ideas and leadership were needed: 'Tell me soon, what else? We have a platform coming. Direct its direction, Eddie. You know what's up and exploding. Drum Time!'

What resulted was a series of seminars with the general title of 'The Arts in the Caribbean Today', on seven successive Sunday mornings, from 16 March to 27 April 1969, in a lecture room at UWI, Mona. The series was advertised as presented by the Caribbean Artists Movement in association with the New World Group of Jamaica, and organised by Dr L Edward Brathwaite.

Marina Maxwell herself spoke at the first seminar on 'Towards a Revolution in the Arts'. She opened with a quotation from Derek Walcott: 'Our origins are subdued in the blood – it is for our poets to provoke them to speak.' The revolution in the arts which she advocated lay in the articulation of origins: 'a persistent "surrealist" drumbeat', 'our African identity' and 'our consciousness of being a vital part of the Third World'.[10] These new forces, or 'lines of blood' were, she claimed, calling for the restructuring of the arts of the Caribbean. The 'unconscious artist' was pointing the way forward, in 'reggae, in pan, in his own tongues – and the rhythmic possession of and by the drum is at the centre'. In contrast, the 'conscious artists' were lagging behind, 'enmeshed in their neo-colonialisms', not listening to, often rejecting, the drum.

Maxwell cited and applauded Edward Brathwaite as an artist who was 'coming home', not only literally but psychologically, quoting from 'Jazz and the West Indian Novel' where he had advocated the search for an authentic West Indian aesthetic and had posed 'the folk' as its basis. Maxwell quoted Elsa Goveia's key passage at CAM's First Conference on the need for West Indian artists to choose their alignment, as she had earlier to CAM in London, but now adding her own equation of the masses with 'the power of the drum', and Brathwaite's alternative tradition with 'the beat, the drum'. Such revolutionary art forms could, she suggested, take root and grow on the UWI campus, but they could do so more importantly off campus. This prompted her to define her use of the terms 'conscious' and 'unconscious' artist, and to accept that they should be reversed. For it is, she explained, in 'our more formal, conscious artists, in particular our published writers [that] this surrealist, synthesising, belly-centred, African identification theme' emerges. Again, she cited Brathwaite: 'Certainly in the fantastic work of Edward Brathwaite who I think today is the central drum sounding the way home among our literary figures' and his trilogy, 'the watershed in our literature [which] poses the synthesis, the alternative tradition.' Lindsay Barrett's *Song for Mumu* seemed to her 'very central' and an example of what she calls the 'surrealist' prose/verse style; the work of Wilson Harris and George Lamming likewise seemed to confirm the emergence of an alternative tradition in fiction. She applauded Edward Baugh's recent review of Barrett's fiction, but claimed that, with very few exceptions, the 'emerging arts' of the Caribbean had no critics at all; that they were 'blinkered by their European orientation and education and are not concerned with listening to the drum', and that they needed to 'enter the *hounfor*' – the holy place in a *vodoun* ceremony.

To Maxwell, the special excitement about this new time of potential revolution in the arts was its quality of 'surrealism', exemplified in carnival. She challenged 'middle-class artists' to stop 'pleasing the European-oriented artists with well-modulated verse and slick theatre, and address themselves to experiment with their own thing, unafraid to fail'. She pressed carnival as 'one of the main sources for the creation of our own conventions in theatre', and as having a serious effect on 'our conscious productions in drama, music and the visual arts'. Her central argument was: 'Emergent too in the West Indies is our own thing – and we have to ground together to attend at the growing, since it was long born before this generation.' In proposing a revolution in the arts, the search for an alternative tradition which builds a 'national and regional culture', they were 'stating, echoing, reflecting and shaping the revolutionary situation in our Caribbean societies'. Using frequent quotations from Frantz Fanon, Maxwell urged the movement from protest literature towards a national culture. As examples of 'cultural guerillas' she cited the Rastas, Derek Walcott, Stanley French, Trevor Rhone, Jerry Small, Eugene McNair. As examples of publications which should be read, she named *Bongo Man*, *Moko*, *Abeng*, *African Youth Move*, referring to the men writing in them as 'political playwrights and poets . . . beginning to write like this because they are more or less involved and committed to their societies'.

Earlier, Maxwell had stated that what was happening in the British West Indies had already happened in Latin America. Now, drawing to a conclusion, she stressed the similarities between the two regions and urged: 'We can draw from this whole store of cultural elements and patterns towards a regional synthesis, a Caribbean culture.' These similarities were more apparent in Trinidad, and she stressed the significance of steelband and, again, of carnival.

Maxwell spoke of her own work as an example of the new revolutionary Caribbean arts which she advocated. Yard Theatre, her experiment in theatre, drew on the tradition of the Little Carib in Trinidad, started by Beryl McBurnie in the 1940s. *Play Mas*, her play based on the Dimanche Gras show was, she said, 'an attempt and an experiment to use carnival as a vehicle for political documentary theatre'; it was written for 'fluid production', but could be performed in a conventional theatre (see Chapter 9). She closed by reading 'The Making of the Drum' from Brathwaite's *Masks*.

Maxwell's central theme – the need for a revolution in the arts based on the indigenous Caribbean folk traditions – opens out to advocate a national, then a regional, culture, then a protest and political culture. She may seem over-insistent on the centrality to Caribbean culture of the drum and of African tradition generally, and her praise for Brathwaite as the exemplary Caribbean writer may seem over-lavish. The paper is of particular value, in the Jamaican context, for its affirmation of Trinidad's lively popular culture and closeness to Latin America. Above all, it is valuable as the firsthand account by an active, innovative creative Caribbean woman of a new sort of drama and a new experiment in theatre. 'Towards a Revolution in the Arts' was considered of sufficient interest and importance to be published as Newsletter Number

One of CAM (Jamaica), in No 10 of the CAM (London) *Newsletter*, April-June 1969, and in *Savacou* 2, September 1970.

Other sessions in this well-attended and highly successful series focused on West Indian theatre, dance, poetry, the novel, the mass media and the arts in the French and Spanish-speaking Caribbean. Brathwaite wrote with delight to Salkey on the afternoon of the second session, on theatre, seeing CAM at work in it:

> Plenty good talk, plenty passion: Lloyd Reckord, Barry ditto, Gordon Rohlehr (over for a week), Trevor Rhone of the Barn, Sheila Hill (Jamaica Playhouse – they chew she up, man) and Stanley French an' Marina. . . . I decide to use CAM for the time being as an invisible divine spark. We going help, encourage and co-operate wid existin' groups as much as we can. In this way, I think we goin' avoid the faction lark and still spread de INFLUENCE.[11]

A Jamaica National Dance Theatre Company 1968 production, 'The King Must Die', Rex Nettleford (bottom right)

The session on dance took place on 18 May, a brilliant lecture-demonstration by Rex Nettleford and members of the Jamaica National Dance Theatre Company, followed by discussion. Brathwaite wrote to Nettleford afterwards:

> Every word that was spoken on Sunday came with love and with a real concern for dialogue of understanding. In face of the present evident failure of our playwrights to catch our dreams within a network of communal experience, the burden of your dancers and the movements that they make will be, for many of us, more grave, more heavy, than they think they ought to be bear or have to make.[12]

Hugh Morrison, of UWI's Radio Unit, taped all the sessions. W Beckles, Acting Resident Extra Mural Tutor in Barbados, planned to edit them for broadcasting.

Yard Theatre

Marina Maxwell had started to put some of her theatre ideas into practice a month before she gave her paper, ideas which were a natural progression from the challenge she had posed in her letter before CAM's First Conference and expressed at CAM's symposium on West Indian Theatre in November 1967. In Maxwell's own words:

> Yard Theatre is an attempt to place West Indian theatre in the life of the people, where the people live, in the yards. It is the bringing together of the conscious and unconscious or trained and untrained artists to attempt to synthesise actively in the performing arts. Perhaps through this experiment we might produce material that is closer to a West Indian audience than what exists now.[13]

One Saturday evening, in early February, the first Yard Theatre production took place, and was described thus, soon afterwards, by a member of the audience:

> A group of men and women from all walks of life – Rastas, semi-academics and academics – gathered together in a cool yard in the shadow of Long Mountain. The atmosphere was gay, informal, excited – for this shadowy place with its flickering candles ranged along the low fence, with its assortment of women in long skirts and African wraps, and men in ties, togas and dashikis – this was the setting where a new theatrical idea found its first expression. Through the doorway, a woman appeared, bearing a hosea drum (Indian) on which was set a lighted candle, shrouded by masses of beads. This advent of the drum was the symbolic way of saying that those present were united by a common spirit, and were concerned to bring to consciousness and share among them, the basic throbbing realities of their present social situation.[14]

Marina Maxwell performing a Xhosa love-song

The simple typed notice for each session was headed, 'Let us ground together at Yard Theatre'. On Saturday 12 April 1969, at 9.00pm, one took place at 12 Princess Alice Drive (Maxwell's home), with 'readings, poetry, drums'. The occasion was 'to remember a brother, Denis Sloley', the radical lawyer; also 'remembering the deaths of other conscious brothers – Che, Marcus Garvey, Fanon, Malcolm X, those who fell in the struggle in the USA, in Vietnam, in Africa, across the Third World'.[15] On Saturday 31 May, at 9.00pm, Yard Theatre was at the home of Mortimo Planno – 'Rasta leader, poet, actor and philosopher'[16] – HIM Haile Selassie, Local 37 EWF Inc, 5 1/2 Brook Street H/Q, off Salt Lane, parallel to the Spanish Town Road, for 'drums, chanting, reggae, poetry, singing, readings'.[17]

In Brathwaite's view the significance of Yard Theatre at the time was considerable: total performance, literally in a yard, geared towards the oral tradition. It was, he reckons, 'the first movement that occurs in Jamaica where experimental theatre becomes possible, and nation language is used, and a combination of music, mime, dance and speech, even masking'. With scripts by Barry Reckord and Trevor Rhone, Maxwell and Brathwaite, 'This becomes a catalyst for what's going to happen in Jamaica. . . . A lot of people who have subsequently become other things were there at the seed-bed of Yard Theatre.' Brathwaite's accounts of Yard Theatre generally and of a particular production such as Marina Maxwell's *Consciousness 1*, are the fullest on record.[18] Otherwise the experiment is, Brathwaite notes, curiously omitted from surveys of drama and dance in Jamaica: 'It doesn't seem to be wellknown. It was a kind of submerged movement.' To Brathwaite as to Maxwell Yard Theatre was a way of 'carrying on the spirit of CAM in another context, adapted to the needs of that context'.

Early 'Savacou'

Brathwaite had been mandated by CAM (UK) not only to try to form CAM in Jamaica, but also to start its long-hoped-for journal. Meanwhile Kenneth Ramchand, newly arrived at the English Department, had begun to formulate his own ideas. Ramchand approached Brathwaite and suggested that they jointly attempt a journal. Ramchand recalls: 'We decided that we would turn it into a magazine that would be the voice of the Caribbean Artists Movement.' According to Brathwaite, and consistent with CAM history: 'He (Ramchand) said he would like to start a magazine, and could I come in? So I said I was starting a magazine anyway, and I wanted it to be a Caribbean Artists Movement magazine. So we agreed to join forces.' Their experience of CAM in Britain had been widely different. Ramchand, in Edinburgh, occasional speaker and correspondent; Brathwaite, in London, founder-member and secretary. Their different views of the new journal's relationship to CAM – for Ramchand, now and in the future, for Brathwaite, integral, building on the past and present – caused problems between them as joint editors from the start, and led eventually to Brathwaite effectively becoming sole editor.

When *Savacou* was being planned, *New World Quarterly*, the journal of the New World Group, had appeared regularly since 1963; it has been described as 'a sophisticated but thoroughly indigenous journal which would contain some of the finest writing on the West Indies during the middle and latter 1960s'.[19] *New*

Ronald Moody's 'Savacou', exhibited outside the Commonwealth Institute before dispatch to its home at UWI in Jamaica

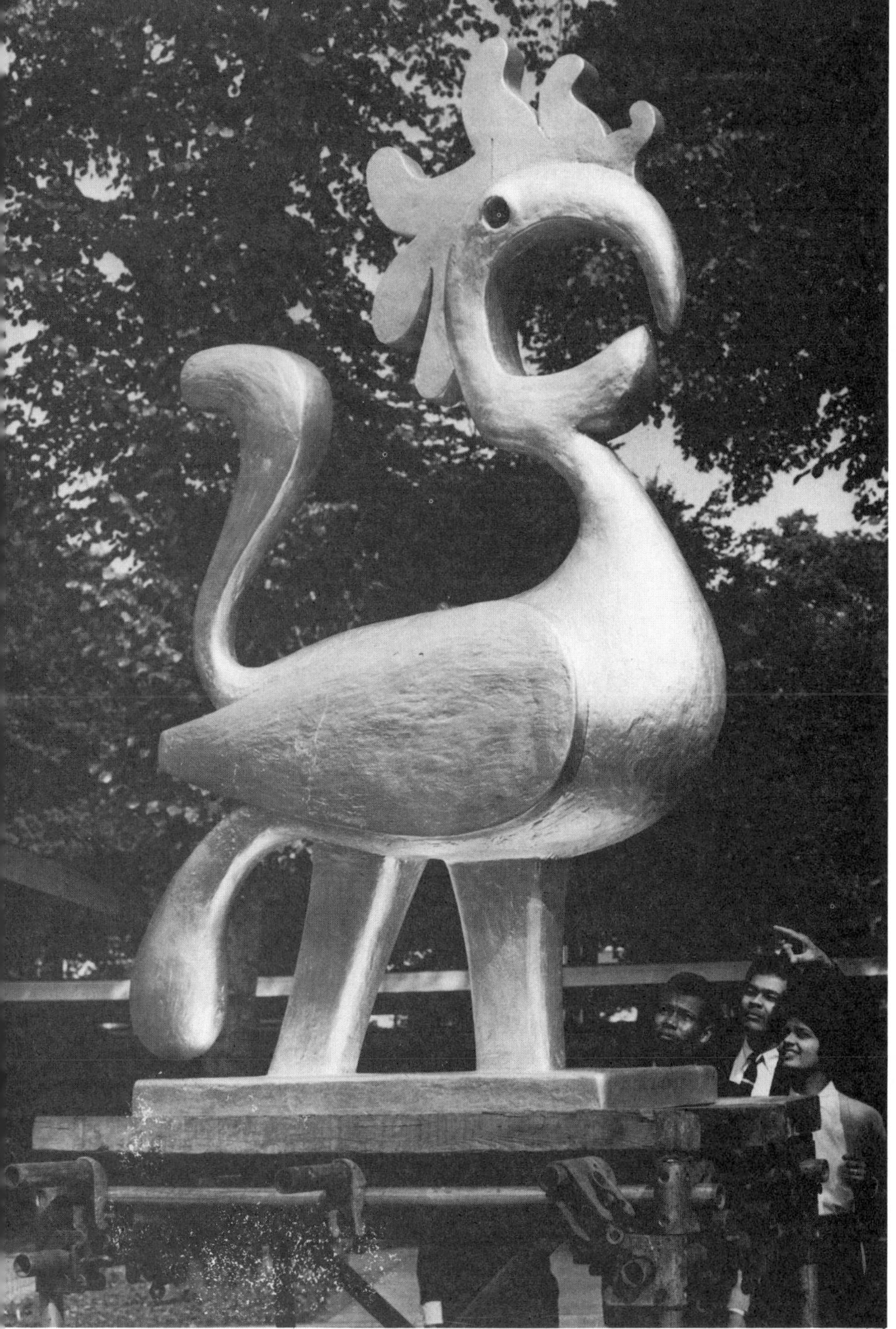

World Quarterly reflected the group's emphasis and perspective: the principal content and editorial comment was economic, political and sociological; the direction was overtly radical. It attempted to bridge academic and popular thought and writing. Its literary content, though regular, seemed secondary, not integrated. *Savacou* might have expected to appear alongside *New World Quarterly*, filling a different space, working for change at another level. In fact *New World Quarterly* ceased to appear after 1968, because of the earlier move to Trinidad of Lloyd Best, its founder, and of a split within the remaining group in Jamaica.

In May 1969, a typed 'Preliminary Brochure, Limited Circulation' announcing *Savacou* was issued, with L Edward Brathwaite and Kenneth Ramchand named as General Editors. They decided rightaway on 'Savacou' as the journal's name. Ronald Moody had told Brathwaite in London about his sculpture of this Carib bird placed outside the Epidemiological Research Unit on the Mona campus. Brathwaite immediately sent six copies of the *Savacou* brochure to Andrew Salkey; he at any rate was concerned to keep *Savacou* close to CAM (London).

> As you see, it's down as edited by me and Ken. This should be extended to include you or John or Donald [Hinds] in London, and an editorial board should also be announced. This present thing was drafted and issued by Ken before I could have a good think about it. I'm also suggesting, since the present format seems more academic than CAM, that there should be alternate academic/creative issues. And since I *hope* to be in London in July, we could all discuss the whole thing properly then.[20]

The printed brochure which followed shows the CAM modifications. The line drawing of the Savacou bird is now signed 'MOODY'; Andrew Salkey's name is added as a General Editor, between the other two; an Editorial Board is announced, with a broad spread of discipline and location: 'Lloyd King and Gordon Rohlehr (Port of Spain); Orlando Patterson and Sylvia Wynter (Kingston); René Piquion (Port-au-Prince); Bobby Moore (Georgetown); John La Rose (London); Hollis Lynch and Paule Marshall (New York); and Cliff Lashley (London, Ontario).'[21] The preliminary 'General Aims' are reduced from six to three, but preceded by a by-line and a purpose: 'SAVACOU is a Journal of the CARIBBEAN ARTISTS MOVEMENT. Its purpose is to bring together the work of creative writers, academics and theoretical thinkers and to provide a forum for artistic expression and thought in the Caribbean today.' Dropped, or subsumed and restated are:

> To describe, comment critically on, and theorise about the Arts in the Caribbean area today; to survey, comment critically on and

> theorise about Caribbean society/societies today; to revalue and reinterpret earlier stages in the evolution of Creole society . . .; to explore and discuss possible influence between the Arts and Society in the Caribbean; through these activities, to help to create an informed and thoughtful public; to contribute to the further development of the Arts; and to suggest orientations for our society and its institutions.

Instead, the General Aims become:

> 1 To present the work of creative writers – established, unknown, in exile or at home.
> 2 To examine and assess the significance of artistic expression through slavery and in the late nineteenth and early twentieth centuries with a view to recognising continuities and submerged or 'lost' traditions.
> 3 To help towards the recognition of the whole Caribbean area as a meaningful historical and cultural entity.

In the concise reworking, almost all references to art and society are omitted; theory and theoretical writing is likewise played down. But creative writing is given greater emphasis, not only by being included in the General Aims, but also by its prominence in the contents of the revised cycle of issues. Initially, three issues a year were proposed, of which one section was to be 'reserved for the publication of creative work by West Indians'; these become four, and the following cycle is promised:

> The fourth issue each year will be devoted to the publication of creative work and artistic criticism. The other issues will concentrate on conceptual ideas, exploring the relationship between the arts, thought and society. Each of these issues will be concerned with a specific topic, the contributions being drawn from various disciplines.

The new journal's distinct differences from *New World Quarterly*, and the hand of CAM, have become more apparent.

The *Savacou* brochure, in its final printed form, continued to promise practical features which, even at the time, must have seemed over-ambitious. In addition to four issues a year, 'a comprehensive listing of current publications by West Indians in each issue' and '*Savacou* will pay for all contributions published.' The magazine never came out four or even three times a year. It appeared twice in 1970 and 1971, and once each year until the end of the decade, except for 1976 and 1978. The promised 'comprehensive listing' never appeared; it had only just been possible in the CAM *Newsletter*, compiled in London. The magazine had some financial backing at the start. Individuals promised 'personal donations or shareholdings'.[22] Elsa Goveia contributed a large sum which set up the journal. Early issues carried a number of advertisements. But, although subscription rates were low, it had to be marketed widely. Unlike *New World* and indeed CAM's *Newsletter*, *Savacou* had no built-in membership subscriptions. Contributors were never paid.

Savacou's first two issues, published in June and September 1970, set the style and format which continued through the decade. They were edited, printed and bound to a high standard, and were more like a book than a journal. They carried a striking cover design by Pat Bishop, a Trinidadian postgraduate student, and a line drawing of Ronald Moody's Savacou bird on the title page. In content they followed the promised cycle and approach, and drew on the academic disciplines of the journal's joint editors. *Savacou 1*, on the specific topic of slavery, is introduced by Elsa Goveia, who places the multi-disciplinary contributions of the issue into the then current debate on the nature of West Indian slave society, in its wider sense. Alongside results of recent research into 'Akan slave rebellions in the West Indies' (Monica Schuler) and 'Francis Williams – Free negro in a slave world' (Locksley Lindo), there are review articles on Alejo Carpentier's *El Reino de este Mundo* (*The Kingdom Of This World*) (James Irish) and CLR James's *Black Jacobins* (Archie Singham), discussing the two books in relation to the slave society of Haiti and the slave revolution in San Domingo; and articles on the language and literature of slave society – by Ramchand and Brathwaite. Letters from Brathwaite to Schuler about her article, early in 1970, show how scrupulous the editors, and Elsa Goveia, were over the preparation of the issue. It was a thoroughbred academic journal, UWI-based, but with inter-disciplinary approaches.

Savacou ***logo. Moody himself held that, in Carib mythology, Savacou was the bird-god with control over thunder and strong winds who later became a star.***

Savacou 2, in contrast, was an all-CAM issue. It included papers from CAM's First Conference – Aubrey Williams, CLR James, Michael Anthony and Louis James; from early CAM meetings – Gordon Rohlehr; and Marina Maxwell's CAM/New World seminar paper. But it also included 1970 work: an introduction by Kenneth Ramchand to the writing of Eric Walrond; 'Timehri' by Edward Brathwaite, which had grown out of his talk when opening the Aubrey Williams exhibition in Kingston in March 1970; 'Meanings' by Derek Walcott, from the programme notes of the first US production of his play, *Dream On Monkey Mountain*, a few months earlier. Like the contributions of Michael Anthony and CLR James, these by Brathwaite and Walcott are classic autobiographical pieces.

Andrew Salkey's name appeared alongside those of Brathwaite and Ramchand as one of the editors on *Savacou* 1 and 2. The 'Editorial Board', promised on the printed brochure, became an Advisory Committee, to which were added, for Number 1: Wilfred Cartey (literary critic), Faye Durrant (librarian), Elsa

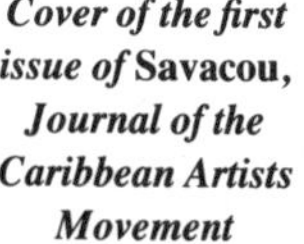
Cover of the first issue of **Savacou**, *Journal of the Caribbean Artists Movement*

Goveia, Oliver Clarke, Aubrey Williams, Marina Maxwell; Lloyd King was dropped. For Number 2, Arthur Drayton and JG Irish were added. There is no evidence of Salkey playing more than a nominal, supportive role as co-editor, as necessitated by distance, nor indeed of the role of the Advisory Committee. For the early issues at least, it was effectively Brathwaite's and Ramchand's journal.

Other CAM-based work

In addition to his work on *Savacou*, Kenneth Ramchand was attempting far-reaching changes in the Department of English, which were influenced by his connections with CAM in Britain. He recalls:

> From the start I went in there in a contentious way, because I knew there was a lot of work to be done to change the structure of the English degree. . . . Armed with my CAM experience, when I came to Jamaica I carried out quite a radical job, transforming the syllabus in English of the UWI.

He also involved himself in departmental politics. He recalls labelling his door, 'Kenneth Ramchand, lecturer in Literature in English', and urging fellow West Indians in the department to apply for the vacant professorship in English, and not accept expatriate English staff as the only choice. For the Department of English, in contrast to that of History, was in the late 1960s still dominated by English expatriates, and the degree syllabus was still wholly concerned with English literature.

In mid-1967, Ngũgĩ Wa Thiong'o had returned to Kenya as a lecturer in the English Department of the University of Nairobi, also influenced by his contact with early CAM. He was soon leading a revolt against the situation there which was similar to that in Jamaica. In October 1968 he and two colleagues – Henry Owuor-Anyumba and Taban Lo Liyong – called for the abolition of the English Department and for a Department of African

Literature and Languages to be set up in its place. Thanks partly to the collaboration of Andrew Gurr, an English colleague, this resulted in the establishment of the Departments of Literature and of Languages, with the emphasis in the Literature Department on modern African, Caribbean and black American literature.[23]

The less sharply-defined colonial situation in the Caribbean seemed not to require such drastic change. Certainly Ramchand claims to have had neither West Indian nor expatriate colleagues who were prepared to join in fighting for such change at UWI in Jamaica. The publication of Ramchand's book, *The West Indian Novel and Its Background* (1970), based on his University of Edinburgh doctoral thesis, greatly consolidated and strengthened his standing, and contributed to a change of syllabus, if not of name, in the Department of English. As the first sustained piece of critical writing on West Indian literature by a West Indian, it provided a historical survey of prose fiction in its social and cultural context. As such, it was unable, Ramchand explained, to deal in depth with all the writers whose work was mentioned and which constituted 'enough relevant and interesting material to justify the establishment of a School of Caribbean Studies at UWI'.[24] Such a school, by 1969, may have seemed a more viable alternative than a Caribbean-focused Department of Literature.

Don Wilson, in the Department of Education, was meanwhile working towards changing the literature syllabus in schools in Jamaica. The 'O' level literature paper was still handled by Cambridge and its set texts taken from English literature. But as part of a Caribbean-wide expansion in secondary education, Jamaica opened, in the late sixties, its Junior Secondary Schools, whereby children without the academic qualifications to progress from primary to high school were able to move on to a specially designed new post-primary three-year curriculum. Wilson recalls how, with a personal interest in literature and fresh from the CAM experience he,

> used to have reading groups of poetry with students. . . . And we decided, the Dip Ed [Diploma of Education] clan of one of the years, to put together an anthology for their own use. When we were half-way through, the Ministry of Education in Jamaica needed a book almost rightaway for use in the new secondary schools. The Ministry was interested in seeing what we had done, we showed it to them, and they said, if we could get it published, they would use it. I spoke to Eddie and Ramchand about it, and they were the first publishers of it.

New Ships, edited by DG Wilson, with a foreward by Edward Baugh, Head of the UWI Mona English Department, was published as the first Savacou book, in 1971. It was bought in bulk by the Ministry of Education and widely distributed in Jamaican schools: in Grades 7–9 of All-Age Schools, and in Forms 1–3 of the new Junior Secondary Schools. Its selection broke new ground, particularly in form and language, by including for study in schools several poems by Louise Bennett and Edward Brathwaite, written in what was then still called 'dialect'. Such choices had been seeded through CAM in early 1967 when Wilson attended Brathwaite's public reading, and took part in the debate following Gordon Rohlehr's talk on calypso.

Brathwaite was himself closely involved in producing textbooks for the new Junior Secondary curriculum, in history. As Series Editor for Longman's three-book course, *The People Who Came*, he helped to structure the content, and contributed substantial and creative editing. Book One (1968), by Alma Norman, was a breakthrough in West Indian school history textbooks. Two-thirds of the book give detailed coverage of the early inhabitants of the Americas, with full chapters on the Maya, Aztec and Inca civilisations of mainland Central and South America, as well as on the Arawaks and Caribs of the West Indian islands; the remaining chapters describe the civilisations of the Africans, East Indians, Chinese and Europeans in their home lands, thus mirroring CAM's broad regional awareness and concern for the rehabilitation of its contributing peoples' cultures. Book 2 (1970), by James Carnegie and Patricia Patterson, opens at the point where traditional West Indian texts begin, with 'discovery' by Europeans; Book 3 (1972), by Edward Brathwaite and Anthony Phillips, opens with the American War of Independence. All three books give regional coverage and emphasis on social and cultural change. Patricia Patterson, Anthony Phillips and Anne Walmsley – the Longmans editor – had all attended CAM's First Conference and worked closely with Brathwaite in carrying out his concept of the series. Brathwaite's keen interest in such work is expressed in his article, 'Writing for Young West Indians – history, geography and slavery', in *Torch*, the Jamaican Ministry of Education journal.

Fellow CAM members, also back in Jamaica, were meanwhile producing material with African or black content which nourished the new mood of black consciousness and pride in Jamaica's African heritage. Lucille Mathurin Mair hosted an 'Africa Night' at Mary Seacole Hall in November 1968. She remembers it as 'a programme of readings, music and drama which was put on by a group of activist staff and students, including Brathwaite, in the aftermath of the traumatic Rodney Affair'. Brathwaite commented later: 'This was the first time that our students had been exposed in any serious way to African art, music, dress, poetry.'[25] He recalls the effect of his reading from Okot p'Bitek's *Song of Lawino*, which, he claims, led to a growing abandonment of

***Covers of* New Ships, The People Who Came The West Indian Novel and its Background**

pressed hair. The production by Lloyd Reckord of Jean Genet's play, *The Blacks*, early in 1970, was regarded as another landmark in the process of black consciousness-making. With a cast of UWI students from a wide spread of the region, it played for almost a month to full houses and was very well reviewed.

Some of the plays which Brathwaite had created in Ghana were performed by Kingston school children in December 1969. A review in the *Jamaica Gleaner* opened thus: 'The "back to Africa" idea is one which produces a great deal of mirth, tinged with scorn, among the so-called middle class which regards it as a dream of a lunatic fringe of some members of our society.'[26] The reviewer, Colin Gregory, went on to describe how moving he found the production by St Andrews Junior School of the play, *The Children's Gifts*, in which the birth of Christ was portrayed in an African setting, and the Magi were African chiefs; how convincing he found *Odale's Choice* – the Antigone story in an African setting – performed by the children of St Peter and Paul (and produced by Betty Wilson). Both schools, as he pointed out, contained a majority of children of 'fair complexion'. Children's plays such as these had never been performed in Jamaica before.

Jamaica's National Theatre Trust had been formed by Lloyd Reckord in 1967 to attract sponsorship for theatrical productions, to make it possible, as he puts it, 'for something worthwhile to happen in the theatre in Jamaica and the Caribbean', by attracting sponsorship and avoiding total dependence on the box office. The Trust enabled a dramatised reading of *Rights of Passage*, produced by Marina Maxwell, to have a short but influential run at the commercial Barn Theatre in November 1970. Meanwhile in May 1970 Bari Jonson returned to Jamaica after 26 years in Britain, to a post as television producer with the Jamaica Broadcasting Company (JBC). He had just finished playing the lead in *Martin Luther King* at the Greenwich Theatre. When his agent heard that he was leaving he said, recalls Jonson, '"Are you mad?" But I desperately wanted to come back to work in Jamaica.' He called to see the Brathwaites only a few days after his return: 'CAM was a link. . . . And I came and found myself, and they steadied me in a way. It was very important.'

The publication at this time of Edward Brathwaite's *Folk Culture of the Slaves in Jamaica*, an expanded version of Chapter 2 of his doctoral thesis, published 'because of its popular interest',[27] provided substance and a context for the new and widespread interest in Jamaica's African heritage. His intention was not, said Brathwaite, to enter into the argument about African 'survivals' within creole society, but to show how the habits, customs and ways of life of former West African slaves, adapted to their Caribbean environment, constituted a 'folk' culture. This folk culture had been increasingly asserted in Jamaica since Independence in 1962, and was now studied by intellectuals and made use of by writers and artists. As in his talk to CAM in December 1967, Brathwaite refers to the theory of a Great Tradition and Little Tradition, and their interdependence in West Indian society.

Brathwaite's affirmation of the Caribbean's Africa-based, creolised folk culture had been most far-reaching since the publication, in 1969, of *Islands*, the third part of his trilogy. From its *vévé* symbol, used in the Haitian *vodoun* ceremony, on the dust-jacket, and the author's note on 'certain Afro-Caribbean religious references which may not be familiar to the reader',[28] to the titles of individual sections based on such religious ceremonies, an African Great Tradition is demonstrated as central to a new Caribbean consciousness. The poem equally articulates and celebrates the creolised, island forms of this tradition, from 'Rites' – a cricket match, to 'Jou'vert' – the start of carnival:

hearts
no longer bound
to black and bitter
ashes in the ground
now waking
making
making
with their
rhythms some-
thing torn
and new [29]

Covers of **Islands, Folk Culture of the Slaves in Jamaica** *and* **Notes to Masks**

Islands is the 'homecoming' of Brathwaite's trilogy. Published just as he had, in reality, returned home, it confirmed his standing as a major Caribbean poet.

The work by Brathwaite and others to rehabilitate Africa in the Jamaican consciousness at this time was much assisted by the return to Mona, in September 1970, of Maureen Warner (now Warner Lewis), directly after two years' teaching in Nigeria. Warner, a Trinidadian, had been a postgraduate student at York from 1966 to 1968, when she became a member of CAM and a friend of the Brathwaites. Thanks to her doctoral research into Yoruba language survivals in Trinidad, followed by firsthand experience of Yoruba culture in Nigeria, she became an active and valuable member of the African Studies Association of the West Indies (ASAWI), founded at Mona in 1966 for furthering the study and knowledge of African history and culture in the West Indies. Warner became editor of its *Bulletin* in 1971. Her collaboration with Brathwaite was highly creative, particularly in their research on kumina religious practice in Jamaica. Her interest in his poetry and its connection with his African experience, together with encouragement from Gordon Rohlehr, led first to an article, 'Odȯmankoma Kyerema Se',[30] and then to her *Notes on Masks* (1977), an excellent introduction to and commentary on the second poem of Brathwaite's trilogy.

The context for CAM: around the Caribbean

CAM activity by individual members flourished. But attempts by Brathwaite to form CAM branches in other Caribbean countries were no more successful than in Jamaica, for similar reasons. In St Vincent he spoke to a group called NAM, which was, he judged, already doing something similar. In Barbados, he remembers starting a group under John Wickham. Wickham had returned home to Barbados in 1967, after 20 years in Port of Spain, London and Geneva. Although by profession a meteorologist, he had been continuously involved in literature as a writer and editor, and belonged to literary groups during his stay in Trinidad. He was one of *Bim*'s most regular contributors; he joined its editorial staff in 1970, having meanwhile become a full-time journalist, as literary editor of the *Nation*. He had already heard a little about CAM from Frank Collymore, and had read the accounts by Anne Walmsley of the First and Second Conferences in *Bim*. He recalls how 'we had a meeting and he [Brathwaite] was really preaching the gospel of CAM'. Yet Wickham also recalls his main impression that CAM in London had a practical, commercial purpose, and that in Barbados it would have to have one too – apparently reflecting how he himself saw a purpose for CAM there. Jill Sheppard and Anthony Phillips had both attended the First Conference and were now working in Barbados. Sheppard, running the Centre for Multi-Racial Studies, Cave Hill, also remembers 'a meeting, supposedly a first meeting of CAM, at the Pelican, with a number of people present'. Then she was away for a while, and found when she got back that 'it didn't exist any more'. Phillips, teaching at the Department of History, UWI, Cave Hill, remembers Brathwaite addressing the meeting, but no more. With Brathwaite only a bird of passage in his own home island, no strong CAM members there, and no shared perception of the need for such a movement, nothing developed.

Trinidad, in April 1968, had seemed to the newly-arrived Gordon Rohlehr as a fertile ground for CAM. He wrote to Brathwaite:

> I'm sure they would like to have anything you do, and maybe roots can be spread in Trinidad where everybody is culture-conscious now that culture has become a political issue. I've only arrived two weeks ago. The English Department here is inefficiently run and generally vague, and my workload is terrific; hence I haven't thought of doing anything. I know one or two people though who

> will be interested, and have no doubt that there is a sort of CAM going in Trinidad already, though not organised on the scale of you cats in London. When I get myself organised, I'll see what can be done.[31]

But Rohlehr soon found that the existing groups and the increasing politicisation of culture allowed little space for CAM. He recalls the main such groups:

> There was the New World movement, and there were a number of young students, some of them not yet at university, who were interested but who were not being given much of a say. They were also more interested in poetry and things like that, and they formed themselves into a group called Unit 16, people like Roger McTair and Victor Questel, which began as a breakaway group from New World: Dave Darbeau was part of that too. Some people were later to become, like Dave Murray, very prominent in the NJAC [National Joint Action Committee]. And after a meeting or two of Unit 16, called that because 16 people attended the first meeting, they changed their name to Pivot, and brought out newsletters which were . . . partly lectures, articles, things which had been done. And I was part of Unit 16, I had spoken to the group, I participated in what they were doing. They held poetry readings and things like that. . . . Some people like Clifford Sealey, who had brought out *Voices* in the period immediately before that, became associated with Pivot, and Eric Roach. Pivot became really what its name suggested: something around which some of the older literary figures gathered. . . . So that we did have something which was beginning to resemble CAM. It unfortunately did not survive the politicising of just about everything in 1970: which ironically is also what was happening to CAM.

Richard Small, introducing Walter Rodney's 1968 speeches, in *The Groundings with my Brothers*, describes the spread throughout the region of 'the slogans, and the thinking accompanying it, of Black Power' and how, by 1969, 'in Trinidad out-of-work "educated" and "uneducated" youth were a part of this ferment. Independently of student activity the young power movement was launched, and now sections of the St Augustine campus are busily engaged in the social issues of Trinidad and West Indian society'.[32] When, in late February 1970, the youth ferment in Trinidad exploded, Unit 16 and other such activities, says Rohlehr, 'did not survive . . . [it was] the death of a lot of such things'.

Guyana 1970

Meanwhile in early February 1970, in Georgetown, Guyana, a number of CAM members found themselves together again: Edward Kamau and Doris Brathwaite, Ken Corsbie, Wilson Harris, John La Rose, Andrew Salkey, Ronald Savory, Sam Selvon, Ivan Van Sertima, Aubrey Williams. The People's

National Congress (PNC) government, under Forbes Burnham, had invited leading Caribbean writers and artists from other parts of the region, from Britain, Canada and the USA, to share in the Republic celebrations, and to participate in a Caribbean Writers and Artists Convention.

The convention was intended to follow on from a one-day Caribbean Writers and Artists Conference, held as part of the Independence celebrations in May 1966. Burnham had then invited 'a number of outstanding Caribbean personalities', and, opening the conference, had 'pledged his word that his government would do its utmost to create the atmosphere which would encourage artists to cease being émigrés and having to go to London for recognition'.[33] The émigrés invited had included ER Braithwaite, Jan Carew, Wilson Harris (though he did not take part), George Lamming, Sam Selvon, Aubrey Williams. An impromptu exhibition of Guyanese art was mounted by Donald Locke at Queen's College, where the conference was held. Writing about the exhibition in the *Guyana Graphic* CLR James pointed out, probably for the first time, connections between the paintings of Aubrey Williams and the fiction of Wilson Harris.[34] But a sense of continuity between the 1966 conference and the 1970 convention was stronger within Guyana itself than in its visitors. CLR James and George Lamming were absent in 1970. Brathwaite, La Rose and Salkey were not invited in 1966.

The ten-day programme for writers and artists in 1970 included educational and cultural events: the opening of the new campus of the University of Guyana at Turkeyn, visits and talks to schools; book and art exhibitions; performances of a historical review, *My Name Is Slave*, assembled by Ken Corsbie, and a choral work, *The Legend of Kaieteur*, with words by AJ Seymour and music by Philip Pilgrim. It also included the annual Edgar Mittelholzer Lectures, in their third year, given by Wilson Harris. *Ascent to Omai* (1970), Harris's ninth novel, was about to be published. His three lectures, on *History, Fable and Myth in the Caribbean and Guianas*, continued to explore and develop ideas which he had put forward at the Second CAM Conference, at the time when his last novel, *Tumatumari*, was published. In these Edgar Mittelholzer lectures he used recent work by Edward Brathwaite and Aubrey Williams – CAM founder-members – to illustrate and exemplify his beliefs. A number of CAM members were in the audience. The lectures may therefore be regarded as part of CAM's continuing influence.

Harris argued in his first lecture that not only JA Froude in *The English in the West Indies, or the Bow of Ulysses* (1888) but also JJ Thomas in *Froudacity, West Indian Fables Explained* (1889) demonstrated the need for a new philosophy of history. Despite

Republic Celebrations, Georgetown, Guyana, February 1970, (l to r) Ivan Van Sertima, Lynette Dolphin, John La Rose, Milton Williams, Forbes Burnham – Prime Minister of Guyana, Donald Locke, Martin Carter, Wilson Harris

CLR James's claim that Thomas 'overwhelms the great historian',[35] Thomas and Froude were equally trapped by the 19th century view of history, since neither could 'supply a figurative meaning beyond the condition he deplored'. Both showed a common suspicion of Haitian *vodoun* and similar religious practices, and thus 'consolidated an intellectual censorship of significant vestiges of the subconscious imagination'. Harris held that 'a philosophy of history may well lie buried in the arts of the imagination', and his intention in these lectures was to concentrate on such vestiges as part of these arts.

He then explored in detail two practices stemming from African myths, which had undergone metamorphosis and become part of a native West Indian imagination: limbo and *vodoun*. Limbo was not only related to Anancy or spider fables – Harris quoted from 'Ananse' in Brathwaite's *Islands* – but also reflected 'the dislocation of a chain of miles'; limbo thus became a gateway between Africa and the Caribbean, and part of an original West Indian architecture which it was still possible to create. Haitian *vodoun* showed a more direct descent from African myth, but it too had undergone West Indian metamorphosis. In stressing the peculiarly West Indian function of *vodoun*, he suggested its potential:

> Haitian *vodoun*, like West Indian and Guianese/Brazilian limbo, may well point to sleeping possibilities of drama and horizons of poetry, epic and novel, sculpture and painting – in short to a language of variables in art which would have a profoundly evolutionary cultural and philosophical significance for Caribbean man.

Risks and caveats were involved for the historian or artist who used such resources, explored such possibilities. But, Harris believed, through the 'gamble of the soul' made by the poet or artist who enters the 'trickster gateway' of limbo, 'emerges the hope for a profoundly compassionate society committed to freedom within a creative scale'. All the variables of limbo – in community, in art – needed to be explored in the complex Caribbean situation of apparent 'historylessness'.

In his second lecture, 'The Amerindian Legacy', Harris pointed to the far greater cleavage between history and art in respect of the Amerindian in the Caribbean, than of the African – and indeed of the Indian from India, the Chinese and the Portuguese. Not only were Amerindians excluded from the Guyana census until comparatively recently, the author of a 1968 publication, *The Amerindians in St Lucia* had written of Caribs' 'cannibalism', of shamans which 'dealt with the devil', of Arawak zemis as 'small idols'.[36] As total contrast to such deprecation and marginalising of the Amerindian legacy, Harris described the 'genuine renaissance of sensibility which has erupted into the work of the gifted Guyanese-born painter, Aubrey Williams, through Amerindian symbols'. Williams was, in his view, unique amongst Caribbean painters in that he attempted to interpret the sensibility of the Amerindian with colour, and his paintings thus 'are involved in the elements as a peculiar, often fantastic scale', and Harris found in them 'a musical imitation . . . a brooding sometimes savage undercurrent of music'. In Williams's paintings,

> a translation of the blood of the past into the scale of the elements is consistent with . . . the reassembly, reconstitution of the muse. . . . In this sense I see Aubrey Williams as a painter of renaissance who has been affected in an original way by an Amerindian 'resurrection' as Edward Brathwaite, for example, has been affected in an original way by an African 'resurrection'.

In the 'rubble of the Carib past', Harris suggested, a new consciousness may be discerned at the time of the Spanish conquest in that its character of conquest was in a state of subconscious erosion. In the wake of the Spanish conquest, the Carib lot became 'something of the sleepwalker of history'; by the beginning of the 19th century Caribs were almost extinct in Guiana. As to Arawak 'zemis', Harris preferred to call them icons, as in iconic turtles, lizards, birds etc, relating their name to 'semi' meaning 'sweet, delicate', so that the resulting correspondences made for new spatial links, a subconscious landscape. Such a vision or form of reality, though occupying certain Latin American writers, was rare in the literature of the British West Indies.

In his third lecture, 'Continuity and Discontinuity', Harris discussed the work of particular West Indian writers and historians. He looked in detail at *Masks* by Edward Brathwaite, 'who possesses, I believe, the greatest potential among Caribbean poets for the revival of poetic folk drama'. Brathwaite had been affected by African images in an evolutionary way, finding an 'oral and visual coincidence in his poems' which 'addresses us through the elements in a manner consistent with West Indian folk consciousness'. Harris contrasted, briefly, recent criticism of the fiction of Michael Anthony and VS Naipaul, showing how the open state of consciousness of the one endowed the *de facto* historical situation with a figurative meaning, and in the other, encircled the imagination. Yet again he lamented the absence of a philosophy of history, in relation to the Third World generally. Such a philosophy was, he believed, essential in the Caribbean:

> In a society which has been shot through by diverse inter-racial features and inter-continental thresholds, we need a philosophy of history which is original to us and yet capable of universal applications. Caribbean man is involved in a civilisation-making process (whether he likes it or not) and until this creative authority becomes intimate to his perspectives, he will continue to find himslf embalmed in his deprivations – embalmed as a derivative tool-making, fence-making animal. As such his dialectic will remain a frozen round of protest.

CLR James and Elsa Goveia were, in his view, the only two West Indian historians to have come close to such a philosophy.

AJ Seymour, introducing the book of Wilson Harris's lectures, links them in specific ways with his series of novels, and believes that they,

> will undoubtedly influence for good the quality and direction of our national and regional intellectual development, and if one does not immediately grasp their plain sense meaning, it is because the lecturer never ceases to be a poet throughout the whole of his dialogue with the ideal reader and throughout his life's work as a committed artist.[37]

Andrew Salkey, in *Georgetown Journal*, records a post-lecture comment from one of the audience:

> Man, the man's mad or what? Why he can't jus' think ordinary thoughts 'bout people, an' put them simple an' straightforward like? What's all this thing 'bout landscape an' the Amerindian swimmin' on dry land, for Gawd's sake, man? Anybody ever swi' on dry land, as far as you know?[38]

Salkey himself writes that he found the lectures stimulating, but Harris's thesis difficult, and the language 'extremely, privately poetic. . . . One either has a vested interest in Wilson, or one doesn't. A few of us, including John La Rose, Edward Brathwaite, Kenneth Ramchand and CLR James, do, and even we find the going hard but rewarding. Not so, many of his critics and non-readers'. Wilson Harris's vision and practice was central to

CAM. But Harris had been wary of CAM's direction since the Second Conference. A question posed by Salkey, after the third lecture, and, Salkey claims, its reference to 'revolution' misunderstood, caused Harris to 'blow his top'.[39] Brathwaite remembers this as quite spectacular. 'He [Harris] attacked several people in turn, reserving his fullest thunder for Andrew. The very breath of revolution seemed to be making him angry.'[40] Harris had, Salkey was told, been under pressure from all quarters.

The visitors were required to take part in the Writers and Artists Convention, for which one day was allocated. Its main purpose was to plan the forthcoming Caribbean Festival of Arts, scheduled to take place in Georgetown in 1971. After a week of staying in Georgetown, there was widespread discontent amongst the assembled writers and artists, ranging from complaints about organisation, accommodation and transport, to the short time allocated for the actual convention. Andrew Salkey's *Georgetown Journal* also includes an account of a 'private and informal writers and artists meeting' which was called on Sunday 22 February, at four o'clock, by Doris Brathwaite, Edward Brathwaite, John La Rose and Andrew Salkey – CAM's key founder members. John La Rose was chairman. The first item of the impromptu agenda was 'Statement of intention', which was never stated, but seems to have been to discuss a strategy for the convention. The second item, 'Formation of a loose union of Caribbean writers and artists, living in the Caribbean and outside the area', was discussed at some length. Earl Lovelace proposed: 'Discussion of the way in which the Caribbean Artists Movement may be of general or specific assistance to the writers and artists in the Caribbean.' Brathwaite gave a 'close, detailed yet brief description of CAM's formation in London in 1967', ending with a proposal not – as seemed promised by the agenda – for CAM to be re-formed on a broad basis, but that 'a similar plan [as in London] might be tried out in Georgetown, linking its own type of CAM, if necessary, to CAM in Kingston and London'. This proposal for a Guyana CAM was then approved (Jan Carew), doubted (OR Dathorne), dismissed (Milton Williams), supported (Beryl McBurnie).

John La Rose, summing up, regretted the absence of Wilson Harris – he had, added Salkey, declined their invitation to attend, but wished the proposition of a Guyanese CAM the very best of luck. Afterwards, Salkey described himself 'pretty badly bruised by our meeting. . . . If CAM, which I believe in, had taken a beating . . . at the meeting . . . my own faith in the renewal of the spirit corporate in the Caribbean had also been assaulted'.[41] His account is at odds with La Rose's more positive memories when he gave a report on the meeting to CAM in London, April 1970 (see Chapter 8). The meeting seemed to confirm that CAM was born of and flourished in a particular time and place, amongst particular people, and could not necessarily be recreated. No Guyana CAM resulted from this meeting. Nothing more was heard of a re-formation of CAM in the Caribbean until Brathwaite raised it at Carifesta in Guyana in 1972, and Marina Maxwell at Carifesta in Cuba in 1979.

Trinidad 1970

The Guyana Republic celebrations and the Writers and Artists Convention were just finishing as the news broke of what came to be called the Trinidad February Revolution. Like the Rodney Affair, it was a landmark in the post-independence history of the Caribbean. It involved CAM members, especially in the Eastern Caribbean, just as had the Jamaica 1968 events. For Gordon Rohlehr, by then in Trinidad for two years, it was the climax of the politicisation of culture, and a turning point in his hopes for the Caribbean, as he was forcefully to articulate and argue the following year.

Salkey's *Georgetown Journal* entry for Friday 27 February records the report of events in Port of Spain the previous day, carried in the *Guyana Graphic*. Headed 'Trinidad students storm bank, cathedral', the report ran:

> Several placard-waving demonstrators were arrested, here, yesterday, following a clash with police when they (the demonstrators) went on a rampage of the Royal Bank of Canada's offices, tearing down decorative articles and overturning potted plants. Some 200 demonstrators, under the vigilant eyes of a mounted police escort, also stormed the Roman Catholic cathedral of the Immaculate Conception, shouting such slogans as 'God is black!' The demonstration, described as a show of solidarity in support of West Indian students charged with rioting at the Sir George Williams University in Canada, was organised by the National Joint Action Committee, here in Port of Spain. . . . The demonstration, made up largely of university students at the St Augustine campus of the University of the West Indies, earlier marched outside the offices of the Canadian and British High Commissions, but made no attempt to enter.[42]

The following day came news of the arrest of five UWI students, with four non-students, charged with disorderly behaviour in a place of worship. These events marked the start of widespread demonstrations in Trinidad led by the National Joint Action Committee (NJAC), 'a committee of about 26 groups – trade unions, students, youth groups, sporting and cultural institutions' which had been formed in March 1969 in order to mobilise dissent.[43] Its chairman was Geddes Granger (now Makandal Daaga), former president of the Students Guild at St Augustine; Dave Darbeau (now Khafra Kambon), then a third-year student and the Guild's publications officer, was also prominent in NJAC's formation. Amongst its objectives were increased employment opportunities for Trinidadians, nationalisation of the oil and sugar industries, for Black Power – primarily in terms of Trinidad's white-controlled economy.

Granger and Darbeau were amongst those arrested on 28 February, remanded to remain in custody for a week. On the day of their release Granger led an estimated 10,000 people in a demonstration march from Woodford Square to Shanty Town, which 'Granger identified as a symbol of "Government indifference" to black people'.[44] Meanwhile a Peoples Parliament under the auspices of NJAC was in continual session in Woodford Square. A week later, on 12 March, several thousand people took part in 'The Long March', 28 miles from Port of Spain to Caroni in the sugar belt, with the slogan 'Indians and Africans Unite Now'. A general strike and march on Port of Spain by sugar, oil, transport and electrical workers as well as Black Power groups was planned to take place on 21–22 April, but was aborted by the Trinidad government's declaration of a State of Emergency on 21 April and arrest of 15 Black Power leaders. A mutiny by part of the army on 21 April, which seized partial control of the Chaguaramas base, collapsed three days later. The State of Emergency was in force until November 1970.

Salkey flew back from Guyana to London on 1 March. La Rose stopped off in Trinidad, from 26 February to 3 March. He wrote to Brathwaite three months later with an account and analysis of the revolution: 'Trinidad is where the action is. One might be inclined to say, "has been".'[45] In the context of CAM, La Rose's comments on the revolution as an 'autonomous and creative' mass movement are significant. He noted how neither Lloyd Best nor James Millette, radical black academics, were active or central to it. 'Lloyd and James', wrote La Rose, 'are the victims of a world which we inherited.'

Jamaica 1970

The Brathwaites returned from Guyana to Jamaica in early March and found UWI at Mona again in crisis. On 22 February, 19 students had occupied the Creative Arts Centre. Their demands were for the 'West Indianisation' of its cultural events and for 'greater student participation in and control of its administration'.[46] The university's administration had followed up its suppression of student protest at Rodney's exclusion order, 18 months earlier, with the removal of several non-Jamaican lecturers, deemed to be provocative and suspect. Students felt they should have more of a share in running the university; so did some of the lecturers, notably James Irish and Sylvia Wynter. The choice of the CAC as a focus of their demands was in line with the steady dismantling of colonial tradition and inheritance, and its replacement by West Indian cultural forms and practice.

By early March the Vice-Chancellor, Roy Marshall, had suspended the 19 students and had sought a court injunction against their occupation as illegal. Brathwaite naturally allied himself with the occupying students. He had played an active role at UWI during the period between the Rodney Affair and the occupation of the CAC, organising younger staff solidarity against the government and UWI administration, which they considered had betrayed them over the Rodney Affair; arranging cultural protest in Yard Theatre and at the CAC, acting as go-between for the students and the Vice-Chancellor. He also drew up and fought for a degree structure based on inter-faculty, interdisciplinary themes, 'so that all of us on campus would have common ground for discussion/conversation';[47] it was effectively rejected by the Arts Faculty Heads of Department. On 9 March he wrote thus to Monica Schuler, the Guyanese historian, a former UWI colleague and now a *Savacou* contributor:

> The Injunction Order has in fact not been served; the students are now in the third week of occupation, the V-C will not compromise on the question of suspension and neither will the students. A group of us staff who sympathise with the students in their protest over the way the Arts Centre has been run; and who feel that protest *must* be allowed, as long as it is reasonable, have been in action to make our case known. We've also been trying to help find a solution. But things at this University are so structured that staff members below the rank of Dean or Senate or Council cannot really get a hearing. We've been called marginal. Plus, of course, the factions that arise within our very group![48]

Because there could be no continuing confrontation, the protest fizzled out. But the period of occupation had given students their first chance to invite to the CAC the performers and art forms of their choice. Brathwaite has recorded how Louise Bennett gave her first appearance there; how Barry Chevannes gave concerts – with solo guitar and voice – of his 'conscious compositions'; how youth from August Town held a concert and craft exhibition, and so on.[49]

Aubrey Williams also went to Jamaica after the celebrations and convention in Guyana. It was his first visit there. He went with Karl Parboosingh, whom he recalled as 'my dear brother, who I still consider is the greatest artist Jamaica has ever produced'. In 1963 Parboosingh, Eugene Hyde and Barrington Watson had formed the Contemporary Jamaican Artists Association, whose headquarters was at The Gallery, 'a kind of artists' cooperative which for several years offered Kingston a focal point for all types of artistic activity'.[50] When it closed, Hyde opened his own John Peartree Gallery, in Constant Spring Road, which specialised in exhibiting forward-looking art. Here, in March 1970, Hyde held a one-man show of Aubrey Williams's paintings. Brathwaite was invited to open it. His speech formed the basis for 'Timehri', published in *Savacou 2* a few months later.

Brathwaite's starting point in 'Timehri' is the West Indian's sense of rootlessness, of not belonging to his landscape. He explains how, for the West Indian intellectual elite – its educated middle class which was involved in the process of creolisation – art has been dissociated from the act of living. Brathwaite cites, and builds on, the following definition by Richard N Adams:

> 'Creolisation' is a socio-cultural description and explanation of the way the four main culture-carriers of the region – Amerindian, European, African and East Indian – interacted with each other and with their environment to create the new societies of the New World. Two main kinds of creolisation may be distinguished: a *mestizo-creolisation*: the inter-culturation of Amerindian and European (mainly Iberian) and located primarily in Central and South America, and a mulatto-creolisation: the inter-culturation of negro-African and European (mainly Western European) and located primarily in the West Indies and the slave areas of the North American continent.[51]

In mulatto America, which includes the West Indian islands, creolisation waned in step with colonialism, and the area's constituent cultures fragmented into 'European, African, indigeno-nationalist and folk': hence its artists' and intellectuals' feelings of rootlessness and of suffering from 'dissociation of the sensibility'. West Indian writers of the 1940s and 1950s described and analysed this cultural problem and made society aware of it. 'The second phase of Caribbean artistic and intellectual life on which we are now entering,' claims Brathwaite, 'is seeking to transcend it and heal it.'

Because his artistic and intellectual concern seemed typical of this second phase, Brathwaite proceeds with an account of his own story, up to his return to Britain in 1965. Then he describes in detail two events from this recent period which he considers to have been 'of central importance to the growth and direction of the West Indian imagination': Stokely Carmichael's visit to London in 1967, and the founding of CAM in 1966. As a result of Carmichael's visit and its repercussions in the Caribbean, a new urgency and significance became evident in Rastafarian and 'primitive' art, in dialect and protest verse. The many-sided, fruitful results of CAM were possible because it came at a time when 'several artists and writers then in London had something new to say'. Artists such as John La Rose, Orlando Patterson,

Andrew Salkey, Marina Maxwell and he himself 'were concerned primarily with the ex-African experience, slavery, the plantation, and their consequences'.

Brathwaite then turns to Wilson Harris and Aubrey Williams, 'both black, both from Guyana, who were contributing if not a different vision, then at least a different approach to that vision'. Because their problem was, unlike that of the West Indian islanders, one of mestizo-creolisation, their starting point was not the negro in the Caribbean but the Amerindian. Quoting Aubrey Williams's statement at the CAM Artists' Symposium, June 1967, Brathwaite claims that Williams was connecting with what many West Indian writers were now trying to do, and, like Harris, was 'extending the bounds of our sensibility'.

Aubrey Williams's life in Guyana, particularly the period which he spent in the North West District, working with the Warrau Indians, had enabled him not only to understand their customs and philosophy, but had given him opportunities to see their ancient art, the *timehri* – rock signs, paintings, petroglyphs – at Tumatumari, carried out by their ancestors, possibly of Mayan origin. The mark of the hand was always etched beside the work and, Brathwaite explains, 'it is from these marks that Aubrey Williams's art begins'. He claims Williams as a modern artist working in an ancient form, and at the same time an ancient artist working in a modern form:

> Form, content, technique, vision – all make a seamless garment for the mind and senses. Like a worshipper possessed at shango or *vodoun*, as with a jazz musician, time past and future speak to the community in the trapped and hunting [sic] moment of awareness. We become the Maya who were already us. Williams is the medium. His paint brush in the door, the *porte cabesse* or central pole, down which the gods often descend into the *tonelle* during *vodoun* worship. Like jazz musicians, still tunnelling the ancient African tone scales and rhythms on European instruments, Williams uses note, tone, rhythm, improvisation. Every one of his paintings is a variation on a central theme; his source's central vision.

Williams's choice of the Amerindian motif does not, Brathwaite claims, exclude the African because he claims ancestry from both, and because the distinction between African and Amerindian in this context is irrelevant:

> What is important is the primordial nature of the two cultures and the potent spiritual and artistic connection between them and the present. In the Caribbean, whether it be African or Amerindian, the recognition of an ancestral relationship with the folk or aboriginal culture involves the artist and participant in a journey into the past and hinterland which is at the same time a movement of

> possession into present and future. Through this movement of possession we become ourselves, truly our own creators, discovering word for object, image for the Word.

'Timehri' follows from and builds on Wilson Harris's recent lectures in Guyana: in what Brathwaite says about the paintings of Aubrey Williams, in the connection, indeed the fusion, which Brathwaite suggests between Williams's use of the Amerindian and his own use of the African past. 'Timehri' triumphantly validates the three-year long association in CAM of major, innovative novelist, painter and poet; it shows how the exposure of their work to each other made possible real movement in creative understanding and exposition.

The creative interaction between Wilson Harris, Aubrey Williams and Edward Brathwaite was reinforced and exposed to a wider audience when Harris was Writer-in-Residence at the Creative Arts Centre, from January to April 1970. His lectures – based on those he had recently given in Guyana – were included in an issue of *Caribbean Quarterly*, which carried a painting by Aubrey Williams on its cover.[52] Brathwaite has stressed how, through these lectures, Harris's 'ideas and word/vision also helped to radicalise the thinking of many students'.[53]

CAM as such had failed to seed in the Caribbean. But several former members were working there, engaged in cultural activities which grew directly from their CAM experience. The central objective of CAM – to enable creative writers and artists to be exposed to each others' work and ideas – had continued, most notably in 1970 at and following the Republic Celebrations in Guyana. And by late 1970 *Savacou*, the journal of CAM, was riding high. *Savacou* 1, June 1970, established it as a progressive academic journal. *Savacou* 2, September 1970, demonstrated the range, quality and vision of CAM members. *Savacou* 3/4, December 1970/March 1971 – the promised issue of new creative writing – was in preparation. It burst on the Caribbean early in 1972, and was to cause confrontation and crisis on as far-reaching and long-lasting a scale as CAM's Second Conference in Britain.

8 Keeping on in Britain
October 1968 - December 1970

The Brathwaites' return to the Caribbean posed CAM in Britain with its most urgent problem after the Second Conference: how to maintain the efficient, many-sided, dynamic organisation which they had initiated and sustained. CAM had had a taste of being without Brathwaite himself earlier in 1968. Key members of the committee felt pessimistic about CAM longterm without him, particularly in the wake of the new directions which some members had requested at the conference. Andrew Salkey recalls:

> Eddie's going left a tremendous emptiness, a tremendous vacuum. John and I really sort of collapsed into each other. It was like two thin cards in a deck of cards missing that third card that propped us up. What are we going to do? How is it going to be carried on?. . . . And it was difficult, because we didn't know: should we take a new direction? What more could we do?

Louis James wrote to Brathwaite in late October 1968, 'I hope CAM goes on. Your leaving will leave a vacuum. We saw this just when you left for a month or two. I wish I was not in such a difficult position, so far from London, and outside the split West Indian group. I don't want to take any initiatives.'[1] Louis James, whom Brathwaite had seen in March 1968 as the most like-minded potential CAM secretary, was aware of his fundamental unsuitability in one respect at least. Not being West Indian mattered increasingly in the autumn of 1968 as outside events occurred and pressures mounted. Nor, given the challenges to CAM at the conference, would an academic have been appropriate as secretary. A new CAM committee had been formed at the Second Conference. John La Rose and Andrew Salkey agreed to act as joint secretaries, with responsibilities carried in specific areas by Jerry Craig and Errol Lloyd (art); Bari Jonson and Evan Jones (drama); Oliver Clarke (treasurer); Louis James (newsletter). Oliver Clarke's public plea to conference participants for help with part at least of the CAM work carried by Doris Brathwaite – typing and dispatching notices of meetings, mailing newsletters and so on – was answered by Anne Walmsley. But La Rose and Salkey could not be secretaries in the Brathwaites' mould. It was not simply a matter of their both being self-employed. From their longer, and longterm, residence in Britain, both had already developed a network of commitments and activism before CAM began which was to make increasing demands on them.

A new CAM committee

In agreeing to become joint secretaries, La Rose and Salkey knew that they would need practical help with much of the day-to-day work involved; hence the decision, probably taken at the new committee's first meeting, in October 1968, to bring in James Berry and Donald Hinds. The choice seemed a good one. Both were practising writers – Berry was beginning to have poems and stories published in magazines and broadcast on the BBC; Hinds, following his work on the *West Indian Gazette*, had written *Journey To An Illusion: the West Indian in Britain*. Both were employed at the Post Office and came, not from the transient postgraduate student number, but from the black immigrant community itself. Neither was particularly wellknown to the committee, nor part of the CAM 'core' which had attended private meetings. Berry was very new to CAM: he joined only in July 1968, and the Second Conference was his first substantial experience of CAM. But he and John La Rose knew each other a little already, through public meetings and poetry readings in various parts of London; it was La Rose who asked Berry to help. Donald Hinds had attended CAM meetings from the start; he was invited to help by Richard Small, who had known him at the *Gazette*. In

Co-opted onto the CAM Committee after the Second Conference, (l to r), Donald Hinds and James Berry

fact, little assistance was asked of Berry and Hinds by La Rose and Salkey in their early months as joint secretaries. They were so used to working together, knew each other so well, that they carried the secretaryship into 1970. There is no record of James Berry taking part in the work of the CAM committee during 1969–70: only of his submitting news and poems for inclusion in the *Newsletter*. His own and others' memories of Berry's part in CAM are from 1971–2.

But Hinds began to play a full part in the work of the new committee early in 1969 when he took over the editorship of the *Newsletter* from Louis James. Louis James had been named, and active, as newsletter editor since early 1968. He had brought out No. 6, January–March, with input and help from Brathwaite and No. 7, April–September, with help from Salkey. With No. 8, October–December, Louis James relinquished the editorship. From the 'editorial' of this and the previous issue, some of the problems are implied. Whereas it had been hoped to include extracts from the Second Conference and subsequent meetings, no help was readily available for the massive job of transcribing them. James announced as his reason for stepping down as editor that he might be leaving the country for a while. Correspondence should, he wrote, be sent to La Rose. But letters between James and Salkey reveal how difficult James had found the role of editor, outside London, and outside the immediate Caribbean circle, with an increasing workload at the University of Kent and with more travel abroad. Despite stalwart help from Salkey on the editorial side, he felt more and more defeated by the problems:

> The office has had a shake-up, and I can't get the secretarial support I used to. (November 1968) I just must go to press by the end of this month, so do send anything relevant you know and I will just do the best I can. After that, Andrew, I will hand over the *Newsletter* to you and John, or whoever will take it on. I can't do as good a job as CAM deserves (December 1968). I can't even in spite of your unstinting help do an adequate job on the *Newsletter* (January 1969)[2]

Donald Hinds was asked to take over, and Christopher Laird to assist him. Together they successfully brought out three issues of a new-look CAM *Newsletter* in 1969: No. 9, January–March; No. 10, April–June; No. 11, July–November; and one in 1970, No. 12, August. Hinds was full of enthusiasm and ideas from the start. To Brathwaite in Jamaica he wrote:

> I won't hold it against you if you cannot remember who I am. The really important thing is that I have been given this most exciting of tasks to edit CAM's newsletters. . . . If possible, I hope to bring it out every other month. What can you tell us about CAM Jamaica or West Indies?. . . . I am thinking of a future newsletter being

> devoted entirely to criticism/reviews. Can you help develop this germ of a thought with Ken Ramchand and other bodies?[3]

Brathwaite replied straightaway: 'It is good that you have taken up the *Newsletter*. Great work can be done through it and it's wonderful to have someone with your talent and enthusiasm and understanding of the problems in charge.'[4] And he sent him material from Jamaica. Hinds's three 1969 issues were well back in the Brathwaite model, with transcripts of talks, reports on meetings; poems, abundant CAM news, and – for the first time – book reviews. Laird gave generous assistance, with 'use of a typewriter which can cut stencils', and especially welcome, with the front cover; he wrote to Hinds, 'I have been soliciting designs for the front cover from some friends. I have asked them to design a cheap and convenient means of reproduction for whatever designs they come up with.'[5] Judith Laird's contribution along with Christopher's is evident in the striking two-colour cover designs of Nos. 9–12.

Covers of the new-look CAM **Newsletter**

CAM (UK) activity, late 1968

At recent sessions at the Students Centre and, most forcefully, at the Second Conference, CAM had been challenged to show more concern for, and to practise closer involvement with, the black immigrant community in Britain. How was CAM to do this and yet retain its essentially apolitical, unaligned character as an artists' movement? John La Rose recalls feeling at the time that the movement might already have come to an end because of pressure for political activity within it. It was not simply the fact of the Brathwaites' returning home. In La Rose's view, the historic moment from which CAM was born was over:

> CAM had been a vibrant movement of artists and intellectuals which sought to reach out to and interact with a larger audience. Having absorbed the vitality of the CAM experience, artists would naturally return to the dedication of their individual creativity.

Other concerns and commitments began to take priority.

Contemporary events, in the Caribbean and in Britain, seemed to many CAM members to require an urgent response. The Jamaican government's ban on Black Power literature had prompted CAM's first collective protest in September 1968. When, in October, the news came through of the expulsion order issued to Walter Rodney, leading members of CAM were amongst those who marched to the Jamaica High Commission and protested inside the building. La Rose, Salkey and Richard Small were arrested. At the first CAM public session in the autumn of 1968, 1 November, the audience at the Students Centre was informed about the events surrounding Rodney's expulsion. Locksley Comrie and Richard Small took the platform, with La Rose and Salkey alongside them. Attendance at this meeting was 'outstandingly large' and its repercussions were far-reaching.[6]

Richard Small had himself taken part, with Walter Rodney, in the Congress of Black Writers at McGill University, Montreal, 11–14 October. Its theme was 'Towards the Second Emancipation: the Dynamics of Black Liberation'. In the words of the organisers the congress was,

> an attempt to recall, in a series of popular lectures by black scholars, artists and politicians, a history which we have been taught to forget: the history of the black man's own response (in thought and in action) to the conditions of his existence in the New World, in short, the history of the Black liberation struggle, from its origins in slavery to the present day . . . to re-discover themselves as the active creators, rather than the passive sufferers, of history's events.[7]

Papers by Caribbean speakers included 'The Fathers of Modern Revolt: Garvey, DuBois' (Robert Hill); 'The History and Economics of Slavery in the New World', 'The Haitian Revolution and the History of Slave Revolt', and, in French, in place of René Dépestre, 'Les Origines et la Signification de la Négritude' (CLR James); 'African History in the Service of Black Revolution' (Walter Rodney); 'Race and Britain and the Way Out' (Richard Small). On the last day Michael Abdul Malik spoke; so, too, did Stokeley Carmichael, on Black Power. Small not only gave the CAM audience an account of the congress, but also a summary of events in Jamaica before and after Rodney was issued with an Exclusion Order.

Locksley Comrie followed with an account of 'new literary activity among the young Rastafarian and black radical writers in Kingston':[8] the new creative ferment among the youth of Jamaica, and the climate in which Rodney's teaching had been so warmly received. La Rose and Salkey read out examples of this new writing which included poems by a Rastafarian, Bongo Jerry (Robin Small, Richard's younger brother), he was also engaged in painting. Rodney had carried examples of this new writing and art to Montreal and given it to Richard Small, who brought it back to London.

Finally, Comrie read out a cable received from Jamaica by Salkey. It was from the Defence Committee of students arrested and refused bail – including Robin Small – and asked for a solidarity demonstration on 7 November and for international coverage. Salkey's notes, in preparation for the CAM meeting, include under 'strategy' several effective ways for CAM to carry out protest and publicity. The meeting passed a resolution, expressing its alarm at recent events in Jamaica arising from the ban imposed on Walter Rodney, and at the 'brutal oppressive action of the Jamaican government which resulted in the death of five persons'; calling on the government to withdraw the ban on Rodney, apprehend and try the murderers, and 'pay compensation to the families of the five deceased workers'; proposing that 'a monument be set up in memory of the five martyrs'.[9] Salkey wrote to Brathwaite the next day:

> We heard about his [Robin Small's] arrest. I read two of his poems last night, at the meeting, and they caused a riot of approval, and I presented some other pieces by three Rasta poets. I also read out some of their political posters. Great! We also showed off three pieces of Rasta artwork, done by Robin's group of Rasta artists up at Irish Town.[10]

Brathwaite had heard in Jamaica of the arrest of La Rose, Salkey and Small, and had written to Salkey in praise and with concern; but, continued Salkey,

> you would have been with us too. . . . And it is easier to be seen protesting, here, for most of us, than it would be at home. . . . John La Rose is thinking, in fact, planning towards a wake business for the five killed at home and for the loss of Walter; it would naturally be a CAM thing, too.

The Rodney Affair kept CAM members in Jamaica and Britain working together.

In contrast to the opening event in CAM's post-conference programme, the second was long-planned, and had been handled, in its preparatory stages, by Brathwaite as CAM Secretary. It was the continuing responsibility of Jerry Craig, and was now causing bitter controversy within CAM. The notice of CAM's November meeting announced:

> *Art Exhibition*
> Under the sponsorship of the British-Caribbean Association, CAM is arranging an art exhibition in the House of Commons from Monday 4 November until Thursday 14 November 1968. The opening ceremony will be performed by the Rt Hon George Thomson, MP, on Monday 4 November at 6.00 pm in the House of Commons.[11]

The decision to go ahead with an exhibition in the British Parliament, which had by a succession of legislative measures shown itself to be so evidently uninterested, even hostile to its Caribbean citizens, seemed to some CAM members to be an act of compromise and collusion.

The idea of such an exhibition had first been mooted in June 1967 by the British-Caribbean Association (BCA), which included several members of parliament, in conjunction with the West India Committee, which represented British trading interests in the region. The BCA plan had, according to its circular letter inviting CAM to take part, 'received the enthusiastic support of the High Commissions for the various West Indian nations'.[12] There is no record of a response by Brathwaite, then CAM secretary, to this initial request. But the matter was reopened by Felicity Bolton, secretary of the BCA, prompted by Graham Norton, a British journalist, who wrote personally to Andrew Salkey in April 1968. Salkey referred it to Brathwaite, considering that 'Jerry Craig and the others might like to know about it at the next [Committee] meeting'. Jerry Craig certainly did; he already had a connection through Chris Chataway, MP, who had asked Craig to donate one of his paintings for a charity show, and – because the painting sold so well – suggested he might like to exhibit in the gallery of the House of Commons. So Craig followed up the BCA invitation, and arranged the CAM exhibition. It contained paintings by himself, Karl Craig, by Art Derry and Aubrey Williams, sculpture by Ronald Moody and Errol Lloyd, plastic panels in laminate by Althea McNish. All except two of Lloyd's exhibits were for sale. The exhibition took place in the Upper Waiting Hall of the House of Commons, and was opened by William Whitlock, MP, Under-Secretary, Commonwealth Office.

Brathwaite had supported the idea to the extent that he took considerable trouble in July 1968 to disentangle crossed wires over the arrangements. But attitudes changed. Craig recalls:

> Aubrey, if I remember, was very much in favour of it to start with, and then had reservations, because even John La Rose and Andrew Salkey – all these people – suddenly were anti it. They said they wouldn't attend it, and there were even talks of boycotting it and having slogans downstairs from more radical members of CAM.

He believes now that Salkey and La Rose were not really against the exhibition, but felt pressurised by the militant faction at the Students Centre. La Rose confirms that he was not against it and took no part in the demonstration. At the time, Craig was personally so hurt by the reaction of people of whom he thought so highly, and by what he saw as the increasing politicisation of CAM, that he withdrew from CAM after the exhibition. Errol Lloyd recalls the dilemma in which he found himself as a CAM visual artist and as a friend, and flat-mate, of Richard Small:

> I was in broad sympathy with his and Locksley's stance over broader participation in the black/immigrant community. I was however out of sympathy with a boycott of the exhibition as I felt it was a kind of interference with free expression of ideas and association of the artist. . . . I resisted any pressure (none was applied directly) not to exhibit, but stayed away from the opening.

Leonard Smith, joint deputy chairman and hon. secretary of the BCA and chairman of the West India Committee and its Public Relations Committee, was of course unaware of the divided views of CAM members; he considered the exhibition a highlight of both organisations' activities.

For the final CAM public session of 1968, on 6 December, a panel of young writers and artists in Britain was assembled. The notice – signed 'John La Rose, Andrew Salkey, Joint Acting Secretaries' – echoed the phrase first used by Wilson Harris, and was perhaps deliberately apolitical:

> Are they seeking and attempting to discern a new vision of consciousness? Young contemporary West Indian poets, playwrights, painters, sculptors and novelists discuss their vision of *their* art and the original idea of the world they seek through it.

The promised line-up of writers and artists drew partly on the Second Conference participants, but also on the Centre, and showed CAM spreading its net amongst the young West Indian student and worker community:

> Winston Benn – painter
> Christopher Laird – painter and poet
> Paul Dash – painter
> Joyce Linton – writer
> Audrey Payne – writer
> Basil Smith – poet
> Sebastian Clarke – poet and playwright
> Winston Branch – painter
> Errol Lloyd – painter and sculptor
> Stephen Kalipha – actor[13]

Those who in fact took part certainly included Marc Matthews, and probably also Winston Best, Tony Matthews and Rudolph Kizerman.

Christopher Laird spoke about the inadequacy of English literary forms and European artistic media, of what he saw as the Caribbean reality, and of his feeling that film alone provided a possible medium for what he wanted to express:

> West Indian world is a world of images of movement, colour, heat and passion. Island raft-like in a throbbing sea, smelly earth, burning, screaming sand, fleshy leaves, dilating moons, shooting stars, hurricanes and mouthfuls of rain in each drop. It is a dramatic world. To write about it in English, feel tied to the English poets who have written intense dramatic verse, Byron, Shakespeare, Coleridge, Marlowe – to write using their idiom is bombast, reminiscent of old forms not appropriate to our infant world.[14]

Basil Smith, rather than make a statement, contributed poems, including:

My heritage is of the night
of dry-thatch cottages
of painted faces
and of drums.

My memory shows strange, snowless winters,
Dry mountain tops,
Green fields and trees
that never grey or die.

So I stand misunderstood, with
My snowless winters and evergreens,
Hated for the thickness of my lips
And my memories of drums.[15]

Two poets have specific memories of the session. Marc Matthews recalls: 'We read and we discussed where we were going: the direction of the writing and the catalyst for it. And I remember that would have been the first time that I was using Guyana language or what we called dialect, "nation language" . . . in this audience.' Sebastian Clarke (now Amon Saba Saakana) contributed a paper which he remembers as being,

> about the artist in relation to his community, and the responsibility of the artist, or writer, to that community. . . . I was thinking that wherever the black man was, he had a responsibility to the community which he came from, whether it was in Europe, America, Africa, the Caribbean. . . . Although I was talking about it theoretically, I don't think I was producing it in my own creative writing, in my poetry, for example. It has taken a very long time for me to transcend that. But at least, theoretically, I was thinking about it.

For a CAM public session to be addressed by such writers and artists, with such contributions, showed the extent to which its concerns were already changing. Brathwaite, in Jamaica, had heard about the session via Anne Walmsley, visiting for Longmans, and wrote to Salkey, 'Anne tells me that London CAM's recent young writers' and artists' thing turned up a lot of exciting material. Is it on tape? Please send copy URGENT.'[16] But neither this, nor the November public session, seems to have been recorded.

Meanwhile the Nottingham branch of CAM continued to flourish. John La Rose accepted its invitation to be guest speaker in October, when he read and talked about his poetry. Louis James, keeping up his initial contacts there, spoke on 'West Indian Literature' in mid-December.

Some of the many venues at which CAM members appeared were listed in the *Newsletter*. On 10 December, Andrew Salkey spoke with Robin Blackburn on 'Che Guevara's Influence on

World Politics', with Lowell Marcus as chairman, at the Lincoln's Inn Students Union, London. And a symposium on 'Afro-Caribbean Culture', held at Las Villas University, Cuba, was attended by CLR James, Barry Reckord, Wilson Harris and George Lamming.

CAM's first break into active protest at the Second Conference was encouraged and followed up by Bryan King. He sent a cutting to Salkey in mid-October, asking, 'I wonder whether CAM might express its concern to the Commissioner for the Eastern Caribbean and ask to be informed of the facts? If the facts officially supplied seem to require protest?'[17] The enclosure presumably referred to recent news that, although British paratroops sent to Anguilla in March 1969 had now been withdrawn, Royal Engineers and policemen were to remain there. King was a life-long campaigner, prodding and protesting wherever he saw cause. The draft of a letter to Enoch Powell of December 1968 was found amongst his papers, part of which reads:

> On the front page of the *Times* yesterday it was stated that an opinion poll of immigrants found 27% feeling that your speeches had made their position more difficult, 55% no difference. In the middle page, of the same poll, it is stated that 55% felt that their position had been made more difficult. This I believe to be the correct figure. This then is the charge against which you have to clear yourself, before your conscience, God, and History. That you have made your 'voluntary' repatriation scheme an evil mockery, – a fleeing from your self-fulfilling prophecy of the wrath to come.[18]

Richard Small continued to urge CAM members to take part in active protest. Before Merle Hodge's talk on Léon Damas on 7 March 1969, Andrew Salkey chaired a meeting to consider reports of recent acts of discrimination against West Indian students at the Sir George Williams University in Montreal, Canada, and discussion of what CAM's response should be. As 'a group of black people working together, discussing black things' the CAM audience should, suggested Small, take some action: protest to the Canadian High Commission, and communicate its solidarity to the students. A wide range of members, from Bryan King to Locksley Comrie, approved and encouraged an activist political role for CAM. But practising artists in CAM did not; they considered that such a role changed its essential character and weakened it. Karl 'Jerry' Craig recalls how,

> I felt the turn in the kind of meetings that grew out of CAM – every time I went to a meeting, it ended in what I would call a political Black Power hassle, and I thought, this is not what I joined CAM about. And if this is what CAM is becoming, I want no part with it.

Andrew Salkey was engaged, in late 1968, in correspondence on another front of proposed CAM activity. Hortense J Spillers, an

Afro-American graduate student in the English and American Literature program at Brandeis University, Massachussetts, USA, had met Salkey and other members of CAM when she lived in London for about six months during 1969. She proposed that CAM (London) participate in a weekend, organised by the university's Afro-American group, 'of cultural events . . . when activists from different parts of the country will converge on campus for a weekend of workshops and special programs'.[19] Her hope was that the university could be persuaded by the Afro-American group to sponsor CAM (London) participation, quoting Pan Am's special group rates for 15 or more, from 14–21 February 1969. But Spillers wrote next in late January:

> The Afro-American society of Brandeis laid siege to the University's communication centre in Ford Hall on the basis of ten demands. We got nine of the ten demands; the one proposal most significant for us we didn't get: that was the demand for an African/Afro-American concentration or department with the right to fire and hire [and] . . . the right to select [its] director. . . . Essentially, Faculty does not want to relinquish its power to students; students, simply, want a piece of the 'power pie'.[20]

The proposed cultural weekend was postponed, though only, Spillers hoped, until April. But in mid-February she wrote: 'Things are apparently at loose ends now; I think it will take us a while to sort ourselves out.'[21] She hoped by 'the next letter' she would have more news about the weekend. No such letter seems to have come. What could have been a seminal CAM experience, on a level with the Havana Cultural Congress – an exposure of Caribbean cultural expression in Britain to the powerful flowering of black arts of the USA in the late 1960s – was obstructed by the very forces that provoked such flowering. 'How,' continued Spillers, 'can an institution call itself "liberal" and humane when it continues to disavow the validity of an ethnic experience?'

Public sessions, 1969

CAM (London), under its joint secretaries, held regular public monthly meetings at the Students Centre throughout 1969. The topics and speakers show CAM's concern with Caribbean arts in an ever-widening context, in Africa, Afro-America, the non-English-speaking Caribbean, and the West Indian immigrant community in Britain. Also, these sessions reflect the increasing interest of CAM members in more popularly-based art forms: dance, film, music. The CAM *Newsletter*, with its new editorial team, once again enabled what was said at CAM public sessions to reach a wider audience. This may have been responsible for ensuring that the majority of 1969 sessions at the Centre were successfully recorded.

'Africa's Unique Dance Culture' was the topic in January. John Akar, founder-director of the Sierra Leone Dance Company, introduced a BBC film about his company by outlining some of the problems faced by a director of African dance when presenting it in a conventional Western theatre to a Western audience. His ambition was, he said, to form a troupe called Afro-World Ballet, with dancers recruited from Africa, the Caribbean, America and South America, with a repertoire of 15–20 hours, and based in the West Indies. Akar had recently returned from a tour of the West Indies, and had observed 'the African cultural renaissance there'. He had been excited by the dancers and musicians, the material and interest which he encountered there; he had 'found some fabulous drummers in the countryside in Jamaica, Trinidad and Dominica', and he expanded on the essential role of the drummer in African dance culture: 'The drum is more than just an instrument of percussion. It is sometimes the voice that dictates, sometimes the teacher, sometimes the dance itself . . . the inner soul.' John La Rose showed himself informed about popular music in Trinidad, and also spoke with understanding of how, in African culture, the carver is possessed by the work he is carving, the drummer by the drum he plays:

John Akar, after talking on African dance to CAM, January 1969

> Out of this is a whole philosophy of life articulated not in words but within an inner kind of preoccupation with the world that is much deeper and more profound than the very statement of that kind of thing in words, and where words fossilise and freeze that kind of idea.

CAM's February public session was on 'Film as an artistic medium'. Evan Jones, the main speaker, introduced himself 'as the West Indian who has more experience of film than most and that I should share this experience'; rather than 'deliver a whole series of generalisations' he made himself available for questions. Horace Ové from Trinidad, already known as a young photographer and film director of outstanding ability, billed to speak with him, did not take part. Ram John Holder shared the platform, and questions. Holder had played a lead part in Evan Jones's 1966 film, *Two Gentlemen Sharing*, which Jones describes as being 'about race relations in England', though it was never screened there. In reply to questions, Evan Jones recounted to the CAM audience how he had got into films and television – as a dramatist. He acknowledged that the film director has more power than the screenwriter. He stressed fundamental problems of film as a medium: the exorbitant costs involved, and the 'stranglehold of the distributors'. Discussion showed the concerns and attitudes of the CAM audience. One member spoke of himself and his friends as 'people who have been trying to sell the continuous revolution', but who 'succeeded so well that we have become successful and

Malcolm X Memorial Meeting at the Students Centre, (l to r) Eric McAlpine – publisher, Andrew Salkey, Rudolph Kizerman – writer, Richard Small, Clifton Jones – actor

Audience for Malcolm X Memorial Meeting, Locksley Comrie seated front row, second from left

rich and middle class'. Another speaker pointed to the consequent challenge for West Indian artists, in terms which echoed Elsa Goveia at CAM's First Conference: 'We are going to reach a crisis stage where every single one of us, in whatever field we're in, has to answer the question: what are we going to do with our talents? At whose disposal should they be? For what purpose?' Another, referring back to the Second Conference, said he believed that 'our own writers and artists refuse to really involve themselves'. A sombre closing note was sounded by a speaker who described the bad situation for blacks in London: 'They're creating another Harlem. . . . Nobody in' goin' no place.'

A filmed documentary about Malcolm X, including an interview, was shown at an additional CAM session in late February: a joint CAM–WISU session to mark the fourth anniversary of his assassination. After the film there were readings by – amongst others – Ram John Holder, Locksley Comrie, Richard Small and Faustin Charles.

Merle Hodge

On 7 March Merle Hodge spoke about Léon Damas in the first of three 1969 public sessions concerned with critiques of, and presentation of, the work of major Caribbean poets, two from the French-speaking West Indies. Less wellknown than his fellow poets of the Negritude movement in Paris in the 1930s, Aimé Césaire and Léopold Senghor, Damas – in his work and life – holds special significance for Caribbean people. Merle Hodge, a Trinidadian, had completed an MA thesis on Damas at University College, London, in 1967, research which, as she says, 'involved looking at English Caribbean, Black America, French Africa, English Africa. Damas himself was the centre of it but it opened up that whole world'. In the 1960s it was fashionable for black intellectuals, especially West Africans, to dismiss Negritude as an unnecessary aberration. But Hodge was well equipped to defend it by placing it in context. She maintained that the main origin and significance of Negritude lay not in French West Africa, but in the French West Indies, a society which had been deprived of its own cultural identity by the slave trade, and which was stratified by degrees of colour.

The life and work of Léon Damas was shown, in Hodge's detailed account, to be of particular interest to the CAM audience and of relevance to its concerns. His ancestry was Negro/European/Amerindian. In his middle-class home he was forbidden to speak creole and to play non-classical musical instruments. Before studying in Paris, he had spent time living among the Bush Negroes of the Guyana interior – descendants of slaves who had reverted to African culture. Later he spent time collecting and disseminating literature from the folk traditions of various negro societies. Books which he published as a student in Paris in the

1930s were confiscated and burned there: a highly critical report on conditions of his home country of French Guiana, and his first collection of poems, *Pigments* (1937). Merle Hodge's talk on Damas, in which she quoted extensively from his poetry, was carried in full in *Newsletters* Nos. 9 and 11.

Tony Matthews and Basil Smith, billed as 'Two Poets of the Revolution', were due to read their poems at CAM's April meeting, but Smith alone seems to have taken part. John La Rose, in the chair, referred back to their part in an earlier CAM session, 'where these younger writers were stating their own vision of the world . . . and what they hoped to do through their creative activity in looking at the world'. Basil Smith, introducing his poems, said that each represented some part of his life and some aspect of his development: as a black man, as a black Jamaican, as a black Jamaican living in London. In discussion, the first and most articulate comment on Smith's poetry came from Locksley Comrie, who saw it as an extension of the current expression by 'black yout' such as Bongo Jerry in Jamaica: 'These boys are eventually breaking loose and destroying all the myths and illusions in the middle class and joining arms together with the working class . . . the rude boys in the fusion which Mr Shearer is so worried about. And,' he added, 'I hope Basil don't mind me calling him middle-class.' Basil Smith did not, and openly acknowledged his gain: 'For me, as a writer, it expanded my scope a hell of a lot more. I was able to see things in the society which I had been deprived of, would possibly still be blind to.' In his presentation of poetry, too, Basil Smith was sensitive to the gap between poet and audience, 'how tiring it gets to have the poet reading down to you, so to speak'. Members of the audience took part in presenting one of his poems.

On 2 May Donald Hinds spoke about his own and other West Indians' experience as 'ordinary immigrants' in Britain, and extracts were read (by Andrew Salkey) from his book, *Journey to an Illusion*. Donald Hinds recalled how he came to write it. Through working on the *West Indian Gazette* and at the BBC, alongside his London Transport job on the buses, he met a number of English journalists. At their encouragement he wrote a piece about young West Indians at school in Britain, which was published in *The Observer*. A few days later he was telephoned by a literary agent, and then signed up by Heinemann for a book. This was, he says, the break he had been hoping for, and it gave him courage to resign from London Transport and become a full-time writer, journalist and researcher. *Journey to an Illusion* remains a classic of the West Indian immigrant experience. With a dedication 'In memory of Claudia Jones and what she stood for', it documents from personal experience the story of West Indians who came to Britain to work, from 1947 onwards. It is based on, and quotes extensively from, conversations with fellow 'ordinary immigrants'. As Hinds writes there: 'Though I was tempted, I kept away from the so-called intelligentsia and spoke to the people who really matter – these people who have been peeped at, poked about like some rare species.'[22] Such West Indian people had appeared as characters in fiction by George Lamming, Sam Selvon and Andrew Salkey. West Indian immigrants had been the topic of work by British sociologists such as Sheila Patterson, RB Davidson. West Indian university students had written about their experiences in *Disappointed Guests*. But Hinds was the first postwar 'ordinary immigrant' to put together a down-to-earth account of the problems they encountered in Britain, and how they learnt to cope. For a CAM meeting to focus on Hinds's book strengthened his role in the new committee, and gave further indication of CAM's increasing emphasis on the West Indian immigrant community.

Record sleeve,* Rights of Passage, *painting by Winston Branch

The work of Aimé Césaire, the great Caribbean poet of the Negritude movement, had been introduced to CAM at its Second Conference. Now, in June 1969, his *Cahier d'un retour au pays natal* was given a dramatic presentation in its entirety at the Students Centre. John La Rose, who had read extracts from the poem at the Second Conference, was responsible for the production and direction of this presentation, the first to take place in Britain.

Introducing it, La Rose quoted widely from a recent interview with Césaire by the Haitian poet, René Dépestre, in particular from Césaire's statements about language and the surrealist approach:

> I wanted to create an Antillean French, a black French that, while still being French, had a black character. . . . It's true that superficially we are French, we bear the marks of French customs; we have been branded by Cartesian philosophy, by French rhetoric; but if we break with all that, if we plumb the depths, then what we will find is fundamentally black.[23]

La Rose recounted, briefly, the history of the *Cahier*'s publication, rediscovery, and its widespread effect since publication. He indicated the relevance of what Césaire said about Martinique in the 1930s to the English-speaking Caribbean of the late 1960s. This reading was, he stressed, a very important occasion: the entire cast of readers was West Indian, and two readers were from Martinique itself. Its effect would be spoilt by movement, so the doors were closed and the audience asked to stay in the room.

Andrew Salkey wrote afterwards that 'the poem was imaginatively orchestrated for nine voices with a wide and constantly changing variety of reading styles' – in French, in Martinican vernacular, and in English translation.[24] La Rose recalls that preparation took several months and included changes to the English translation, made in consultation with Merle Hodge and Jacques Compton, where he considered the translation not exact or poetic enough. For La Rose it was a counterpart to his presentation of Brathwaite's reading of *Rights of Passage* in March 1967, and another important milestone in his CAM activity. It marked the Caribbean breaking out of its imprisonment in a single language – whether Dutch, French, Spanish or English – and reaching out to itself across language barriers.

Another long Caribbean poem was given its first complete London reading to CAM, on 29 September: *Islands*, just published, read by Brathwaite himself – over from Jamaica on three months' leave, for study and to take part in Poetry International at the Royal Festival Hall. Unlike his reading of *Masks* a year before, to a small group at his home, this was a public reading to a large, attentive audience at the Students Centre. Brathwaite's many-voiced poem of return to the Caribbean islands, where he recognises and rejoices in a continuing African presence and accepts the islands as home, worked on the CAM audience as a contemporary and accessible counterpoint to Césaire's poem. A few months earlier, Brathwaite's reading of *Rights of Passage* (recorded in 1967) had been published by Argo. The sleeve of the pair of discs carries a painting of a West Indian by Winston Branch; Branch recalls their first meeting at an exhibition in 1967 at the Arts Lab, how Brathwaite told him about CAM and later invited him to do the sleeve of these records.

Femi Fatoba and Tony Evora

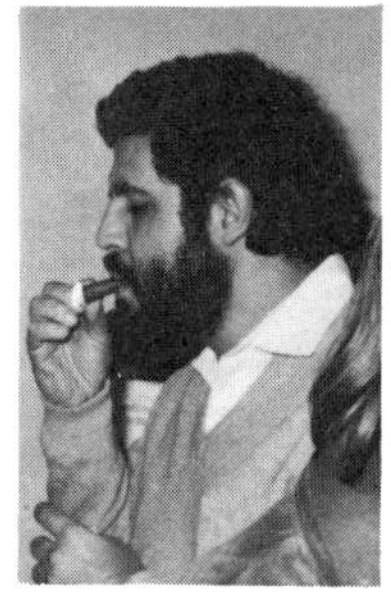

The role and nature of African drumming, introduced at the January session, were more fully described and demonstrated in November. Femi Fatoba, Nigerian poet and actor, a former member of Wole Soyinka's 'Orisun' drama group, and Tony Evora, Cuban graphic designer, spoke about and played 'The tonal drums of the Yoruba': as preserved in their homeland, as transferred to the Caribbean.

This was CAM's last session in 1969. There was no session in October or December, perhaps a sign that the organisation of regular sessions each month was already more than La Rose and Salkey could manage, at a time of increasing pressure from their other involvements.

Two weeks before Brathwaite's reading, Ivan Van Sertima again addressed CAM. In *Astride Two Visions* he gave personal memories and assessments of Cheddi Jagan and Wilson Harris, who, he claimed, 'have had the most profound effect upon the thinking life of my generation, my community . . . who have thrown the longest shadows over the social and spiritual landscape of Guyana in the fifties and sixties'.[25] He spoke in particular of their effect on 'the poets and men of sensibility' of his time. Whereas Jagan had since become discredited, half-forgotten, 'in those early years he acted as a catalyst for the very best in our community', and Van Sertima made detailed reference to Jagan's role in the political events of British Guiana in the 1950s. Poets such as Martin Carter had kept alive Jagan's anger and sense of high purpose; his poems had enormous appeal for the youth of Guyana.

Van Sertima confessed to having been haunted, ever since the 1950s, by fear that their revolution had failed, not just from pressures and ostracisation from outside, but from their own 'internal unpreparedness for any true revolution'. Now he could accept that revolution meant 'not merely a movement of the mass but a movement within the man'. This was the revolution to which Wilson Harris was dedicated:

> He more than any of us realised that if the masses were not to end up trapped in the old cycle of things there was a need for a native and original vision of community, a vision that would make sense of our complex heritage on that continent, our African, Indian, Amerindian and European presences. . . . He knew that this translation of our legacies, of our grassroots, this reorientation of our consciousness, this dialogue between the society and its original spirits, was not a peripheral cultural issue, not, as some of the leaders said, something that could be attended to afterwards. It was, he knew, central and urgent to that revolution.

Van Sertima admitted that it had taken him years to appreciate what Wilson Harris was about: 'To me, as to many, he was at first a great enigma.' He described their meetings in Guyana, and gave a vivid account of how, in the autumn of 1958, Harris camped out in an empty house in Georgetown while working on *Almanac of a Jumbi* – one of three novels, never published, which came before *Palace of the Peacock*[26] – and read aloud from it to the young writers who hung about him there: Milton Williams, Sydney King (now Eusi Kwayana), Van Sertima himself.

Van Sertima closed by reading an extract from *Palace*, and stressed the significance of Harris's concept of character as having 'implications not only for the novel but for what we have been speaking of: this vision of a community rising out of a broken and dislocated past and tradition'. Ivan Van Sertima's exposition of Wilson Harris's creative purpose echoed and reinforced that of Brathwaite; implicit in his poetry, explicit in his talks to CAM.

The CAM–WISU Symposium

As in the two previous years, CAM's programme of monthly public sessions was interrupted, and strengthened, by a summer conference. Requests and attempts to hold a non-residential conference in London had been unsuccessful in 1968, but were realised in 1969. In mid-August a weekend symposium was held at the Students Centre, organised jointly by CAM and WISU; this was regarded by CAM members as its Third Conference. Since October 1968 La Rose and Salkey had, as CAM joint secretaries, worked increasingly closely with WISU. The topics and speakers at this symposium reflected topical concerns shared by the two organisations: 'Africa in the Caribbean' (Edward Brathwaite); 'The Negritude Movement and Black Awareness' (Merle Hodge and Andrew Salkey); 'The Development of Black Experience and the Nature of Black Society in Britain' (John La Rose); 'The Threat to the Education of the Black Child in Britain and what to do' (Jack Hines and Augustine John).

Gary Burton, current president of WISU and overall chairman of the symposium, explained that this joint venture with CAM was by the 'new, revolutionary WISU' which realised that as students they should 'shed the illusion of a middle-class, white identity, and go straight back to our black brothers and sisters, those who catch hell in this community'. Under the leadership of Jack Hines, its discussion officer, WISU had decided to found a 'teaching and social service corps' to meet the needs of the black community, 'within the new concept of the world-wide black revolution'. The symposium was its first venture in presenting 'the new approach to black history, seen by black people interpreted through the black experience'. Because the symposium was intended as the start of a course, Burton urged the audience to take notes and approach it in an academic way. At the same time, the audience should not be intimidated: 'Let's sort of make it cool, cosy, intimate and black, black, real black, you know, like back home, so that you throw your ideas out.' He was disappointed to see 'not many black sufferers in the audience', on whose side WISU, he stressed, stood firm.

Speaking for CAM, John La Rose welcomed the audience and, in particular, Edward Brathwaite, 'one of the principal founders of CAM'. Brathwaite's talk on 'Africa in the Caribbean' was, in its core thesis, similar to the one he had given at the CAM public session in December 1967. Again he affirmed the existence of an alternative, living tradition in the Caribbean, ignored or denied by the European-oriented, intellectual tradition – a folk continuum which was the basis of Caribbean society, although no anthropological study had yet been made of it. Again he listed evidence from his own research on the continuation of African tradition in Caribbean everyday life, often at odds with the scholastic, academic tradition. Again he urged the necessity of going back to the catastrophe of slavery, by way of 'certain imaginative explorations'. Again he pointed to the artist as an important ally of this alternative tradition, in that he went instinctively to the folk.

But Brathwaite's thesis was now presented without Redfield's theoretical framework of a Great and Little Tradition; it had become confidently his own, and was illustrated throughout with firsthand examples from the Caribbean. The intellectual tradition continued to be imposed, he said, through the mass media, and at UWI, where 'West Indian literature in English, which is our literature, does not yet have a central and permanent place in the curriculum', and there was no Institute of Caribbean Studies. The 'watershed of the Rodney crisis' had enabled a polygamous West Indian family structure to be discussed openly in the Jamaican press for the first time. Speaking of the need to recognise the centrality in Caribbean society of African religious practice, whereby the participant in a ceremony becomes possessed, undergoes a change and is drawn into communion with his fellows, he cited Rex Nettleford's attempt to recapture this in dance choreography. He praised recent New Beacon publications as examples of the alternative tradition in action. His overall message was that Caribbean people should acquire their own analytical framework, formulate an aesthetic which could encompass European and African art, accept the validity of their own folk, oral tradition, in short undergo a 'revolution of consciousness'.

At the opening of his talk Brathwaite stated his belief that 'it is in the imagination of the West Indian first of all that this revolution which we talk about and which we hope for can take place'. Towards the end he identified a parallel revolution of imagination and consciousness in the Black Power or black consciousness movement which had started in the United States, moved to the Caribbean, and become an international movement. His final plea was for the link with the creole folk culture of the Caribbean to be re-established in Caribbean society 'at the deep detonating level of our peoples' consciousness. Then, in my opinion, the Caribbean would be transfigured, its energies liberated, and a new green unleashed for our possession'.

Brathwaite seemed attuned to the atmosphere set by the WISU chairman. After replying to a few questions and comments on his talk, he requested discussion 'so that people other than myself might express views'. He dealt briefly with questions from the audience on problems for the exiled writer, details of African culture, what sort of Black Power should be sought. Aubrey Williams was in the audience, and had intervened early and substantially. He thanked Brathwaite for two concepts, particularly that of a 'beautiful, utopian hope of cultural renaissance' – but wondered whether 'the stronger shoots of resurgence, if they did come now or in the future, would not be like the seeds of weeds coming up in a landscape that has been treated for weeds'.

Brathwaite thoroughly explored Williams's question and brought it into other replies so that it became the key discussion theme. His response was again informed by a year back in the Caribbean. Yes, society was increasingly mechanised and Americanised, with many consequent dangers – of the continuing projection of an outside image, of the folk tradition being regarded as irrelevant, of its being taken over by 'operators'. There was still hope in the individual, and especially in the artist. Brathwaite warned against wanting TV sets and a high standard of living, thus 'denying a chance for this renaissance to grow on its own terms, admitting the very influence you're supposed to be fighting against'. Industrialisation, in which 'the logic of European culture ends', would not necessarily improve the social wellbeing of the people.

John La Rose saw this as part of a wider problem: 'The moment you attempt to subvert solutions you enter the field of creative originality, and it's this that we're attempting to do by looking at a society in a different way from all the assumed ways of looking at societies.' A questioner took this to mean that 'instead of rooting up the past' in order to make the present more effective and real, they should work on new principles. But Brathwaite stressed the importance of examining and mapping out their past, and how past and present are continuous. A question was raised on what was to become a burning issue, in the Caribbean and in Britain: the relation of Black Power to socialism. Brathwaite, aware of the complexities involved, replied that the topic required a whole session to itself, and invited the questioner to give a talk on it; his own comment was that Black Power was 'autonomous, a thing in its own right and not a side issue'. Again La Rose came in, showing how such considerations were part of the same problem of creative originality, and that the term 'socialism' was 'itself a terminology which we've inherited. The very fact of attempting to recreate or to reconceptualise implies questioning an inheritance, means you invent as you go along. But to invent, you've got to be autonomous'.

Before taking questions, Gary Burton stressed his concept of the session's purpose: 'What we're trying to do here tonight is to create the foundations for a revolutionary Black Power, and that cannot be ready-made.' Brathwaite's year back in Jamaica, and the continuing dialogue between CAM founder members, provided the audience at the Students Centre with a level of practical creative endeavour and political wisdom won from experience which were far removed from Black Power rhetoric and revolutionary jargon.

Two speakers were listed for the second session of the symposium, 'The Negritude Movement and Black Awareness'. But there is no record of what Merle Hodge said in amplifying, no doubt, the claim in her Damas talk that the socio-political implications of Negritude continue today. Salkey introduced his paper on black awareness with a statement of indebtedness to Brathwaite including quotations from *Islands*, for awareness of the Caribbean Great Tradition, its native, folk tradition, and how 'our Caribbean present must be informed by it, shot through by it and revitalised accordingly'.

The 'working definition of black awareness in the Anglophone Caribbean' with which Salkey began was overtly political: from the realisation of West Indians' unique value in the economic expansion of Europe during slavery to recognition of 'our contemporary, neocolonialist years. . . . Abused client states, that's all we really are'. He distinguished himself from artists who were unaware of the political context and influences of their work. His definition ran thus:

> Black awareness in our Caribbean terms is the will to make concrete and viable our vision of ourselves as an initiating, self-protecting, inventive, courageous, productive and ultimately culturally enriched people. Black awareness is the beginning of our search and definition of revolution.

Such revolution would enable Caribbean people to 'make a dynamic contribution not only to their own history, but to world history'.

Salkey indicated recent sources of this 'new black awareness': early Rastafarian groups and the 'ensuing artistic aftermath'; Malcolm X and his influence on the arts in black America; the work and influence of Walter Rodney; the cultural impact of Jamaica-based CAM. He went on to name Caribbean writers, publications and institutions which he considered had made a contribution towards the new black awareness, in Britain and the Caribbean. The poets he included were very few: Brathwaite, Sebastian Clarke, Frank John, John La Rose, Tony Matthews, Basil Smith; so too were the novelists: Lindsay Barrett, Jan Carew, Roger Mais, Vic Reid, Sam Selvon, Orlando Patterson – here his strict political criteria made room for Selvon's 'comic genius', yet excluded Wilson Harris, George Lamming and VS Naipaul. Playwrights included Marina Maxwell, but again omitted Derek Walcott. Lamming was also excluded from the essayists. Gordon Rohlehr alone was cited as a critic with black awareness. The newspapers were those which came 'out of the Rodney supercharge'. New Beacon, Frank John's publications, and Black Dimensions were the only publishers. His exemplary single volumes were the Arusha Declaration, *Froudacity*, Goveia's historiography, *Black Jacobins* and the Havana Declaration – 'all pride-making narratives'. And the Students Centre was singled out as an establishment of black awareness, 'with Locksley Comrie and Richard Small. . . . through now with Gary Burton, Ansel Wong, Jack Hines, Earl Green'.

Finally Salkey indicated the way forward, primarily for the artist: 'As our Caribbean man begins to change, so must his vision, his language, his techniques, his objectives, and the uses of these in the arts.' Caribbean communities themselves must be the new centres for approval, not the metropolitan centres – as when he began to write – and Salkey warned of their new guises and continuing dangers: 'Neocolonialism has many faces.' He called on artists for a new alignment: 'Our struggle for change in the arts must be all of a piece with the new intention of our young people in the Caribbean.' Salkey closed by quoting a statement by Elsa Goveia that slaves and free men and women who 'demanded political equality . . . and championed the rights of man, were all alike in being essentially subversive. . . . The object of all their endeavours was radical change.' Salkey heard, he said, echoes of this statement in Brathwaite's paper, which was for him personally, 'a very clear call to revolution'.

John La Rose was the fourth speaker, with a paper on 'The Development of Black Experience and the Nature of Black Society in Britain'. He began with early Caribbean history: how Columbus and his successors had found and destroyed the Carib/Arawak civilisation of the Caribbean, and had attempted, but failed, to subordinate Amerindian civilisations elsewhere; how not long after, 'the first African ancestors were dragged away in that "ferry of infamy"'. The burden of his paper was 'the consequences, including our presence here today'.[27]

La Rose gave a succinct account of the way in which the use of African slave labour formed the basis for 'an entire structure of Empire': through commercial, then industrial capitalism. The unpaid labour of 'our African ancestors' enabled the first West Indians in Britain – white planters and slavers – to live in luxury, to build splendidly, to collect art, and so on. Africans came to Britain in small numbers soon after the slave trade began. Although the status of slavery had no recognition in English law, the social and occupational status of negroes was slow to change. Using late 19th century quotations from Joseph Chamberlain and Cecil Rhodes, La Rose showed how the Empire was unashamedly regarded as a market for British products, and hence essential to the living standards of Britain's own expanding population. He linked the hippie who tried to withdraw from industrial society, the Afro-American who shouted 'burn baby, burn', the act of possession in African religious practice in the Caribbean, as different forms of flight from 'this virus of destruction'.

La Rose demonstrated how Empire also rested on the contempt of the coloniser for the colonised, so that the self-confidence of the colonised was eroded and his self-contempt deepened. VS Naipaul was cited as the product of such contempt, Prospero/Caliban, Crusoe/Friday relationships in the work of Shakespeare and Defoe as reinforcing the ideology of colonisation: 'Here the thrust is to appropriate and manipulate the intimate subconscious of the conquered and to wean him away from himself and toward the great universalising Euro-centred tradition which CLR described at great length at the first CAM conference.' La Rose quoted Derek Walcott's poem, 'A Far Cry from Africa' as an expression of the colonised intellectual; he cited Aimé Césaire's *Cahier* and Jacques Roumain's 'A Long Road to Guinea' as 'profound poetic revelation' of 'the journey of the exile from the source', linking them with the art of possession in pocomania and shango, as 'a flight from destruction into the circle of light'.

The contemporary dilemma of West Indian peoples was described by La Rose in the 'Prosepoem for a Conference' which formed part of his paper:

> A people of exile, living in the permanence of tragedy and dispossessed hope. We are the wanderers and a wonder of this world. . . . We are, such as we are, living tissue of contemporaneity caught in our islands, or thicker land masses, plying our own triangular trade in ourselves; exporting ourselves from hopelessness into hope. . . . Fragments of roots, scorned in the night of self-contempt – spring to rebirth, the seeds of renewal. Exile paid its premium in self-awareness. We begin to know, a message of hope and contradiction, but such is my message.[28]

This, explained La Rose, was the tension into which stepped the black abolitionist, the black maroon, black slave rebels, and their 'perception of creative originality'. Similar originality was shown by JJ Thomas, in 'validating the new languages which the Africans developed in the Americas to appropriate the world in their own terms through their own vision of experience. . . . This was Caliban and Friday preserving the intimacy of their vision, rebelling and asserting their being, scorning contempt and dissolving self-contempt'.

This joint symposium was the first CAM event at which John La Rose and Andrew Salkey were main speakers. Although wellknown at the time respectively as poet and novelist, their roles at CAM sessions and conferences until now had been as chairman or a participant in discussions; despite repeated requests from the committee, they chose not to make formal presentations themselves. Now, after a year as joint secretaries, they spoke alongside Brathwaite. Just as Brathwaite's paper was informed by his year in Jamaica, so were theirs by the year in Britain: by their programme of CAM events, by their close cooperation with WISU and the Students Centre, and by their close involvement in black community issues. The papers by Salkey and La Rose must surely, like that of Brathwaite, have been followed by discussion, but it seems not to have been recorded. The three papers themselves were recorded, and that of La Rose reproduced in *Newsletter* No. 11. They show the very different yet inter-related approaches of CAM's three founder-members to Caribbean society and the artist's role within it. All three spoke from concern and involvement with the West Indian community, with none of the apparent defensiveness when they were challenged at the Second Conference, only a year earlier.

A complete account of the symposium is further impaired by other peoples' papers apparently not having been recorded. The absence of what was said by Jack Hines and Augustine (Gus) John in 'The threat to the education of the Black child in Britain and what to do' is particularly regrettable. Jack Hines was a Jamaican law student who became involved with the struggle against banding in schools and with the supplementary schools movement; he helped to found the Caribbean Education Association (see below). Augustine (Gus) John, born in Grenada, had come to Britain in 1964, to train as a novitiate of the Dominican order. As the only black student priest at Blackfriars Priory in Oxford, he quickly came, as he puts it, 'face to face with British racism in terms of my own personal experience as well as what was actually happening in terms of the English law'. He worked with the Oxford Council for Racial Integration, and was specially active on its education sub-committee, helping to organise the children of Caribbean workers at the Cowley car factories, and of Asian communities in Oxford. In 1967 he decided to leave the Dominicans, for reasons to do with their involvement in South Africa, and because his evolving Marxism made it seem inconsistent to continue as a member of the church. He came to London, worked at a youth centre in a crypt in Paddington, and became involved in the network of activities around the Students Centre, particularly, he recalls,

> with a group of younger and older people, passionately interested in education and what was actually happening to our children. . . . There were problems of children coming to this country from the Caribbean to join parents . . . and the difficulties of the British people not really understanding the nature of the West Indian education system and introducing tests which were culturally biased and discriminatory.

CAM members' other involvements

John La Rose, in particular amongst CAM members, shared the interest in West Indian children's education demonstrated by WISU and spoken about at the symposium by Jack Hines and Gus John. Introducing CAM's April session La Rose had brought to the attention of the audience the 'dangerous threat which is hanging over the heads of children of West Indians in the Haringey area of North London', and read out a leaflet issued by the North London West Indian Association (NLWIA):

> ALL WEST INDIAN PARENTS . . . . BEWARE
> YOUR CHILD'S FUTURE IS THREATENED
> It's time to get up and get NOW
> We are all ambitious for our children. No mountain is too high. Some people think we are too ambitious.
> SO WE HAVE TO DO SOMETHING ABOUT IT
> The HARINGEY EDUCATION COMMITTEE proposes to introduce changes which will affect *YOUR* child
> * Children are going to be "banded"
> * Schools are going to be "streamed"
> * Black children will be dispersed
> One of the main reasons given for this "DRAMATIC CHANGE" by Haringey Education Committee is the HIGH PROPORTION OF BLACK CHILDREN IN HARINGEY SCHOOLS
> This is just the smoke!
> More in the mortar beside the pestle!
> UNITE AND FIGHT FOR YOUR RIGHT

La Rose was a speaker, along with Jeff Crawford and others, at a meeting on 23 April called by the North London West Indian Association, paralleled by a signature campaign and followed by another demonstration at Haringey Civic Centre. Their aim was to coordinate protest at the new policy of 'banding' which Haringey Borough Council was on the point of adopting. 'Banding' had been recommended by a Council committee as the basis for distributing pupils in Haringey secondary schools into its 11 newly established comprehensive schools. Ostensibly banding would ensure that each school had a spread of pupils in bands of above average, average, and below average ability. But a secret document, leaked to leaders of the NLWIA, revealed the real reason. 'On a rough calculation half the immigrants will be West Indians at 7 of the 11 schools, the significance of this being the general recognition that their IQ's work out below their English contemporaries. Thus academic standards will be lower in schools where they form a large group.'[29] To the leaders of the NLWIA it was clear that the proposed spreading of the West Indian children population through banding would stop this concentration and make it possible to ignore their lack of success in the education system. John La Rose and Winston Best, Barbados-born teacher, were part of the working group which formulated a response to the Council and coordinated the protest. The NLWIA campaign resulted in the Council ultimately withdrawing its banding proposals.

In March 1969, shortly before this campaign was getting under way, John La Rose and Sarah White moved into their new home at 2 Albert Road, Finsbury Park. Its downstairs front room became the New Beacon Bookshop. During 1969 La Rose was involved in establishing the George Padmore and Albertina Sylvester Supplementary Schools, amongst the first 'supplementary schools' for West Indian children; it was held in the new bookshop after school on Mondays, Fridays and Saturdays.[30] In the summer of 1969, La Rose, Gus John, Jack Hines and others formed the Caribbean Educational Association (CEA), later renamed the Caribbean Educational and Community Workers Association (CECWA).

The education issue was regularly on the agenda at the Students Centre. At a 3–10 pm meeting on 27 April, titled 'Towards Our Freedom', the first item was 'The threat to black children's education in Britain'. Other topics ranged from 'Britain's Racism In Anguilla', 'Problems Confronting Black West Indian Students In Canada' and 'Biafra' to the 'International Black Struggle'. Almost all the participants had also taken part in CAM events: Cosmo Pieterse, Richard Small, Calvin Hernton, Tony Matthews, Basil Smith, Winston Best – and as always, La Rose and Salkey. The following month, on 18 May, in a 4–10 pm meeting, La Rose spoke on 'Haringey's Ghetto Schools'. The meeting was another anniversary celebration of Malcolm X's death, now named 'Black Prophet El Malik El Hajj Shabazz', with the words, 'It's time for Black People to come together on the basis of what we have in common . . . *OUR BLACKNESS*.' After La Rose, Ansel Wong spoke on 'Black Cultural Nationalism'. Other speakers were as before: Pieterse, Matthews, Smith, Hernton, and Salkey. They came together for a final session: 'Our common bonds'.

Increasingly the consciousness and thrust of these WISU meetings was of the black struggle as an international one: cultural, educational and political. Its climax was UNITY WEEK, 25 August – 1 September, following immediately after the weekend CAM–WISU symposium. With the title, 'Unity – The Time Is Now' – and a cover drawing of hands from Africa joined with a hand from the Caribbean below a profile from the southern USA – the booklet of the week's events contains many statements and quotations. The statements relate to contemporary issues for the black community in Britain: Gary Burton, chairman of the Students Centre's House Committee on the 'opening up of the West Indian Students Centre to all black people and my own efforts to broaden the definition of a student'; Tony Hug, chairman of the National Federation of Pakistani Associations in Great Britain, on the need for a militant black people's front; Hortense Spillers, on her observation of racism in Britain during her stay in London. The programme's quotations are all Afro-American: Langston Hughes, Carolyn F Gerald, Jorge Rebelo, Nikki Giovanni, Ron Karenga, Claude Brown. Such forceful consciousness of blackness was only just beginning to be articulated by West Indians in Britain: poems by June C Doiley, a young Jamaican student, and by Basil Smith are included.

The programme, which was drawn up by the students, shows substantial input by members of CAM: CLR James and Cosmo Pieterse were amongst those speaking on 'The Black International Struggle'; Errol Lloyd and Horace James spoke on 'Our Cultural Heritage', Donald Hinds on 'The West Indian In Britain'. Andrew Salkey presented three films from revolutionary Cuba and took part in an 'assessment of programmes and policies of the West Indian Students Centre – new directions for the future'. Exhibitions included arts and crafts (Errol Lloyd), books (John La Rose of New Beacon): also photography (Denis Stafford Chung). Performances included Jacques Compton reading West Indian short stories 'by writers who are essentially folk poets'; Faustin Charles, Tony Matthews, Basil Smith and others reading their poetry; Bari Jonson's one-man show. There was also a performance by the Black Arts Dance Company, a play by the Black Arts Workshop, a compilation of 'jazz, poetry and mime' – for all of which Ansel Wong was mainly responsible. Members of the Black Arts Workshop, in particular, Femi Fatoba, June Doiley and Ansel Wong, attended CAM meetings.

CLR James was presented with a bust of himself by Errol Lloyd, with, La Rose recalls, 'a most moving speech'. Lloyd's sculpture had been cast in bronze thanks to the efforts of a small committee of Cris Le Maitre, La Rose, Small and Lloyd. A special presentation was made by the House Committee of the Students Centre, 'on behalf of *all Black People*', to Jessica Huntley, as one of 'several brothers and sisters [who] have offered their services, expertise and advice to us in our struggles to discover ourselves'. Huntley had herself typed and brought out papers in connection with the Centre's 1968 seminar, was now seeking funds for publication of statements from a recent conference on black power in Bermuda, and was about to bring out the book of speeches and essays by Walter Rodney, *The Groundings with my Brothers*, edited by Ewart Thomas, with an introduction by Richard Small and cover design by Errol Lloyd. The book was published under a new imprint with deliberate double resonance: Bogle-L'Ouverture, an imprint whose publications were soon to make a unique and significant impact alongside those of New Beacon.[31]

The New Beacon Bookshop and publishing company had considerably more space and prominence in its new home at 2 Albert Road. Peter Fraser recalls how 'it was quite splendid going to a bookshop in somebody's front room. And having such a wonderful bookshop owner to speak to, about not only the literature, but

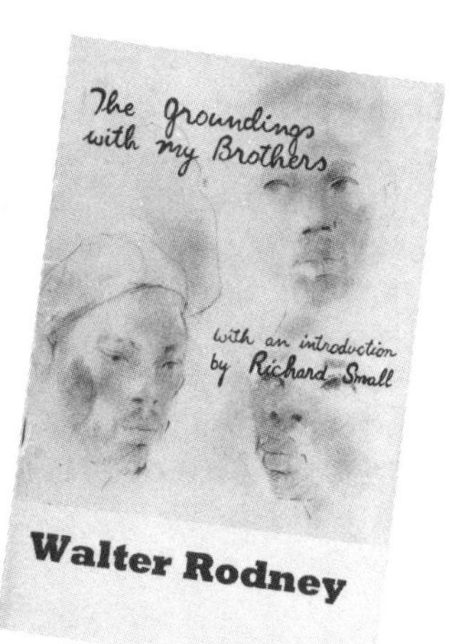

Cover, **The Groundings with my Brothers,** ***drawings by Errol Lloyd***

Bust of CLR James by Errol Lloyd

also the politics and culture of the Caribbean'. New Beacon was now so well established in the West Indian community, and such an integral part of events at the Centre, that John La Rose was given space to write about it in the Unity Week programme. His statement is consistent with his deeply rooted and long-lasting intent, and worded in typical La Rose style, avoiding all fashionable contemporary jargon:

> New Beacon is an attempt to end the constant hiatus in certain areas of Caribbean life; to end the imprisonment in English, in Spanish, in French, in Dutch which accordingly denies areas of experience which, if made available, would immediately disclose the total specificity of Caribbean life; and to make each new generation aware that they are not starting from scratch. As distributors of books (Caribbeana, Afro-Americana, Africana) New Beacon sets out to assist in the recovery of a past held in contempt, and to establish an awareness of the dangers and pitfalls which lie ahead if facile solutions are expected or attempted. More autonomous appropriation of the Word through publishing is what is needed. We have only taken a small step.

Former WISU officers remember the practical help which they received from CAM members. Ansel Wong, chairman of the House Committee in the late 1960s, acknowledges the support and guidance of La Rose and Salkey in activities at the Centre. Locksley Comrie, outgoing president of WISU in May 1969 recalls how, when he heard of a charge being trumped up against him,

> the first person I went to was Andrew Salkey. I said, 'Andrew, somebody's trying to frame me – somebody from the audience, the Students Union.' Andrew followed me to the Police Station, went in and said, 'Is there a charge or do you intend to press a charge against Locksley?'. They said, 'No, but there have been certain reports.' And Andrew said, 'Can I have it?' and it was given. And Andrew handled that case and the police apologised and we went our ways.

Given John La Rose's work in education with his supplementary school and the CEA on top of his publishing and bookselling, Andrew Salkey's active role with the Students Centre on top of his radio and other journalistic work, and his own writing, their continued input in CAM and its programme throughout 1968 and 1969 was remarkable. Salkey also carried the main burden of CAM correspondence. He took on Brathwaite's earlier role of encouragement, thanks and support to fellow CAM workers, gave helpful critical comment to fledgling writers, assisted with and contributed to the *Newsletter*, fielded requests for CAM's help with events and exhibitions.

CAM (UK) activity, 1970

The CAM Committee received a further blow in January 1970: another early, core member, its hard-working and efficient treasurer, Oliver Clarke, returned to Jamaica, his accountancy studies complete. Like the Brathwaites, he seemed irreplaceable. CAM was now no longer the buoyant organisation of October 1968, and Clarke's long-serving committee colleagues were tired and overstretched. A letter from Salkey to Brathwaite shows how it was:

> The Treasurer's bit re CAM is quite a problem; nothing was ever settled before Oliver's departure, and everything has been dumped on yours truly. I have asked Kelvin (Kelly) Saul, Secretary/Treasurer of the West Indian Students Centre's Board of Governors and a chartered accountant himself, (Guyanese) to be our new Treasurer for CAM. He has agreed. I will see him on Saturday for the big handover.[32]

Salkey amended the membership fee reminder form with Kelvin Saul's name replacing Oliver Clarke's. Anne Walmsley ran it off, ready to put in with notices of the next meeting; she also attempted to update the membership list. But with the lull in CAM activity, membership lapsed, and there was little for the new treasurer to do.

Donald Hinds chaired and introduced CAM's first public session in February 1970, on 'Contemporary African Poetry', with two African poets, Femi Fatoba (Nigeria) and Cosmo Pieterse (Namibia). La Rose had proposed the session; since he first met Ngũgi at an early CAM private meeting, he had been looking for ways, as he puts it, 'to bring the Africans closer to us'. Fatoba had already taken part in a CAM session on Yoruba drumming; Pieterse had attended and participated in the Second Conference. Now they read and commented on poetry by their contemporaries, including: David Diop, Léopold Senghor, Gaston Bart-Williams, Gabriel Okara, Christopher Okigbo, Dennis Brutus, Jorge Rebelo, Agostinho Neto, D'Andrade, Wole Soyinka, Ouloguem Yambo, JP Clark, Kofi Awoonor, Okot p'Bitek, Taban lo Liyong,

Tchic'aya U'Tamsi, Malangatana, John Okai. Their reading also included traditional oral African poetry, and their own poems.

CAM's joint secretaries were away from London in February, attending the Guyana Republic Celebrations and Convention of Writers and Artists. In early April, they held two CAM public sessions for reports on their visit. They were joined by Ivan Van Sertima and Sam Selvon for the first session, when they gave their impressions of Guyana. Although the session was not recorded, Sebastian Clarke (now Amon Saba Saakana), who had been in the audience, interviewed La Rose the following day about his observations in Guyana. Introducing the published interview, Saakana described its significance being 'that it re-evaluates and re-appraises all traditionally accepted norms of what art is, how it is to function etc, anything, but true to the life styles of Black people.'[33] La Rose had asked to be allowed to see Afro-centred traditions, and attended a queh-queh wedding and a cumfa religious ceremony. He pointed out the difficulty which musicians trained in 'a certain kind of musical notation' had in writing down the music of the first; the element of drama in the second reminded him of *Maria Antonia*, the dramatic production which he had seen in Havana, 'where there's a long tradition . . . of studying the folk . . . and especially the Afro-centred folk traditions' – beside which the Theatre Guild production which he saw in Georgetown, *My Name is Slave*, 'really looked quite cardboard'. To Saakana's question as to whether there were 'any signs of a cultural awakening in terms of the mass population, African and Indian', La Rose described the 'very fierce mental culture . . . centred in Georgetown but . . . based upon the world' of which Martin Carter and Wilson Harris were part. He also mentioned a new poetry magazine called *Expression* edited in rotation by recent school-leavers who included John Agard and Janice Lowe (now Shinebourne). Georgetown was, he said, 'a very African town'. Although there were Indian writers and producers of plays and so on, he confessed not to know what was happening in cultural terms among the Indians on the plantations.

At the second session the same speakers, plus Aubrey Williams, less Selvon, spoke about the focus of their visit – the convention and its proposals for a Caribbean Festival of the Arts. La Rose prefaced his account with mention of the earlier convention in 1966, and of the leading figures and publications of Guyana's cultural scene: Lynette Dolphin and Arthur Seymour, Chairman and Vice-Chairman of the National History and Arts Council of Guyana, pianist and poet respectively; *Kyk-over-al*, in which Martin Carter, Wilson Harris and Ivan Van Sertima were first published, and now *Kaie*.[34] He stressed the lack of continuity between the two conventions because leading figures in Caribbean arts who attended the 1966 Convention were absent in 1970. The list of artists present in 1970 was, however, long and varied, and included writers, painters, musicians, actors and dramatists, and a dancer.

La Rose went on to give his account of the meeting called, the day before the official convention, by the Brathwaites, Salkey and himself. Their account of CAM had stressed 'the informal nature of its structure which we think absolutely necessary for a community of artists and people interested in the arts, if they are to retain their independence and function effectively'. After discussion, stated La Rose, 'people felt there should be a Caribbean CAM. This was expressed especially by some of the people who had never participated at all in CAM's work. So they were exploring the possibility of a Caribbean CAM and how it could be structured.' La Rose's account of the meeting and its outcome is consistent with his initial concept of the purpose and character of CAM. It is markedly more positive and optimistic than Salkey's account in *Georgetown Journal*.

The purpose of the convention was to discuss and prepare for a Festival of Caribbean Arts in 1971 or 1972. La Rose gave a detailed account of it, summarising the conclusions of the sub-committees, each concerned with a different aspect of the arts. There was much evidence of contributions by CAM members: from the Literature Committee, that the convention should have been more broadly-based to include academics like Elsa Goveia, Gordon Rohlehr, Kenneth Ramchand, so that inter-disciplinary dialogue would have taken place; from the Music and Drama Committee, that instead of a four-yearly festival there should be continual 'participation of the artists in the life of the society', with the emphasis on young people; from the Art Committee – of which Aubrey Williams was rapporteur – that Amerindian work should be included, and that the visual arts should contribute to other art forms. Moreover, 'we in CAM', affirmed La Rose to this CAM meeting in London, 'propose to pursue this question of festivals continuously with the people back in Guyana'. He urged the audience to contribute their ideas and suggestions, and send them to Georgetown. La Rose's overall concern was to ensure that the Festival should be fully and widely contributed to by Caribbean people, in the way that CAM events were, and not simply controlled by official festival sub-committees.

The convention's definition of the Caribbean was that initiated by the New World movement and adopted by CAM: 'the area which extends from Cuba to the Guianas, which crosses language and discovers specificity in ourselves.' La Rose indeed recalls Salkey and himself insisting that artists from the non-Anglophone Caribbean be invited to participate in Carifesta; that, despite political difficulties, Cuba must culturally be part of it. When, after the convention, Martin Carter and Arthur Seymour were passing through London, they met together in Salkey's flat and La Rose again stressed that Carifesta must be pan-Caribbean. Later, La Rose recalls supplying names and addresses in Haiti, Cuba, Martinique and Guadeloupe, at Lynette Dolphin's request.

Andrew Salkey, at La Rose's request, spoke about the 'concealed fundamental benefits' to Caribbean societies of such a festival. It would not simply display Caribbean creative arts, but would make 'a fundamental statement about our lives through our art', because culture, in CAM's definition was 'an umbrella term for all the efforts we make, all the acts we perform to enhance our lives and the results accruing from these efforts', in contrast to 'that strange, middle-class concept of culture'. The Guyana proposal for an Arts Festival was revolutionary because it was based, Salkey believed, 'on majority participation, on total Caribbean mobilisation'. The cultural gains would be many: to combat Euro-centred statements about Caribbean culture,[35] and to provide a parallel to the energy being unleashed by small groups throughout the area. The Guyana proposal was 'our Caribbean revolution, through the arts, aimed at the dismantling of our underdevelopment and exploitation and what John correctly calls our mimetic cultural position'. And his hope was that the Festival would become 'a dynamic continuing reality'.

Ivan Van Sertima's response was altogether more cautious and sceptical. The festival plans looked to him like 'government bulletins'; the convention 'like a great circus'. After the bitter Guyanese experience of 1953, he warned against entering into this festival with naive hopes of a revolution. For a real cultural breakthrough, there had to be revolution inside the people themselves – hence the importance of 'a continuous, vital contact with the people' by the artists and writers of the region. The recent convention, the proposed festival, were indeed signs of things starting to change in Guyana, but they must be sure that 'this thing runs right through the lives of the people'. Once again, as at the Second Conference, he spoke out against the fact that no West Indian novels or poetry were used in Guyanese schools, that there was no course in Caribbean literature at the University of Guyana.

Aubrey Williams, who spoke last, was less worried about this first Festival of Caribbean Arts: 'The important thing is that it be done. It must start and afterwards we would grow on that.' But he was perturbed to find scant coverage of the convention in the Caribbean press, of what was 'a unique occurrence . . . [that] a democratic government should choose to make its coming republican status by holding a conference of the arts' – a consequence of the 'very profound sympathy and understanding of the creative arts' which had grown over the past four years in Guyana's President, Forbes Burnham. Williams was eager to talk about his first visit to Jamaica, afterwards. He was deeply affected by its landscape and its people, especially by the very poor. Whereas in other countries they seemed poverty-stricken,

> in Jamaica, this was never so. In the lowest level of the peasantry, I found something that I've always had a hunger for in other countries of the Caribbean, a striking personal pride. . . . I have to go back to Jamaica again and again because I feel that here is the human template for a Caribbean people.

The Rastafari people, and Rastafarian art were, he said, 'one of the shocks of my visit to the Caribbean this time'. He had spent a night with a group of them, called Charter 15, smoking and drinking 'the root, the weed'. The leader impressed him most of all. 'The truths in his statements come slowly home to me.' Williams played extracts from a tape of his night with Chapter 15.

During questions and discussion, reference was made to the recent Black Power demonstrations in Trinidad. La Rose promised another meeting in ten days' time when more information would be given, because 'we need to understand what is going on'. La Rose, too, commented at length on the absence of any Rastafarian artist at the recent convention, and the lack of discussion of music from 'our real traditions', such as those of bongo and shango. CAM was, he stressed, attempting to give convention and festival a 'much larger creative dimension' than had been proposed. Because of the authoritarian tradition in Caribbean society, there was a tendency to leave things for people with authority to do: hence the need for CAM's intervention in a way that would be effective.

John La Rose continued to feel buoyant about CAM in Britain. Writing to Brathwaite in May 1970, he reported news of the latest New Beacon publications – Brathwaite's *Folk Culture of the Slaves in Jamaica* and the reprint of *Creole Grammar* by JJ Thomas, and continued: 'The work goes on. We had two sessions on Guyana, on the 3rd and 10th March [sic; in fact, April]. They were both very good. We had Sam [Selvon], for the first time, with us.'[36]

No further CAM meetings are on record, or remembered, for the balance of 1970. Demands on the joint secretaries from their other involvements increased, and CAM's activities as such went into abeyance. Eight months into 1970, Donald Hinds and Christopher Laird brought out *Newsletter* No. 12, containing part two of the transcript of Van Sertima's talk the year before, two book reviews, six poems by James Berry, and a listing of members' awards and new publications. With CAM so dormant, there was very little news.

John La Rose's activity in publishing was, during 1969–70,

matched by Andrew Salkey's activity as a writer. His fourth novel, *The Adventures of Catullus Kelly*, set in London, was published in 1969, and followed in 1970 by *Havana Journal* and a new children's book, *Jonah Simpson* – with demonstrable CAM influence in the change of jacket artist and illustrator from William Papas to Karl 'Jerry' Craig. Salkey's novel, *Come Home, Malcolm Heartland*, was not published until 1976. But from its opening quotations – from a 1969 interview with Alejo Carpentier and from Césaire's *Cahier*, to its references – to the Haringey schools issue and to Enoch Powell, it is in theme and context a book of the 1968–1970 period. The Centre, so important to the book's main characters and the scene of much of the action, though here set in Brixton, shares recognisable features with the Students Centre in Earls Court: a facade of a 'converted Victorian mansion', with a bar 'which was typically crowded', and a main lecture hall with double doors.[37] Malcolm talks about 'the change that had come about at the Centre, from the period when it was an inoffensive students' hideaway to its present exciting climax of a confused revolutionary forum'. He remembers 'that the place had provided its members and uninvited floating groups of droppers-in with a variety of cultural and specific political activities'. The Students Centre was the centre of Salkey's activism, cultural and political, and his vivid record of it in this period was part of that activism.

As 1970 progressed, events in Britain claimed more and more of La Rose's and Salkey's time and energy. The fight against the 'banding' of black children, successful in Haringey, 'spread to other areas, and became incorporated in the programmes of black political organisations'.[38] Meanwhile the NLWIA, concerned for some time by the question of West Indian children in ESN (Educationally Sub-Normal) schools, had taken the Haringey Borough Council to the Race Relations Board on grounds of racial discrimination. After a year's investigation the Board 'agreed that there were in fact a disproportionate number of pupils of West Indian origin' in such schools.[39] In 1970 CECWA held a conference, which La Rose was involved in organising..

Other CAM members were concerned with the effects of apparently racist attitudes and practices not only in education but in British society at large. Ambalavaner Sivanandan was librarian at the white liberal Institute of Race Relations (IRR); a Sri Lankan Tamil, he had come to Britain with his Singalese wife in 1958, just at the time of the Notting Hill riots. He had joined CAM through knowing Richard Small in CARD. The IRR staff, led by Sivanandan, considered the Institute's presentation of race issues to be exclusively academic, and to avoid awareness and analysis of the race relations on its doorstep in Britain. In 1970 they began to work for fundamental change at the IRR.

Confrontations between the police and the black community were meanwhile on the increase, including attacks on individuals and on black institutions. The Black House, a cultural group newly set up by the Racial Action Adjustment Society (RAAS), was raided by the police in February 1970 and closed down. The Mangrove Restaurant, in Notting Hill, 'a meeting place and an eating place, a social and welfare club, an advice and resource centre, a black house for black people', was repeatedly raided by the police, who harassed its customers and persecuted its owner, Frank Critchlow.[40] A demonstration on 9 August in protest at its proposed closure was met with police violence, against which the blacks fought back. A number were arrested, and nine were subsequently charged with riot, affray and assault. Preparations and support for the defence of the 'Mangrove 9' absorbed much energy of leading CAM members from August 1970 until the trial in the autumn of 1971. CAM poets read at many of the defence meetings.

1970 was a crucial year, a turning point, for the black community in Britain. CAM activity inevitably became more diverse and dispersed in the urgent concerns which faced its members, and in which its joint secretaries, La Rose and Salkey, were especially involved.

9 CAM Continuing
At Home 1971 - 1982

1971–1972

At home in the Caribbean, where all attempts to seed CAM as such had failed, 1971–2 saw continued flowering of its offshoots, and at the same time, the entrenchment of divergent directions. In Jamaica, Yard Theatre developed more substantial, less frequent, productions. *Savacou* broke new ground with its collections of creative and academic writing. In 1971, Karl 'Jerry' and Christine Craig returned home. Christine was at last able to develop her interest and gifts in writing, first stimulated through CAM in London. Jerry was appointed Director of the Jamaica School of Art, where he brought the CAM experience into all aspects of art education and training. Clifton Campbell had meanwhile been appointed Art Inspector in the Ministry of Education, enabling his CAM experience to be brought into schools. A short but high profile visit by Ronald Moody, and annual, longer visits by Aubrey Williams, with frequent exhibitions, enabled their work and ideas, their particular 'vision of consciousness' – familiar to CAM members in Britain – to be known in Jamaica.

Also in 1971 Christopher and Judith Laird returned home to Trinidad, and began to prepare the ground for opening Kairi House and its magazine, *Kairi*, both of which recognise CAM roots. And Guyana, in 1972, was host to the first Carifesta, a fully regional celebration of all the Caribbean arts, to which CAM people and ideas had contributed, which CAM people attended, and at which Brathwaite held another CAM session.

ACLALS papers, 'Savacou' poems

Early in 1971, CAM members' work was most visible in the field of literature. In January, the UWI Mona campus hosted the triennial Conference of the Association for Commonwealth Literature and Language Studies (ACLALS). Sessions were held at the Creative Arts Centre. This was ACLALS' first conference to be held in the Caribbean; for the English Department on all three UWI campuses, and especially for Mona, it was important as the first chance for the now substantial body of Caribbean literature in English to be critically discussed together with longer established literatures of the Commonwealth; it was the first airing of the younger Caribbean critics in an international forum. VS Naipaul was invited as guest speaker, and accepted. Edward Kamau Brathwaite was invited to give the opening paper. In 'The Function of the Writer in the Caribbean' Brathwaite's theme, as he summarises it, was:

> That the writer should [get to] know his society, and history, and do what he could to heal the dichotomies, especially between folk and elite, folk being defined (for me) as the black masses without the exclusion of the folk from other cultural groups; and that the healing process had to begin with a recognition of the resources of the folk, we ourselves turning our eyes from overseas back to the ground of ourselves.[1]

Naipaul was asked to 'respond' to Brathwaite's paper. Neither paper nor response has ever been published; nor has a full record appeared of the ensuing discussion, which Brathwaite describes as causing the conference to 'split into "Academics", upholding the tradition . . . and "Gorillas" . . . hammering home the new gospel of indigenisation'.[2] Anti-Naipaul statements made during the debate have been unfairly attributed to Brathwaite.

Papers given at the ACLALS Conference by Kenneth Ramchand and Gordon Rohlehr, like that of Brathwaite, reflected the debate at CAM sessions in London and Canterbury and indicated the directions in which their critical thought had been developing since. Ramchand, in 'History and the Novel: A Literary Critic's Approach' sets out to show how, 'even when they are concerned with contemporary reality, nearly all West Indian novels are engaged with history'.[3] With side-glances at Lamming's *Season of Adventure* and Naipaul's *A House for Mr Biswas*, and a more detailed look at Anthony's *The Year in San Fernando*, he concludes that 'the imaginative writer, trying to produce a historical novel as such, runs an unnecessary risk, and that the writer who is alive to his time and in his time is automatically involved in a dialogue with the past and the future'. As in his talks to CAM in 1967, Ramchand continues to defend Anthony as an exemplary writer of fiction. The bulk of his paper is concerned with 'one of the best-known historical novels', Vic Reid's *New Day*, contrasting attitudes towards it by literary critics (Louis James and Gerald Moore) and the historian Roy Augier, and pointing to the possibilities which may result from 'a form of collaboration' between the work of the historian and the work of the novelist. Rohlehr, in 'The Folk in Caribbean Literature', attempts to redefine the much-used term 'the folk' and West Indian writers' relation to it. He sees their main problem as 'one of understanding and expressing the flow between rural "folk" sensibility and experiences of semi or total urbanisation'.[4] Because 'folk' has most insistently been applied to the work of Selvon, Rohlehr looks especially at *A Brighter Sun* and *The Lonely Londoners*, in order 'to point out the variety and consequently the inadequacy of the term'. He quotes Selvon's prose alongside calypso lyrics to demonstrate that both relate to the same oral tradition which comes 'out of the process of acculturation in the town'. Similarly, he shows how Louise Bennett's verse comes from the same tradition as Sparrow's calypsos. Rohlehr has consolidated and expanded the ideas which he expressed to CAM in 1967.

Simultaneously with the ACLALS Conference, Gordon Rohlehr's article 'Islands' appeared in the January 1971 issue of *Caribbean Studies*.[5] This was the first sustained piece of critical writing to consider Brathwaite's three long poems as a trilogy, and Rohlehr's first substantial exposition of Brathwaite's poetry. He opens with a bold assertion: 'Together these books are the monumental epic of a race, a kind of *Aeneid* or *Iliad* for Black people'; he goes on to state that they reveal 'Brathwaite's concern as an Afro-West Indian who is both professional historian and poet, with coming to terms with his own history'. Rohlehr's knowledgeable exposition and careful, sympathetic analysis of each poem in content, language and form, defend and illuminate his assertions. The deeply shared cultural understanding between writer and critic which began in Britain through CAM is here in flower.

Two months later, *Savacou* 3/4, December 1970/March 1971, was published, a 'special issue', 'New Writing 1970': the fourth issue, as promised, 'devoted to the publication of creative and artistic criticism'. It is, in fact, all creative work, with no criticism, and it altogether fulfils the first of the journal's 'General Aims': 'To present the work of creative writers – established, unknown, in exile or at home.'[6] The bulk of the issue – 176 pages, a double issue – consists of new work by 'established' writers: extracts from novels in progress by John Hearne ('Slave Ship' from *The Sure Salvation*) and George Lamming (from *Natives of my Person*); poems by Martin Carter, John Figueroa, Cecil Gray, Nicolas Guillen (in translation – the only non-English-speaking Caribbean writing), AL Hendriks, and Derek Walcott. Also, it contains work by younger writers whose work had already been published in other Caribbean literary journals: extracts from novels in progress by Timothy Callender, 'Martin's Bay' (not published) and 'Circle' by James Carnegie, from *Wages Paid* (1976); poems by James Berry, Wayne Brown, Dennis Craig, Marc Matthews, Anthony McNeill, Mervyn Morris, Victor Questel, Basil Smith, Bruce St John, Dennis Scott; an account of a visit to Cuba by Barry Reckord, and 'White Fridays in Trinidad', extracts from an anonymous diary which records at firsthand the events and mood of the Trinidad February Revolution.

This substantial amount of undisputably literary material is prefaced by and interspersed with a handful of aggressively non-literary contributions by young Jamaicans. Unknown to readers of literary journals, they had been given quite a hearing in Kingston, in performance at Yard Theatre and similar venues, and in the many grassroots publications which had sprung up and circulated in Jamaica from 1968 onwards, such as *Bongo Man*, *Ital*, *Rasta Voice*, *Abeng*. Brathwaite had been excited by them from the time of his return. His letter of December 1968 which described the 'fiasco of the exploratory CAM meeting' had told Salkey more about the young writers and their publications, first introduced to CAM in London at its November 1968 meeting:

> Little pamphlets, broadsheets, broadsides, good journalism, interesting poems. And what I like about these boys: they are cool. They are gentle and quiet. They seem to be listening; watching; waiting. We may have the Revolution with this generation or the next or the next. But there is certainly a change; a difference. I am trying to make up a collection to send to you; for your archives. But they are v. difficult to find; and if found, to keep.[7]

Brathwaite had gone on to quote to Salkey the first part of 'The Youth' by Bongo Jerry, which appears as the fourth poem in *Savacou* 3/4:

> I want to know the truth.
> But they tell me to wait.
> Wait till when?
> Till I'm seventy.
> Or eighty and eight.
> I can no wait.
> Because dem tek young people fe idiot.
> To them truth is when you don't tell lie or when you face
>   don't show it.
> Hoping that they could hide the truth and I would never know it.
> Dem cold.
> For the truth will out.
> Because I the youth will shout.

Three other poems by Bongo Jerry, alongside two poems and two prose pieces by Audvil King, and a prose 'Comment' by Ras Dizzy, appear in *Savacou* 3/4. Placed at the start of the journal, immediately before and soon after 'White Fridays in Trinidad', they have maximum impact as voices of the black, dispossessed, youth of the Caribbean. Jerry and King in particular articulate the feelings and experience of the youth in post-independent Jamaica, drawing on black consciousness, Rastafarian language and imagery, reggae rhythm, disc jockey style, in their verse and prose experiments.

Brathwaite took pains in the 'Foreward*', annotated '*sic' to

Savacou 3/4 to defend the selection, and particularly these early contributions, against charges of sacrificing 'literary' standards to the current wave of black consciousness:

> The consciousness we are speaking about is also very largely a Black Consciousness; and this is what scares the pants off those who talk about 'Racism'. But Black Consciousness is not concerned with excluding people, but with filling a void. . . . The Consciousness is 'black', too, because the majority of the people in the area who are and who feel the burden of non-possession, are black; and because the majority of those who possess nothing and who are articulate about it in song, dance and poetry, are black.[8]

This explains, in particular, the wide selection of poems in 'dialect': not only the contributions by the three young Jamaicans, but also poems by Marc Matthews (Guyana) and Bruce St John (Barbados), who had been using it for some time. A little later, Brathwaite continues:

> This does not mean that to be West Indian one has got to be black. But it does mean that one must become increasingly aware of what *cultural authenticity* implies. For a growing and large number of people 'black' has now become the ruling agent of their creolisation. The pervasive use of dialect in this issue of *Savacou* is just one more indication of this.

The 3/4 'Foreward' closes with a reference to the ACLALS Conference, and the 'mature contributing audience who demand to share in the artistic exploration of our terrain. Not you and me, but us'.

Bongo Jerry's work had been published in *New World Quarterly*. But its appearance, and that of work by Audvil King – Public Health Inspector, editor and writer, and Ras Dizzy – Rastafarian artist, poet and journalist, in a serious journal of literature raised a furore in some quarters, and provoked a fierce and reverberating debate about contemporary Caribbean literature. This began when *Savacou* 3/4 was reviewed in the *Trinidad Guardian* in July 1971 by the poet Eric Roach. He criticised the work of these young Jamaican writers with comments such as:

> Colour, trumpeted on so many pages, gives the impression that one is listening to 'Air on the nigger string' or to the monstrous thumping of a mad shango drummer. . . . We must write out of the totality of our history, our environment and our feeling. To thrash out wildly like [Audvil] King and [Bongo] Jerry in the murky waters of race, oppression and dispossession is to bury one's head in the stinking dunghills of slavery. . . . We have been given the European languages and forms of culture – culture in the traditional aesthetic sense, meaning the best that has been thought, said and done.[9]

He 'stressed the artist's need to learn his craft and to write out of the fullness of his experience' finding most of the poetry in the issue, 'bad, fanatical, boring and naive'. Syl Lowhar, a young Grenadian poet, living in Trinidad, replied, questioning the assumptions about 'culture' and 'history' on which Roach's review seemed to be based.[10] Roach, in turn, replied that his review was not concerned with racialism or nationalism, but with bad versus good verse, and with standards of judging poetry.

The poems of Eric Roach, born in Tobago in 1915, were wellknown and highly regarded, and had been widely anthologised from the 1950s onwards. Brathwaite later described him as 'one of our most respected and beloved poets'.[11] Although his poems use standard English language, rhythm and form as was common with his generation, they are expressed with bold, memorable lyricism, and in startling Caribbean imagery. Poems such as 'I am the archipelago' reveal his bitter consciousness of the black West Indian condition, made explicit in his note to accompany 'Homestead' in an anthology of 1968: 'The slave ancestry disgusts him [the West Indian] and he attempts to flee from himself but is trapped in the world outside his islands. Europe resents him. Africa does not recognise the long-absent, much-changed prodigal with his European language and attitudes. He is condemned to plod along the limbo edges of the world, rootless, displaced, marginal'.[12]

A month later Gordon Rohlehr published a massive review of *Savacou* 3/4, which occupied all four pages of the Literary Supplement of *Tapia* – the tabloid newspaper produced by Tapia House, founded by Lloyd Best on his return home to Trinidad from Jamaica in 1968 as an attempt to re-form the New World Group. Rohlehr used Roach's review and exchange with Lowhar as his starting point, and held up Roach's articulated criticism and implicit attitudes to unsparing scrutiny. Roach seemed to Rohlehr to exemplify a colonial, elitist approach to literature modelled on the great English poets, in the European cultural tradition. Rohlehr is not uncritical of the *Savacou* issue; the selection should, he believes, have been more stringent, and, while its strong Jamaican flavour was understandable, it should have accommodated more young Trinidadian writers alongside Victor Questel and Roger McTair: in particular, Abdul Malik and Anson Gonzalez. But he recognised that the editorial policy had been deliberate: 'As broad a cross-section of what is actually being written, good or bad, so as to indicate as many trends as are current in the feeling, sensibility and creative effort of the period.'[13] He goes out of his way to welcome features common to the young writers whose work offended Roach: 'The confidence with which young writers are trying to shape ordinary speech, and to use some of the musical rhythms, which dominate the entire Caribbean environment.' Also, pointing to the Rastafarian presence in the popular music of Jamaica, painting and sculpture, and how the Rastafarian dream provides the poor with 'some ground of hope, and the ability to translate hardship into myth', Rohlehr justifies the inclusion of work by Ras Dizzy and Bongo Jerry.

Roach had stated a specific objection to Bongo Jerry's poem 'Sooner or Later', which he saw simply as 'clap-trap':

> so have-gots, have-nots,
> trim-heads, comb-locks, dreadknots
> is sheep from goat.
> find ourself, row your own boat,
> be ready for the day

Rohlehr explained Roach's objection as arising from a lack of sympathy for the tradition out of which the poem grew. Indeed, he points out that the average reader of *Savacou* also 'comes from a world in which proverbs and aphorisms are meaningless' – and he expands into a detailed account of Jamaican patois popular songs, and the Rastafarian roots of Bongo Jerry's work, including the name 'Bongo'. He stresses that such work makes its point most effectively when read aloud. Rohlehr also points to the way in which Roach's hostility to certain poems in the journal seem to have blinded him to other work which should meet his criteria of poetry, so that he ignores the carefully crafted poems of Anthony McNeill, and fails to remark on the great variety of style in Derek Walcott's work, which the *Savacou* selection illustrates. Finally, Rohlehr attempts to answer Roach's question as to the fate of the young poets to whom he so violently objects. He does so by quoting a poem by Roach himself, showing it to be rhetorical and imitative, and continues:

> In answer to Mr Roach's question about the possible fate of today's generation of 'soap box bards', I'd venture that in 20 years' time, their fate may be no worse than his. The experience of living in the West Indies is sufficiently chastening to temper most rhetoric into reticence.

The piece thus becomes the first scholarly, substantial and sympathetic defence for a new direction in Caribbean poetry, which has since become widely practised. Rohlehr's understanding of the pressures which conditioned the poets most fiercely criticised by Roach, and the contemporary culture which shaped their poems, justifies their inclusion in *Savacou*, and champions the new directions which the CAM journal was charting. Although *Savacou* 3/4 may have seemed at the time startling and revolutionary, threatening and destructive, now, in retrospect, in the context of CAM and the complete series of its journal, it demonstrably reflects CAM's consistent confidence in the wide creative potential of Caribbean people, the need for a change of consciousness, and for opportunities for this change to be articulated, explored and shared, by writer and by reader, and also by performer and audience.

Savacou 3/4 editors were stated again as Edward Brathwaite, Kenneth Ramchand, Andrew Salkey; Salkey may well have been responsible for the creative work from writers 'in exile in Britain': James Berry, Marc Matthews. Brathwaite has acknowledged 'some help in the early stages from the (then) co-editor of the journal, Kenneth Ramchand'.[14] In his recollection, he and Ramchand 'parted company on the selection of material for that anthology'. Ramchand, however, claims that it was not until later, with *Savacou* 7, that he 'began to have misgivings about the direction in which the thing was going'.

Publications and productions

The second *Savacou* of 1971, 5, *Creolisation*, created no similar stir. Edited by Ramchand – in theory, at least, the editors alternated issues – its content follows the policy of interdisciplinary studies. Two of the papers – by Sylvia Wynter and Ramchand himself – were given at the January ACLALS Conference. The theme of this issue, as stated in the half-page foreword, attempts to override the recent storms: 'Whatever their differences as to the means and steps by which it is to be achieved, the writers agree on the need for a society and a culture that are genuinely creole, that is island-born whatever the distant origins.' Brathwaite's book *The Development of Creole Society in Jamaica, 1770–1820* had just been published. Based on his doctoral thesis, it provides evidence that the people who came to live and work in Jamaica had, by the early 19th century, begun to form a society with its own distinctive 'creole' character, and that the process of 'creolisation' was still active in Jamaican, and hence, Caribbean, society. It proposes acceptance of a creole basis for Caribbean society. Lucille Mathurin Mair contributed a substantial review-article of Brathwaite's book to this issue of *Savacou*, discussing it as the work of historian, poet and literary critic. 'Solid scholarship supports his vision; the result is a challenging statement of the perspective which finds in the Jamaican past, and implicitly, in its future, material for "a difficult but possible creole authenticity".'[15]

Savacou 6 was published in 1972, subtitled New Poets Series – I, *Reel from 'The Life Movie'*, a collection of poems by Anthony McNeill. It is introduced by 'Notes on a correspondence' between Dennis Scott, poet, playwright, producer, and McNeill – both Jamaicans then studying in the USA. Their work had been widely anthologised and included in all the recent collections, including

Savacou 3/4, *Seven Jamaican Poets* (1971) edited by Mervyn Morris, and *Breaklight* (1971) edited by Andrew Salkey. McNeill, born in 1941, was regarded as a young poet of great promise. He came from a privileged middle-class background – his father was then Minister of Home Affairs – but wrote, claims Scott, 'as someone familiar with his Kingston', in whose poetry 'the language of the urban poor is grappled into new and subtle forms'.[16] McNeill presents the culture of the black dispossessed, particularly Rastafarianism and music, with highly conscious and finely worked literary skill. There could be no cause here for the furore raised by poems of 'the yout'' included in *Savacou* 3/4. After publication, McNeill claimed that his text had been misrepresented and falsely edited. To avoid further recriminations and bitterness, Brathwaite withdrew the first edition, and reprinted it with corrections, all of which taxed *Savacou*'s slim resources.

Kenneth Ramchand selected and introduced his own choice of poetry in *West Indian Poetry: an Anthology for Schools* (1972). Cecil Gray, senior lecturer in education at UWI and himself a poet and short story writer, contributed questions for discussion. Its contents range from Claude McKay and Tom Redcam to Dennis Scott and Anthony McNeill, and Ramchand's accompanying commentaries 'attempt to chronicle in broad outline the development of West Indian art in verse'.[17] The only women whose work is included are Una Marson, Louise Bennett and Alma Norman – Canadian teacher of history and author of *The People Who Came* Book 1. There are no poems by the young, dispossessed youth, in their own language. But in a section called 'Dialect into Poetry', Louise Bennett's poem 'Colonisation in Reverse' appears alongside, amongst others, Brathwaite's 'The Dust' and Dennis Scott's 'Uncle Time', echoing the session on West Indian poetry at CAM's First Conference. The cover is also a product of CAM, based on 'Night Landscape', a painting by Karl (Jerry) Craig which Anne Walmsley, the book's publisher, bought at the Commonwealth Institute/CAM exhibition early in 1971.

Yard Theatre continued to mount landmark productions each year. In 1971, *One Love* was put on at the INAFCA African Museum Yard. It was the largest show they had mounted. The day before it opened, Marina Maxwell wrote:

> Over forty-six performers ranging from Count Ossie's Rastafarian Drummers, Cedric Brooks' Mystic Revelations, and an Afro-Jazz group of musicians, actors reading from Bogle L'Ouverture's *One Love* publication of new material and from Caribbean Artists Movement's *Savacou* anthology. Guitar singers, Shango chanters and drummers and Mackie Burnett's United African Jamaica All-Star Steel band. We're trying [sic] it altogether into one statement with the theme, 'Bongo Man Ah Come', which is one of

> Count Ossie's popular recording chants. It's working. Toes crossed for tomorrow tonight. The theme poem recurring also throughout is Audvil King's 'God Chile Wipe Yuh Eye'.[18]

The establishment theatre critic view of the production was less than enthusiastic. Archie Lindo, in *The Star*, who referred to Yard Theatre 'becoming more established', said he liked the music – 'some very effective drumming, saxophone playing and very good singing' – the variety of readers, the use of torch lights, but he felt that tighter production would have been more effective.[19] He lamented, too, 'the tendency to be vitriolic and bitter', and made a personal plea for a change of subject matter and 'some more light-hearted moments'. It was not everyone's idea of theatre.

Marina Maxwell's own play, *Play Mas*, was at last performed in 1971, by the University Players at the Creative Arts Centre. A production had been scheduled to open in October 1968, but postponed because of the tension following the Rodney Affair. Its producer, Keith Noel, wrote in the programme that he was attracted by the novelty of the play's approach, by its ideological base, and by the use of carnival as a vehicle for its ideas. 'M.M.' (Mervyn Morris), reviewing the production in the *Gleaner*, described the play as 'viable theatre,' but 'not so much a play as a dramatic pamphlet'. He considered it deserved a more vigorous production at another venue; at the Arts Centre 'it tends to remain merely another theatrical happening' whereas it 'ought really to be performed for audiences mainly of the disaffected, whom it might stir to productive anger'.[20]

In 1972 Frank Hasfal, who had contributed the story 'Sajinna Truth' to *One Love* (published by Bogle-L'Ouverture in 1971), wrote and mounted a play, *Black Destiny*, for Yard Theatre. He attempted, wrote Marina Maxwell, to 'synthesise Rasta belief and the puberty rites of the Ashanti in symbolic statement'.[21] That is the last Yard Theatre production on record. *Persistent Plantations* – echoing the title of George Beckford's book, *Persistent Poverty*, was planned for 1973, again for Lloyd Reckord's National Theatre Trust. It was to have been Maxwell's most ambitious production, with her usual groups joined by performers from Zambia, and students and staff from Jamaica's School of Art. But, Brathwaite records, 'unfortunately the proprietor of the Garden Theatre suddenly felt, a few hours to opening, that he couldn't really take all those sufferers and drums, and closed the premises, according to report, on a technicality'.[22] When, in the mid-1970s, Marina Maxwell left Jamaica and went to live and work in Trinidad, her home island, Yard Theatre went with her. Edward Kamau Brathwaite was regarded by her as 'a moving light from scratch, and Doris, his wife, meets all our emergencies' (Doris in fact also took part in several productions);[23] but there was no question of

Edward Kamau and Doris Brathwaite in Jamaica, 1977

Brathwaite's keeping it going in Jamaica. He comments: 'It was not my idea, and it was not my style, either, that particular performing arts aspect.' But the influence of Yard Theatre lived on in Jamaica, with the founding of Harambee Theatre by Frank Hasfal in 1972, and particularly with the opening of the Cultural Training Centre in 1975. There its ideas for theatre were carried on by Dennis Scott, Rawle Gibbons, Honor Ford-Smith, Thom Cross.

Programme, **Play Mas** *by Marina Maxwell*

Maureen Warner's work with ASAWI was extended when, in 1971, she founded a dance group amongst UWI students, called 'Omo Ajini' (Children of Guinea/Africa). The group performed in the open air and at the Creative Arts Centre at Mona, always in the round, using the concept of the circle as in traditional African dance. It attempted in particular to recreate the grace and subtlety of Yoruba dance, and thereby, as she explains, 'to rid people of the idea that all African dance was hot and fiery'. Members of the group danced and sang, using Yoruba dances which Warner had learnt in Nigeria and Yoruba songs recorded during her research in Trinidad, and the programme included a section of drumming.

In August 1972 Ronald Moody was back in Jamaica for three weeks, as guest of the Festival 10 Arts Committee. His main engagement, on 6 August, was to open Art '72, a huge exhibition, both retrospective and contemporary, of Jamaican art, mounted in the Assembly Hall of UWI at Mona. The *Sunday Gleaner* carried an article, 'Ronald Moody, Jamaican Sculptor', signed 'Kamau'. Brathwaite added the name 'Kamau', and used it alongside or, preferably, in place of 'Edward', after visiting Kenya early in 1971 as guest of Ngũgĩ wa Thiong'o and the Department of Literature, University of Nairobi; Ngũgĩ's grandmother gave Brathwaite the

Gĩkũyũ name. Kamau Brathwaite took the opportunity to write at length about Moody's background, life, work and personality, for Moody was, he claimed, 'literally unknown in Jamaica'. He also highlighted Moody's CAM connection. Describing the Savacou bird on campus, Brathwaite continued:

> Ronald Moody regards it as one of the most rewarding moments of his life when in 1964 he was invited home to set up his celebration of the island's past. Since then, the Caribbean Artists Movement (CAM) of which Moody is a founder member, has named its journal *Savacou*, in tribute to him.[24]

In an interview for *Jamaica Journal* Moody spoke of the contrast in the Jamaican art scene now, in 1972, compared with his visit eight years earlier. Then he was conscious of the great variety of wood at hand for sculpture, and amazed that no one was using it. On this trip, he said,

> I have seen a terrific sort of explosion, this excitement not only in the use of woods but in the art as a whole. The Rastafarians have made an impact that will develop and give the West Indies . . . you know, the Mexican Rivera and the impact he had? . . . The same sort of thing can happen here in Jamaica.[25]

Poster of 'Contemporary 12' group exhibition in Jamaica, July 1976,

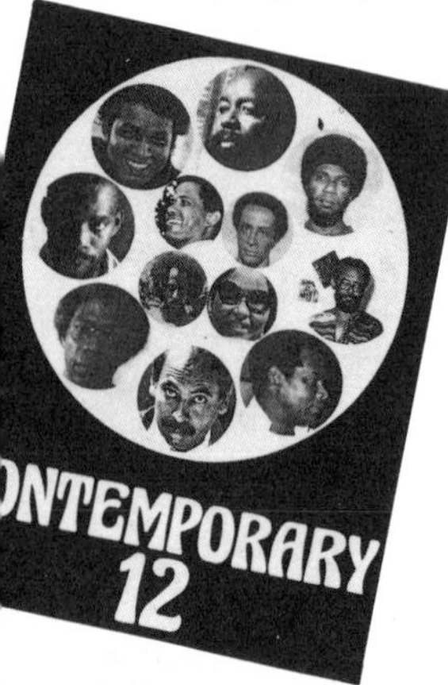

clockwise: on the hour, Barrington Watson; quarter past, Karl Parboosingh; twenty past, Aubrey Williams; half past, Erwin De Vries; quarter to, Eugene Hyde

Moody went on to make statements in line with what he had said to CAM in 1967 and 1968, now in the Jamaican context and to a Jamaican audience:

> The artist's job is to remind the people of certain eternal laws and values, in art there is no progress. . . . Here in Jamaica there is a difference in the art [from Europe]. . . . There is a sanity here that the artists show because the artist has a very direct relationship to the society. . . . Growth is only growth when it represents the connecting-up of inner experiences.

After Aubrey Williams first visited Jamaica in 1970, he spent several months there each year for many years. During the early 1970s he stayed and worked alongside Karl Parboosingh at his home in Sligoville and at a place near Port Antonio which they hoped to make, as Williams recalled, 'a haven for Caribbean artists', where writers, painters, musicians and sculptors could stay and complete whatever they were working at. Such a community of artists at least found some sort of realisation when in 1974 the Olympia International Art Centre was opened in Kingston, designed and owned by the architect, artist and art collector AD Scott. Williams stayed there and worked alongside leading Jamaican artists and the Surinam painter, Erwin de Vries, exhibiting with them as the 'Contemporary 12' group. He also had one-man shows at the Olympia and at the Gallery Barrington, owned by Barrington Watson. In Jamaica, Williams's work found ready purchasers and patrons amongst individuals and institutions.

Carifesta '72

In Guyana, meanwhile, plans laid at the Writers and Artists Convention of February 1970 for a Caribbean Festival of the Arts had been gathering momentum. They were shaped by a conscious change in government policy towards cultural activity, resulting from the country's newly proclaimed status as Co-operative Republic. 'Government is seeking to awaken a new sense of identity in the mass of the people and to promote indigenous forms of art,' wrote Celeste Dolphin, editor of *Kaie*, the Official Organ of the National History and Arts Council of Guyana (NHAC), in a special issue, *The Vision of Carifesta*, December 1971. The previous month a Carifesta Secretariat had been established at the offices of the NHAC, with Lynette Dolphin, Celeste's elder sister, as Director, and Frank Pilgrim as Commissioner: all three members of wellknown middle-class families, of the cultural establishment of Guyana. *Kaie* led off with a summary of the address given to the NHAC by the Minister of Information and Culture; he charged it to 'create and organise a programme which would involve the masses', after stating: 'We have to ensure that people do not come to view the NHAC as a group of well-educated people enjoying themselves.' Provisional plans for Carifesta, printed in *Kaie*, seem predictable and conservative – with one exception: 'In the special field of folk music it is proposed to introduce to Carifesta audiences a Rastafarian orchestra which has developed into an important element of the Jamaican music scene.' CAM's criticism of the absence of Rasta culture in Carifesta plans was answered – probably as a result of Frank Pilgrim hearing the Mystic Revelation of Rastafari orchestra when he visited Jamaica. Evidence of official encouragement for folklore in Guyanese culture appears in the reproduction of four paintings by Aubrey Williams depicting Guyanese myths and legends, accompanied by an article by Roy Heath on 'The Function of Myth', and by the retelling of a Guyanese legend, 'Ole Higue and Young Samaan' by Doris Harper Wills.

Arthur Seymour

Creative work and concepts familiar to CAM are most startlingly apparent in an article by AJ Seymour – founder and editor of *Kyk-over-al*, and the leading literary figure in the establishment group – modestly titled, 'A Note on Literature and Caribbean Society'. A *Times Literary Supplement* interview with VS Naipaul, earlier in the year, after winning the Booker Prize with *In a Free State* (1971), provided Seymour with a range of statements against which he could project the aims of Carifesta.[26] Whereas Naipaul, 'as an ex-colonial writing in the English literary tradition', said he found it nearly impossible to have the pleasure of a direct response from an audience; claimed he would not have become a writer without London; confessed to finding himself in a kind of limbo, a refugee, peripheral, in London, Carifesta proposed to dissipate the Caribbean writer's sense of placelessness. Seymour contrasted Naipaul's development 'in the colonial cocoon' with the 'change in our regional and colonial situation' which Carifesta was designed to make. He went on to mention new relationships between literature and Caribbean society: 'Manifestations emerge in folk dance and usages in dance, in dialect and in creole techniques; in the debating bodies to be found in the Rastafarian movement; in a greater interest in the literary values of the calypso-carnival world.' Seymour proposed to send these 'Notes' as an Open Letter to a number of his friends and colleagues – Derek Walcott, Edward Brathwaite, Kenneth Ramchand, John Hearne, EM Roach, Martin Carter, Wilson Harris, and Andrew Salkey, 'who has become one of the models of the successful expatriate West Indian writers'. Seymour, like CAM in its UK sessions, saw Naipaul as the antithesis of Caribbean writers who were concerned with creative change in Caribbean society. Recognition of new, folk-based, literary criteria which embrace dialect, creole forms such as calypso, is shared with CAM by Seymour, and offered to EM Roach for further dialogue.

Participants from Cuba and Haiti at Carifesta '72

At last, from 25 August to 15 September 1972, Carifesta happened. Guyana was host to a range of artists, offering a variety of cultural manifestations, from a spread of countries around the Caribbean, on a scale and of a diversity far exceeding the early plans. For three weeks these artists took part in a multi-faceted programme – partly scheduled, partly spontaneous – which drew audiences at times in their thousands: partly of visitors, largely of Guyanese people. In all, 1000 artists were reckoned to have taken part, from 28 countries: the English, French, Spanish and Dutch-speaking Caribbean, countries of Central and South America which bordered the Caribbean Sea; and countries of South America such as Brazil and Peru with which Guyana had since Independence established diplomatic relations, or signed cultural agreements.

The scheduled programme included, for the visual arts: an International Art Exhibition, with paintings and sculpture from 14 countries; one-man exhibitions by three Guyanese painters – Stanley Greaves, Philip Moore, Aubrey Williams; an exhibition of work by 'outstanding Jamaican painters', selected by Edna Manley; exhibitions of tapestries from Brazil, of children's art, and of photographs. For literature: a two-day conference on the theme, 'The Creative Writer in Society with Special Reference to the Third World'; poetry and prose readings, an anthology of *New Writing from the Caribbean* (1972), edited by AJ Seymour, designed to introduce writers of the wider Caribbean to senior school, undergraduate and adult students – the first of its kind; an exhibition of over 500 books containing literary work by such writers. For drama: a variety of plays from the English-speaking Caribbean.

Carifesta '72, logo

But it was in the performing arts of music and dance that Carifesta was most adventurous and memorable. Lynette Dolphin, herself an accomplished pianist, trained in the European classical tradition, wrote afterwards, in her official Carifesta report, about 'Music at Carifesta':

> Of the many sounds of Carifesta, the drums emerged as a significant element. The carved Apinti drums of Suriname, the painted Assater drum of Haiti and the drums of Cuba, Jamaica, Bahia and Trinidad, created the compelling rhythms of the folk manifestations in song and dance which entertained and thrilled the large audiences at the Cultural Centre, the National Park and Queen's College. In many instances the only music was that supplied by the drum, ranging skilfully from the soft and tender to the energetic. The drum was frequently heard in the streets of Carifesta as Steel Bands and Masquerade Dancers from Nevis, Montserrat and Guyana displayed their skills to the crowds.[27]

She describes performances of *The Legend of Kaiteur*, recitals by Ray Luck (piano) and Ian Hall (organ), a Cuban orchestra, and then continues:

> But music was inextricably mingled with dance and song at Carifesta as in the presentations of Martinique's Chorale de Francois, the Kingston Chorale of St Vincent, and folk singers of Antigua, Dominica and Grenada. And after the public shows ended and the performers returned to Festival City, there were strains of music as groups from different countries played their instruments, sang their songs and danced – Festival City did not sleep until dawn.

Such integrated art forms, free of language barriers, accessible to all, made a deep and lasting impression at Carifesta.

A number of CAM members took part in Carifesta: Karl 'Jerry' Craig, Ronald Savory and Aubrey Williams; Michael Anthony, Edward Kamau and Doris Brathwaite, Sam Selvon; Kenneth Ramchand, Gordon Rohlehr and Ivan Van Sertima; Doris Harper Wills. Their participation in the Carifesta programme was almost entirely in CAM's strongest fields – literature and the visual arts – with one exception: Doris Harper Wills, a trained dancer and choreographer, who 'writes', as she often says, 'with bodies'. Other CAM members were noticeably absent: CLR James and George Lamming, who had participated in the initial planning in 1966; Salkey and La Rose who, with fellow members, had ensured that at the more specific planning for Carifesta in 1970, CAM concepts and ideas were articulated, and had insisted on pan-Caribbean participation.

Doris Harper Wills dancing with Gora Singh at the Guyana National History and Arts Council, with Aubrey Williams's 'Guyana' on the wall behind them

In addition to the twice-weekly series of poetry readings and a special session for prose readings, Brathwaite was asked to do a special, full reading of *Rights of Passage*. He in turn persuaded AJ Seymour who, as a Carifesta organiser, was not down to read, to give a complete reading of his poem 'Over Guiana, Clouds' – wellknown on the page but seldom heard.

At the conference convened by AJ Seymour, papers were read by Kenneth Ramchand and Gordon Rohlehr. A special issue of *Kaie* reprinted most of the papers: on contemporary Puerto Rican, Brazilian and Haitian literature, and on French Caribbean literature; on 'The Importance of our literature in Caribbean secondary education'; on 'Music in Society', on 'Art and Society'. Seymour, in his introductory paper, describes political independence as empty unless, as artists, they come out from under the 'former domination of the Euro-centred traditions and assess the new and gathering strength of the values of the Afro-centred past, no longer recessive and welling up from the deeps into the dignity of contemporary life'.[28] He refers to the need for 'resurrection of the image of the African slave, but invested with a power and dignity not known before'. After thus echoing the persistent theme of Brathwaite's talks to CAM, Seymour makes overt reference to his work:

> Brathwaite who has reversed the Middle Passage would lead us back to a comprehension of our roots in African history; the Rastafari will make us understand the value of syntax disregard and of explosion when poetry is composed at certain social levels.

Again, as in *Kaie* of 1971, Seymour comes out on the side of the 'cultural gorillas', champions the new literary work in *Savacou* 3/4.

Kenneth Ramchand's paper, Seymour states, unfortunately

could not be reproduced. It was concerned with literature in education – a topic close to Seymour's heart, and one on which Ramchand was, by 1972, equipped to speak with firsthand, innovative experience. From Seymour's brief paragraph of summary, Ramchand's main points seem to have been that the education system and process should focus upon literature as a communal art illuminating the whole society; that those passing on the values of literature should be properly equipped to do so; that a distinction should be made between imaginative literature and literature which represents social commentary; that if literature was to assist in the regeneration of West Indian society, writers must ensure that they make an honest projection of their society, striving for the discovery of values rather than mere documentation of what is known.

Gordon Rohlehr's paper, 'The Creative Writer and West Indian Society', is printed in full, over 30 pages. It is concerned to show 'how several West Indian writers' notions of the potential of Caribbean peoples are shaped by their presumptions concerning the history of the area'.[29]

Rohlehr starts with the Beacon group in Trinidad in the 1930s and its concern to 'develop that current of consciousness which had always been there in the West Indies'. This alternative current was kept alive in Trinidad by,

> the presence of a living oral tradition of the calypso, and a rich variety of rhetorical games. For in Trinidad since Emancipation a peculiar relationship had sprung up between various classes, which found its forum on the streets at carnival time, and in the rapidly developing calypso tents during the second quarter of the 20th century.

The development of a West Indian awareness was 'paralleled by the beginnings of a literature rooted in the language and experience of the area'. It led, too, to the desire to reappraise and rewrite West Indian history: CLR James and Eric Williams.

Rohlehr finds parallels to Eric Williams's attack on British historians in *Capitalism and Slavery* in George Lamming's 'preoccupation with the moral and physical consequences of colonialism in almost everything that he has written', and in Lloyd Brathwaite's analysis of social stratification in Trinidad.

> One discipline echoes the other. Discovery on one plane influences enquiry on any other plane. An unacknowledged wholeness exists in Caribbean creative exploration, whether it be conducted on the level of literature, music, dance, historiography or social anthropology. Because of the wholeness of sensibility, one can start virtually anywhere in a lecture such as this. Had I, for example, begun by talking about 'dread' in Jamaican music, or political calypsos in Trinidad during the period of Independence, I would almost

certainly have ended with observations on Jamaican politics, or on the poetry of Bongo Jerry and Edward Brathwaite, or on the later plays of Walcott, or on Naipaul since *A House for Mr Biswas*.

Scrutiny of the poetry of Martin Carter is carried out in the context of British Guiana, 1953–57. Rohlehr recommends Ivan Van Sertima's paper to CAM of 5 September 1969, in *Newsletter* Nos. 11 and 12, as an accurate assessment of the period, and reminds his audience that 'Carter was much closer to [the] skeleton of politics than any other West Indian writer besides, perhaps, Roger Mais, and the internal shattering of Guyana was a more terrible thing than anyone who has not known it can possibly realise'.

Meanwhile Trinidad in the mid-1950s was experiencing 'the new sense of history and destiny' which Eric Williams, as Prime Minister, seemed to offer. Sparrow, at 21, won the calypso crown. 'The oral tradition was flowering . . . both on the stage and on the political platform.' Of particular importance for the poets and novelists of the Caribbean was 'the dream of Federation' which seemed, in the mid-1950s, shortly to be realised – only to evaporate into political disillusionment with its break-up in the early 1960s. This is shown as the context for landmark work by Lamming, Harris and Naipaul. Rohlehr finds that Naipaul in *The Middle Passage* 'completely dismissed the notion that Caribbean peoples had any potential', and could be linked to Martin Carter's 'powerful sense of fatalism'. This sense of fatalism seemed indeed to have grown during the 1960s and to be now 'an inescapable part of the Caribbean scene'. Yet the work of Wilson Harris indicates 'quite a different set of possibilities'. Rohlehr's account of *Palace of the Peacock* is enriched by comparisons with Herman Melville's *Moby Dick* and particularly with Joseph Conrad's *Heart of Darkness*. It concludes:

> The importance of Harris is that he keeps open the possibility of a personality which can be explored, and the concept of a new ground for faith after the inevitable shatter and waste of politics. The difficulty of Harris's dream is one of relating it to historical situation, channelling it into time and place.

After glances at Guyana (and more about Carter), and Jamaica, in the 1960s, Rohlehr describes how in Trinidad 'Walcott emerged as an articulate, enraged, despairing voice'. Poems in *The Castaway* (1965) and *The Gulf* (1969), and essays of the 1960s, signal Walcott's feelings of isolation and of the need to withdraw. Walcott seems to regard carnival as a negative force, and he shows particular awareness of the dangers of state patronage of folk culture.

So to the 1970s and, asks Rohlehr: 'On what can the West Indian artist build a fresh faith? . . . What positives, if any, have appeared in the commentaries and essays of artists in the period?' He finds none in Naipaul, whom he dubs 'a determinist in history, a nihilist in politics; and an absurdist in aesthetics'. In Lamming he recognises a ground for new hope 'in a conception of history as growth and possibility', particularly in acceptance of roots in Africa. Rohlehr points to a similar recognition, together with acceptance of the concept of a mulatto West Indian culture, in Walcott's 'What the Twilight Says' (1970). In Wilson Harris's statements of the mid-1960s, 'his aim is to keep open the sense of man's possibility in the face of his diminishment'.

It is in the poetry of Edward Kamau Brathwaite that Rohlehr claims to find the most positive view of Caribbean man's potential. He quotes from *Islands* to show how although the Caribbean ground is 'broken', it is rich and ready for cultivation; how although 'the future returns', it also lies open, and can be 'refashioned'.

> This open-endedness in Brathwaite's work is, to my mind, one of the finest gifts which he offers to the Caribbean literary scene. . . . The shards of history are material for building in the present, and the artist/citizen redeems the past and reclaims it by creating in the present.

Rohlehr's continuing historical sense is evident alongside his close knowledge of Caribbean literature, both enriched by his CAM experience. Four years in Trinidad have given him intimate knowledge of its society, and enabled him to expand and deepen his interest in calypso and the oral tradition.

The conference paper on 'Art and Society' was given by Denis Williams. Aubrey Williams had no opportunity to speak formally, but he and his two fellow artists 'were present for the greater part of the exhibition at their respective sites and were able to explain to interested viewers the background to their work'. Twelve of Aubrey Williams's paintings were on view at the Critchlow Labour College, entitled (and numbered within each series) 'Warrau', 'Carib' and 'Arawak' – the three main Amerindian peoples of Guyana. His exhibition catalogue also gives details of the murals at Timehri Airport which he had completed in 1970, and which were seen by all Carifesta visitors on arrival. Painted in brilliant but durable colours, the four external murals and one internal mural cover a total area of 130 square yards, and depict Amerindian motifs: Tumatumari, Kamarau, Kaietuma, Maridowa, Itiribisi. Aubrey Williams's long and deeply felt concern with recreating the iconography of the region's pre-Columbian cultures pervaded Carifesta. May it have been responsible for the 20 foot-high Aztec pyramid prominent at the Opening Ceremony?

Writing afterwards about Carifesta, Brathwaite recalled: 'Children were everywhere.'[30] The official report made much of the substantial participation of children and young people. The Pageant of Youth involved some 640 children; it included a depiction, through costume, music and movement, of festivals peculiar to the various races of Guyana – and for this Doris Harper Wills was mainly responsible.

Carifesta seemed another golden opportunity to discuss the possible re-formation of CAM in the Caribbean, but this time Brathwaite had to put the case on his own. He recalls:

> When I got there I was distressed to find that the organisers did not know anything about CAM, or didn't seem to care. And here was an opportunity to have people doing what CAM did: which is not only to be performing, but to get together and talk. So eventually I persuaded Arthur Seymour to set up a CAM meeting, which we did have. And there I was able to tell the various people from all over the region about CAM. We set up this thing, and it was well attended, people were very keen. But then what happened is what I expected to happen. The Carifesta Secretariat felt that they would be the best people to deal with it, and it was therefore agreed that CAM would be run by Pilgrim from the Carifesta desk at CARICOM and that was the end of it. We haven't heard of it since. And this is just what would happen, once you become involved with governments.

Yet the terms in which he afterwards wrote about Carifesta reflect throughout his CAM experience, his CAM aspirations. In Brathwaite's view, Carifesta was remarkable as 'Emancipation Day come true'; it demonstrated that the metropolitan style of control, seized at Independence, did not work, 'because there was no "kingdom of ourselves". The Caribbean did not know itself'. Although it had been a long time coming, Brathwaite could now perceive 'a profound reassessment among Caribbean people about themselves. Explosions inward: Soul, Afro, Drum, Rock, Haiti with *vodoun*, Martinique with Césaire, Trinidad with steelband, Jamaica with reggae, Surinam with Dobru, Chin a Foeng and Michael Slory'. What was implicit in Carifesta was that home is here and now. Brathwaite stressed that Carifesta involved those present in a sense of cultural wholeness. But such a sense of wholeness tended to bring Caribbean people face-to-face with fragments of the past that exist within them. Only a renewal of consciousness could bring about the sort of change sought by an independent Caribbean:

> The Alpha and Omega of the new legislation is consciousness: the kind of spiritual energy, craft and insight we saw released and made manifest at Carifesta: to conceive of change; to interpret it; to give it form and content; and above all, to provide it with protection.

It was 'the tension between politics and culture, nationhood and race, government and people' which, in Brathwaite's view, 'makes the Caribbean fragile, complex, so unique'. He continued: 'The central creative problem in the Caribbean is how to use and resolve this tension: how to achieve a multi-cultural synthesis of man, soil and sunlight. Carifesta was conceived as a significant step towards this.'

From the omnipresent drum to the integrated performance arts; from the reinstatement and celebration of forms of indigenous folk culture to full acceptance of the idiom, rhythm and form of peoples' speech-based literature; from the wider Caribbean representation to the interchange with its literature; from the dialogue between artists, between artists and public, to concern for a wider audience – Carifesta reflected all the cultural endeavour of Caribbean people which was nurtured within CAM.

1973–1982

Edward Kamau Brathwaite's attempt in 1972 to interest Carifesta participants in re-forming CAM came to no more than the attempts of he and his fellow CAM founders in 1970. The Caribbean writers, artists and intellectuals whom they addressed were almost all only visiting Guyana; their places of work – at home, in exile – were too scattered, their concerns were too disparate. Moreover, in 1972 the Carifesta Secretariat promised to fulfil the role of CAM within the Caribbean Community Secretariat.

No mention of CAM seems to have been made at Carifesta '76 in Jamaica. But Marina Omowale Maxwell made a further attempt at Carifesta '79, in Cuba, when she presented a paper to its Writers Symposium. She spoke of artists' need for 'a network, a community of support, to FREE AND TO DEVELOP our own Caribbean Cultural Identity', and to 'form our own organisation outside of the frames of the reactionary governments of the region'.[31] She proposed a Carifesta Resolution to set up a committee to work out how 'a network, a movement of Caribbean artists' could be founded, with funding from, she suggested, such sources such as OPEC, CARICOM, OAS and UNESCO. Her aims of 'a Caribbean Artists Movement coming out of Carifesta' ranged from providing technical expertise for workshops and summer schools, a cultural magazine in all the languages of the Caribbean, a Caribbean library and documentation centre, a Caribbean publishing house and publication facilities for writers, artists, educators, to promotion and organisation of Third World and Caribbean festivals and travelling exhibitions.

The aims encompassed those of CAM in its early, ambitious days, and took them much farther. Maxwell's vision of CAM would indeed have required massive funding and a complex bureaucracy. It would have been ostensibly at the service of, but fundamentally at odds with, the character of CAM and its belief in artists' freedom and independence. This, the final CAM initiative, also came to nothing, in terms at least of a regional movement. But Maxwell also encouraged the formation, in 1979/80, of the Writers' Union of Trinidad and Tobago, which included 'poets, novelists, critics, playwrights, journalists, radio and TV script writers, film scripters and textbook writers'. Associations were also developed in Trinidad following Carifesta '79 for dance, music, and drama. But there was none for visual arts; no interdisciplinary artists' group; no on-going regional network. Maxwell's hope was that during and after Carifesta '81, in Barbados, 'similar bodies be formed in each Caribbean territory so that artists organise themselves for creativity, survival, action and growth – and that these bodies move towards amalgamation in each unit into Caribbean Artists Movement (CAM) chapters'.[32] Maxwell chronicled no further moves towards CAM 'chapters'. Carifesta '81 was the last for more than a decade.

Another significant cultural group formed by CAM people in the Caribbean in the 1970s was Kairi in Trinidad, inspired by Christopher and Judith Lairds' experience of CAM in London. This was a multi-faceted arts group, formed in 1974 round a theatre cooperative, and based at Judith Laird's family house in Belmont, Port of Spain, renamed Kairi House. The formation of Kairi had been prompted by Rawle Gibbons's drama group, *Is We*, which met and rehearsed in the Lairds' home. *Is We* had in turn been much influenced by *Dem Two* which played in Trinidad in early 1974 during its first Caribbean tour. Marc Matthews's and Ken Corsbie's initial two-man programme of Caribbean oral material in performance was soon followed by *All Ah We*, when John Agard and Henry Muttoo joined them. At Kairi House, in Judith Laird's view, 'all the creative arts that we had learnt came to fruition': in the drama productions, in her painting and design classes and activities with young children, and in the arts magazine *Kairi*. Early issues of *Kairi* were produced loose-leaf, on different sizes and colours of paper, for flexible use and display, and included posters and T shirts – clear follow-up of ideas expressed by Christopher Laird at CAM's Second Conference. *Kairi* pioneered publication of new, young voices from the Eastern Caribbean: Victor Questel, Rawle Gibbons, Paul Keens-Douglas, and Christopher Laird himself. *Kairi* also published first collections of poems by Bruce St John and Abdul Malik. John La Rose recalls how, on his visit to Trinidad in March 1970, Laird introduced Abdul Malik's poetry to him, letting him hear a tape recording of Malik reading his 'Panrun'. On a later visit Laird described to La Rose what Ken Corsbie and Marc Matthews were doing in *Dem Two* and insisted that it 'went beyond the orality of

Kairi House, 1974, (l to r), Paul Keens-Douglas, Trevor Millette, Michelle Sogreen, Judith Laird, Christopher Laird

poetry, that this was performance poetry – not what you were doing in London'. 'Performance poetry' was practised in the Caribbean before it became widespread in Britain.

Brathwaite's Carifesta '72 attempt to re-form CAM was his last. But the preparation and publication of the journal *Savacou* continued through the 1970s and constituted mainstream CAM work. *Savacou* 7/8, 1973, was a special issue and the one which Ramchand claims marked the end of the shared editorship. It was planned by Brathwaite as a 70th birthday tribute to Frank Collymore. It contains tributes to and valuable information about *Bim* and its editor, plus reprints of highlights of its back issues and new writing by *Bim* contributors: a celebration of the longest-lasting of Caribbean literary journals and its much-loved editor. Brathwaite invited John La Rose and Andrew Salkey to be guest editors of *Savacou* 9/10, 1974, sub-titled *Writing Away from Home* (see Chapter 10). *Savacou* 13, 1977, was another special issue. Sub-titled *Caribbean Woman*, it is dedicated to Una Marson, and edited by Lucille Mathurin Mair, who had, in 1974, at last successfully completed her PhD thesis, *A Historical Study of Women in Jamaica, 1655–1844* – researched and written whilst she taught history at Mona and was warden of Mary Seacole Hall. The contents of this issue of *Savacou* are a characteristic mix of academic and new creative writing of quality, all by women – the first Caribbean publication to be so, and a foretaste of the many significant women writers and critics who were to appear as a major feature of the 1980s: Jean Goulbourne, Marjorie Thorpe, Merle Hodge, Lorna Goodison, Judy Miles, Opal Palmer, Peta-

***Record sleeve,* Marc-up, *featuring Marc Matthews with* Dem Two *and* All Ah We**

Anne Baker, Christine Craig, Maureen Warner Lewis.

Savacou 11/12, 1975 – *Caribbean Studies* – contains a new approach to a new academic subject. Introducing the issue Herman McKenzie, UWI Mona lecturer in sociology, welcomed its spread beyond exclusively social science studies to papers concerned with 'the Caribbean writer and with the societal milieu', and the attempted assimilation of theories and concepts in the social sciences and the arts. The one piece of purely creative writing is exemplary, in quality and presentation: Olive Senior's 'Ancestral Poem', printed over a light green batik flower design. Brathwaite's contribution, 'Caribbean Man in Space and Time', part prose-poem, part academic paper, is a seminal staging-post in his mid-1970s research, thought and action. *Savacou* 14/15, *New Poets from Jamaica*, reflects some of the creative change that had come about in Jamaica by the late 1970s. It contrasts with *Savacou* 3/4, *New Writing 1970*, in several ways: in content – all poetry; in arrangement – a selection of work by 13 people; in origin – all from Jamaica, all young. The black and Rasta thinking, the popular music rhythms, the people's speech, have been accepted and skilfully refined, Michael Smith and Oku Onuora appear instead of Bongo Jerry and Audvil King. Now, too, more than half the contributors are women, Christine Craig and Lorna Goodison amongst them. Again, Brathwaite's introduction points to what the collection is and does, describing its writers as 'weaving a "creole" synthesis'.

During the 1970s and early 1980s *Savacou* also published books: poetry, short stories, essays in a 'Cultural Heritage' series, and bibliographies, on a cooperative basis. This expansion was made possible largely because Doris Brathwaite had equipped herself early with word processing and desktop publishing skills. *Savacou* was a forum for much of the new interdisciplinary, Caribbean-centred research and writing in Jamaica in the 1970s; equally it was a platform for the new creative writing, particularly by young urban blacks and by women, much of which used forms, rhythm and language drawn from the oral tradition. It shared CAM characteristics, and is remembered as creating something of a CAM group, by contemporaries at UWI such as Bridget Jones, lecturer in the Department of French, who describes the *Savacou* phase as having been 'very positive in cultural terms. This is why I measure Brathwaite's achievement in intangibles – very many black students, especially women – were given a stronger sense of self-worth'.[32]

In the decade which followed Brathwaite's last attempt to re-form CAM in the Caribbean – at Carifesta '72 – *Savacou* was CAM in all but name.

10 CAM Continuing
At Home Away From Home
1971 - 1982

1971–1972

There were no further CAM meetings in London in 1970 after the two in April. Donald Hinds and James Berry in particular felt that CAM should be revived, with a planned programme for 1971. So on 1 January 1971 Hinds sent members of the committee a handwritten, duplicated note:

> Howdy: 1970 was a lethargic year for CAM. Suggest we meet at John La Rose's to plan CAM's 1971 programme, on Tuesday 12 January at about 8.30 – no, 'Mek Dat' 8.30 P-R-E-C-I-S-E-L-Y. Your silence will be taken to mean you *CAN* make it.[1]

La Rose and Salkey agreed to this initiative. The continuing core of CAM answered the summons: founder members John La Rose and Sarah White, Andrew Salkey, Aubrey Williams; CAM committee members James Berry, Christopher Laird, Anne Walmsley; and Paul Dash. It was, as Anne Walmsley reported to the Brathwaites the following month:

> A real good CAM reappraisal. We were all missing it and wanted it to be alive again. The first three years had been new and great and flowering. But the big open meetings at the Centre were ended. We must go on with the same structure (yes, we came back to the necessity of a non-Committee, non-Officers, non-Agenda, Minutes etc) but into new directions. Seemed our future meetings might be of three sorts, for which we'll use well-worn names for want of better: 1 MAXIs – for wider audience and CAM fringers *when* there's an event or person to warrant one. Not held regularly, not always organised by John and Andrew. 2 MIDIs – for selected CAM members and friends. . . . 3 MINIs – when anyone who wants to ask a few people round to read, talk about their work, and talk.[2]

There was no question of trying to revive CAM as it had been. The Students Centre, which housed its public meetings from March 1967 to April 1970 and whose members, activities, viewpoint and philosophy had become increasingly entwined with those of CAM, could no longer be used. Not that the West Indian government-backed Centre turned CAM out, as might be suspected, because of its political activism; WK Hynam, the then warden, has stated that he received no directives 'to refuse permission for CAM meetings to be held there'.[3] The decision seems to have been reached by the CAM leadership itself. The political crisis of 1970 made a continuing association with the Centre unacceptable. Also, the programme of monthly meetings had, from October 1968 until April 1970, been largely arranged and convened by La Rose and Salkey. Neither any longer had the time, energy or commitment to sustain such a programme. Smaller spontaneous or *ad hoc* meetings, yes. But a revival of CAM public meetings would be dependent on finding another suitable venue, and on other committee members' taking initiatives and responsibilities.

The occasion for a small *ad hoc* CAM session arose in early February 1971. Beryl McBurnie, pioneer of dance in Trinidad and founder of its Little Carib Theatre movement, was passing through London. John La Rose invited her to speak and demonstrate, in the ground-floor room of his house, 2 Albert Road – the New Beacon Bookshop – on a Sunday night. Twenty or thirty CAM members came, summoned by phone because of a postal strike. Paul Dash remembers the occasion and thinking to himself,

> something extraordinary is happening. The place was absolutely packed. John had a through lounge and of course that's where his bookshop started, and we were surrounded by all these books. And I remember we sat on the floor, and I brought a friend of mine, a chap called Alfred Hutchinson who wrote a book called *The Road To Ghana*, he's South African. And I introduced him to John La Rose that evening. I remember Beryl McBurnie dancing to illustrate the points she was trying to make. And I thought, what an incredible character!

CAM's revival was generally strengthened by a CAM-assisted event, seeded and germinated during the early phases of CAM. From 22 January–14 February 1971 the Commonwealth Institute mounted a major exhibition of Caribbean art, 'Caribbean Artists in England'. The catalogue, which simply lists the artists whose work was displayed and contains no introduction, makes no mention of CAM's assistance. But Donald Bowen, then curator of the Institute's Art Gallery, had contacted Brathwaite as early as July 1967. He was, he wrote, interested to hear of the establishment of CAM, he wished it prosperity, and wondered, 'if at some time in the future we could, with your cooperation, mount an exhibition of Caribbean art'.[4] The gallery was fully booked for 'a year or two ahead', but could Brathwaite meet him in order to discuss the idea? They met in October, and Bowen confirmed the details to Brathwaite: an exhibition of painting and sculpture by Caribbean artists during the summer of 1970.

> So that you can place before your Committee some details of this proposal, I would suggest that the exhibition consists of not more than about a hundred works, preferably by 15–20 artists. In that way, each artist can be represented by a small body of work. The selected artists should, I feel, be drawn from both those resident here or away from home, and of course from those still living in the Caribbean. Anything like 'complete representation' will almost certainly produce an exhibition with little impact.[5]

Bowen went to CAM's exhibition at the Students Centre in May 1968 and took photographs of several of the works on show. He remembers the 'invaluable help' which CAM gave him. He did not know a lot of the artists, he welcomed guidance on what work an individual did, and where to find him. 'I'm sure a great deal of the credit must go to CAM.' Jerry Craig, responsible for CAM's May and November 1968 exhibitions, liaised with Bowen and regards the CI show as having been 'the ultimate of the CAM exhibitions'.

At the Commonwealth Institute in January 1971, 17 artists exhibited, nine of which had a CAM connection: Winston Branch, Karl 'Jerry' Craig, Paul Dash (not listed), Art Derry, Errol Lloyd, Keith Simon, Aubrey Williams – paintings; Althea McNish – fabrics, Ronald Moody – sculpture. Other Caribbean artists whose work hung alongside that of CAM artists were Althea Bastien – fabrics, Owen R Coombs, Daphne Dennison, George Lynch, Vernon Tong, Ricardo Wilkins (now Kofi Kayiga), Llewellyn Xavier – paintings; Donald Locke – ceramics. The combination of those recommended by CAM, and those selected by Bowen, made for a more truly representational exhibition than if it had simply been of CAM artists. Bowen had independent contacts; also, as a practising artist himself, and a member of the staff at the Commonwealth Institute since 1953 – first as exhibition adviser, later as gallery director – he brought professional expertise and a disinterested, objective eye to the selection of artists and their work. The exhibition was, in effect, an example of just the sort of cooperative venture with a British institution which CAM had initially sought. Bowen shares this view:

Caribbean artists in Lond

Aubrey and Eve Williams at the Commonwealth Institute/CAM Exhibition, 1971, with 'Warrau'

> I would have hoped in the first instance that it would have done those artists some good. First of all, they would have had a showing, to their advantage, in a very nice gallery. They wouldn't have had a lot of expense – it was virtually nil. . . . There was a big distribution of the catalogue – it was sent to libraries and places all over the world. We would have circulated the press and all sorts of local newspapers and so on and so forth: dealers, critics. Perhaps only a few but anyway some of them would have come to the exhibition. And we would hope in that way that the exhibition itself and the artists who made it up would get some benefit.

The young Caribbean artists found the show of special interest and value. Paul Dash remembers,

> thinking it was so different to the things I was seeing at Chelsea [School of Art] because there were these painters coming from a different tradition whose approach to painting was so very different to everyone else's. And many people would say, 'Oh a lot of it was naive', but I remember thinking, it's different and it's interesting. Some of it I didn't like, but then I can go to an exhibition of work by almost any painter and not like a lot of it, David Hockney or whatever.

The Commonwealth Institute exhibition prompted part of another CAM 'mini' session on 7 March, at Anne Walmsley's flat, just off Bedford Square in central London. Andrew Salkey and Aubrey Williams shared the meeting, on 'New Directions in Caribbean art'.[6] First Andrew Salkey told how he had been asked to take part in a BBC 2 'Late Night Line Up' programme on the recent Commonwealth Institute exhibition. His handwritten notes for what he planned to say show how the exhibition acted as stimulus and encouragement to CAM founder-members, but how it also met with establishment constraints and distortion. Salkey had drawn the BBC's attention to the exhibition, had been asked to do something on it. But when he met the television team at the Commonwealth Institute Gallery, he found 'TV camera concerns dominating all artistic and literary considerations'; work was chosen for 'camera convenience'.[7] Moreover, he claimed that his prepared script suffered 'severe editing' – and he read to the CAM meeting his original script in its entirety, 'without the so-called necessary editorial cuts and reworking'. But this at least gave some mainstream publicity to the exhibition. Salkey was clearly disappointed at how little coverage the show received, and suggested a whole range of contacts that should be made: from Caribbean and other Third World correspondents in Britain, to domestic British correspondents, editors and producers. The exhibition prompted Salkey to think longterm about Caribbean art in Britain:

> I'd like to make a suggestion or two about doing something about the . . . need for a continuing *historical record* of our Caribbean painting, sculpture, ceramics, fabric designing, mural and poster work, engraving and the other allied visual graphic and plastic arts. Not only book publication but the publication of posters, postcards and greeting cards as Jessica Huntley's Bogle L'Ouverture publications has been doing.

Salkey's suggestions are reminiscent of those of Brathwaite and Louis James at the start of CAM: creative, farsighted and desirable, but requiring considerably more funds and administrative input than CAM – certainly in 1971 – could dream of mustering.

Aubrey Williams followed Salkey, with a report on the recent work of two artists in Guyana. He himself had just completed his murals at Timehri, Guyana's new international airport: a Guyana Government commission, to be ready for Carifesta '72. Then, as Williams said when interviewed in Guyana shortly afterwards, 'I could hardly finish the murals before cutting out to see my old friend and mentor, Denis Williams, who lives there [Issano, in the interior]'.[8]

Denis Williams, also born in Georgetown – three years before Aubrey Williams – had, unlike Aubrey, gone directly to Britain to study art soon after he left school. By 1953, when Aubrey arrived, Denis was a Lecturer at the Central School of Art, Holborn, and Visiting Tutor at the Slade School of Fine Art, and had exhibited in Paris and London. In 1957, when Aubrey was getting established, Denis left for Africa. He spent five years in Khartoum, Sudan, and from 1962 worked in Nigeria, first at Ife, then at Lagos; in addition to teaching, he carried out research in African antiquities, painted, and wrote.[9] In 1968 he returned to Guyana. Denis had been at Issano for two years by the time Aubrey visited him there and reported:

> He had never held a cutlass in his life before, he'd never seen a venomous Guyanese snake in his life. This is an intellectual, a supreme intellectual in the high European sense who suddenly decided to fill a big gap in his life and do something for his country and all that. He went to Issano with this dream but didn't exactly know what he would do. He had some experience in peanut culture in Africa, and he decided that he would plant peanuts.

Aubrey spent ten days with Denis at Issano. He had taken his paints – 'I can't live without painting' – and turned the school at Issano into a studio: 'Denis came down, he picked up a brush or two, and he's better than ever. I was terribly inhibited working with the great man just watching the colours come out on the surface.'

Questioned as to whether Denis Williams's venture was artistic or agricultural, Aubrey Williams answered:

> You have to know the man. He lives his life totally. . . . You can't divide it up: the agricultural from the scientific, from the archaeological, from the creative in the sense of his sculpture and painting. Incidentally he is sculpting in hard jungle woods and stone now for the first time in his life and I've seen some fantastic pieces.

Asked how he rated Denis Williams among Guyanese artists, Aubrey insisted, 'He's our first painter – I mean, everybody knows that Denis Williams is our first painter, you shouldn't ask a question like that. But I had qualms about his *oeuvre*, what was happening? But I think he's better than ever.' Aubrey spoke of some of the work that Denis was currently engaged in: a portrait, and a book, on Dr Gigliogi – the man responsible for eradicating malaria in Guyana in the 1930s; assemblng and investigating old Amerindian artefacts. These last would, Aubrey considered, contribute to 'a true Guyanese identity' which 'must naturally come out of our primordial life in this country', echoing the theme of Denis Williams's Edgar Mittelholzer Lectures, *Image and Idea in the Arts of Guyana*, in January 1979.[10] Aubrey Williams's final prediction of the work in which Denis Williams was engaged was:

> Denis Williams is going to build a monument to Guyanese art, philosophy, identity in the jungle at Issano – he is going to build it out of Guyanese wood and stone, he is going to decorate it with Guyanese sculpture and painting.

This was a memorable, rich meeting, for the few CAM members who came to it.

The new CAM initiative

Meanwhile Donald Hinds and James Berry were following up their New Year initiative. A further committee meeting was held on 7 February; a draft agenda, in Donald Hinds's hand, runs:

> *BUSINESS*
> Who does what?
> Finance?
> Programmes?
> Structure?
> Current account £19
> Deposit account £89.89
> Total: £108.89 [6/2/71]

'Structure?' appears again below, underlined. Anne Walmsley's brief notes from the meeting indicate that CAM's structure was indeed the focus of discussion. James Berry: 'lack of structure and pattern very unsatisfactory'; Errol Lloyd: 'CAM not broad enough. Too elitist. No new blood. No attraction for the young.' Donald Hinds lamented that CAM was reduced to mini sessions only. John La Rose questioned whether CAM might have exhausted the stage of monthly meetings, and pointed to offshoots of CAM in contemporary black theatre. Louis Marriott – a newcomer to the CAM committee – challenged CAM to 'reach the whole West Indian community'. In London from Jamaica since 1964, Marriott worked as a journalist, mainly for the BBC; he was a board member of the Dark and Light Theatre Company, established in Brixton in 1969.

Members summoned to a meeting at John La Rose's house on 27 June were presented with a typed agenda, which named Donald Hinds as 'Acting Secretary' and James Berry as 'Acting Chairman'. The formality of an agenda was new to CAM; so was the role of chairman, separate from that of secretary. This first crucial meeting of the new-style CAM was attended not only by CAM's joint secretaries, La Rose and Salkey, but also by CAM's first organising secretary Edward Kamau Brathwaite and his right hand, Doris Brathwaite – on leave from UWI; also by Sarah White, Christopher Laird, Paul Dash, Femi Fatoba and Yulisa (Pat) Amadu Maddy, the Sierra Leonean dramatist, and Jessica Huntley. (Apologies from Anne Walmsley: her father had just died.) The agenda contained ten items. After introductions and tributes came the core item, 'The adopting of "Suggestions for CAM's future programmes" into a working programme for CAM's future activities.'

These 'Suggestions', 16 in all, were listed on three accompanying sheets of paper, and prefaced by the chairman with a 'brief explanation of how they came to be drafted'. They were not suggestions for discussion, but for adoption. An alternative agenda, prepared by Hinds for himself and Berry alone, states as their objectives, 'to adopt as many of the suggestions as possible' and 'to discuss and adopt the committee's ideas to improve suggested programmes': 'The latter [JB] will try to get certain items which follow the usual CAM mould adopted within half an hour – forty minutes time limit.' It was *their* programme, and the committee was to approve it, in effect, rubber stamp it. When the suggestions for CAM's future programme reappeared at the next meeting, a month later, only slight changes had been made to it. Donald Hinds's notes on the meeting indicate that in fact adoption of his and Berry's suggested topics was not straightjacketed into the time allocated, but formed a springboard for lengthy and constructive discussion:

> Everyone made a contribution and within three hours of stimulating discussion some 22 clear ideas as a workable programme emerged. CAM's public meetings which have been at the red light for over a year had finally got to gear and when Eddie gets it into top speed quite soon, it should cruise along easily for at least two years. It was most interesting to see emerging from the discussion the shape of what we wanted from CAM, the stuff we expected it to supply to meet both our intellectual and artistic needs.

This new CAM programme of suggested meetings was very thorough, comprehensive, and made some attempt to meet new interests. Although the topics, predominantly literary, were divided into the four traditional genres, they included 'Caribbean Women Writers', and under 'Poetry', experimental readings of new poems with instruments – drum, pan, guitar or saxophone. Art topics included 'West Indian Art and its Progressive Trends'. Some subject areas were new to CAM: music, sport, and 'ethics, philosophy and mysticism'. Other topics sound strangely old-fashioned, and smack of a lingering colonial approach: under drama, reference to the Greek classical model, under art, an introduction to Great European Painting. A new committee was needed to implement the programme: to select the first three topics and speakers, and most importantly, to decide where the meetings should be held. Item 8 of the agenda was 'The business of securing a room at the Camden Arts Centre as CAM's new headquarters'; according to Hinds's private agenda, they were expecting a report from Aubrey Williams, but he was not present.

At the next meeting, 25 July, the agenda was shorter. With the programme of meetings agreed – a revised and shortened version was circulated – and the first two topics selected, the place for CAM's meetings was the main item. After CAM's experience of the Students Centre, everyone agreed that the choice of venue was all-important: not just a place where CAM held meetings, nor even its headquarters, but a residence and a home. Neither of the Brathwaites was present this time, but Aubrey Williams, Anne Walmsley and Judith Laird, Femi Fatoba again, Ray Luck, and some Afro-American students were there. Although Aubrey Williams reported positively on the suitability and availability of the Camden Arts Centre, members were more attracted by John La Rose's report of a 'positive alternative'. This was the Keskidee Centre, opened in Islington the previous year. Oscar Abrams, its founder and director, had worked with La Rose since they were together in the Islington CARD in the early 1960s, and recently over black supplementary schools. The building in Gifford Street, close to the Caledonian Road, Kings Cross, was initially thought of by Abrams as providing simply such a school. But because of its spacious accommodation – a large and a small hall, four sizeable rooms and a kitchen – and because of the demonstrable need by

the local West Indian community for a more broad-based centre, he set up a Trust to acquire the building and to run it as a 'Centre providing educational, social and cultural activities'.[11] Such an institution – existing for, and used by, the immigrant community – seemed a more appropriate and enriching home for CAM than a mainstream British arts institution like the Camden Arts Centre, on the Finchley Road in Hampstead. Hinds's notes record full participation by La Rose and Salkey in all items on the agenda; Salkey annotated his copy of the revised programme, and noted the date and place of the next committee meeting.

But neither Hinds nor Salkey kept any record of the meeting on 5 September. The main item on its agenda was:

> Reorganising CAM's administration
> a) a re-examination of CAM's aims and objects [sic]
> b) a drafting of standing orders to guide CAM's administration
> c) a reorganising of the Committee
> d) ordinary membership reviving old interests, stimulating new.

This was accompanied by two pages setting out what the acting chairman and secretary proposed; under a heading, 'The Working of the Movement', were specified a committee of 12 with titles for six; a fixed term of service; how new committee members were to be appointed. Under another heading, 'Meetings', the document proposed regular two-monthly committee meetings, an AGM, and outlined the roles of chairman and secretary. La Rose and Salkey had gone along with the new-style committee meetings, but such rigid rules and insidious bureaucracy would, they felt, work against the essential spirit of CAM. The next committee meeting, planned for 10 October, was cancelled. There are no further agendas or notes of committee meetings; no evidence indeed of any further such meetings.

CAM public meeting at the Co-op Hall, September 1971, Edward Kamau Brathwaite on **New Cultural Signals in the Caribbean** *(close-ups of Nadia Cattouse, Ronald Moody, Gerald Moore, Sam Selvon, Donald Hinds, Andrew Salkey, Bernard and Phyllis Coard)*

CAM did, however, hold two public meetings in the autumn of 1971, at the Cooperative Hall, Seven Sisters Road, which resulted directly from the new committee and its programme. On 22 September Brathwaite spoke on 'New Cultural Signals In The Caribbean'. In their original suggestions, Berry and Hinds had hoped that he would combine 'A review of CAM's work in London and the West Indies, since founded, with programme and plans for the future' with 'a review of the cultural development of the Caribbean since the era of Independence and present outlook for the future'. But Brathwaite himself did not regard this as an occasion for retrospection, and certainly not about CAM. He was more concerned to share with his London audience the creative ferment in the Caribbean, of which he was now part. The talk was not recorded, but it was fully covered in *West Indian World* by James Berry, who prefaced his report with a detailed biography, highlighting Brathwaite's work in CAM.[12]

Brathwaite is reported as having introduced his talk with the, to CAM audiences, now familiar thesis that the dominant European culture in colonial Caribbean society which his generation had inherited, was, since Independence, being increasingly challenged by Caribbean peoples' constituent cultures: African, Indian, Amerindian, Chinese. Although Caribbean governments were now black, they tended to react to the emergence of new cultural forms of expression in similar ways to their white predecessors. As examples of such establishment reaction, Brathwaite related in detail the recent watershed confrontations between black youth and government in the Caribbean: the Rodney Affair in Jamaica, the February Revolt in Trinidad. He also recounted a confrontation of another sort: that between establishment academics and writers and critics pursuing the folk tradition, at the Commonwealth Literature Conference in Jamaica in January 1971 (the ACLALS Conference), seeing this as part of the same pattern. In Berry's report,

> those reactions were opposed to his identification with the restless search of the masses, their intense desire to redefine their position, to move from the automatically lowest strata of their society. He saw that there was a great need for the developed sensibilities of the community to be linked with those of the uneducated and the underdeveloped.

He reported, too, how Brathwaite emphasised that a redefinition of the position of the racial majority in the Caribbean, ie people of African origin, did not only provoke the black establishment, but also aroused feelings of insecurity among the Chinese, Indian and white West Indians. They, too, must redefine their position, deciding whether they sought to revert completely to their parent cultures, and thus force the Caribbean into further fragmentation, or 'be guided into unity with all the richness of its multi-cultures'. And that, said Brathwaite, as reported by Berry, 'depended entirely on the wisdom of the social reformers, the artists, the intellectuals, the politicians'.

Discussion seems to have been as substantial as the talk itself, in the best CAM tradition. It led Brathwaite to outline the changing forms of cultural expression, mentioning Derek Walcott's Theatre Workshop of Trinidad, Barry and Lloyd Reckord's theatre work in Jamaica, Rex Nettleford's Jamaica National Dance Theatre Company, and Marina Maxwell's Yard Theatre; also, 'he touched on the expressive aspects of ska and the reggae'. It also provoked Brathwaite into a clear definition of his own direction:

> Three members of the audience, in support of each other, voiced their disappointment that Dr Brathwaite had given no indication of a specific lead towards a violent revolution. He replied that this dichotomy at the end of a meeting was not infrequent. In any case, if he should even take it upon himself to give a list of what to do towards a revolution, he doubted if anything would work out. He had not come to talk about a bloody revolution. His talk was about new cultural signals in the Caribbean, which he hoped would lead to a positive redefinition of West Indian identity.

Three years on from CAM's Second Conference, Brathwaite's examples of cultural change were in drama, dance, and music – neglected or ignored in CAM's early phase. The confrontation which he now met was more radical, more aggressive than that posed by Richard Small, Locksley Comrie and Lowell Marcus, and mirrored the mood of anger and frustration amongst young blacks in Britain in the early 1970s. James Berry's report makes clear his own identification with and concern for the uneducated masses.

On 29 October – the traditional CAM spot of the last Friday in the month – came the promised evening of poetry and music. Those advertised as taking part included Mustapha Matura, James Berry, T-Bone Wilson, Louis Marriott, and Marc Matthews, with guitarist and folk singer Ray Blair; Archie Markham was not listed but remembers reading his poetry. Matthews was just passing through London. His return to Guyana had, he recalls, 're-energised a lot of things Guyanese and Caribbean in me and it was always hearing that voice again and hearing the intonations and the language again'. Matthews's example as a performance poet, his and other poets' use of Caribbean rhythm and language – the combination was a breakthrough for CAM, and heralded a new era. Several members also performed earlier in October 1971, at the Faraday Hall, on the Sunday before the opening of the trial of the Mangrove Nine. Brathwaite, who had not yet returned to Jamaica, appeared with La Rose and others, alongside Black

Reading in support of the Mangrove Nine, the night before their trial began, (l to r) John La Rose, Edward Kamau Brathwaite, Marc Matthews, T-Bone Wilson

Panther activists Althea Jones (now Lecointe-Jones) and Darcus Howe, in 'a kind of pre-trial wake of poetry, song and sound'.[13]

The 1971 CAM public meetings at the Cooperative Hall attracted large audiences. For Brathwaite's talk, intended to launch the new CAM, members of the audience were invited to sign if they would like to receive future CAM literature: 80 did so. They included CAM stalwarts, new and long-established writers and artists, former Students Centre officers. Marc Matthews remembers 'a very full house' at the poetry evening. The audience for both meetings included a number of people involved in the current educational struggle, for meetings of the Caribbean Education and Community Workers Association were also held at the Cooperative Hall. Like the Students Centre before it, that venue too was responsible for bringing in its own audience.

The black education movement had gained momentum and publicity from the appearance, in 1971, of Bernard Coard's book, *How The West Indian Child Is Made Educationally Sub-Normal In The British School System*. Published for CECWA by New Beacon (with substantial support and help from individuals and West Indian organisations – see Coard's note of indebtedness), it was subtitled 'The scandal of the black child in schools in Britain', and produced evidence – authenticated from Coard's own research and experience – of the large numbers of West Indian children placed in ESN schools in Britain. According to Coard, this was partly because of the cultural and class bias of the tests to which they were subjected, partly because of attitudes of teachers and children. He maintained that once so placed, most children remained in such schools, with consequent permanent harm to their education and to their job prospects. Coard identified the particular harm to black children caused by the white middle-class curriculum which ignored the black child's history, language, culture and identity. His concluding recommendations to West Indian parents – the book is dedicated to ' . . . all Black parents who value their children's education and opportunities in life above all else' – included a call to open black nursery and supplementary schools; to read West Indian story books and books about black people – and provided a 'booklist for parents' of 'West Indian literature for children'; all titles were said to be obtainable from New Beacon Books (Bogle-L'Ouverture did not start to sell books until 1974). At least half the books on the list are by CAM members: Salkey's four children's novels and his collection of short stories; Michael Anthony's novels of childhood; Kenneth Ramchand's and Anne Walmsley's school anthologies; the first of the new Caribbean school histories edited by Brathwaite, and his Ghana plays for children. CAM's reading public was now extended from the audiences at its meetings to West Indian parents and children, largely thanks to John La Rose and Sarah White's bookselling and publishing enterprise and involvement with CECWA. The list in Coard's book was reprinted in *The Times Educational Supplement* in May 1971, headed 'Black booklist' – in the belief that teachers, too, would find it helpful.[14]

Covers of **Breaklight** *and* **One Love,** *based on paintings by Karl 'Jerry' Craig and Errol Lloyd*

Breaklight, An Anthology of Caribbean Poetry chosen, edited and introduced by Andrew Salkey, was also published in 1971, in a handsome hardback edition, by a prestigious British publisher, Hamish Hamilton. It included none of those poets who read and performed at the CAM session in October 1971. Yet it attempted, in Salkey's words, to present 'the discovery of a new light throughout our society; and the promise, now, offered us by our young poets . . . of spiritual and social redefinition. . . . In our Caribbean, these poets are essentially poets of revolution, because they are poets of hope.'[15] Salkey placed young, unpublished or little published poets alongside older, better known poets, Caribbean-based alongside British-based. They included many who had taken part in, or been in touch with, CAM: Elliott Bastien, Edward Brathwaite, Jan Carew, Faustin Charles, Sebastian Clarke, Wilson Harris, Evan Jones, Knolly La Fortune, John La Rose, Ian McDonald, Tony Matthews, Marina Maxwell, Mervyn Morris, Dennis Scott, Sam Selvon, Basil Smith, Ivan Van Sertima. The absence of James Berry, Marc Matthews, Archie Markham, T-Bone Wilson shows how fast creative expression in Britain was moving in the late 1960s, early 1970s. By the time *Breaklight* was published, it was already, in a sense, out of date. But it was a landmark book as the first collection of Caribbean poetry to span the Caribbean and Britain, to include so many of the new generation of writers in both. And it was very much a CAM book, not only through its editor and contributors, but in its title – by Knolly La Fortune, and its cover – by Karl Craig, based on his earlier drawing for the cover of *Newsletter* No 7.

Another landmark collection of Caribbean writing published in 1971, also introduced by Andrew Salkey, was *One Love*, Bogle-L'Ouverture's second published book, again a group effort by Jessica Huntley and 'fellow workers'.[16] It contains prose and poetry by Audvil King, Althea Helps, Pam Wint and Frank Hasfal, all born in Jamaica in the 1940s and 1950s, all active there in the 'Black Movement'. Salkey points out and salutes its landmark features: its use of 'our authentic voice . . . mainly urban proletarian Jamaican and Rastafarian in essence and detail', its political meaning 'because it defines and illustrates the waiting power of Blackness in our Caribbean', discussion and illustration of 'our women recapturing their depressed revolutionary consciousness and putting it once again in an assertive position'. *One Love* exposed many readers in Britain for the first time to the literary ferment and growth of black consciousness in Jamaica in the wake of Walter Rodney, and to the new voices of urban youth, of Rastafarians. and of women.

Errol Lloyd's painting, itself titled 'One Love', a full-face image of a black woman with a strong decorative element, reminiscent of African prints, is reproduced – in black and white – on the cover of the book. It was one of several paintings by Errol Lloyd and fellow Caribbean, and African, artists to be reproduced in full colour by Bogle L'Ouverture as greetings cards, from 1971 onwards. In a contemporary interview Huntley said: 'The first time we did them people were a bit shocked. Black faces on a card. But,' she added, 'there's a need for them, for us.'[17] Bogle had preceded the cards with a series of posters by Rastafarian artists, starting with a self-portrait by Ras Daniel Heartman. Visual imagery was thus added to the written and spoken word in the expression of black consciousness.

CAM at Keskidee

When at last the Keskidee Centre was available to CAM, at the beginning of 1972, there was no new committee to take full advantage of it. The CAM meetings which were held there, although all topical and lively, were one-off occasions, on random dates. There was no apparent CAM programme or purpose. They depended again on La Rose and Salkey. In February, a panel of speakers discussed Barry Reckord's BBC TV play, *In The Beautiful Caribbean*, called a 'Reggae play' because it drew on the then new Jamaican musical form. In March, 'A Tribute to Ronald Moody' was arranged and presented by Errol Lloyd. Slides of Moody's work were shown and commented on by Lloyd and La Rose; Moody was present but did not speak publicly. In June,

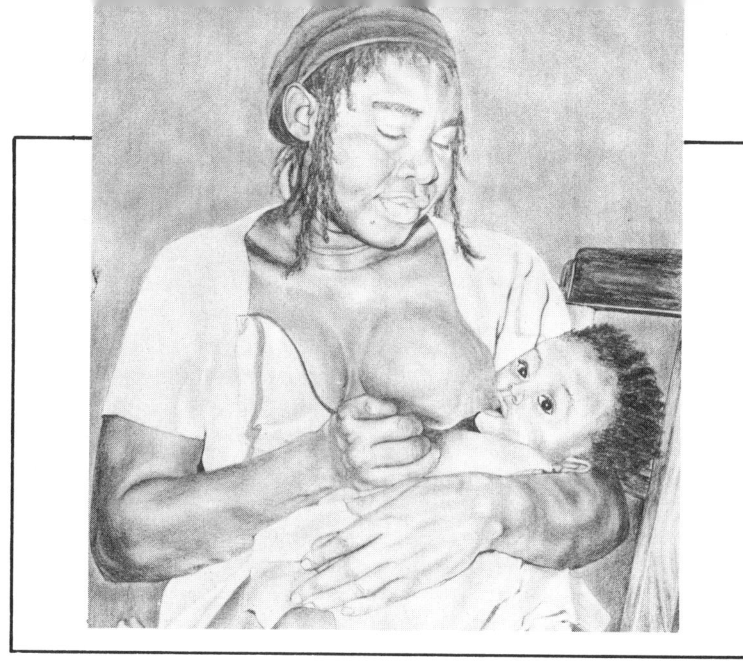

Poster by Ras Daniel Heartman

Dennis Sardinha (on leave from UWI's Cave Hill campus in Barbados) gave a talk on Nicolás Guillén. In July Pio Zirimu, Lecturer in the Department of Literature at Makerere University, Uganda, spoke about the context of Okot p'Bitek's already classic poem, *Song of Lawino*. Zirimu's was the one other name which Ngũgĩ had mentioned to La Rose as also involved in the campaign to change the perspectives of literature teaching at the universities of East Africa. Zirimu was a close friend and colleague of p'Bitek; his talk followed shortly after a performance of *Lawino* in mime at Keskidee.

Less formal CAM-like occasions at Keskidee at this time are remembered by Yvonne Brewster (then Jones), back in London from Jamaica – and the very successful Barn Theatre, as a professional theatre producer and director. On Sunday afternoons La Rose, Salkey, Shake Keane, Pat Amadu Maddy, Emmanuel Jegede and others would have what she describes as the equivalent of a Caribbean 'tea meeting'; she recalls Andrew Salkey reading from his most recent books.

Keskidee as a cultural centre was enriched by CAM's activities in 1972, as the Students Centre had been in the late 1960s. Oscar Abrams recalls how 'it helped us to become more interested in what was written about the Caribbean and by Caribbean people, and begin to read, to collect, to look around. CAM's contribution was vital, and in fact it helped Keskidee because literature and drama were both in it.' In turn, CAM meetings at Keskidee brought in, as had been hoped, an audience from the West Indian community. Linton (now Kwesi) Johnson's experience of CAM was mainly at the Keskidee. He had left school in 1970, aged 18, with 'O' levels, and by 1972 was studying for 'A' levels while doing

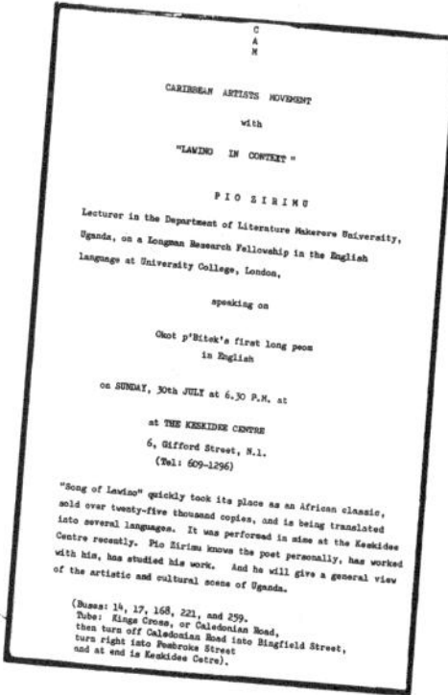

C
A
M

CARIBBEAN ARTISTS MOVEMENT

with

"LAWINO IN CONTEXT"

P I O Z I R I M U

Lecturer in the Department of Literature Makerere University, Uganda, on a Longman Research Fellowship in the English language at University College, London,

speaking on

Okot p'Bitek's first long poem
in English

on SUNDAY, 30th JULY at 6.30 P.M. at

at THE KESKIDEE CENTRE
6, Gifford Street, N.1.
(Tel: 609-1296)

"Song of Lawino" quickly took its place as an African classic, sold over twenty-five thousand copies, and is being translated into several languages. It was performed in mime at the Keskidee Centre recently. Pio Zirimu knows the poet personally, has worked with him, has studied his work. And he will give a general view of the artistic and cultural scene of Uganda.

(Buses: 14, 17, 168, 221, and 259.
Tube: Kings Cross, or Caledonian Road,
then turn off Caledonian Road into Bingfield Street,
turn right into Pembroke Street
and at end is Keskidee Cetre).

Notice of CAM public meeting at the Keskidee Centre, 1972

clerical jobs. He had become a member of the Black Panther Movement's Young League, taking the Ghanaian name 'Kwesi' ('born on Sunday' – as indeed he was), and had begun to discover Afro-American literature. A study group and a discussion group at a Brixton youth club, both of which he had helped to form, needed books; he went to New Beacon and got to know La Rose, who invited him to CAM meetings. Johnson remembers CAM's 'Evening of poetry and music' at the Cooperative Hall in late 1971, and 'Jamal Ali, T-Bone Wilson and Mustapha Matura, the angry black poets of the day',[18] and particularly the Keskidee meetings in 1972. He recalls how stimulating they were for him, 'as a young person just discovering that there was such a thing as black literature, as Caribbean literature'. His connection with the Keskidee, begun in CAM, developed in all sorts of ways. He became librarian, on a voluntary basis, and began to take part in its dramatic productions. 'The Keskidee in those days was an important centre for black cultural activity and I began attending other events there and soon found myself at the centre of black creativity in London.'

In 1972 La Rose and Salkey were guest editors, at Brathwaite's invitation, of *Savacou* 9/10, a special CAM (UK) issue. Many of its contributors had been active or associated with CAM in Britain: James Berry, Faustin Charles, Stuart Hall, Donald Hinds, Linton Kwesi Johnson, Christopher Laird, Judith Laird, John La Rose, Louis Marriott, Horace Ové, Orlando Patterson. Almost all were still in Britain; so too were most of the other contributors: Jamal

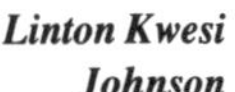
Linton Kwesi Johnson

Ali, Roy Heath, Frank John (now Nkemka Asika), Rudolph Kizerman, EA Markham, Jimi Rand, T-Bone Wilson – and VS Naipaul. The issue constituted, in effect, the first anthology of black British writing, not yet recognised as such. It contains photographs by Ové of the August 1970 Mangrove Nine Demo, and carries a cover design by Aubrey Williams, 'Jaguar'. The issue's subtitle, *Writing Away from Home* suggests the continuing ambivalence of some of its contributors, despite CAM's increasing orientation towards the Caribbean community in Britain. Its Introduction, signed by La Rose and Salkey, claims 'manifold evidence of Caribbean cultural inventiveness' in the two-fold context of being 'here in Britain': 'the crucial pressures of racism and class antagonism' and 'the darkness of our "voluntary exile", out of the alienated physical and spiritual responses away from home'.

In their Preface, the guest editors present CAM as a movement very much alive, poised to take off on a new course. All the meetings since October 1968 are listed and all the people who have taken positions of responsibility in CAM, from their fellow founder members, to 'Donald Hinds and James Berry who have undertaken much of the continuing and expanding work of the Movement in London'. They report:

> That there is a renewed interest in the continuing work of CAM (UK) on the part of our Caribbean communities here, and that it is being shared by our musicians, singers, actors and popular entertainers, even though they haven't yet found it convenient to participate, as fully as they would like, in the sessions of their choice.

There is no suggestion that the CAM session listed as the most recent – on Ronald Moody, March 1972 – was almost the last.

CAM's 'disappearance'

In April 1972, La Rose and Salkey were interviewed by Adrian Mitchell in *The Guardian*.[19] Again, their references to CAM are all in the present continuing tense. The concept of CAM is still that of its founder members. La Rose:

> CAM starts by saying that liberation begins in the imagination. We don't have an official membership. We don't have officer responsibility but worker responsibility. People find this structure hard to grasp.

Salkey:

> It's an almost mirage-like structure. The only thing we've ever planned is that we always look as if we're disappearing. You know why? Our history has been full of authoritarians. But the work gets done.

By 1972 a CAM committee was almost non-existent; the CAM programme of activities was very thin, and ceased altogether after the summer. Donald Hinds and James Berry had attempted in 1971 to construct a new programme for CAM and to attract new membership. But their approach seemed out of keeping with the character of CAM and was found inappropriate by CAM's founder-members; they were discouraged from going further. Berry makes light of their failed attempts:

> I proposed various things at the time. . . . We had regular monthly meetings where we used to come together and talk. And then I remember the Keskidee ideas came up strong, and then it was decided that that phase of CAM had probably served its purpose and would now grow in other ways.

Hinds recalls what went wrong more specifically:

> It [the proposed new CAM programme] was mainly his [Berry's] thing. But CAM wasn't really set up for that sort of programme. It was a much more spontaneous thing. James wanted to have a structured meeting, when we could look forward to seeing what was going to happen and so on. He wanted a more planned intellectual discussion on a lot of themes, and so on.

Hinds had thought that CAM would continue to evolve, and was quite prepared for it to keep on changing its shape. 'I think that this is where I differ from James Berry: he had a plan and he thought that this was what we were going to do and so on.' La Rose recalls that he could not convince Berry that CAM was not bureaucratic.

La Rose and Salkey, and CAM's five-year-long members, participants, and fringers, continued CAM in whatever they did. As Brathwaite puts it in his Postscript to *Savacou* 9/10: 'Those away from home, keeping the faith, continue to express themselves in multi-variate ways within CAM and its offshoots.'[20] But the absence of a visible and definable CAM presence after 1972 meant that, to the regret of many, there was no CAM for those who came after.

1973–1982

1972 proved in many ways to be the end of an era in the life of West Indians in Britain, and 1973 a year of new beginnings. This was the year in which the 1971 Immigration Act came into force, bringing all primary black immigration to an end. The Caribbean community gradually became less one of immigrants or exiles, more one of black British. West Indian children born in Britain began to outnumber those who had come over to join their parents; it is reckoned that, by the mid-1970s, two out of every five black people in Britain were born there. Chris Mullard's book

Black Britain (1973) was the first by a member of the new generation of young blacks born and brought up in Britain. The New Beacon Bookshop became more accessible to the black community in 1973 when it moved from La Rose's home into premises with a shop front on the Stroud Green Road in Finsbury Park, North London. Bogle-L'Ouverture added bookselling to its book, poster and card-publishing in 1974, and opened its shop (renamed the Walter Rodney Bookshop in 1980), just off the Uxbridge Road in Ealing, West London.[21] At the IRR, major confrontations in 1972 between council and staff led to the disbandment of the existing Institute and the formation of a new council in March 1973, which included amongst its teachers, university lecturers, community workers: 'Augustine John, author and youth worker at University of Manchester', and 'John La Rose, poet and publisher of the New Beacon press'.[22] La Rose was elected chairman of the new council during this crucial period when the IRR was establishing its independence, and moving from Jermyn Street, Piccadilly, to premises in Kings Cross.

By 1974, when *Savacou* 9/10 was finally published (delays from the printer in Jamaica), there was no more CAM activity as such to report, no further CAM statement to make from London. So Brathwaite added a Postscript, in which he lists publications, exhibitions and other work by *Savacou* 9/10 contributors, and by CAM members, over the previous two years. Salkey had three publications out in 1973 alone. A letter from La Rose of January 1974, which Brathwaite quotes and amplifies, tells of his cultural work on many fronts: with the black education movement; of co-production with Horace Ové of a film on the Mangrove Nine; of producing a live 90-minute BBC/TV programme in which the work of several CAM writers and artists was featured; and of New Beacon's new and forthcoming publications. The letter closes: 'Meanwhile keep going and watch the perils of the dawn as it comes over our horizon.'[23]

CAM (UK) was central to the special edition of the BBC 2 television programme, Full House, 'featuring the work of West Indian artists, writers, musicians and film-makers', on Saturday 3 February 1973.[24] John La Rose and Nigel Williams – now a wellknown playwright – were Associate Producers. Williams was responsible for internal BBC liaison, and La Rose for the devising, directing, and control of the programme, subject only to the BBC Executive Producer. La Rose was able to insist that Canute James, not an English actor, should present it. The majority of items were concerned with performance and had wide popular appeal: extracts from Lindsay (Barrett) Eseoghene's 'Black Blast' – an exploration of Caribbean history through music, mime and dance, and from Mustapha Matura's play 'Bakerloo Line'; a service at the

Pentecostal Church of God at the Angel, Islington (produced by La Rose and directed by Tony Laryea) and a Sunday lunchtime session of kaiso music at the Coleherne, a pub in Earl's Court (filmed by Horace Ové); a performance by Count Prince Miller of reggae, described in the *Radio Times* billing as 'the latest musical craze to come out of the West Indies and achieve a wide popularity'. A sequence of poetry and prose devised by La Rose contained work by CAM members from 1966 to 1972, by writers in Jamaica and Britain. Evan Jones, Jamal Ali, John La Rose, Sam Selvon, Linton Kwesi Johnson and T-Bone Wilson read their own work; Edward Kamau Brathwaite's 'Wings of a Dove' was read by Yvonne Brewster and Bongo Jerry's 'Sooner or Later' by Andrew Salkey. An equivalent CAM sequence of art was planned; La Rose saw this as being central to the programme and commissioned Althea McNish to arrange it. McNish contacted fellow CAM artists and selected work by ten, including herself. In the televised programme, the paintings, sculpture and fabrics simply appeared as studio background, to the artists' disappointment and disgust. Television's showbiz instincts and need for a mass audience favoured the popular performance arts. But in all the programme was a critical event, giving public recognition to all the arts which CAM members had been able to accomplish, and presenting them to a mass audience. It reflected the movement in Caribbean arts since CAM was launched with Edward Kamau Brathwaite's public reading of *Rights of Passage*, six years earlier.

CAM seemed finally to disappear when the second of its three founders left Britain. Andrew Salkey was invited to the USA in 1974 by Robert Hill, to work with him at Northwestern University, Evanston, on a play based on the recently-released papers of Marcus Garvey's trial in 1925. As a result of giving readings and talks at other American universities, Salkey was offered, two years later, a professorship in writing at Hampshire College, Amherst, Massachusetts. He left London in August 1976, believing that after the initial two-three year contract, he would return. But longer contracts were proposed. As for many of his Caribbean writer contemporaries, North American universities offered a base and livelihood, appreciation and response, not offered in Britain and difficult to refuse. Salkey left an irreplaceable void in the CAM network, and in the larger black community, in Britain.

John La Rose's cultural work in Britain's black community developed and expanded throughout the 1970s. Harry Goulbourne, Jamaica-born, Britain-educated academic writes of La Rose's 'profound commitment to the emergence of a new community in post-imperial Britain for all who regard Britain as *home*'.[25] New Beacon continued to be the base for his many-sided activities: further publications – reprints of more Caribbean classics, first volumes of poems by Mervyn Morris and James Berry, new fiction by Erna Brodber and Carl Jackson; more widespread bookselling – to schools and libraries in Britain, and into the Caribbean; and intensified concern with education and youth work – the Black Parents Movement and the Black Youth Movement emerged in 1975 from the George Padmore Community School.

In 1982 New Beacon joined with its fellow black publisher-bookseller Bogle-L'Ouverture and publisher Race Today to plan and hold, in and around Islington Town Hall, North London, the First International Book Fair of Radical Black and Third World Books. Its opening by CLR James, introduced by John La Rose, thanked by Jessica Huntley, was a historic moment, marking 60 years since James first arrived in Britain, 15 since the formation of New Beacon Books and of CAM. Edward Kamau Brathwaite opened the Third Book Fair, in Acton, West London, in March 1984. Introducing him, La Rose described CAM as the Book Fair's ancestor. CAM which in 1972 had seemed to disappear was now revealed only to have gone underground, a submerged source and spring for the onward movement of Caribbean creative endeavour.

CLR James opened the First International Book Fair of Radical Black and Third World Books, Islington Town Hall, April 1982

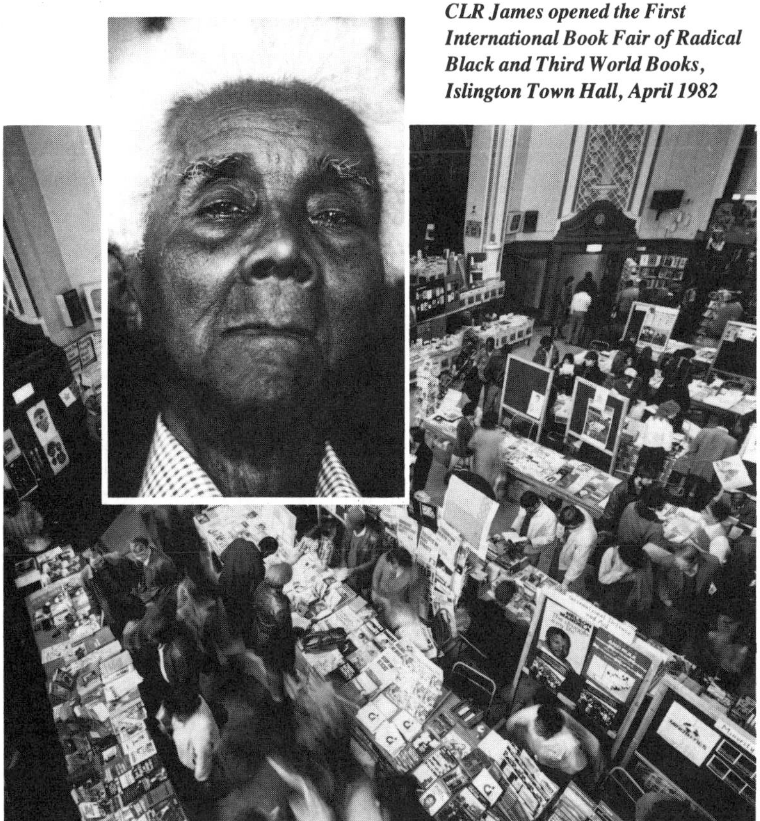

11 Postscript

The formation and operation of CAM was itself an act of creativity; its members saw CAM as a means of bringing about change in Caribbean people and Caribbean society. CAM embodied the ideas and beliefs of its active members – where they converged and where they were different, hence its inner dynamic. Its outward face reflected the changing scene in Britain and in those parts of the Caribbean where it tried to take root. But the essential character of CAM remained constant: a community of men and women deeply involved with Caribbean arts and culture, a community concerned with rehabilitating and extending Caribbean consciousness. This is the CAM which has lived on, long after its formal existence as an organisation ceased. It is part of a continuing movement for change, with its own identifiable ancestors and relatives. Its legacy is varied and demonstrable, in the present, into the future.

The character of CAM

CAM was formed in late 1966 by practising writers, artists and critics from the former British West Indies, who were working or studying in or in reach of London. They felt a need to know each other and each others' work. As John La Rose explains: 'Artists together means that they develop a vulnerable interaction on the basis of where they wish to go with their ideas.' They considered that the art of their newly independent nations had reached something of an impasse; although the content of its fiction and poetry, its painting and sculpture, had become 'nativised', its forms continued to be those inherited from European art. Several writers and artists, working separately, knowing little or nothing of each others' work, had already started to change the pattern: Edward Kamau Brathwaite and John La Rose in poetry, Wilson Harris and Orlando Patterson in fiction, Aubrey Williams in painting, Ronald Moody in sculpture. They were the creative core of CAM, the informal group with which CAM began, and which continued, with the exception of Patterson, throughout, and beyond, CAM's visible life. Other writers and artists, and drama people, were drawn into the CAM group; so too were critics, sympathetic readers and viewers.

Some of CAM's founder members believed from the start that CAM should be more than an informal group: that its writers and artists should be accessible to a wide audience in Britain, and that their work and ideas should have a public platform, so that Caribbean literature and art, particularly in its revolutionary new forms, would reach and activate a new range and generation of people. Brathwaite in particular was determined that CAM should 'go public' as early as possible. Thus the study-group character of CAM's small, private sessions was paralleled by one of an open university. The model of Eric Williams's University of Woodford Square was recreated in Earls Court and at Canterbury. Public CAM also came to fulfil something of the purpose of the black supplementary schools of the 1970s. The essential concept of CAM was that private group should interact with public organisation. Only such a two-layered movement could hope to implement CAM's belief in its artists and equally in the creative potential of Caribbean people.

Brathwaite, 'organising secretary' and spokesman for CAM in its first phase, defined further objectives which required CAM to go public: to facilitate Caribbean writers and artists' 'meeting our readers, viewers and listeners, and setting up dialogue with them', 'to provide a forum of discussion between ourselves and artists and intellectuals from outside the Caribbean', 'linking the West Indian artistic communities abroad to the rich soil of their origins back in the West Indies'.[1] CAM's programme evolved in order to fulfil these objectives: monthly public sessions, annual conferences; art exhibitions; the recording of talks, readings and discussion; a newsletter.

For CAM as a public organisation to fulfil all these objectives, and to carry out its programme, involved it in outside contacts which seemed to endanger – to some members at least – compromising its freedom as a group of writers and artists. The Students Centre provided an appropriate venue for CAM's public sessions, but its student and immigrant audience at times interrupted these sessions in ways that some CAM members did not welcome. At the Second Conference, these interruptions came to a head when CAM artists were challenged directly to relate to and identify with the immigrant community in Ladbroke Grove and Brixton; as a result key artists withdrew from CAM, notably Wilson Harris and Karl 'Jerry' Craig. While the University of Kent provided a welcome venue for CAM's public residential conferences, it involved academic contacts – non-Caribbean grounded lecturers and uncertain responsibility for tapes of sessions – which caused some members to feel that their autonomy as Caribbean artists and intellectuals was endangered. The West Indian High Commissions seemed to some members an appropriate source of assistance and funding. But Brathwaite's invitation to the Jamaican High Commissioner to open CAM's first art exhibition caused a split within the CAM group, and Brathwaite himself ceased further requests when help offered by the Jamaican High Commission was tied to acceptance of its own selected and sponsored Jamaican students' CAM membership. CAM's acceptance of the British Caribbean Association's invitation to exhibit in the House of Commons deepened the split, with some members threatening to demonstrate outside while their fellow members exhibited within. As CAM became better known it was called on to cooperate with British cultural and media events. La Rose agreed to work with the BBC on its TV Full House programme, but he and other CAM members felt that British media demands compromised the presentation of their work, particularly that of the artists.

La Rose had foreseen such dangers. His concept of CAM from the start, and consistently to the end, was primarily of a group of artists. In attempting also to be a public organisation he knew that CAM was vulnerable. His political experience had taught him that self-reliance and independent operation were the only way to effective action. La Rose had already founded New Beacon Publications when CAM began; he expected far less of CAM as an organisation than Brathwaite did.

For CAM to function as a public organisation required some definition of responsibility. But, claimed La Rose: 'We don't have officer responsibility, but worker responsibility.'[2] In fact, two offices in CAM were designated all the way through, those of secretary and treasurer. Both were in the main self-appointed. Brathwaite took on the role of secretary early in CAM; La Rose and Salkey took on the role when Brathwaite returned to Jamaica, insisting at first on being 'acting secretaries', later accepting 'joint secretaries'. In a sense, Brathwaite was always *the* CAM secretary. Oliver Clarke took on the role of treasurer as soon as CAM went public; he knew that the organisation would need funds so volunteered to round up subscriptions, raise money for CAM, and keep its accounts. CAM with other secretaries, or a self-styled chairman, did not flourish – with Marina Maxwell early in 1968, with James Berry and Donald Hinds in 1971. Only the founder members had a consistent and united concept of what CAM was about and how it should operate. They insisted on what La Rose called the movement's 'informal structure' which was, he said, commending CAM to the 1970 Convention in Guyana, 'absolutely necessary for a community of artists and people interested in the arts, if they are to retain their independence and function effectively'.[3] After a year of being CAM secretary, with this informal structure, Brathwaite confessed: 'If you have a sense of community, you have to share your power with the community, and this is why CAM is structured in this strange way.'[4]

The part played by women within this informal structure was apparently small, but significant. Of the women artists active in London at the time that CAM was formed, none was invited to the founding meetings. But when Brathwaite first left for Jamaica in January 1968, the key job of secretary was entrusted to Marina Maxwell, writer and theatre person. Her short period in this role seems to have been somewhat divisive – the result of her being outside the original founding group and not fully sharing its ideas and approach, plus the difficulty of taking over from Brathwaite despite his careful attempts to brief her. But from the moment of her arrival in Jamaica she regarded herself as a CAM person, working with and speaking to the New World group as such. She developed Yard Theatre as a CAM-related activity. Her enthusiasm for establishing CAM in the Caribbean lasted throughout her years in Jamaica and back home in Trinidad, with plans set out on a grand scale at Carifesta '79. She remained loyal to a concept of CAM, though it tended to be her own concept, and not necessarily that of the group. The participation of Elsa Goveia, Jean Franco, Althea McNish, Pearl Connor, Yvonne Brewster and Doris Harper Wills was highly valued. Jessica Huntley was never a CAM member, but through her closely related cultural activism, particularly in publishing, she was assumed to be part of CAM, attending at least one committee meeting; in *Savacou* 9/10 she was thanked for editorial assistance during its early stages. Anne Walmsley published accounts of CAM's first two conferences, and, from late 1968, attended committee meetings and assisted with clerical work.

The most valuable work by women for CAM was done by the founder members' wives. Nerys Patterson suggested CAM's name, and took an active part in all early sessions. Pat Salkey was warmly hospitable and supportive to the frequent CAM gatherings which Andrew held at their flat. Sarah White was involved from the start, as John's partner, and through her work with New Beacon; the importance of her efficiency and hard work, her calm approach and ready sense of humour, can never be overestimated. Central and supreme was Doris Brathwaite – although she would certainly have denied it. No other woman had a significance in CAM which was similar in any way. This was in part a result of her work as co-secretary with Edward Kamau Brathwaite. During London CAM she kept up the membership list, fielded enquiries and correspondence, registered and listed participants at the conferences, transported and supervised the tape recorder, and many more such tasks; in Jamaica, she shared all the *Savacou* work, training and equipping herself in all ways which could be of benefit to it. But her significance was above all a result of how she carried out CAM work, and what she herself was. She had her own strong ideas about the creative function of CAM, her own firm belief in what CAM could achieve – evident in her radiant face at the First Conference, her frequent interventions in discussion at the Second. Everyone in CAM remembers her work and presence with special admiration and affection. In 1987, the year after her death, Knolly La Fortune contributed an assessment of CAM, 'In revered memory of Mrs Doris Brathwaite, the first secretary of CAM'.

The concept behind CAM's informal structure was that of a community. Brathwaite, interviewed in 1973, said: 'I was working on the African concept of the community.'[5] CAM's efficacy and its dynamism came from individuals each carrying out the parts suited to their own capacity and character. It took pains to nurture and care for all the members of its community. Copies of Brathwaite's letters show how he would write after spotting someone at a public session, encouraging him or her to join CAM; how he wrote to speakers whom he invited to a session with a welcome beforehand, and in warm, generous, appreciative terms afterwards, each one individual and specific. After each conference, his fellow CAM members also received such letters. If he sensed too long a gap in hearing from one of them, he would drop a line: 'Missin' you, man! Long time no hear or see!'[6] Salkey took on a similar role after the Brathwaites' departure, always responding promptly with appreciation for all CAM work that was done. Isolation was indeed overcome. The fragmentation of which Caribbean artists were so conscious – in their history, in their scatter of island and mainland communities, each itself divided – found some wholeness within the membership of CAM.

All its members, not simply its practising artists, felt that they mattered and were part of the movement for creative change. CAM demonstrated that a community could be more creative, effect more change, than the individual alone. CAM speakers tried to make it clear that the audience was as important a part of the session as they were. Discussion following a talk was less a matter of addressing questions to the speaker than of group discussion and discovery. This was particularly evident at the Second Symposium on the Havana Congress and at the Second Conference, of which Brathwaite wrote afterwards to Stuart Hall that 'its outstanding feature . . . was the standard, scope and sense of involvement of the discussion'.[7] When Brathwaite spoke at the 1969 joint CAM/WISU Seminar he invited his audience to take part from the start, and requested discussion, not questions, afterwards.

The openness and non-exclusivity of CAM, its broad membership, was also in character with CAM as a community. Anyone who shared CAM's thinking and concerns, and who wanted to take part, was welcome. White members' fears that the evident mood of black consciousness would exclude them proved unfounded. Allegations, such as that by Amon Saba Saakana that CAM's membership was predominantly middle-class cannot be denied.[8] It began so, and its core members were always so. But the CAM audience at the Centre, at the Cooperative Hall and at Keskidee, included an increasing number of 'ordinary immigrants'. And CAM's concern was consistently for creative change which involved the black majority and was in their interests: 'the people' of the Caribbean, 'the ghetto' of Britain. When asked in 1973 about attempts 'to bring the West Indian workers in to CAM', Brathwaite replied:

> We didn't get near the workers. That's a thing we were moving into but it all got complicated by the politics which came in soon after. You know, the specialised Black Power, not our Black Power movement but the more strident one which tried to deny the importance of the cultural revolution.[9]

La Rose considers that attempts to politicise CAM were responsible for its intense, creative phase coming to an end after the Second Conference. That CAM as a visible organisation lasted for so short a time – fully operative for three years, coming and going, as Salkey said in 1972, 'like a mirage', for two – was entirely in character, and what La Rose at any rate expected. He comments:

> I knew that once an organisation like that has lasted for a bit it becomes a bureaucratic organisation, it does not become a profoundly creative, artistic experience. . . . After that people proceed to do what they have to do as they were doing it before but profoundly affected by their experience.

John La Rose considers that by the time the organisation ceased, CAM had served its real purpose.

The founder members named themselves as a 'movement', but had no group ideology and defined no manifesto. They saw CAM as part of a wider movement for change in Caribbean society. As artists, they were concerned with specific change in the thinking and hence the creativity of Caribbean people: from a concept of their history as fragmented to one that is continuous, from a concept of their society as being without indigenous culture or tradition to one which is rich in both; from the self-contempt and dependency of a colonised people to belief in their own creative achievements and ability; from mimetic, derivative cultural forms to authentic and original creativity.

The key to much of this change was, they believed, through change in the consciousness of Caribbean peoples. Harris, Williams, Brathwaite and La Rose all spoke of their awareness of the submerged, forgotten memories in the subconscious of Caribbean people, and of the urgent need for such memories to be revived and rehabilitated. Such a 'vision of consciousness' – a phrase first used by Harris, quoted by CLR James, echoed by La Rose and Brathwaite – had, they believed, freed the creativity of a few Caribbean artists and would enable others to change their creative practice. La Rose recalls Harris referring to people who shared such a vision as a 'community of consciousness'.

A first step towards this change in consciousness was what CAM members called 'a theory of unmaking'. Rehabilitation and unmaking were seen as part of the process of creolisation. To Gordon Rohlehr, the work of Selvon, Louise Bennett and Sparrow exemplified the creolisation of their Caribbean experience; Brathwaite called for a 'social creole ideology' as the direction for new Caribbean creativity. This ideology involved a changed attitude towards tradition. Many CAM members believed that a traditional culture was alive in the Caribbean, but was not yet fully recognised or built on – referred to by Harris as the 'native tradition' and by Brathwaite as the 'Little Tradition'. So the emphasis in CAM thinking was on using art forms which related to folk or native culture – on kaiso, calypso and carnival, and religious practices – *vodoun*, shango and kumina. As native/folk culture was the culture of 'the people', the majority, it would be 'popular' at least in the sense of its base. These new art forms should attempt to find a folk/native 'voice': in language, rhythm, form and presentation.

At the First Conference CAM artists were challenged by Elsa Goveia to exercise responsible choice in their art forms if they were to effect radical change in Caribbean society. The areas of culture in which CAM's founder members worked were primarily areas of art or 'high culture': literature – fiction, poetry and a little drama; art – painting, sculpture and fabric design. These were the arts most familiar and accessible to the educated elite of the colonies, therefore those most dominated by the European Great Tradition; they allowed very limited access to a Caribbean audience. But CAM's founders had, from the start, shown themselves deeply concerned with extending the audience for Caribbean arts – Brathwaite, insisting that CAM 'go public', La Rose, through New Beacon Books. Although their poetry was published in books, accessible only to a literate audience, both men were vitally engaged with literature drawn from, and presented in, the Caribbean oral, performance tradition. Poetry was read or performed throughout the life of CAM in London, at Yard Theatre in Jamaica, at Kairi House in Trinidad. Painting and sculpture by CAM artists was seen and discussed by a wide audience, not normally exposed to 'art', through its exhibitions at a wide variety of venues, including artists' homes and studios. And CAM became increasingly concerned with the performing arts of drama and dance, and with music – arts which could build more directly on the native or Little Tradition of the 'folk', and reach and involve a mass audience. CAM recognised other areas of activity as essential to its artistic work, and as part of Caribbean cultural practice: history, criticism, publishing and bookselling, education, youth work. In all these areas there was, during the lifespan of CAM, startling development and impressive expansion. CAM's essential characteristic of movement is as evident in the steadily widening areas of its cultural practice, as in the changing forms and approaches within them.

CAM in a sequence of movements

In thought and impulse, in activities and character, CAM had much in common with other arts movements which have taken place since World War One – in the USA, in Caribbean countries, and in European capitals.

New York, and especially its Harlem district, was the scene of the first of these movements. After World War One, Afro-Americans and Caribbean people who had recently settled there shared a sharpened sense of the racial prejudice and injustice of American society and a new black self-consciousness and assertiveness. This found expression in a wide range of artistic, intellectual and cultural work, in part encouraged by the then new appreciation of African culture and civilisation and the critical re-evaluation of Western civilisation. Such work sought to create a positive self-image for black people, to explore their own ethnic identity and heritage, and to assist in the 'negro's coming of age'. The New Negro Movement of the 1920s comprised two strands, separate but related. Literary Garveyism, the movement so named by Tony Martin,[10] was centred in the many cultural activities of the Universal Negro Improvement Association and particularly in the high literary content of its newspaper, *Negro World*. The Harlem Renaissance, whose 'remarkable outpouring of literature, art and music', in the words of its historian, Nathan Huggins, ' . . . symbolised black liberation and sophistication – the final shaking off of the residuals of slavery in the mind, spirit and character'[11] was assisted by American publishers and sponsors. They encouraged black US and Caribbean writers living in the USA and enabled them to reach a wider audience: Langston Hughes and Countee Cullen, Zora Neale Hurston and Eric Walrond, and, pre-eminent, though not wishing himself to be aligned with either movement, Claude McKay.

In Cuba, during the late 1920s, the predominantly Spanish culture was broken into by African-based arts: negro ballet, chamber music with themes from African music, and, most significantly, literature which introduced and experimented with African rhythms, language and themes. Prompted by a wish to build a national identity and an indigenous Cuban culture which reflected its ethnic mix, now that it had gained independence from Spain, and encouraged by the then current fashion amongst the European avant-garde for negro art, the white Cuban writers Alejo Carpentier and Emilio Ballagas, and particularly the mulatto poet, Nicolás Guillén, led the influential movement of Negrismo or Afro-Cubanism.

Haitians meanwhile increasingly felt that they had been recolonised since the USA occupied their country in 1915. *La Revue Indigène* was published on the wave of mounting opposition to the Occupation; its six issues of 1927–8 launched the *Indigéniste* movement.[12] Younger writers, from the black majority rather than the mulatto elite, had, like their Cuban contemporaries, benefited from the intellectual upheavals and new interest in African culture in Paris in the 1920s; they showed themselves determined to revolutionise the style of Haitian literature and to create literary authenticity. Their work was distinctive not simply from an infusion of local colour and expression of the diversity of the Haitian experience but by its belief that cultural wholeness was to be found in the traditions of the folk. Strengthened by the research and writings of Jean Price-Mars, and by literature of the Harlem Renaissance, they – in particular Carl Brouard and Jacques Roumain – recognised the possibility of Africa as a cultural matrix.

A bid for a more radical break with the French literary tradition, and a more positive and complete embrace of African culture, was made in Paris in the 1930s by students from French Caribbean and African colonies. In the journal *Légitime Défense*, founded in 1932 by Etienne Léro and two fellow Martinican students, Léro affirmed the association of politics and poetry, denounced the intellectual bastardisation of his Caribbean homeland society, and urged his readers to 'think black'.[13] Thus were sown the seeds of the widely influential and long-lasting movement founded by Léopold Sédar Senghor (Senegal), Aimé Césaire (Martinique) and Léon Damas (French Guiana) with their journal *L'Etudiant Noir* of 1934 and their subsequent literary work. The Negritude movement was named after Césaire used the word *négritude* in his *Cahier d'un retour au pays natal*, extracts of which were first published in Paris in 1939. Here Césaire was himself the first great exponent of Negritude, using the new techniques of surrealism to explore the black subconscious and the black experience.

After World War Two, further movements arose in Cuba and the USA, echoing those which had occurred there before but taking them much farther. Whereas Afro-Cubanism had in part been introduced and practised by white Cubans, looking at their country's African culture from the outside, the new Negrismo movement of the 1960s was entirely led by Afro-Cubans themselves, thanks to the wider opportunities for education and literacy introduced by the revolution. Afro-Cuban culture indeed seemed the most dynamic in Cuban society at the time of the 1968 Havana Congress; as La Rose put it, it was an expression by black intellectuals of 'the interior life of the African sensibility inside the Revolution'.[14] Meanwhile in the USA, the widespread mobilisation and increased confidence amongst Afro-Americans which accompanied the Civil Rights and the Black Power movements gave rise to a renewed and extended flowering of black arts, from the mid-1950s to the early 1970s, which came to be known as the Second Black Renaissance, or the Black Arts Movement. While it combined elements of both earlier traditions in its mass appeal and participation, in its self-definition and organisation, and in its setting up of autonomous institutions, it seemed to spring more directly from the Garvey tradition than that of the Harlem Renaissance, but with bolder experimentation and innovation in form and expression, and more accomplished, conscious crafting.

The situations in which all these movements occurred were ones in which people of African descent had until recently been, or continued to be, oppressed – as external colonies or neo-colonies, or as internal colonies within a predominantly white society. Intellectuals and artists set out to celebrate African culture and African values. They recognised that political and economic freedom or independence had little substance unless supported or accompanied by the liberation of peoples' consciousness. The movements were thus radical in political as well as in cultural terms, and often referred to themselves as revolutionary. In literature, this flowering was characterised by a search for new forms, language and rhythms. Each movement produced or brought into prominence major writers, and in turn helped them to reach a wider readership or audience. Thus the poetry of Langston Hughes and Countee Cullen, the novels of Claude McKay, influenced the founders of Negrismo in Cuba and the young *indigéniste* writers in Haiti. Senghor, Césaire and Damas and their fellow African and West Indian students in Paris in the 1930s knew and admired their work and were personally acquainted with these and other writers of the Harlem Renaissance.[15] Their work continued to inspire the young Afro-Americans in the Black Arts Movement. Work by the Negrismo writers Carpentier and Guillén and by the Negritude writer Césaire was influential on CAM writers Harris, Brathwaite, La Rose; poetry and drama from the Black Arts Movement, especially that of Calvin Hernton and LeRoi Jones was a force behind younger poets in CAM – Marc Matthews, Amon Saba Saakana, Linton Kwesi Johnson. From Negritude was born the Présence Africaine publishing house and bookshop in Paris in 1947, and its series of international congresses: of Negro Writers in Paris (1956), of Negro Writers and Artists in Rome (1959) and of Negro-African Literature in Dakar (1963).

CAM was in the mainstream tradition of such movements and shared many of their characteristics; it was also significantly different, partly in consequence of its place and time. Like the proponents of Negritude, CAM's initiators were Caribbean people in their metropolitan centre, meeting there for the first time with fellow West Indians (though as confined to the Anglophone as those in Paris had been to the Francophone), and with people from Africa. Like their French counterparts, CAM writers and would-be writers found distinct examples of European-modelled literature against which to rebel. They too began as an elite, intellectual group, in part academically-based. But CAM's London of the 1960s was far in time from Negritude's Paris in the 1930s. Postwar migration had created a Caribbean community in Britain. Two of CAM's initiators were not temporary students, but residents; La Rose and Salkey represented and became increasingly aligned with that community. CAM's core writers' and artists' group was inseparable from its public membership and organisation. Like the Black Arts Movement, and Literary Garveyism before it, CAM became increasingly concerned with arts which communicated with and involved 'the masses' – hence recognition, which some members were slow to grasp, of the potential for drama. In its thinking CAM, with its stress on creolisation, on the cross-cultural imagination, on a Caribbean and not a black aesthetic, seems closer to the *indigéniste* movement of Haiti than to *negrismo* in Cuba.

Again, like its Afro-American counterparts, CAM was concerned with other art forms besides literature, and with discovering its own aesthetic, although it did not seek out and define one with the thoroughness of the Black Arts Movement. The ambivalence within CAM towards cooperation with British institutions paralleled on the one hand the white patronage of the Harlem Renaissance, and on the other the search for autonomy and black institutions of Garveyism and the Black Arts Movement. CAM artists might have expected to receive from British intellectuals something at least of the acclaim experienced by Negritude writers in France. But there was no English equivalent of André Breton's preface to Césaire's *Cahier* in 1945, nor of Jean-Paul Sartre's introduction to Senghor's *Anthologie de la nouvelle poésie nègre et malgache* [Anthology of the New Black and Malagasy Poetry] in 1948, and to Fanon's *Les damnés de la terre* [The Wretched of the Earth] in 1961. As La Rose comments, 'England, indeed Britain, was not like that.'

The particular significance of CAM in this sequence of movements comes partly from its dual orientation: towards cultural work in the Caribbean, and amongst the Caribbean community in Britain. It also comes, most obviously, from CAM as the first arts movement of the whole English-speaking Caribbean. But it was also the first genuinely Caribbean-wide cultural movement: with its emphasis on the recognition and rehabilitation of Amerindian as well as African ancestry; its composition and its concept, in membership and activities, of the Caribbean as a region, one people among the continuing barriers of language. And CAM was uniquely participatory. Almost all the equivalent movements were launched with or published a periodical as a vehicle for their members' new work and new ideas. Garvey's *Negro World* reached the widest audience (200,000 at its peak), and its high proportion of literary content was open to all contributors who shared its ideology. But CAM's *Newsletter* reflected its activities as a public organisation, with open membership, by recording the talks and discussion and the poems read at its sessions, carrying them to a wider audience, so that the audience was itself part of the movement. The sessions themselves, at their best, led to participatory and collective thinking. The focus, the ideal, of CAM's aspiring art-forms was participation: individual understanding and creative response to a writer's fiction or poetry, to an artist's painting or sculpture; corporate creative participation in new performing art forms.

The legacy of CAM

The precise legacy of CAM is difficult to define. During the CAM period, the late 1960s and early 1970s, much cultural reappraisal and reconstruction was taking place in the Caribbean and in Britain. But specific institutions claim ancestry from CAM, and individual writers and artists acknowledge the seminal influence of CAM on their development. General trends in Caribbean arts since then demonstrate the CAM inheritance, especially those in poetry. Much of the critical evaluation of Caribbean literature which has developed over the past 20 years began in CAM sessions and conferences, and in subsequent continuing debates. The teaching of Caribbean literature in schools and universities, in the Caribbean and in Britain, began at the time of, or soon after, CAM, and was much assisted by members' initiatives and teaching, and by publication of their critical texts and anthologies. Likewise teaching of and research into Caribbean history has benefited from members' work. A number of books openly state their debt to CAM. Thanks to CAM, a generation of Caribbean people, involved directly in its public programme, was educated in Caribbean literature and art, and their historical and socio-political context. As members of a CAM audience, they felt themselves to be part of the creative process.

New Beacon's early publications were closely linked with the evolving CAM programme; its bookselling began through CAM. Now, 25 years on, New Beacon as both publishing and bookselling operation is vigorous and expanding. The International Book Fair of Radical Black and Third World Books – held annually in London since 1982, also in Manchester and Bradford since 1985, and in San Fernando and Port of Spain, Trinidad, in 1987 and 1988 – openly acknowledges CAM as its ancestor. Its week-long programme of talks and symposia, its public poetry readings and sessions for schools, are as integral to the Fair as the actual book displays. Creation for Liberation, formed by Darcus Howe and Linton Kwesi Johnson in 1975 as the cultural arm of the Race Today Collective, became an active black arts organisation; Johnson states that it 'tried to follow in the footsteps of CAM'. Its poetry readings, art exhibitions and discussion forums played a significant part in the evolving black arts movement in Britain. The Minority Arts Advisory Service (MAAS), and its inter-cultural arts magazine, *Artrage*, have developed in part as a result of the CAM experience of people who set it up, worked with it or have been closely associated with it – Naseem Khan, Errol Lloyd, James Berry, Peter Fraser, Pearl Connor. The Nigerian Society of African Artists was formed in London after Uzo Egonu, Femi Fatoba and Mercian Omodeinde Carrena attended CAM sessions and got to know CAM people; it selected the London-based artists who exhibited at FESTAC in Lagos, 1975.

In the Caribbean, Yard Theatre and *Savacou* – journal and cooperative publishing house – regarded themselves as CAM activities. Kairi House and arts magazine resulted from Christopher and Judith Lairds' experience of CAM. Kairi was succeeded by Banyan, whose weekly television programme *Gayelle*, produced for Trinidad and Tobago Television by Christopher Laird from 1985 to 1990, continued CAM concerns in the programme's broad cultural coverage and regional cooperation. Laird was largely responsible for a 13-part television series, *Caribbean Eye*, broadcast in 1991–2, the first documentary series about the Caribbean to be made within the region. As Laird has stated: 'CAM's philosophy still buoys my work.'[16] CAM followed up its contribution to the first Carifesta with significant participation by individual members at those which followed.

CAM's influence on individual creativity has been claimed most positively by young writers and artists. For its core creative artists, already producing major work when CAM began, the movement's value was to provide a forum for critical discussion, to build an understanding audience. As Aubrey Williams put it, 'CAM helped create an intellectual atmosphere for everybody to be creative and relate to each other.'[17] Several young or beginner writers and artists claim that CAM was formative in their development. Not all: Amon Saba Saakana (then Sebastian Clarke), aligning CAM writers with those of the 1950s, claims to have received no encouragement or help from them – in contrast with what he found amongst black writers in the USA when he lived there in the early 1970s:

> I couldn't really connect with most of the Caribbean writers who were based in this country, who were working here – in terms of the physicality of their speech, the middle-class orientation of their minds, and they did not have – as far as I was concerned – any organic connection with younger writers, as against the situation in America.

But James Berry is appreciative of what CAM gave him:

> It was very important for me because I did not come from an academic background. . . . And so, coming into contact with the circle of CAM, which had people who . . . were informed, had contact with the Caribbean cultural roots and were motivated politically – it helped to give me focus and direction.

For Faustin Charles, falling between the Berry and Saakana generations, 'CAM gave encouragement, the sort of encouragement that I think young writers need. And not only in getting published, but in bringing you from that isolation into meeting other writers. You read each others' works, and you learn.' Linton Kwesi Johnson, then a Tulse Hill, Brixton, school-leaver, states: 'I just don't think my poetic development would have been stimulated in the way it was in the absence of CAM.' John La Rose advised him to read Brathwaite, enabling him to discover 'that the Caribbean poetic vision is much broader than the Great Tradition of England, and includes all kinds of nuances from our oral tradition which has always been there but has always been suppressed'. Johnson remembers hearing Andrew Salkey read 'Mabrak' and 'Sooner or Later' by Bongo Jerry, and poems by Audvil King, and then reading them himself in the controversial *Savacou* 3/4. He used to take his early poetry to Salkey and La Rose for criticism. Christine Craig claims that it was through CAM and its writers – particularly Andrew Salkey – in London that her own wish to write was first kindled; back in Jamaica, *Savacou* encouraged and nurtured her writing through opportunities for publication.

Caribbean artists who, at the time of CAM, were students or

recent art school graduates, make comparable claims about CAM. Winston Branch:

> It gave me a forum, a kind of springboard to know that I was not alone in the field, and the fact that there were other people painting, making sculpture, that they were involved in a similar activity to what you were in, you had something from which to go forward. Because I didn't feel I was doing something for the first time. . . . There were other people who were travelling down that road, the writers as well as the artists.

Paul Dash:

> It made me aware – because don't forget I was isolated in this world of mainstream European painting and sculpting. It introduced me to black painters, artists and intellectuals – the heavyweights at that time, some of them. And it helped me to look at myself and to question myself: where I was going, what I was trying to do with my work.

Errol Lloyd:

> The idea of there being a group of people who could actually make a living through their art, and who were actually creating a sort of art which was unique in my opinion, would have come through Aubrey Williams and Art Derry and Karl Craig, all those people who were a generation before me, whom I met in CAM. I think that without them there's little doubt I certainly would not have got involved.

It was during the period of CAM that literary forms and styles now dominant in Caribbean writing first became apparent. Each of the novelists whose work was discussed in CAM – Orlando Patterson, Wilson Harris, Michael Anthony and Lindsay Barrett (Eseoghene) – was taking the novel in a distinctive new direction. The novels of Sam Selvon were held by CAM members as exemplary for their creolisation of the Caribbean experience. Since this period, the quantity of new Caribbean fiction has markedly declined, but some of its most innovative and acclaimed writers have built on those new directions, in particular, Earl Lovelace, Erna Brodber, Merle Collins. Meanwhile Harris has continued to write and publish work which exemplifies 'a radical new art of fiction' in which the cross-cultural imagination is always apparent, his range of context now widened from the Guyana interior to Mexico, Brazil and Britain. When CAM was formed, poetry lagged far behind fiction in the so-called 'Caribbean literary renaissance' surrounding Independence. It was still mainly the preserve of educated people, written in Standard English and using traditional English form and rhythm. But an alternative poetry, forging new traditions as radical as the work of Harris in fiction, was at the centre of CAM and, by the time CAM ended, widely in evidence. The three long poems by Edward Kamau Brathwaite, read to CAM and published at that time, demonstrated the possibilities of a poetry which employed a wide continuum of language, drew on folk traditions of a range of cultures, and came to full life in performance. The explosion of new poetry which Brathwaite encountered in Jamaica and Rohlehr in Trinidad, and which followed in Britain, was encouraged and published by, amongst others, Salkey, La Rose and Brathwaite. CAM sanctioned acceptance of poetry which broke with the inherited English tradition in language, rhythm and content, and was written primarily to be heard. 'Nation Language' – the term introduced by Brathwaite – is widely used in place of 'dialect' and 'creole' to describe the language in which much of the new Caribbean poetry is written.[18] A wide range of Caribbean poets, many of whom were in CAM or published in CAM-related books and journals, developed and found a receptive audience for their distinctive directions: James Berry, Linton Kwesi Johnson, Marc Matthews, Lorna Goodison, Michael Smith. And Brathwaite himself has in a second trilogy of long poems, and in shorter poems, continued to explore his own Caribbean 'vision of consciousness'.

In art, the continuing impact of CAM has been less apparent. No revolution in style, no new trends, can be claimed as CAM's legacy to Caribbean painting and sculpture. CAM made no corporate impact in the Caribbean. But Aubrey Williams's continuing work and regular exhibitions in Jamaica from the 1970s until his death in 1990 impressed his fellow artists, delighted his patrons and purchasers, and widened Jamaicans' concept of Caribbean art. Karl 'Jerry' Craig, in addition to his evolving work as a painter, brought the CAM experience into art education, first as Principal of the Jamaica School of Art from 1971 to 1981, now as Lecturer in Art and Craft at the School of Education, UWI, and as Assistant Chief Examiner in Art and Craft for the Caribbean Examination Council (CXC). In Britain, Errol Lloyd developed a unique role as organiser of exhibitions of Caribbean art, as propagator of the work of fellow Caribbean artists, partly through his work with MAAS. He has become the link between CAM and the younger group of black artists, who are aware that they cannot draw on the Caribbean imagery of Art Derry and Althea McNish, or the pre-Columbian motifs of Aubrey Williams. McNish's designs continue to be in wide, international demand; her recent work includes a huge mural (1990) and hangings and banners (1991) for two liners of the Royal Caribbean Cruise Line sailing in the Caribbean.

Aubrey Williams's two major exhibitions in London in the 1980s – *Paintings on the Music of Shostakovich* and *The Olmec Maya and*

Now – brought his powerful forms, his radiant canvases to a wide range of viewers. Creation for Liberation invited Williams to speak at, and Errol Lloyd to chair, a forum in conjunction with its 1987 exhibition at Brixton Village, which enabled interaction of ideas and dialogue between Williams and young black artists, in the CAM tradition.[19] Ronald Moody's work was almost invisible after CAM, even at the time of his death in 1984. But the exhibition *The Other Story: Afro-Asian Artists in Post-War Britain* at the Hayward Gallery in late 1989 opened with a room devoted to Moody sculptures; a new generation was held by their stillness and the intensity of their vision. In March 1992 the Tate Gallery purchased Moody's large wooden sculpture, 'Johanaan'.

CAM members were from the start concerned to establish a Caribbean aesthetic for their arts, to define criteria of their own for cultural work. They were aware that for too long they had depended on outside validation. New Beacon's work in publishing was thus an act of independent Caribbean literary judgment. The young university lecturers and postgraduate literature students who introduced and discussed Caribbean literature in CAM, from Sparrow to Harris, were amongst the first fledgling professional Caribbean literary critics. Through their university posts, Kenneth Ramchand and Gordon Rohlehr in the Caribbean, and Louis James in Britain, continued to develop their ideas about Caribbean literature and to subject individual writers' work to close scrutiny, as in CAM. Rohlehr's *Pathfinder: Black Awakening in 'The Arrivants' of Edward Kamau Brathwaite* and *Calypso and Society in Pre-Independence Trinidad* are testimony to the continuing evolution of ideas which Rohlehr first explored in CAM. Because all three hold university posts they in turn have trained later generations of Caribbean critics such as Victor Chang, Carolyn Cooper, Patricia Ismond, the late Victor Questel and Jennifer Rahim in the Caribbean, Valerie Bloom, Fred D'Aguiar, Denise deCaires Narain, Susheila Nasta and Akua Rugg in Britain.

The complaint heard often in CAM that Caribbean literature was not taught in schools or universities has been abundantly remedied. Kenneth Ramchand and Gordon Rohlehr were at the forefront of the introduction of Caribbean literature courses on the Jamaica and Trinidad campuses of UWI and of its spread in secondary schools; Rohlehr has also been closely involved in the literature syllabus of the CXC. Courses in Caribbean and African literature introduced by Louis James at the University of Kent have introduced other British students, black and white, to wider perspectives and the particular qualities of Caribbean literature. When the Association for the Teaching of Caribbean, African and Asian Literatures (ATCAL) was formed (at a conference at the

University of Kent at Canterbury in September 1978, organised by Lyn Innes, a specialist in African and Afro-American Literature), Louis James and Anne Walmsley were active members, and contribute regularly to ATCAL's journal, *Wasafiri*. The whole movement towards multicultural education in Britain continues aims and aspirations expressed in CAM and practised by the publishing and bookselling of New Beacon and Bogle-L'Ouverture.

Research into and the teaching of Caribbean history was already well under way by the time CAM started. But the contributions of historians – from CLR James and Elsa Goveia to Douglas Hall and Edward Kamau Brathwaite – informed CAM members and directed their focus. CAM members who went on to take up university posts in history – Brinsley Samaroo in Trinidad, Peter Fraser, first in Trinidad, then in Britain, Ivan Van Sertima in the USA, Brathwaite in Jamaica – acknowledge CAM's influence in their perspectives on history. Van Sertima finds continuity in his experience of CAM and his current work in tracing evidence of an early African presence in the Americas and other parts of the world. Brathwaite succeeded Elsa Goveia as Professor of Caribbean Social and Cultural History at UWI; thanks to Goveia's recommendation, he is Caribbean representative on the UNESCO world history project. The courses in African and Caribbean history which Gerald Moore and Donald Wood pioneered at the University of Sussex at the time of CAM have contributed to wider historical perspectives in education and research.

Several books were born alongside or as a result of CAM. Brathwaite's *Creole Society*, was researched, thought out and largely written between 1965–68, and is dedicated in part to CAM. Dennis Sardinha's book, *The Poetry of Nicolás Guillén: an Introduction*, 'had its birth in a request to address members of the CAM in London'. *Facing the Sea: A New Anthology from the Caribbean Region* – the first to introduce to schools the writing of the French, Spanish and Dutch-speaking Caribbean alongside the English – grew from Anne Walmsley's introduction to the work of Carpentier, Guillén, Césaire and Damas in CAM. A book on the art of Aubrey Williams, *Guyana Dreaming*, resulted from the artist's friendship through CAM with its compiler, Anne Walmsley. James Berry has continued to promote the work of fellow West Indian-born and Black British poets through his anthologies – *Bluefoot Traveller* and *News from the Babylon*, the *Bluefoot Cassettes* – in the CAM tradition.

Personal bonds created in CAM have lived on. There is continuous interaction and evidence of working friendships amongst CAM members. Following Aubrey Williams's death in April 1990, a Memorial Exhibition of his work at the Centre of

Contemporary Art in Kingston, Jamaica, was opened by Edward Kamau Brathwaite; at an Aubrey Williams Celebration at the Commonwealth Institute in London, Wilson Harris, John La Rose, Errol Lloyd, Marc Matthews, Andrew Salkey (through his son, Jason), and Anne Walmsley were amongst those who gave tributes. *Foundations of a Movement*, the book presented to John La Rose on the occasion of the 10th Book Fair in March 1991, contains many contributions by people associated with CAM. In his piece Brathwaite writes of CAM as 'the most important happy happening to Caribbean artists in the second demarche of the 20th century, and a friendship which, now that I think about it, has been the fundament on which not only me but an ever-increasing number of us have rooted/greened our various achievements on'.[20]

Rex Nettleford, trade unionist and educator, essayist and editor, dancer and founder of the Jamaica National Dance Theatre Company, was first aware of CAM through its *Newsletter*, then through core members who returned to Jamaica and involved him in the CAM-New World seminars. He recognises the character and legacy of CAM:

> The operative word is 'Movement'. So that even without the advantage of bricks and mortar, or even a kind of established sort of hierarchy of leader and led and officers, CAM carried with it a force, and it is that force which inspires, catalyses and instils new hopes and possibilities for this articulation, this creating, this confidence in self, which I believe are so critical. . . . One has to work on several levels at the same time. . . . Paths are made by walking, and while one is walking one has to be cutting the path. That's our job now, and CAM must be seen as part of that process.

Appendices

CAM Meetings January 1967–July 1972

1967

6 Jan, Patterson's home
Is there a West Indian aesthetic?
Orlando Patterson

3 Feb, Patterson's home
Extracts 'The West Indian Jazz Novel'
Edward Brathwaite

3 March, Jeanetta Cochrane Theatre
Reading of 'Rights of Passage'
Edward Brathwaite
Presented by London Traverse Theatre Company and New Beacon Publications, regarded as a CAM event

10 March, West Indian Students Centre
New Directions in West Indian Writing
Michael Anthony, Wilson Harris, Louis James, Orlando Patterson, Kenneth Ramchand
Andrew Salkey (Chair)

7 April, Students Centre
Sparrow and the Language of the Calypso
Gordon Rohlehr
John La Rose (Chair)

14 April, Williams's studio
Discussion with Edward Brathwaite, Wilson Harris, John La Rose, Andrew Salkey
Aubrey Williams

21 April, Patterson's home
Poetry Reading
Antony (John) La Rose, Faustin Charles

5 May, Students Centre
Childhood in the West Indian Novel: Michael Anthony v. Camara Laye
Kenneth Ramchand
Colloquy: 'Sisyphus' and 'Ruins'
Orlando Patterson, John Hearne
Gerald Moore (Chair)

2 June, Students Centre
Symposium: West Indian Artists
Karl Craig, Althea McNish, Ronald Moody, Errol Lloyd, Aubrey Williams
Gerald Moore (Chair)

25 June, Theatre Royal Stratford
Exhibition and Performance: Poetry, dancing, satirical sketches, folksongs
Produced by Activists for the Theatre Royal, Stratford, by Bari Jonson et al with CAM participation

7 July, Students Centre
The Contribution of the West Indies to European Civilisation
C.L.R. James
Bryan King (Chair)

? Sept
'Song for Mumu'
Lindsay Barrett

27 Sept, Brathwaite's home
Reading of 'Masks'
Edward Brathwaite

13 Oct, Students Centre
Symposium: Communications Media in and to the West Indies
George Lamming, Jeremy Verity, John La Rose, Jon Stallworthy, James Currey
Edward Brathwaite (Chair)

10 Nov, Students Centre
Symposium: West Indian Theatre
Stanley French, Evan Jones, Ram John Holder, Marina Maxwell, Lloyd Reckord, Celia Robinson, Frank Thomasson
Jeremy Verity (Chair)

1 Dec, Students Centre
An Area of Experience – West Indian Poetry
Edward Brathwaite
Andrew Salkey (Chair)

1968

6–7 Jan, Nottingham
Weekend School on West Indian Literature
Kenneth Ramchand, Louis James
Robert Reinders (Organizer)

2 Feb, Students Centre
Spanish and French West Indian Literature Today
Jean Franco
Michael Follet-Foster (Introduction)
Andrew Salkey (Chair)

1 March Students Centre — *The Origins of Jazz: the Franco-American Culture of the New Orleans Free Negroes*
Robert Reinders
Andrew Salkey (Chair)

5 April Students Centre — *Cuba of the Third World: First of two symposia on the International Cultural Congress held in Havana 4–11 January*
C.L.R. James, Alba Grinan, Andrew Salkey, John La Rose
Edward Brathwaite (Chair)

19 April Nottingham — *The West Indian Writer in Britain*
Peter Figueroa

3 May Students Centre — *Second symposium on Havana Congress*
Douglas Hall, Irving Teitelbaum, Andrew Salkey, John La Rose
Edward Brathwaite (Chair)

7 June Students Centre — *Colonialism and colour in the British West Indies*
Douglas Hall

5 July Students Centre — *Evening of Poetry and Prose from the Third World in memory of Dr Martin Luther King*
C.L.R. James, Calvin Hernton, George Awoonor Williams, Dennis Brutus, Bari Jonson, John La Rose and others

October Nottingham — *Recordings and Meanderings*
Poetry Reading featuring John La Rose

1 Nov Students Centre — *Black Writers Conference McGill University October 1968*
Richard Small

New Literary Activity among the Young Rastafarian and Black Radical Writers in Kingston, Jamaica
Richard Small, Locksley Comrie

6 Dec Students Centre — *Symposium: Are they seeking and attempting to discern a new vision of consciousness?*
Winston Benn, Christopher Laird, Paul Dash, Joyce Linton, Audrey Payne, Basil Smith, Sebastian Clarke, Winston Branch, Errol Lloyd, Stephen Kalipha, Winston Best, Marc Matthews, Tony Matthews, Rudolph Kizerman
John La Rose (Chair)

13 Dec Nottingham — *West Indian Literature*
Louis James

1969

17 Jan Students Centre — *Africa's Unique Dance Culture; BBC film on internationally famous Sierra Leone Dancers*
John Akar

7 Feb Students Centre — *Film as an artistic and educational medium in the Caribbean*
Evan Jones, Horace Ove

21 Feb Students Centre — *In Memory of Malcolm X*
filmed interview and documentary; anthology of readings by:
Clifton Jones, Ram John Holder, Locksley Comrie, Rudolph Kizerman, Richard Small, June Doiley, Faustin Charles

March – April UWI Mona Jamaica — *The Arts in the Caribbean Today*
series of seminars organized by Edward Brathwaite, presented in association with New World Group of Jamaica.

16 March UWI Mona Jamaica — *Towards a Revolution in the Arts*
Marina Maxwell

7 March Students Centre — *Léon Damas, Poet of Negritude*
Merle Hodge

11 April Students Centre — *Two Poets of the Revolution reading their own work*
Tony Matthews, Basil Smith
John La Rose (Chair)

2 May Students Centre — *The West Indian in Britain* with extracts from his book 'Journey to an Illusion' by Donald Hinds read by Andrew Salkey

16 May Nottingham — *Unreason and Violence*
Wilson Harris

6 June Students Centre — *Reading of Aimé Césaire's 'Cahier d'un retour au pays natal'*
John La Rose (Introduction)

Film, *Rhodesia Count Down*

5 Sept Students Centre — *Astride Two Visions: A Personal Testament*
Ivan van Sertima

29 Sept Students Centre — *Reading of 'Islands'*
Edward Brathwaite

7 Nov Students Centre — *The Tonal Drums of the Yoruba*
Femi Fatoba, Tony Evora

1970

20 Feb Students Centre — *Reading of poems which represent Contemporary Writing of African Poetry*
Cosmo Pieterse, Femi Fatoba
Donald Hinds (Introduction)

3 & 10 April Students Centre — *Impressions of Guyana during the Republic Celebrations, and the Caribbean Writers and Artists Convention held in Georgetown, Guyana, 24 February*
Andrew Salkey, Sam Selvon, John La Rose, Aubrey Williams, Ivan van Sertima
John La Rose (Chair)

1971

17 Feb New Beacon 2 Albert Road — *Caribbean Dance: demonstration lecture*
Beryl McBurnie

7 March Anne Walmsley's flat — *BBC TV programme Caribbean Artists in Britain*
Andrew Salkey
New Directions in Caribbean Art
Aubrey Williams

22 Sept Co-op Hall, Seven Sisters Road — *New Cultural Signals in the Caribbean*
Edward Brathwaite

29 Oct Co-op Hall — *An Evening of Caribbean Poetry*
T-Bone Wilson, Marc Matthews, James Berry, Louis Marriott, Mustapha Matura, Archie Markham, Roy Blair (guitarist and folk singer)

1972

21 Feb Keskidee Centre, King's Cross — *Panel discussion of BBC-TV presentation of Barry Reckord's reggae play 'In the Beautiful Caribbean'*

10 March Keskidee Centre — *Ronald Moody: Slides of his work presented by*
Errol Lloyd, John La Rose

26 May Keskidee Centre — *Nicolas Guillén, Poet of Cuba*
Denis Sardinha

30 July Keskidee Centre — *Okot p'Bitek's 'Song of Lawino'*
Pio Zirimu

CAM Conferences

First CAM Conference
University of Kent
15–17 September 1967

16 Sept — *The Socio-Cultural Framework of the Caribbean*
Elsa Goveia

Claude McKay: The Early Phase of West Indian Literature
Kenneth Ramchand

The Predicament of the Artist in the Caribbean
Aubrey Williams

Commentary on slides of his paintings
Clifton Campbell

West Indian Literature in the 30s
C.L.R. James

Growing Up in Writing
Michael Anthony

Readings from Caribbean Literature
Calvin Hernton, George Lamming, Doris Harper Wills, Kwabena Amoako, Peter Figueroa, Edward Brathwaite, C.L.R. James, John La Rose, Knolly La Fortune

17 Sept — *The Poetry of the West Indies*
Louis James

Natives of My Person
George Lamming

Performing in the West Indies and in Britain
Bari Jonson, Lloyd Reckord, Horace James

Second CAM Conference University of Kent 31 August – 2 September 1968

31 Aug *West Indians in Britain*
Stuart Hall
Andrew Salkey (Chair)

Aimé Césaire and the French Caribbean
Clive Wake
Louis James (Chair)

Symposium: New Directions in Caribbean Arts
Christopher Laird, Joyce Linton, Karina Williamson, J.A. Ramsaran (Chair)

Late Night Soundings: Readings and Music
John La Rose and Daniel Moreau
Introduction of and readings (in French and English) from Césaire's *Cahier d'un retour au pays natal*;
Hope Howard and A. Deer (Nottingham CAM)
Songs with guitar

1 Sept *The Void of History in the Caribbean*
Ivan Van Sertima
John La Rose (Chair)

The West Indian Presence in Africa
Gerald Moore
Andrew Salkey (Chair)

Symposium: The Artist in the Caribbean
Karl Craig, Errol Lloyd, Ronald Moody, Edmund Gill

Poetry Reading
John La Rose
creation poem from Mali;
Edward Brathwaite
from *Masks*, *Rights of Passage*, *Islands*

CAM 'Business' Meeting: The Purpose and Future of CAM

2 Sept *The Amerinidan Presence in the Caribbean Novel*
Wilson Harris
Kenneth Ramchand (Introduction and Chair)

Some Thoughts on West Indian Writing: a 'Proletarian' View
Henry Swanzy
Andrew Salkey (Chair)

Conference Resolutions and Round-up

Third CAM Conference, WISU and CAM Symposium, West Indian Students Centre 15–17 August 1969

15 Aug *Africa in the Caribbean*
Edward Brathwaite

16 Aug *The Negritude Movement and Black Awareness*
Merle Hodge, Andrew Salkey

17 Aug *The Development of Black Experience and the Nature of Black Society in Britain*
John La Rose

The Threat to the Education of the Black Child in Britain and what to do
Jack Hines, Augustine John

CAM Art Exhibitions

1967	
25 June Theatre Royal, Stratford	*New Art and Sculpture presented by the Caribbean Artists Movement*
June King's Road studio	*Clifton Campbell: special exhibition for the CAM Committee*
July Theatre Royal, Stratford	*CAM Exhibition* Aubrey Williams Karl Craig Ronald Moody Errol Lloyd Althea McNish
16–17 Sept University of Kent	*First CAM Conference: Art Exhibition* Paintings: Aubrey Williams – Guyana Clifton Campbell – Jamaica Art Derry – Trinidad Sculpture: Ronald Moody – Jamaica Errol Lloyd – Jamaica
12 Dec West Indian Students Centre	*Paintings by Members of the Caribbean Artists Movement* selected by Karl Craig for display at a reception given by the Students Centre for donors to its appeal which

stated that the Centre hoped to be 'a showpiece for West Indian arts and crafts'.
Aubrey Williams
Clifton Campbell
Art Derry

1968

Feb/March
Digby Stuart College

West Indian Art Exhibition
arranged by Karl Craig
Clifton Campbell
Karl Craig
Errol Lloyd
Althea McNish
Aubrey Williams

Feb/March
London School of Economics

West Indian Art Exhibition
West Indian Society,
arranged by Karl Craig
Winston Benn
Clifton Campbell
Carlisle Chang
Karl Craig
Edmund Gill
Errol Lloyd
Althea McNish
Peter Minshall
Aubrey Williams

21–26 May
Students Centre

Exhibition of West Indian Art
Paintings
Winston Benn – Trinidad
Clifton Campbell – Jamaica
Ronald Savory – Guyana
Karl Craig – Jamaica
Art Derry – Trinidad
Aubrey Williams – Guyana
Paintings and Sculpture
Errol Lloyd – Jamaica
Ronald Moody – Jamaica
Fabric and Plastic laminate panels
Althea McNish – Trinidad
Sculpture
(unlisted) Karl Broodhagen – Barbados

31 Aug – 2 Sept
University of Kent

Second CAM Conference: Art Exhibition
Paintings
Karl Craig – Jamaica
Edmund Gill – Barbados
Clifton Campbell – Jamaica
Art Derry – Trinidad
Paul Dash – Barbados
Aubrey Williams – Guyana
Sculpture
Errol Lloyd – Jamaica
Ronald Moody – Jamaica
Pottery
Madge Rivers – Jamaica

4–16 Nov
House of Commons, Westminster

Caribbean Artists Movement Exhibition
in association with the British-Caribbean Association,
Karl Craig: paintings
Art Derry: paintings
Errol Lloyd: sculpture
Althea McNish: plastic laminate panels
Ronald Moody: sculpture
Aubrey Williams: paintings

1971

22 Jan–14 Feb
Commonwealth Art Gallery, Commonwealth Institute

Caribbean Artists in England
Althea Bastien: fabrics
Winston Branch: paintings
Owen R. Coombs: paintings
Karl Craig: paintings
Daphne Dennison: paintings
Art Derry: paintings
Errol Lloyd: paintings
Donald Locke: ceramics
George Lynch: paintings
Althea McNish: fabrics
Ronald Moody: sculpture
Keith Simon: paintings
Vernon Tong: paintings
Ricardo Wilkins: paintings
Aubrey Williams: paintings
Llewellyn Xavier: paintings
(unlisted) Paul Dash: paintings

CAM Journals

CAM NEWSLETTER
No 1, March/April 1967, pp 1–4
No 2, April/May 1967, pp 1–6
No 3, June/July 1967, pp 1–12
No 4, August/September 1967, pp 1–12
No 5, October/November 1967, pp 1–14
No 6, January/March 1968, pp 1–16
No 7, April/September 1968, pp 1–8
No 8, October/December 1968, pp 1–6
No 9, January/March 1969, pp 1–14
No 10, April/June 1969, pp 1–18
No 11, July/November 1969, pp 1–16
No 12, August 1970, pp 1–18

CAM NEWSLETTER (Jamaica)
No 1, March 1968, pp 1–14

SAVACOU: A JOURNAL OF THE CARIBBEAN ARTISTS MOVEMENT

No 1, June 1970: *Slavery*, pp 1–108

No 2, September 1970: *CAM Conference Papers*, pp 1–100

No 3/4, December 1970/March 1971: *New Writing* 1970, pp 1–176

No 5, June 1971: *Essays around the Idea of Creolisation*, pp 1–128

No 6, New Poets Series – I: Anthony McNeill, *Reel from 'The Life Movie'*, introduction by Dennis Scott

No 7/8, January/June 1973: *Tribute to 80 Frank Collymore*, pp 1–156

No 9/10, 1974: *Writing Away From Home*, pp 1–134

No 11/12, September 1975: *Caribbean Studies*, pp 1–120

No 13, Gemini 1977: *Caribbean Woman*, pp i-xvi, 1–90

No 14/15, 1979/80: *New Poets From Jamaica* – an anthology, edited with an introduction by Edward Kamau Brathwaite, Poets Series – 5

No 16, 1989: Edward Kamau Brathwaite, *Sappho Sakyi's Meditations*

Manuscripts and Oral Source Material

1 Audio-cassettes of talks at CAM sessions and conferences, copied from contemporary recordings on reel-to-reel tapes and transcribed. Tapes held by Edward Kamau Brathwaite, Donald Hinds, Louis James, John La Rose, and University of Kent; cassettes held by John La Rose and Anne Walmsley; transcriptions held by Anne Walmsley.

2 Contemporary typescripts of talks given at CAM meetings and conferences, either prepared by speakers, or transcribed soon afterwards from recordings; typescripts held by Edward Kamau Brathwaite, copies by Anne Walmsley.

3 Letters from CAM files held by Edward Kamau Brathwaite, Donald Hinds, Andrew Salkey; copies held by Anne Walmsley.

4 Notices and programmes of CAM meetings and conference and related events held by Edward Kamau Brathwaite, Donald Hinds, John La Rose, Andrew Salkey; copies held by Anne Walmsley.

5 Unpublished contemporary accounts of CAM and CAM-related events, of talks given by CAM founder-members; typescripts held by Edward Kaman Brathwaite, copies by Anne Walmsley.

6 Interviews conducted by the author with people who were members of, or associated with CAM, as listed below; tapes and transcripts held by Anne Walmsley.

Oscar Abrams London, 8.10.87
Michael Anthony Port of Spain, Trinidad, 24.7.86
Diana Athill London, 9.7.87
Winston Benn London, 8.2.87
James Berry London, 17.1.86
Felicity Bolton Brighton, England, 23.7.87
Denis Bowen London, 9.8.90
Donald Bowen London, 2.7.87
Winston Branch London, 18.3.87
Edward Kamau Brathwaite Irish Town, Jamaica, 15.3.86
Clifton Campbell Mona, Jamaica, 11.3.86
Faustin Charles London, 27.1.87
Oliver Clarke Kingston, Jamaica, 10.3.86
Locksley Comrie New York, 23.3.86

Pearl Connor London, 25.2.87
Ken Corsbie Bridgetown, Barbados, 1.8.86
Christine Craig Kingston, Jamaica, 12.3.86
Karl 'Jerry' Craig Kingston, Jamaica, 12.3.86
James Currey London, 9.7.87
Paul Dash London, 24.2.87
Art Derry Chesterfield, England, 24.6.87
Uzo Egonu London, 15.8.90
Peter Figueroa Southampton, England, 15.7.87
Peter Fraser London, 2.7.87
Stuart Hall London, 8.10.87
Wilson Harris Chelmsford, England, 11.2.86
Leila Hassan London, 11.12.85
Antony Haynes London, 21.9.87
Donald Hinds London, 19.2.86
Merle Hodge St. Augustine, Trinidad, 29.7.86
Ram John Holder London, 21.7.87
Darcus Howe London, 16.1.86
Eric Huntley London, 28.4.86
CLR James London, 3 & 11.12.85
Louis James London, 27.5.87
Gus John London, 15.2.88
Linton Kwesi Johnson London, 18.6.86
Bridget Jones Reading, 2.3.90
Evan Jones Bath, England, 3.7.87
Bari Jonson Mona, Jamaica, 22.4.91
Naseem Khan London, 15.11.87
Carl Kirton London, 30.10.87
Knolly La Fortune London, 29.1.87
Christopher Laird Port of Spain, Trinidad, 24.7.86
Judith Laird Port of Spain, Trinidad, 24.7.86
John La Rose London, 22.11.85 & 14.2.86
Errol Lloyd London, 24.1.86 & 29.4.86
Wally Look Lai Port of Spain, Trinidad, 26.7.86
Lucille Mathurin Mair Kingston, Jamaica, 20.4.91
Marc Matthews London, England, 23.11.87
Ian McDonald London, 27.6.86
Althea McNish London, 1.2.87
Vida Menzies London, 25.3.87
Mervyn Morris Mona, Jamaica, 12.3.86
Rex Nettleford Mona, Jamaica, 17.3.86
Patsy Patterson Kingston, Jamaica, 12.3.86
Orlando Patterson Kingston, Jamaica, 18.3.86
Anthony Phillips St Joseph, Barbados, 1.8.86
Frank Pike London, 29.6.87
Kenneth Ramchand St Augustine, Trinidad, 29.7.86
Lloyd Reckord Mona, Jamaica, 12.3.86
Gordon Rohlehr Tunapuna, Trinidad, 28.7.86
Akua Rugg London, 1.10.87
Amon Saba Saakana London, 5.2.87
Andrew Salkey Amherst, USA, 20.3.86
Brinsley Samaroo St Augustine, Trinidad, 28.7.86
AD Scott Kingston, Jamaica, 17.4.91
Sam Selvon London, 23.10.86
Jill Sheppard Bridgetown, Barbados, 1.8.86
Vishnudat Singh St Augustine, Trinidad, 29.7.86
Ambalavaner Sivanandan London, 22.9.87
Richard Small Kingston, Jamaica, 13.1.89
Leonard Smith London, 16.9.87
Yvonne Sobers Irish Town, Jamaica, 16.3.86
Jon Stallworthy Oxford, England, 30.9.87
Henry Swanzy Bishop's Stortford, England, 1.7.87

Ivan Van Sertima New Brunswick, USA, 24.3.86
Maureen Warner Lewis Kingston, Jamaica, 10.3.86 & 23.4.91
Ngũgĩ Wa Thiong'o London, 16.3.87
Barrington Watson Yallahs, Jamaica, 18.4.91
Sarah White London, 24.9.87
John Wickham Bridgetown, Barbados, 31.7.86
Aubrey Williams London, 28.3.72 & 4.9.86
Karina Williamson Oxford, England, 17.7.87
Doris Harper Wills London, 19.3.87
Don Wilson Mona, Jamaica, 13.3.86
Betty Wilson Mona, Jamaica, 13.3.86
Ansel Wong London, 16.6.87
Donald Wood London, 21.9.87

Notes

Material quoted in the text comes from two main sources: transcripts of recordings, or contemporary typescripts, of talks given at CAM sessions; interviews conducted by Anne Walmsley with people who were members of, or associated with, CAM (see Appendix, 'Manuscripts and oral source material'). Because quotations from these two sources are numerous and obvious, they are not identified with notes.

1. The Background

1 Ronald Moody quoted by Cynthia Moody, 'Ronald Moody: A Man true to his Vision', *Third Text: Third World Perspectives on Contemporary Art and Culture* 8/9, Autumn/Winter 1989, pp.6–7.

2 Margaret Busby, 'C.L.R. James, a Biographical Introduction', C.L.R. James, *At the Rendezvous of Victory*, p. vii.

3 Elsa Goveia, 'Study Group on the Economic History and Development of the West Indies', *The W.I.S.U. Newsletter*, Vol I No 1, December 1946, p.5.

4 R.L.C. Aarons, 'Una Marson: A True Trail-blazer', *The Jamaica Gleaner*, 22 December 1974, p.10.

5 Rhonda Cobham, 'The *Caribbean Voices* Programme and the Development of West Indian Short Fiction: 1945–1958', *The Story Must be Told: Short Narrative Prose in the New English Literatures*, ed. by Peter O. Stummer (Bayreuth, Germany: Koningshausen + Newmann, 1986), pp. 146–7.

6 Quoted by Peter Fryer in *Staying Power: The History of Black Power in Britain* (London: Pluto Press, 1984), pp. 350–1.

7 Figures stated by Peter Fryer, ibid., p. 372.

8 George Lamming, *The Pleasures of Exile*, p. 212.

9 Michael Anthony, 'Growing up in writing', *Savacou* 2, p. 64.

10 ibid., p.65.

11 V.S. Naipaul, *Finding the Centre: Two Narratives* (London: Andre Deutsch, 1984), pp. 15, 21, 22.

12 *Caribbean Voices: An Anthology of West Indian Poetry*, Volume 2, *The Blue Horizons*, ed. by John Figueroa (London: Evans, 1970), footnote, p. 3.

13 Edward Kamau Brathwaite, *Savacou* 14/15: *New Poets from Jamaica*, p. iii.

14 Margaret Garlake, *New Vision 56–66* (Jarrow, Tyne and Wear: Bede Gallery 1984), p. 4.

15 ibid., p.30.

16 Eric Newton, *The Listener*, 1959.

17 'Stravinsky's Rite of Spring', published as 'Mulatta' in Figueroa, ed., op. cit., p. 191.

18 *Poetry From Cambridge 1947–1950*, ed. by Peter Morris Green (London, Fortune Press, 1951), pp. 9–13.

19 Hinds relates how the distinction was impressed on him by an official at the West Indies High Commission, who forbad Hinds to continuing reading the newspapers there. Donald Hinds, *Journey to an Illusion*, p. 198.

20 *London Calling: the West Indian Students' Centre*, brochure of the 1960s, p. 2.

21 Letter from W.K. Hynam to Anne Walmsley, 25 September 1987.

22 Claudia Jones, 'The Caribbean Community in Britain', *Freedomways*, Summer 1964, reprinted in Buzz Johnson, *'I Think of My Mother': Notes on the Life and Times of Claudia Jones* (London: Karia Press, 1985), p. 152.

23 ibid., p. 23.

24 Donald Hinds, 'People of all Races pay Homage to Claudia Jones', ibid., p. 162.

25 Claudia Jones, op. cit., p. 152.

26 Paul Buhle, *C.L.R. James: The Artist as Revolutionary* (London: Verso, 1988), p. 145.

27 David Pitt, 'We Lost a Freedom Fighter', Buzz Johnson op. cit., p. 167.

28 Edith Clarke, *My Mother Who Fathered Me: A study of the family in three selected communities in Jamaica* (London: Allen and Unwin, 1957).

29 Roger Hill, *The Evening Standard*, quoted by Cynthia Moody, op. cit., p. 19.

30 Cynthia Moody, op. cit., p. 19.

31 ibid., p. 20

32 Namba Roy was also a writer. His second novel, *Black Albino* (London: New Literature, 1961; Longman, 1986), was published a few months before his death. His first novel, *No Black Sparrows* (Oxford: HEB, 1989), was rejected by the publishers to whom he submitted it in the mid 1950s.

33 Edwin Mullins, *Sunday Telegraph Arts Review*, 1963, p. 12.

34 Bridget Jones, 'Orlando Patterson (1940 –)', *Fifty Caribbean Writers: A Bio-Bibliographical Critical Source book*, ed. by Daryl Cumber Dance (Westport, Conn., USA: Greenwood Press, 1986), pp. 368–376.

2. The Beginnings of CAM

1 John La Rose, '20 years of New Beacon books', *New Beacon Review* Nos 2/3, November 1968, p. 158.

2 John La Rose, 'The Politics of Culture: Writing and Publishing Today', Islington Public Library, London, 25 May 1985, Anne Walmsley's notes.

3 ibid.

4 ibid.

5 John La Rose, 'Back into Time', *Caribbean Essays* ed. by Andrew Salkey, p. 51.

6 Eric Williams, 'Four Poets of the Greater Antilles', a lecture to the Trinidad and Tobago Literary League of Cultural and Debating Clubs, Port of Spain, 4 April 1952, *Caribbean Quarterly* Vol. 2 No. 4, 1952, pp. 8–15.

7 John La Rose, 'Address at the Inauguration of Lennox Pierre Auditorium of the OWTU [Oilfield Workers Trade Union] "House of the People", 143 Charlotte Street, Port of Spain, Trinidad and Tobago, 2 July 1988, unpublished typescript, p. 6.

8 John La Rose, Islington Public Library, op. cit..

9 Edward Kamau Brathwaite, 'The Living Poet', talk on BBC Radio 3, producer Joan Griffiths, 21 April 1982, unpublished transcript, p. 6.

10 ibid., p. 7.

11 Gordon Rohlehr, 'West Indian Poetry: Some Problems of Assessment', *Tapia* No 20, Literary Supplement, 29 August 1971, p. 14.

12 Edward Kamau Brathwaite, Comments on Working Draft 1 (September 1990) of this book, 23 December 1990 – January 1991, p. 19.

13 ibid., p. 20.

14 Edward Kamau Brathwaite, 'John the Conqueror', *Foundations of a Movement* ed. by John La Rose Tribute Committee, p. 20.

15 Edward Baugh, 'Introduction', *An Index to 'Bim'* (St Augustine, Trinidad: UWI Extra-Mural Unit, 1973), p. 16.

16 V.S. Naipaul, *Finding the Centre: Two Narratives* (London: Andre Deutsch, 1984) pp. 23, 25.

17 L.E.B. [L. Edward Brathwaite], review of *A Quality of Violence* by Andrew Salkey, *Bim* 31, July–December 1960, pp. 219–220.

18 Letter from Edward Brathwaite to Bryan King, 30 November 1966.

19 Letter from Edward Brathwaite to Edward Lucie-Smith, 12 December 1966.

20 Letter from Bryan King to Edward Brathwaite, 3 December 1966.

21 Edward Lucie-Smith, 'Notes About the Writers', *The Sun's Eye* ed. by Anne Walmsley, p. 130.

22 Letter from Edward Lucie-Smith to Edward Brathwaite, 17 December 1966.

23 Letter from Edward Brathwaite to Edward Lucie-Smith, 12 December 1966.

24 Edward Brathwaite, 'Movement to Overcome Isolation of West Indian Artists', *Jamaica Weekly Gleaner*, 4 February 1968.

25 Letter from Edward Brathwaite to Edward Lucie-Smith, 28 December 1966.

26 Edward Brathwaite, *Jamaica Weekly Gleaner*, op. cit..

27 Bridget Jones, 'Some French influences in the fiction of Orlando Patterson', *Savacou* 11/12, p. 27.

28 Letter from Kenneth Ramchand to Edward Brathwaite, 4 January 1967.

29 Letter from Louis James to Edward Brathwaite, undated.

30 Letter from Gordon Rohlehr to Edward Brathwaite, 12 January 1967.

31 Letter from Edward Brathwaite to Louis James, 16 January 1967.

32 Edward Brathwaite, 'Jazz and the West Indian Novel', I, *Bim* 44, January–June 1967, pp. 275–284; II, *BIM* 45, July–December 1967, pp. 39–51; III, *Bim* 46, January–June 1968, pp. 115–126.

33 Gordon Rohlehr, *Pathfinder*, p. 5.

34 ibid., pp. 73, 75, 77.

35 Robert Hewison, *Too Much: Art and Society in the Sixties, 1960–75* (London: Methuen, 1986) pp. 105, 112.

36 Letter from Edward Brathwaite to Colin Rickards, 6 February 1967.

37 Letter from Edward Brathwaite to Randolph Stow, 22 February 1967.

38 Peter Blackman's poem, *My Song is For All Men*, published in a single volume (London: Lawrence & Wishart, 1952), does not attempt the ambitious scale of Brathwaite's poem and is far shorter.

39 Letter from Louis James to Edward Brathwaite, undated.

40 Letter from Edward Brathwaite to Gordon Rohlehr, 6 March 1967.

3. CAM goes Public

1 Programme for reading of *Rights of Passage*, 3 March 1967, p. 4.

2 Wilson Harris, *Tradition and the West Indian Novel*, intro. by C.L.R. James (London: London West Indian Students' Union, 1965); reprinted in Wilson Harris *Tradition, the Writer and Society*.

3 Letter from Michael Anthony to Edward Brathwaite, 13 March 1967.

4 Letter from Edward Brathwaite to Michael Anthony, 12 March 1967.

5 Letter from Gordon Rohlehr to Edward Brathwaite, 12 January 1967.

6 Letter from Edward Brathwaite to Gordon Rohlehr, 6 March 1967.

7 Gordon Rohlehr, 'Sparrow and the Language of Calypso', *Savacou* 2, pp. 87, 88. Later quotations also from transcript of recording, and from Rohlehr's own typescript, part of which appears in *Newsletter* No. 2.

8 *Newsletter* No. 2, p. 1; No. 3, p. 7.

9 *Newsletter* No. 4, pp. 8–11; *Caribbean Quarterly* Vol. 14, Nos. 1 & 2, 1968, pp. 90–96.

10 John La Rose and Raymond Quevedo, *Kaiso: A Review*.

11 For a more detailed account of the reading and discussion see Anne Walmsley, 'John La Rose: A Poet of the Caribbean Artists Movement', *Foundations of a Movement*, pp. 173–180.

12 Letter from Kenneth Ramchand to Edward Brathwaite, 18 April 1967.

13 Bridget Jones, 'Orlando Patterson (1940–)', 1986 op. cit., p. 272.

14 *Newsletter* No. 3, p. 8.

15 Letter from Kenneth Ramchand to Edward Brathwaite, 8 April 1967.

16 Letter from Edward Brathwaite to John Hearne, 8 May 1967.

17 Letter from John Hearne to Edward Brathwaite, 12 May 1967.

18 Letter from Sir Roland Penrose to Edward Brathwaite, 4 May 1967.

19 Edward Kamau Brathwaite, 23 December 1990 – 1 January 1991 op. cit., p. 3.

20 Letter from Edward Brathwaite to Bryan King, 2 June 1967.

21 Letter from Edward Brathwaite to Louis James, 11 June 1967.

22 Letter from Edward Brathwaite to C.L.R. James, 29 May 1967.

23 Letter from C.L.R. James to Edward Brathwaite, 20 June 1967.

24 C.L.R. James, 'The Contribution of the West Indies to European [sic; but James specified 'Western'] Civilisation', *Newsletter* Nos. 3, 5, and 6 for quotations.

25 Letter from Edward Brathwaite to Wilfred Cartey, 22 July 1967.

26 Letter from Bryan King to Edward Brathwaite, 30 November 1966.

27 Letter from Bryan King to Edward Brathwaite, 22 March 1967.

28 Letter from Edward Brathwaite to W.K. Hynam, 12 April 1967.

29 Letter from Gordon Rohlehr to Edward Brathwaite, 12 January 1967.

30 Letter from Kenneth Ramchand to Edward Brathwaite, 4 January 1967.

31 Letter from Kenneth Ramchand to Edward Brathwaite, undated.

32 Letter from Edward Brathwaite to Douglas McFarlane, 26 May 1967.

33 Letter from Edward Brathwaite to Kenneth Ramchand, 28 December 1966.

34 Letter from Edward Brathwaite to Marina Maxwell, 12 January 1968.

35 Letter from Edward Brathwaite to Gordon Rohlehr, 11 March 1967.

36 Letter from Gillian Shears to Edward Brathwaite, 15 April 1967.

37 Letter from Edward Brathwaite to Lee Metcalfe, 2 May 1967.

38 Letter from Edward Brathwaite to Joan Lewis, 3 July 1967.

39 Letter from Edward Brathwaite to Gordon Rohlehr, 26 May 1967.

40 David Widgery, 'Politics and flowers: the anniversary of the 1967 Dialectics of Liberation conference is a reminder that the sixties produced ideas as well as music', *New Society*, 10 July 1987, p. 12.

41 David Cooper, ed., *The Dialectics of Liberation* (Harmondsworth: Penguin, 1967) p. 9.

42 Stokely Carmichel, 'Black Power' in ibid., p. 156.

43 ibid., p. 158.

44 Gordon Rohlehr quotes from this speech in *Pathfinder*, pp. 300 & 301, citing his source as Susan Craig, *Black Power Groups in London 1967–69*, University of Edinburgh, April 1970, unpublished mimeo, pp. 34–35.

45 C.L.R. James, 'Black Power: its Past, Today and the Way Ahead', *Spheres of Existence*, p. 223.

46 Edward Brathwaite, 'Timehri', *Savacou* 2, p. 40.

47 Benjamin W. Heineman, Jr., *The Politics of the Powerless: A Study of the Campaign Against Racial Discrimination* (London: OUP for the IRR, 1972), p. 180.

48 Manning Marable, *Race, Reform and Rebellion: the Second Reconstruction in Black America, 1945–1982* (London & Basingstoke: Macmillan, 1984), p. 86.

49 Edward Brathwaite, 'Timehri', op. cit., p.40.

4. A Wider Audience

1 Edward Brathwaite, 'Artists Hold Conference on W.I. Arts', *Barbados Advocate*, 24 September 1967.

2 Letter from Edward Brathwaite to Louis James, 11 June 1967.

3 Preliminary notice of conference, June 1967.

4 Letter from Edward Brathwaite to J.W. Lambert, 7 September 1967.

5 Elsa Goveia, 'The Social Framework', *Savacou* 2, pp. 7–15, for this and subsequent quotations.

6 Rex Nettleford, 'Foreword', *Caribbean Quarterly*, Vol. 30, Nos. 3 & 4, September–December 1984, p. v.

7 Aubrey Williams, 'The Artist in the Caribbean', *Savacou* 2, pp. 16–18, for this and subsequent quotations.

8 C.L.R. James, 'Discovering Literature in Trinidad: The Nineteen-Thirties', *Savacou* 2, pp. 54–60, for this and subsequent quotations.

9 Michael Anthony, 'Growing Up with Writing', *Savacou* 2, pp. 61–66, for this and subsequent quotations.

10 C.L.R. James quoted by Anne Walmsley, 'First C.A.M. Conference', *Bim* 46, January–June 1968, p. 82.

11 Louis James, 'Caribbean Poetry in English: Some Problems;, *Savacou* 2, pp. 78–86, for this and subsequent quotations.

12 Brathwaite, *Barbados Advocate*, op. cit.

13 Letter from Marina Maxwell to Edward Brathwaite, August 1967.

14 Letter from Edward Brathwaite to John La Rose, 19 September 1967.

15 Letter from Edward Brathwaite to Sir Lionel Luckhoo, 19 September 1967.

16 A.R., 'Caribbean Culture Visits Canterbury', *Daily Telegraph*, 18 September 1967.

17 Letter from Edward Brathwaite to the Editor, the *Daily Telegraph*. September 1967.

18 Letter from Don Wilson to Edward Brathwaite, 16 October 1967.

19 Letter from Edward Brathwaite to Don Wilson, 5 November 1967.

20 Letter from John La Rose to Edward Brathwaite, 24 September 1967.

21 Letter from Edward Brathwaite to George Lamming, 2 October 1967.

22 Letter from Edward Brathwaite to Diana Athill, 2 October 1967.

23 Letter from Diana Athill to Edward Brathwaite, 3 October 1967.

24 Letter from Edward Brathwaite to Don Wilson, 5 November 1967.

25 Courtney Tulloch, 'Notting Hill Festival', *International Times*, 5–20 October 1967, p. 3.

26 Letter from Edward Brathwaite to Ram John Holder, 22 October 1967.

27 Winston Best, 'John La Rose: The man and the idealist and the shrewd political operator', *Foundations of a Movement*, p 13.

28 Letter from Oliver Clarke to Edward Brathwaite, 12 November 1967.

29 Letter from Ken Corsbie to Doris Brathwaite, 20 December 1967.

30 Letter from Edward Brathwaite to Louis James, 17 November 1967.

31 Letter from Edward Brathwaite to Jeremy Verity, 15 November 1967.

32 Letter from Alain Rickards to Edward Brathwaite, 29 September 1967.

33 Letter from W.K. Hynam to Edward Brathwaite, 21 December 1967.

34 Letter from Bryan King to Edward Brathwaite, 7 November 1967.

35 Letter from Louis James to James Currey, 21 September 1967.

36 Visnudat Singh, 'The Canterbury Conference', *Enquiry*: The Trinidad and Tobago Society – U.K. Newsletter, Vol. 1 No. 4, October 1967, p. 8.

37 Letter from Edward Brathwaite to Antonio de Castro, 21 August 1967.

38 Draft letter from Edward Brathwaite addressed 'Dear Sir', 22 August 1967.

39 Phyllis Allfrey, *The Star of Dominica*, 16 September 1967.

40 Letter from Edward Brathwaite to Don Wilson, 5 November 1967.

41 Letters from Edward Brathwaite to Kenneth Ramchand and Christopher Laird, 8 December 1967.

5. A Broader Context

1 Letter from Edward Brathwaite to Pierre [?], 10 January 1968.

2 Students Centre House Committee notice quoted by Edward Brathwaite in letter to Bryan King, 6 January 1968.

3 Letter from Edward Brathwaite to Marina Maxwell, January 1968.

4 Letter from Marina Maxwell to Louis James, January 1968.

5 Letter from Louis James to Edward Brathwaite, undated.

6 Letter from Louis James to Edward Brathwaite, undated.

7 Letter from Louis James to Marina Maxwell, undated.

8 Letter from Edward Brathwaite to Robert Reinders, 25 March 1968.

9 Letter from Edward Brathwaite to V.S. Naipaul, 11 October 1967.

10 Letter from V.S. Naipaul to Edward Brathwaite, 17 October 1967.

11 Letter from Andrew Salkey to Edward Brathwaite, 26 October 1967.

12 Letter from Edward Brathwaite to Jean Franco, 11 October 1967.

13 Jean Franco, 'Caribbean Writing in French and Spanish', *Newsletter* No. 6, pp. 8–11, for this and subsequent quotations.

14 Césaire's *Cahier* first appeared as extracts in the Paris-based journal *Volontés* (Wishes) in 1939. It was published complete in Paris by Bordas in 1945, with a preface by André Breton, leader of the surrealist movement. See also Note 10, Chapter 6.

15 Quoted by Manning Marable, *Race, Reform and Rebellion*, p. 116.

16 Andrew Salkey, *Havana Journal*, p. 110.

17 ibid.

18 ibid., p. 104.

19 Pedro Perez Sarduy, 'A friend of mine and a friend of Cuba', *Foundations of a Movement*, p. 160, for this and subsequent quotations.

20 Quoted by Edward Brathwaite in 'Caribbean Report, January/March, 1968', *Newsletter* No. 6, p. 2.

21 ibid., pp. 2–5, for this and subsequent quotations.

22 Letter from Edward Brathwaite to Andrew Salkey, 20 November 1967.

23 Letter from Edward Brathwaite to Gordon Rohlehr, 27 March 1968.

24 Edward Brathwaite, 'Movement to overcome isolation of WI artists', *The Jamaica Weekly Gleaner*, 14 February 1968; reprinted, with slight amendments, *Caribbean Quarterly*, Vol. 14 Nos. 1 & 2, 1968, pp. 57–59.

25 Letter from Edward Brathwaite to Don Wilson, 23 March 1968.

26 Letter from Edward Brathwaite to Gordon Rohlehr, 27 March 1968.

27 Rosey E. Pool, *Beyond the Blues: new poems by American negroes* (Lympne: Hand & Flower Press, 1962).

28 Letter from Edward Brathwaite to Gordon Rohlehr, 27 March 1968.

29 Notice of CAM session, 5 April 1968.

30 Typescript by Edward Brathwaite, pp. 1–2, also transcript of recording.

31 Letter from Edward Brathwaite to Sir Laurence Lindo, 21 May 1968.

32 Letter from Edward Brathwaite to Jerry Craig, 21 May 1968.

33 Letter from Ronald Savory to Anne Walmsley, 24 July 1986.

34 Ronald Moody, 'Clifton Campbell', typescript 14 May 1968.

35 Letter from Douglas Hall to Doris Brathwaite, 17 May 1968.

36 Letter from Andrew Salkey to Edward Brathwaite, undated.

37 Letter from Michael Kustow to Andrew Salkey, 9 May 1968.

38 Letter from John La Rose to Edward Brathwaite, 25 June 1968.

39 Gus John, 'Resolute, Radical and Revolutionary', *Foundations of a Movement*, p. 76.

40 Letter from Locksley Comrie to Edward Brathwaite, undated.

6. Confrontation and Crisis

1 Cable from John La Rose to Aimé Césaire, 26 June 1968.

2 Letter from Edward Brathwaite to Bobby (Robert) Moore, 18 June 1968.

3 Doris Brathwaite prepared lists of participants for the First and Second Conferences. Both include 'occupation' but only that for the Second, 'country'.

4 Michael Gilkes, *Wilson Harris and the Caribbean Novel* (London: Longman, 1975), p. 120.

5 Louis James, ed., *The Islands in Between*, p. 12.

6 John La Rose, ed., *New Beacon Reviews*, 1968, p. 1.

7 Ivan Van Sertima, *Caribbean Writers: Critical Essays*, back cover.

8 Henry Swanzy kept diaries throughout his working life, which he refers to as his 'ego books'.

9 Henry Swanzy, entry in 1968 diary for 2 September, typescript, with handwritten corrections.

10 Aimé Césaire, *Return to My Native Land*, French/English bilingual editions, trans. by Emile Snyders (Paris: Présence Africaine, 1968); English edition, trans. by John Berger and Anna Bostock (Harmondsworth: Penguin, 1969).

11 Wilson Harris, *The Far Journey of Oudin*, pp. 72–73.

12 Wilson Harris, *The Secret Ladder*, pp. 36, 52–53.

13 Wilson Harris, *Palace of the Peacock*, pp. 57–59.

14 Wilson Harris, *Heartland*, p. 62–65.

15 Derek Walcott, 'The Voyage Up River (for Wilson Harris)', *The Castaway* (London: Jonathan Cape, 1965), p. 50.

16 Wilson Harris, 'Art and Criticism', *Tradition the Writer and Society*, pp. 7–12.

17 Henry Swanzy, op. cit., entry for 31 August.

18 Letter from Edmund Gill to Marina Maxwell, 2 March 1968.

19 Letter from Robert Reinders to Louis James, 28 May 1968.

20 No recording of the CAM 'business' meeting exists. Anne Walmsley took detailed notes in preparation for her article on the Second Conference, *Bim*, 48, January–June 1969, pp. 233–236.

21 Both newspapers are quoted by Anne Walmsley in ibid., p. 233.

22 Edward Kamau Brathwaite, 23 December 1990 – January 1991, op. cit., p. 41.

7. Grounding in the Caribbean

1 Edward Brathwaite, 'O Dreams O Destinations', *Rights of Passage*, p. 61.

2 Letter from Edward Brathwaite to Andrew Salkey, September 1968.

3 Norman Girvan, 'After Rodney: the Politics of Student Protest in Jamaica', *New World Quarterly*, Vol. 4 No. 3, High Season 1968, pp. 59–68. The above account is mainly based on this article.

4 Richard Small, 'Introduction', *The Groundings with my Brothers*, p. 7.

5 Letter from Andrew Salkey to Edward Brathwaite, 2 November 1968.

6 Edward Kamau Brathwaite, *The Love Axe/1: Developing a Caribbean Aesthetic 1962–1976*, unpublished typescript (longer and more detailed than the three parts in *Bim* 61, 62, 63) dated April 1975 – October 1976, p. 29.

7 Letter from Edward Brathwaite to Andrew Salkey, 18 December 1968.

8 New World Group membership form.

9 Letter from Marina Maxwell to Edward Brathwaite, undated, for this and subsequent quotations.

10 Marina Maxwell, 'Towards a Revolution in the Arts', *Savacou 2*, pp. 19–32, for this and subsequent quotations.

11 Letter from Edward Brathwaite to Andrew Salkey, 23 March 1969.

12 Letter from Edward Brathwaite to Rex Nettleford, 22 May 1969.

13 Marina Maxwell, *Newsletter* No. 10, p. 11.

14 Anonymous, 'Yard Theatre', ibid., p. 13.

15 Notice of Yard Theatre, 12 April 1969.

16 Edward Kamau Brathwaite, 'The Love Axe/1', Part One, *Bim* 61, June 1977, p. 57.

17 Notice of Yard Theatre, 31 May 1969.

18 Edward Kamau Brathwaite, 'The Love Axe/1', Part Three, *Bim* 63, June 1978, pp. 182–3.

19 Ivan Oxaal, *Black Intellectuals and the Dilemmas of Race and Class in Trinidad* (Cambridge, Mass., USA: Schenkman, 1982), p. 286.

20 Letter from Edward Brathwaite to Andrew Salkey, 8 May 1969.

21 Printed brochure for *Savacou*, p. 4.

22 Letter from Edward Brathwaite to Andrew Salkey, 8 May 1969.

23 James Ngũgĩ, Henry Owuor-Anyumba, Taban Lo Liyong, 'Appendix: On the Abolition of the English Department', Ngũgĩ wa Thiong'o, *Homecoming*, pp. 145–150.

24 Kenneth Ramchand, *The West Indian Novel and its Background* (1970), p. xi.

25 Edward Kamau Brathwaite, 'The Love Axe/1', *Bim* 61, June 1977, p. 59.

26 Colin Gregory, 'Of this and that: Back to Africa', *The Daily Gleaner*, 15 December 1969, p. 10.

27 Edward Brathwaite, *The Folk Culture of the Slaves in Jamaica*, back cover.

28 Edward Brathwaite, 'Note', *Islands*, p.ix.

29 ibid., pp. 112–3.

30 Maureen Warner Lewis, 'Odomankoma Kyerema Se', *Caribbean Quarterly*, Vol. 19, No. 2, June 1973, pp. 51–99.

31 Letter from Gordon Rohlehr to Edward Brathwaite, 4 May 1968.

32 Richard Small, 1969, op. cit., p. 10.

33 'Report on the Caribbean Writers and Artists Conference', *Kaie* No. 3, December 1966, p. 3.

34 C.L.R. James, 'An Hour's Harvest of Unique Art', *Guiana Graphic*, 21 June 1966; reprinted in *Guyana Dreaming*, comp. by Anne Walmsley, pp. 79–80.

35 Wilson Harris, *History, Fable and Myth in the Caribbean and Guianas*, for this and subsequent quotations.

36 The Revd. C. Jesse, *The Amerindians in St Lucia (Iouanalao [sic])* (Castries: Voice Publishing Co., 1953; revised edn, St Lucia Archaeological and Historical Society, 1968).

37 A.J. Seymour, 'Introduction', Harris, *History, Fable and Myth*, p. 4.

38 Andrew Salkey, *Georgetown Journal*, pp. 170–1.

39 ibid., p. 182.

40 Edward Kamau Brathwaite, 26 December 1990 – 1 January 1991 op. cit., p. 55.

41 Andrew Salkey, *Georgetown Journal*, p. 241.

42 ibid., p. 328.

43 Susan Craig, '1970 Confrontation: Trinidad and Tobago', *Contemporary Caribbean: A Sociological Reader* Vol. 2 ed. by Susan Craig (Port of Spain: Susan Craig, 1982), p. 40.

44 Quoted by Ivor Oxaal in 'Race and Revolutionary Consciousness: A Documentary Interpretation of the 1970 Black

Power revolt in Trinidad', 1971, in *Black Intellectuals*, p. 223.

45 Appendix E: 'A Letter from John La Rose to Edward Brathwaite, London 25.5.1970', in Salkey, *Georgetown Journal*, p. 403.

46 Edward Kamau Brathwaite, 'The Love Axe/1', Part One, *Bim* 61, p. 60.

47 Edward Kamau Brathwaite, 26 December 1990 – 1 January 1991, op. cit., p. 50.

48 Letter from Edward Brathwaite to Monica Schuler, 9 March 1970.

49 Edward Kamau Brathwaite, *The Love Axe/1*, unpublished typescript, p. 30.

50 Note on Eugene Hyde, catalogue for *Remembrance: An Exhibition of Jamaican Art*, 31 August – 25 September 1983, Art Gallery, Commonwealth Institute, p. 4.

51 Edward Brathwaite, 'Timehri', *Savacou* 2, pp. 35–44, for this and subsequent quotations.

52 *Caribbean Quarterly*, Vol. 16, No. 2, June 1970.

53 Edward Kamau Brathwaite, *The Love Axe/1*, unpublished typescript, note 15, p. 3.

8. Keeping on in Britain

1 Letter from Louis James to Edward Brathwaite, 21 October 1968.

2 Letters from Louis James to Andrew Salkey, November and December 1968, 25 January 1969.

3 Letter from Donald Hinds to Edward Brathwaite, 2 March 1969.

4 Letter from Edward Brathwaite to Donald Hinds, 28 March 1969.

5 Letter from Christopher Laird to Donald Hinds, 27 February 1969.

6 John La Rose and Andrew Salkey, Preface, *Savacou* 9/10, p. 8.

7 Richard Small, 'Congress of Black Writers, Montreal, 1968', *Newsletter* No. 8, p. 5.

8 John La Rose and Andrew Salkey, op. cit., p. 8.

9 Typescript, 'Resolution' and 'Proposal', in Andrew Salkey's CAM files.

10 Letter from Andrew Salkey to Edward Brathwaite, 2 November 1968.

11 Notice of CAM meeting of 1 November 1968.

12 Letter from Shirley Wrigley, Nominated Chairman Sub-Committee for Art Exhibition, British Caribbean Association, 2 June 1967.

13 Notice of CAM meeting, 6 December 1968.

14 'CAM's December Meeting', *Newsletter* No. 9, p. 4.

15 'My Heritage', *Newsletter* No. 10, p. 14; also 'Evening', pp. 14–16

16 Letter from Edward Brathwaite to Andrew Salkey, 18 December, 1968.

17 Letter from Bryan King to Andrew Salkey, 10 October 1968.

18 Handwritten draft of a letter from Bryan King to Enoch Powell, 4 December 1968.

19 Letter from Hortense Spiller to Andrew Salkey, 16 December 1968.

20 Letter from Hortense Spiller to Andrew Salkey, 25 January 1969.

21 Letter from Hortense Spiller to Andrew Salkey, 12 February 1969.

22 Donald Hinds, *Journey to an Illusion*, p. xii.

23 'An Interview with Aimé Césaire', *Discourse on Colonialism* (Paris: Présence Africaine, 1955; New York, Monthly Review Press, 1972), pp. 67–8.

24 Andrew Salkey, 'A report on the premier presentation of Aimé Césaire's *Return to my Native Land (Cahier d'un retour au pays natal),* in a spoken recital, at the West Indian Students Centre, on Friday, June 6th, 1969', *Newsletter* No. 10, pp. 16–17.

25 Ivan Van Sertima, 'Astride Two Visions (A personal testament)', *Newsletter* No. 11, pp. 1–7, No. 12, pp. 11–17, for this and subsequent quotations.

26 Harris writes: '*Almanac* was one of three novels that came before *Palace* with which I was dissatisfied and which were eventually scrapped. However the latter part of *Almanac* was important as it brought into play certain rhythms and dimensions that led into *Palace*? (Letter to Anne Walmsley, 6 September 1991).

27 John La Rose, 'The Black Experience and the Nature of Black Society in Britain', *Newsletter* No. 11, pp. 9–13, for this and subsequent quotations.

28 Reprinted as 'Prose Poem for a Conference: for Andrew Salkey', *Race Today*, May 1974, p. 157.

29 Quoted by Winston Best, *Foundations of a Movement*, p. 17.

30 Roxy Harris in ibid., p. 58; he explains the names thus: 'George Padmore after the Trinidadian revolutionary who worked with Nkrumah, and Albertina Sylvester after a local

woman from Grenada who was an important activist in the black education movement and some of whose children attended the school.'

31 The names of the imprint are explained thus in its catalogue: **Bogle-L'Ouverture Publications** commemorates two outstanding revolutionary heroes of the Caribbean and dedicates itelf to upholding the high ideals for which they lived and died. **Paul Bogle** was born in slavery in about 1820. He was a Baptist Preacher and a great source of inspiration to the people of Stony Gut, in the Parish of St Thomas, Jamaica. He organised and led the Morant Bay Rebellion in 1865 and was among the 436 fighters slaughtered by the order of the Government of Jamaica. **Toussaint L'Ouverture**, like Bogle, was the son of a slave. At 45 he joined the revolutionary movement and soon became its leader, defeating the British, Spanish and French in battle. He was tricked aboard a French ship and died from cold and starvation in Fort de Joix prison on 7 April 1803. Two years later, in October 1805, his successor declared San Dominique the independent state of Haiti.

32 Letter from Andrew Salkey to Edward Brathwaite, undated.

33 'John La Rose – Statements', interviewed by Sebastian Clarke, Guest Editor, *Journal of Black Poetry*, Vol. 1, No. 17, Summer 1973, pp. 25–28.

34 *Kyk-over-al* started in 1945 as the organ of the B.G. Writers Association and publisher of talks by the B.G. Union of Cultural Clubs. When both organisations ceased to function *Kyk's* editor, A.J. Seymour, continued to edit and publish it independently 1945–1961; with Ian McDonald, 1984–1989, who has edited it alone since Seymour's death in 1989. *Kaie* is the Official Organ of the National History and Arts Council of Guyana.

35 Salkey referred specifically to what William Walsh had written about 'the usage of language of folk culture of the Caribbean and about the folk culture itself in nine studies of Commonwealth writers', referring to the essay on VS Naipaul in William Walsh, *A Manifold Voice: Studies in Commonwealth Literature* (London: Chatto & Windus, 1970).

36 'A Letter from John La Rose to Edward Brathwaite, London 25.5.1970' in *Georgetown Journal*, p. 407.

37 Andrew Salkey, *Come Home, Malcolm Heartland* (London: Hutchinson, 1976), p. 114, for this and subsequent quotations.

38 A. Sivanandan, *From Resistance to Rebellion: Asian and Afro-Caribbean struggles in Britain* (London: Institute of Race Relations, 1986), p. 134.

39 Winston Best, op. cit., p. 18.

40 A. Sivanandan, op. cit., p. 136.

9. CAM continuing: at home

1 Edward Kamau Brathwaite, *Love Axel/1*, unpublished typescript, p. 40.

2. ibid., p. 41.

3 Kenneth Ramchand, 'History and the Novel: A Literary Critic's Approach', *Savacou* 5, pp. 103–113. (Text of address at the ACLALS Conference, Mona, Jamaica, January 1971).

4 Gordon Rohlehr, 'The Folk in Caribbean Literature' and 'Samuel Selvon and the Language of the People', *Critics on Caribbean Literature* ed. by Edward Baugh (London: Allen & Unwin, 1978) pp. 27–37, 153–161, from 'The Folk in Caribbean Literature', *Tapia*, 17 December 1972. (Revised version of a paper presented at the ACLALS Conference, Mona, Jamaica, January 1971).

5 Gordon Rohlehr, 'Blues and Rebellion: Edward Brathwaite's *Rights of Passage*', Baugh ed. op. cit., pp. 63–74. (From 'Islands', *Caribbean Studies* X, January 1971).

6 'General Aims', printed brochure and back inside cover *Savacou* 1–13.

7 Letter from Edward Brathwaite to Andrew Salkey, 18 December 1968.

8 Edward Brathwaite, 'Foreward [sic]', *Savacou* 3/4, p. 8.

9 Eric Roach, *Trinidad Guardian*, 14 & 18 July 1971, as quoted by F. Gordon Rohlehr in Note 13 below.

10 Syl Lowhar, *Trinidad Guardian*, 17 July 1971, as quoted in Note 13 below.

11 Edward Brathwaite, *The Love Axel/1*, unpublished typescript, p. 70.

12 Eric Roach, 'Notes About the Authors', *The Sun's Eye*, ed. Anne Walmsley, p. 132.

13 F. Gordon Rohlehr, 'West Indian Poetry, Some Problems of Assessment', *Tapia* No. 20, 29 August 1971, *Literary Supplement*, pp. 11–14.

14 Edward Brathwaite, *The Love Axel/1*, unpublished typescript, p. 66.

15 Lucille Mathurin Mair, 'Creole Authenticity: a review of Edward Brathwaite's *The Development of Creole Society in Jamaica*

1770–1820. Clarendon Press, Oxford, 1971', *Savacou* 5, p. 120.

16 Dennis Scott, 'Introduction', Anthony McNeill, *Reel from 'The Life Movie'* (Mona, Jamaica: Savacou, 1972, 1975), p. 3.

17 Kenneth Ramchand and Cecil Gray, *West Indian Poetry: An anthology for schools* (Trinidad & Jamaica: Longman Caribbean, 1971), p. vii.

18 Marina Maxwell, unpublished typescript '"Bongo Man Ah Come!" or Inside Yard Theatre' addressed to 'Sebastian', undated, p. 2. Sebastian Clarke (Amon Saba Saakana) visited Jamaica from New York in the summer of 1971 and saw Maxwell; he received a letter similar to this typescript.

19 Archie Lindo, *The Star*, 9 September 1971.

20 M.M., 'Topical Righteous Anger', *The Sunday Gleaner*, 1971, p. 32.

21 Marina Maxwell, 'Work Yard', unpublished typescript, 1974, quoted by Edward Brathwaite, *The Love Axe/1*, Part Three, *Bim* 63, June 1978, Note 58, p. 191.

22 Edward Brathwaite, ibid., Note 59, p. 191.

23 Marina Maxwell, unpublished typescript op. cit., p. 2.

24 Kamau [Edward Kamau Brathwaite], 'Ronald Moody', Jamaican Sculptor', *The Sunday Gleaner*, 6 August 1972.

25 Dawn Ritch, 'An Evening with Ronald Moody', *Jamaica Journal*, September 1972, p. 65.

26 A.J. Seymour, 'A Note on Literature and Caribbean Society', *Kaie: the Vision of Carifesta*, No. 8, December 1971, pp. 12–15.

27 Lynette de W. Dolphin, 'Report on Organisation and Events of Carifesta '72', unpublished typescript, p. 10.

28 A.J. Seymour, 'We must hear our Brothers speak', *Kaie* No. 11, August 1973, p. 5.

29 Gordon Rohlehr, 'The Creative Writer and West Indian Society', ibid., p. 48, for this and subsequent quotations.

30 Edward Kamau Brathwaite, 'Doing it our way: Carifesta '72', *West Indies Chronicle*, April 1874, pp. 104–5; 'Carifesta '72', eight articles, *Advocate-News* (Barbados), 16 October – 3 December 1972, for this and subsequent quotations.

31 Marina Ama Omowale Maxwell, 'Towards Psychic Integration & Wholeness: Towards a Caribbean Artists Movement (CAM) Network to free and develop our cultural identity', *About Our Business*, p. 93.

32 Letter from Bridget Jones to Anne Walmsley, 10 March 1990.

10. CAM continuing: at home away from home

1 Donald Hinds, handwritten and photocopied letter, 1 January 1971.

2 Letter from Anne Walmsley to Edward and Doris Brathwaite, 15 February 1971.

3 Letter from W.K. Hynam to Anne Walmsley, 25 September 1987.

4 Letter from Donald Bowen to Edward Brathwaite, 20 July 1967,

5 Letter from Donald Bowen to Edward Brathwaite, 12 October 1967.

6 John La Rose and Andrew Salkey, 'Preface', *Savacou* 9/10, p. 7.

7 Andrew Salkey, typescript notes for this and subsequent quotations.

8 Typescript of interview in Guyana with Aubrey Williams, 1971, p. 1.

9 Denis Williams, *The Third Temptation* (London: Calder & Boyars, 1968), *Icon and Image: A study of sacred and secular forms of African classical art* (London: Allen Lane, 1974).

10 Denis Williams, *Image and Idea in the Arts of Guyana*, The Edgar Mittelholzer Memorial Lectures, Second Series, January 1969 (Georgetown: National History and Arts Council, 1969).

11 *The Keskidee Centre*, contemporary brochure, p. 2.

12 James Berry, 'Focus', *West Indian World*, 8 October 1971, p. 4.

13 Letter from John La Rose to Edward Brathwaite, 29 January 1974, quoted by Brathwaite, 'Postscript', *Savacou* 9/10, p. 133.

14. 'Book List for Parents: West Indian Literature for Children', Bernard Coard, *How the West Indian child is made educationally sub-normal in the British school system* (London: New Beacon, for CECWA, 1971); reprinted as 'Black booklist', *Times Educational Supplement*, May 1971.

15 Andrew Salkey, 'Introduction', *Breaklight*, pp. xvii–xix.

16 Audvil King, Althea Helps, Pam Wint, Frank Hasfal, *One Love*, intro. by Andrew Salkey (London: Bogle–L'Ouverture, 1971).

17 'Lindsay Mackie talks to Jessica Huntley', *The Guardian*, 16 August 1973.

18 Linton Kwesi Johnson, tribute to John La Rose, *Foundations of a Movement*, pp. 81–2.

19 Adrian Mitchell, 'Adrian Mitchell talks to Jamaican novelist Andrew Salkey and Trinidadian poet John La Rose', *The Guardian*, 4 April 1972.

20 Edward Brathwaite, 'Postscript', *Savacou* 9/10, p. 132.

21 The bookshop was renamed in memory of Walter Rodney after his sudden death and suspected assassination in Georgetown, Guyana, 13 June 1980.

22 'IRR Council at 31 March 1973', Appendix IV, A. Sivanandan, *Race and Resistance: The IRR story* (London: Institute of Race Relations, 1974).

23 Letter from John La Rose to Edward Brathwaite in *Savacou* 9/10, p. 133.

24 *Radio Times*, 3–9 February 1973, p. 15.

25 Harry Goulbourne, tribute to John La Rose, *Foundations of a Movement*, p. 55.

11. Postscript

1 Edward Brathwaite, 'Movement to overcome isolation of WI artists', *Jamaica Weekly Gleaner*, 14 February 1968.

2 Adrian Mitchell, op. cit.

3 Transcript of recording of CAM session, 10 April 1971.

4 Transcript of recording of CAM session, 1 December 1967.

5 Paullette Perrier, 'Harmattan: Whose Ancestor Am I?' *Journal of Black Poetry* Vol. 1, No. 17, Summer 1973, p. 22.

6 Letter from Edward Brathwaite to Louis James, 17 November 1967.

7 Letter from Edward Brathwaite to Stuart Hall, 11 September 1968.

8 Amon Saba Saakana, *The Colonial Legacy in Caribbean Literature*, p. 106.

9 Paullette Perrier, op. cit., p. 21.

10 Tony Martin, *Literary Garveyism: Garvey, Black Arts and the Harlem Renaissance* (Dover, Mass., USA: the Majority Press, 1983).

11 Nathan Huggins, *Voices from the Harlem Renaissance* (New York: OUP, 1976), pp. 3–4. Huggins's comprehensive and authoritative account is contained in *Harlem Renaissance* (New York: OUP, 1971).

12 See Chapter 3: The Indigenous Movement, J. Michael Dash, *Literature and Ideology in Haiti, 1915–1961* (London & Basingstoke: Macmillan, 1981).

13 Dorothy S. Blair, *African Literature in French* (Cambridge: Cambridge University Press, 1976), p. 145.

14 Transcript of recording of CAM session, 5 April 1968.

15 See Chapter 5, 'Black Students in Paris and the Harlem Renaissance', Lilian Kesteloot, *Black Writers in French: A Literary History of Negritude* trans. by Ellen Conroy Kennedy (Philadelphia, USA: Temple University Press, 1974).

16 Christopher Laird, tribute to John La Rose, *Foundations of a Movement*, p. 101.

17 Rasheed Araeen, 'Conversation with Aubrey Williams', *Third Text: Third World Perspectives on Contemporary Art and Culture*, No. 2, Winter 1987/88, p. 35.

18 Edward Kamau Brathwaite, *History of the Voice: The Development of Nation Language in Anglophone Caribbean Poetry*.

19 The Creation for Liberation Open Exhibition, *Art by Black Artists*, was organised by Eddie Chambers, Chila Burman and Eugene Palmer, whose own work was included in it. Aubrey Williams showed a portrait, uncatalogued, of the jazz musician Charles Mingus, and donated a prize for the 'best exhibit'. The forum on 29 October 1987 was entitled 'Seeking a Black Aesthetic', and followed a screening of Imruh Bakari's film on the life and work of Aubrey Williams, *The Mark of the Hand* (1986).

20 Edward Kamau Brathwaite, 'John the Conqueror', *Foundations of a Movement*, p. 20.

Select bibliography

Books by, or with substantial contributions by, CAM people

ANTHONY, Michael, *The Games were Coming* (London: Deutsch, 1963; HEB, 1977)
The Year in San Fernando, intro. by Paul Edwards and Kenneth Ramchand) (London: Deutsch, 1965; HEB, 1970,
Green Days by the River, (London: Deutsch, 1967; HEB, 1973)
BARRETT, Lindsay, *The State of Black Desire* (Paris: Alemeon, 1966)
Song for Mumu (London: Longman, 1967)
Veils of Vengeance Falling (Enugu, Nigeria: Fourth Dimension, 1985)
BERRY, James, *Fractured Circles* (London/Port of Spain: New Beacon, 1979)
Lucy's Letters and Loving (London/Port of Spain: New Beacon, 1982)
Chain of Days (London: OUP, 1985)
Bluefoot Traveller: Poetry by West Indians in Britain (London: Limestone Publications, 1964; revised edition: Harrap, 1981; Nelson, 1985)
News for Babylon: The Chatto Book of West Indian-British Poetry (London: Chatto & Windus, 1984)
BRATHWAITE, Doris Monica *EKB: His Published Prose and Poetry 1948–1986: A Checklist* (Mona: Savacou, 1986)
A Descriptive and Chronological Bibliography (1950–1982) of the Work of Edward Kamau Brathwaite (London/Port of Spain: New Beacon, 1988)
BRATHWAITE, Edward, ed., *Iouanaloa: Recent Writing from St Lucia* (Castries: Department of Extra Mural Studies, June 1963)
Four Plays for Primary Schools (London: Longmans Green, 1964)
Odale's Choice (London: Evans, 1967)
*Rights of Passage** (London: OUP, 1967)
*Masks** (London: OUP, 1968)
*Islands** (London: OUP, 1969)
The Arrivants: A New World Trilogy, Brathwaite's first three poems* (London: OUP, 1973)
The Folk Culture of the Slaves in Jamaica (London/Port of Spain: New Beacon, 1970; revised edn, 1981)
The Development of Creole Society In Jamaica 1770–1820 (Oxford: Clarendon Press, 1971)
and Anthony Phillips, *The People Who Came, Book 3: Longman Secondary School Histories for the Caribbean*, Series Editor: Edward Brathwaite (Trinidad/Jamaica/London: Longman Caribbean, 1972)
Caribbean Man in Space and Time: A Bibliographical and Conceptual Approach (Mona, Jamaica: Savacou, 1974)
Contradictory Omens: Cultural Diversity and Integration in the Caribbean (Mona, Jamaica: Savacou, 1974)
Mother Poem (Oxford: OUP, 1977)
Sun Poem (Oxford: OUP, 1982)
X-Self (Oxford: OUP, 1987)
History of the Voice: The Development of Nation Language in Anglophone Caribbean Poetry (London/Port of Spain: New Beacon, 1984)
CHARLES, Faustin, *The Expatriate: Poems 1963–1968* (London: Brookside Press, 1969)
Crab Track (London: Brookside Press, 1973)
Days and Nights in the Magic Forest (London: Bogle-L'Ouverture, 1986)
CORSBIE, Ken, *Theatre in the Caribbean*, intro, by Trevor Rhone (London: Hodder & Stoughton, 1984)
CRAIG, Christine, *Quadrille for Tigers: Poems* (Berkeley, California, USA: Mina, 1984)
CRAIG, Karl, *Emmanuel and his Parrot* (London: OUP, 1970)
Emmanuel goes to Market (London: OUP, 1971)

FIGUEROA, Peter M.E. and Ganga Persaud, eds, *Sociology of Education: A Caribbean Reader* (Oxford: OUP, 1976)
GOVEIA, Elsa V., *A Study of the Historiography of the British West Indies to the End of the Nineteenth Century* (Mexico City: Instituto Panamericano de Geografía e Historia, 1956)
Slave Society in the British Leeward Islands at the End of the Eighteenth Century (New Haven, Conn.: Yale, 1965)
HALL, Douglas, *Free Jamaica* (New Haven, Conn.: Yale, 1959)
HALL, Stuart and Paddy Whannel, *The Popular Arts* (London: Hutchinson, 1964)
and Tony Jefferson, eds, *Resistance through Rituals: Youth subcultures in postwar Britain* (London: Unwin Hyman, 1975)
et al, *Culture, Media, Language: Working Papers in Cultural Studies, 1972–79* (London: Hutchinson, in association with the Centre for Contemporary Cultural Studies, University of Birmingham, 1980)
HARRIS, Wilson, *Eternity to Season* (Georgetown, 1954; London/Port of Spain: New Beacon, 1978)
*Palace of the Peacock** (London: Faber, 1960)
*The Far Journey of Oudin** (London: Faber, 1961)
*The Whole Armour** (London: Faber, 1962)
*The Secret Ladder** (London: Faber, 1963)
Heartland (London: Faber, 1964)
The Eye of the Scarecrow (London: Faber, 1965)
Tradition, the Writer and Society: Critical Essays (London/Port of Spain: New Beacon, 1967)
The Waiting Room (London: Faber, 1967)
Tumatumari (London: Faber, 1968)
Ascent to Omai (London: Faber, 1970)
History, Fable and Myth in the Caribbean and Guianas:
The Edgar Mittelholzer Memorial Lectures, third series, February 1970) (Guyana: National History & Arts Council, 1970)
Black Marsden (London: Faber, 1972)
Companions of the Day and Night (London: Faber, 1975)
Da Silva da Silva's Cultivated Wilderness and Genesis of the Clowns (London: Faber, 1977)
The Tree of the Sun (London: Faber, 1978)
The Angel at the Gate (London: Faber, 1982)
Carnival (London: Faber, 1985)
The Infinite Rehearsal (London: Faber, 1987)
The Four Banks of the River of Space (London: Faber, 1990)
Explorations: A Selection of Talks and Articles 1966–1981 (Aarhus, Denmark: Dangaroo Press, 1981)
The Guyana Quartet, Harris's first four novels* (London: Faber, 1985) with 'A note on the genesis of *The Guyana Quartet*'
HEARNE, John, *Voices Under the Window* (London: Faber, 1955)
Stranger at the Gate (London: Faber, 1956)
The Faces of Love (London: Faber, 1957)
The Autumn Equinox (London: Faber, 1959)
Land of the Living (London: Faber, 1961)
The Sure Salvation (London: Faber, 1981)
ed., *Carifesta Forum: An Anthology of 20 Caribbean Voices* (Kingston: Carifesta 76, 1976)
HINDS, Donald, *Journey to an Illusion: The West Indian in Britain* (London: Heinemann, 1966)
HODGE, Merle, *Crick Crack, Monkey* (London: Deutsch, 1970)
and Chris Searle, *'is freedom we making': the New Democracy in Grenada* (Grenada: Government Information Service)
'Challenges of the Struggle for Sovereignty: changing the world versus writing stories', in *Caribbean Women Writers: Essays from the First International Conference*, ed. by Selwyn R. Cudjoe (Wellesley, Mass., USA: Calaloux Publications, 1990), pp 202–208.
JAMES, C.L.R., *Minty Alley*, intro. by Kenneth Ramchand (London: Secker & Warburg, 1936; New Beacon, 1971)

World Revolution 1917–1936: The Rise and Fall of the Communist International (London: Secker & Warburg, 1937)
The Black Jacobins: Toussaint L'Ouverture and the San Domingo Revolution (New York, Dial: 1938; revised edn, London: Allison & Busby, 1980)
A History of Negro Revolt (Britain: Independent Labour Party, 1938; revised edn Washington, USA: Drum & Spear Press, 1969; London: Race Today, 1985)
Mariners, Renegades and Castaways: The Story of Herman Melville and the World we Live in (USA: 1953; Berwick, Detroit, Mich., USA: Berwick Editions, 1978)
Facing Reality (USA: Correspondence Publishing Company, 1958; Berwick, Detroit, Mich., USA: Berwick Editions, 1974)
Beyond a Boundary (London: Stanley Paul Hutchinson, 1963)
The Future in the Present: Selected Writings, intro. by Margaret Busby (London: Allison & Busby, 1977)
Spheres of Existence: Selected Writings, intro. by Margaret Busby (London: Allison & Busby, 1980)
At the Rendezvous of Victory: Selected Writings intro. by Margaret Busby (London: Allison & Busby, 1984)
JAMES, Louis, *Fiction for the Working Man: 1830–1850* (London: OUP, 1963)
ed., *The Islands in Between: Essays on West Indian Literature* (London: OUP, 1968), intro. by Louis James, pp 1–49
JOHN, Gus, commentary in Derek Humphry, *Police Power and Black People* (London: Panther, 1972), pp 209–239
Race in the Inner City (London: Runnymede Trust, 1971)
JOHNSON, Linton Kwesi, *Voices of the Living and the Dead* (London: Race Today, 1974)
Dread Beat and Blood, intro. by Andrew Salkey (London: Bogle-L'Ouverture, 1975)
Inglan is a Bitch (London: Race Today, 1980)
Tings and Times (Newcastle: Bloodaxe, 1992)
JONES Evan, *Protector of the Indians: A Life of Bartolomé de Las Casas* (London & Harlow: Longman, 1973)
et al, *Junior Language Arts for the Caribbean: A Five-Year Course (Trinidad/Jamaica/London: Longman Caribbean, 1978–82)*
Tales of the Caribbean Books 1–4 (Aylesbury: Ginn, 1984)
KHAN, Naseem, *The Arts Britain Ignores: The Arts of Ethnic Minorities in Britain* (London: Arts Council, Gulbenkian Foundation & Community Relations Commission, 1976)
LA FORTUNE, Knolly, *Moments of Inspiration* (Port of Spain, Trinidad: Guardian Printery, 1947)
Legend of T-Marie (London, privately printed, 1968)
The Schoolmaster Remembers (London, privately printed, 1979)
LAMMING, George, *In the Castle of My Skin* (London: Michael Joseph, 1953; Longman, 1970)
The Emigrants (London: Michael Joseph, 1954)
Of Age and Innocence (London: Michael Joseph, 1958)
Season of Adventure (London: Michael Joseph, 1960)
The Pleasures of Exile (London: Michael Joseph, 1960)
Water with Berries (London: Longman, 1971)
Natives of My Person (London: Longman, 1972) – 'Politics and Culture' in K. Drayton & G. Lamming, *The Most Important People* (Bridgetown: Cedar Press, 1981)
LA ROSE, Antony (John), *Foundations: a book of poems* (London/Port of Spain: New Beacon, 1966)
ed., *New Beacon Reviews: Collection One*, 1968
ed., *New Beacon Review: Number One*, July 1985
ed., *New Beacon Review: Numbers 2/3*, November 1986
and Raymond Quevedo, *Kaiso: A Review* (St Augustine, Trinidad: Extra Mural Department, UWI, 1983)
LA ROSE, John, Tribute Committee, ed., *Foundations of a Movement: A Tribute to John La Rose on the occasion of the 10th International Book Fair of Radical Black and Third World Books* (London: John La Rose Tribute Committee, 1991) See contributions by Winston Best, pp 12–19; Kamau Brathwaite, pp

20–23; Aggrey Burke, pp 25–31; Matthew Butler, pp 32–33; Femi Fatoba, pp 40–41; Stanley French, pp 43–44; Wilson Harris, pp 65–66, Louis James, p 72; Gus John, pp 73–79; Linton Kwesi Johnson, pp 80–82; Christopher Laird, pp 101–103; Errol Lloyd, pp 104–107; Archie Markham, pp 113–116; Adrian Mitchell, 119–120; Andrew Salkey, pp 155–157; Pedro Perez Sarduy, pp 159–160; Anne Walmsley, pp 169–180; John Wickham, p 188.

LEWIS, Maureen Warner, *Notes to Masks* (Benin City, Nigeria: Ethiope, 1977)

Guinea's Other Suns: the African Dynamic in Trinidad Culture (Dover, Mass.: Majority Press, 1991)

LLOYD, Errol, 'Introduction: an historical perspective', in catalogue for *Caribbean Expressions in Britain – An Exhibition of Contemporary Art*, Leicestershire Museum and Art Gallery, 16 August-28 September 1986, reprinted *Artrage* No 15, Winter 1986.

LOOK LAI, Wally, 'The Road to Thornfield Hall: An analysis of Jean Rhys's novel *Wide Sargasso Sea*', *New Beacon Reviews*, ed. by John La Rose, Collection One, 1968, pp 38–52

MARKHAM, E.A., *Human Rites: Selected Poems 1970–1982* (London: Anvil Press, 1984)

ed., *Hinterland: Caribbean Poetry from the West Indies and Britain* (Newcastle-upon-Tyne: Bloodaxe, 1989)

MATHURIN MAIR, Lucille, *The Rebel Woman in the British West Indies during Slavery* (Kingston: Institute of Jamaica for African-Caribbean Publications, 1975)

'Recollections of a Journey into a Rebel Past', in *Caribbean Women Writers: Essays from the First International Conference*, ed. Selwyn R. Cudjoe (Wellesley, Mass.: Calaloux Publications, 1990), pp 51–60

MATTHEWS, Marc, *Guyana My Altar: Poetry*, preface by Edward Kamau Brathwaite (London: Karnak House, 1987)

MAXWELL, Marina Ama Omowale, *About our own Business* (Trinidad: Drum Mountain, 1981)

McDONALD, Ian, *The Hummingbird Tree*, intro. by Gordon Rohlehr (London: HEB, 1969; 1974)

MOORE, Gerald, *The Chosen Tongue: English Writing in the Tropical World* (London: Longman, 1969)

MORRIS, Mervyn, ed., *Seven Jamaican Poets* (Kingston: Bolivar, 1971)

The Pond: A Book of Poems (London/Port of Spain: New Beacon, 1973

Shadowboxing: Poems (London/Port of Spain: New Beacon, 1979)

and Pamela Mordecai, eds, *Jamaica Woman: An Anthology of Poems* (Kingston/Port of Spain: Heinemann, 1980

ed., *The Faber Book of Contemporary Caribbean Short Stories* (London: Faber, 1990)

NETTLEFORD, Rex M., *Mirror, Mirror: Identity, Race and Protest in Jamaica* (Kingston: Collins & Sangster, 1970)

Dance Jamaica: Cultural Definition and Artistic Discovery. The National Dance Theatre Company of Jamaica, 1962–1983, foreword by Edward Kamau Brathwaite (New York: Grove Press, 1985)

NGUGĨ WA THIONG'O, *Homecoming: Essays on African and Caribbean Literature, Culture and Politics* (London: Heinemann, 1972)

PATTERSON, H. Orlando, *The Children of Sisyphus* (London: Hutchinson New Authors, 1964; Longman, 1982, 1986)

The Sociology of Slavery: An Analysis of the Origins, Development and Structure of Negro Slavery Society in Jamaica (London: MacGibbon & Kee, 1967)

An Absence of Ruins (London: Hutchinson, 1967)

Die the Long Day (New York: Morrow, 1971)

Slavery and Social Death: A Comparative Study (Cambridge, Mass./London: Harvard, 1982)

PATTERSON, Patricia and James Carnegie, *The People Who Came, Book 2: Longman Secondary School Histories for the Caribbean*, Series Editor: Edward Brathwaite (Kingston/Port of Spain/London: Longman Caribbean, 1970)

RAMCHAND, Kenneth, ed., *West Indian Narrative: An Introductory Anthology* (London: Nelson, 1966; revised edn 1980)

The West Indian Novel and its Background (London: Faber, 1970; new edn, Heinemann, 1983)
An Introduction to the Study of West Indian Literature (London: Nelson, 1976)
and Cecil Gray, eds, *West Indian Poetry: an Anthology for Schools* (Harlow/Trinidad/Jamaica: Longman Caribbean, 1971; new edn 1989)
Best West Indian Stories (Walton-on-Thames: Nelson, 1982)
ROHLEHR, Gordon, *Pathfinder: Black Awakening in 'The Arrivants' of Edward Kamau Brathwaite* (Tunapuna, Trinidad: Gordon Rohlehr, 1981)
Calypso and Society in Pre-Independence Trinidad (Port of Spain: Gordon Rohlehr, 1990)
SAAKANA, Amon Saba, (as Sebastian Clarke) ed., *New Planet: Anthology of Modern Caribbean Writing* (London: Karnak House, 1978)
and Adetokunbo Pearse, eds, *Towards the Decolonization of the British Educational System* (London: Frontline Journal/Karnak House, 1986)
The Colonial Legacy in Caribbean Literature Vol I, preface by Ngũgĩ wa Thiong'o (London: Karnak House, 1987)
SALKEY, Andrew, *A Quality of Violence* (London: Hutchinson New Authors, 1959; New Beacon, 1978)
ed., *West Indian Stories*, (London: Faber, 1960)
Escape to an Autumn Pavement (London: Hutchinson New Authors, 1960)
Hurricane (London: OUP, 1965; Penguin Puffin, 1980)
ed., *Stories from the Caribbean: an Anthology* (London: Elek, 1965)
Drought (London: OUP, 1966)
Riot (London: OUP, 1967)
ed., *Caribbean Prose*, (London: Evans, 1967)
The Late Emancipation of Jerry Stover (London: Hutchinson, 1968; Longman, 1982)
The Adventures of Catullus Kelly (London: Hutchinson, 1969)
Jonah Simpson (London: OUP, 1969)
Havana Journal (Harmondsworth: Penguin, 1971)
ed., *Breaklight: An Anthology of Caribbean Poetry*, (London: Hamish Hamilton, 1971; New York: Doubleday, 1972)
Georgetown Journal (London/Port of Spain: New Beacon, 1972)
ed., *Caribbean Essays: An Anthology*, (London: Evans, 1972)
Jamaica (London: Hutchinson, 1973; Bogle-L'Ouverture, 1983)
Anancy's Score (London: Bogle-L'Ouverture, 1973)
Come Home, Malcolm Heartland (London: Hutchinson, 1976)
ed., *Writing in Cuba since the Revolution: an Anthology of Poems, Short Stories and Essays* (London: Bogle-L'Ouverture, 1977)
In the Hills where Her Dreams Live (Havana: Casa de las Americas, 1979; California: Black Scholar Press, 1981)
Away (London: Allison & Busby, 1980)
Joey Tyson (London: Bogle-L'Ouverture, 1980)
Danny Jones (London: Bogle-L'Ouverture, 1980)
SELVON, Samuel, *A Brighter Sun* (London: Allan Wingate, 1952; Longman, 1971)
An Island is a World (London: Allan Wingate, 1955)
The Lonely Londoners (London: Alan Wingate, 1956; Longman, 1972)
Ways of Sunlight (London: MacGibbon and Kee, 1957; Longman, 1973)
Turn Again Tiger (London: MacGibbon and Kee, 1958)
I Hear Thunder (London: MacGibbon and Kee, 1963)
The Housing Lark (London: MacGibbon and Kee, 1965)
Moses Ascending (London: Davis-Poynter, 1972)
SMALL, Richard, 'Introduction', in Walter Rodney, *The Groundings with my Brothers* (London: Bogle-L'Ouverture, 1969), pp 7–11
TAJFEL, Henri & John L. Dawson, eds., *Disappointed Guests: Essays by African, Asian and West Indian Students* (Oxford: OUP, for the IRR, 1965). See contributions by Mervyn Morris, pp 5–26; Kenneth Ramchand, pp 27–37; Elliott Bastien, pp 38–54
VAN SERTIMA, Ivan, *Caribbean Writers: Critical Essays* (London/Port of Spain: New Beacon, 1968)
They Came Before Columbus: The African Presence in Ancient America (New York, Random House: 1976)

WALMSLEY, Anne, ed., *The Sun's Eye: West Indian Writing for Young Readers* (London: Longman, 1968; new edn 1989)
and Nick Caistor, eds, *Facing the Sea: A New Anthology from the Caribbean Region*, preface by Edward Kamau Brathwaite (London: HEB, 1986)
'Charting New Directions: Caribbean Literary Journals and Creative Change – *Savacou*, Journal of the Caribbean Artists Movement', in *Aspects of Commonwealth Literature*, Vol I, Collected Seminar Papers No 39 (University of London, Institute of Commonwealth Studies, 1990), pp 127–139
ed., *Guyana Dreaming: The Art of Aubrey Williams* (Aarhus, Denmark:Dangaroo, 1990)
WILSON, Betty and Pamela Mordecai, *Her True-True Name: An Anthology of Women's Writing from the Caribbean* (Oxford: HEB, 1989)
WILSON, Donald, ed., *New Ships: An Anthology of West Indian Poems for Junior Secondary Schools* (Kingston: Savacou, 1971; London: OUP, 1975)
WILLIAMSON, Karina, *Voyages in the Dark: Jean Rhys and Phyllis Shand Allfrey*, Occasional Papers in Caribbean Studies No 4 (Coventry: University of Warwick Centre for Caribbean Studies, 1987)
WOOD, Donald, 'John Jacob Thomas: A brief biography', in J.J. Thomas, *Froudacity: West Indian Fables Explained* (London/Port of Spain: New Beacon, 1969)
Trinidad in Transition (Oxford: OUP, 1968)

Select discography

Records and cassettes of poetry written and spoken by, or collected by, CAM people

BERRY, James and Alistair Bamford, eds, *Bluefoot Cassettes* (London: British Library National Sound Archive, 1990, contributors include James Berry, EA Markham, Linton Kwesi Johnson.
Isn't My Name Magical? Poems for Children (BBC/Longman Listening and Reading Cassettes)
BRATHWAITE, Edward Kamau, contributor to *The Poet Speaks*. Record Ten, ed. by Peter Orr (London: Argo, 1968)
Rights of Passage (London: Argo, 1969)
contributor to *Poetry International '69*, recorded at the Queen Elizabeth Hall, London, 1969, ed. by Peter Orr (London: Argo, 1970)
contributor to *Poets of the West Indies reading their own works*, ed. by John Figueroa (New York: Caedmon Records, 1971)
Masks (London: Argo, 1972)
Islands (London: Argo, 1973)
Palabra de esta America: Poemas (Havana, Cuba: Casa de las Americas, 1976)
Edward Kamau Brathwaite's Mother Poem, a reading and discussion recorded at Annual Conference of the Association of Teachers of Caribbean and African Literature, University of Warwick, 1980 (London: ATCAL, 1980)
Atumpan, intro. by Carolivia Herron (Washington, D.C.: Watershed Foundation, 1990)
JOHNSON, Linton Kwesi, *Dread Beat and Blood and Poet and the Roots* (London: Virgin Records, 1978)
Forces of Victory (London: Island Records, 1979)
Want Fi Goh Rave (London: Island Records, 1979)
Bass Culture (London: Island Records, 1980)
Di Black Betty Booshwah (London: Island Records, 1980)
LKJ in Dub (London: Island Records, 1980)
Making History (London: Island Records, 1983)
Reggae Greats (London: Island Records, 1985)
Linton Kwesi Johnson in Concert with the Dub Band, recorded at the Queen Elizabeth Hall, London, 1984 (London: LKJ Records Production, 1986)
Tings and Times (London: Sterns Records, 1991)
LA ROSE, John and Linton Kwesi Johnson, eds, *An Evening of International Poetry* (London: Alliance Records, 1983), contributors include James Berry, Linton Kwesi Johnson, EA Markham, Pedro Perez Sarduy.
MATTHEWS, Marc, *Marc-Up: Marc Matthews and Friends* (Prospect, St James, Barbados; Theatre Information Exchange, 1978), contributors include Ken Corsbie, Marc Matthews.

Index

Aarons, RLC, 166
Abeng, 197, 262
Abrahams, Peter, 139
Abrams, Oscar, 144, 290, 297
Adams, Sir Grantley, 111
Adams, Richard N, 220
Adelphi Theatre, 13
Africa Centre, 13, 32, 125
Africa Unity House, 27–8
African and Caribbean Social and Cultural Centre, 6–7
African Studies Association of the West Indies (ASAWI), 209, 269
African Youth Move, 197
Afro-Cubanism, *see* Negrismo
Agard, John, 253, 280
Akar, John, 234
Alan Wingate Ltd, 9
Albertina Sylvester Supplementary School, 249
Ali, Jamal, 298, 302
Alex Pascall Singers, 33
All Ah We, 280
Allfrey, Phyllis Shand, 110, 125
All Nations Club, Hackney, 92
Amoako, Kwabena, 109, 124, 153, 159, 169
Amnesty International, 146
Andrade, Carrera, 108
Andre Deutsch Ltd, 30, 44, 91, 113–4
Anouilh, Jean, 140
Anthony, Michael, 10, 30, 44, 53, 65–8, 75–6, 78, 85, 90–1, 96, 101–4, 113, 145, 204, 215, 260, 274, 295, 318
Arcade Gallery, 7
Archer Gallery, 16
Architectural Association School, 18
Argo Record Company, 127, 239
Armstrong, Louis, 134
Artrage, 316
Art Teachers' Movement, Trinidad, 18
Arts Council, 49, 54, 62, 80, 95, 124, 159
Arts Lab, Drury Lane, 59, 239
Arts Review, 17
Association for Commonwealth Literature and Language Studies (ACLALS) 259–61, 263, 266, 292
Association for the Teaching of Caribbean African and Asian Literature (ATCAL), 320
Athill, Diana, 44, 112–3
Attila the Hun (Raymond Quevedo), 70
Augier, Roy, 260
Austen, Jane, 46, 69
Avery Hill College of Education, 80
Awoonor, Kofi (Awoonor-Williams), 152–3, 252

Baker, Peta-Anne, 281
Ballagas, Emilio, 312
Ballet Nègre, 4
Banyan Ltd, Trinidad and Tobago, 316
Barbados Advocate, 94, 110
Barbados Arts Council, 125, 140
Barbados National Theatre Workshop, 140
Barker, JS, 112
Barn Theatre, Kingston, 140, 198, 208, 297
Barrett, Lindsay (Esoghene), 126, 196, 244, 301, 318
Bart-Williams, Gaston, 252
Basement Theatre, Trinidad, 117, 140
Bastien, Althea, 285
Bastien, Elliott, 157, 295
Baugh, Edward, 196, 206
Beacon, The, 9, 33, 36, 38, 102, 275
Beckford, George, 39, 42, 195, 268
Beckles, W, 199
Bellay, Deputé, 84
Benn, Winston, 29, 135, 150–2, 230
Bennett, Louise, 60, 68, 87, 105–6, 139, 207, 219, 261, 267, 310
Berry, James, 4, 5, 7, 153, 159, 169, 181, 224–5, 256, 261, 266, 282, 288–91, 295, 298, 300, 303, 306, 316–7, 319, 321
Best, Lloyd, 194, 202, 218, 248, 264
Best, Winston, 119, 230, 249
Betaudier, Patrick, 158, 179
Bim, 9–10, 19, 42, 46, 53, 55–6, 111, 139, 210, 281
Bishop, Pat, 201
Bishop's High School, Georgetown, 39
Black Arts Dance Company, 250
Black Arts Movement, USA, 313–4
Black Arts Workshop, 250
Blackburn, Robin, 231
Black Dimensions, 244
Black House, The, 258
Black Panther Movement, 155, 294, 298
Black Parents Movement, 303
Black Unity and Freedom Party, 155
Black Youth Movement, 303
Blair, Ray, 293
Blake, William, 177
Bloom, Valerie, 320
Bogle-L'Ouverture Publications, 156, 250, 267–8, 286, 295–6, 301, 303, 321
Bolton, Felicity, 159, 185, 229
Bongo Man, 197, 262
Bookers McConnell, 48, 50
Bowen, Denis, 16–7
Bowen, Donald, 284–5
Bowling, Frank, 32, 50, 80, 182
Branch, Winston, 29, 176, 230, 239, 285, 317
Brandeis University, Massachussetts, USA, 233
Braithwaite, ER, 131, 212
Brathwaite, Doris Monica (Wellcome), 34, 39–43, 49, 51, 54, 57–8, 89, 129–30, 143, 152, 155, 157, 159, 171, 185, 188, 190, 193, 195, 211, 216, 218, 223, 252, 254, 268, 274, 282–3, 289, 307–8
Brathwaite, Edward Kamau, 1, 10, 19–20, 34–5, 39–43, 46–76, 78–80, 83, 86, 88–91, 93–5, 97, 105–15, 119–31, 133–5, 137, 139–43, 147–51, 153–7, 159–62, 164–5, 167–72, 174, 180, 182–5, 188–91, 193–8, 200, 202, 204, 207–23, 225–6,

228–9, 231, 239, 241–7, 252, 254, 256, 260–4, 266–70, 272, 274, 277–9, 281–6, 289, 292–5, 298, 300–10, 313, 317–9, 321–2
Brathwaite, Lloyd, 275
Breton, André, 314
Brewster, Yvonne (Jones), 140, 297, 302, 307
Brierre, Jean, 37
Bristol Old Vic School, 13
British Broadcasting Corporation (BBC), 5–7, 9–13, 15, 28, 36, 43, 45, 47, 50, 61, 91, 103, 112–4, 165, 224, 234, 237, 286, 301, 306
British Caribbean Association (BCA), 159, 228–30, 306
British Council, 13, 19–20, 48, 95, 127
British Guiana Chronicle, see Guyana Chronicle
British Museum, 2, 45, 90
Brixton Technical College, 29, 154
Brixton Village, 320
Brodber, Erna, 303, 318
Broodhagen, Karl, 18, 150
Brooks, Cedric, 267
Brotherston, Gordon, 143
Brouard, Carl, 312
Brown, Claude, 250
Brown, Rap, 136
Brown, Wayne, 139, 261
Brutus, Dennis, 152–3, 252
Bryden, Ronald, 62
Buhle, Paul, 23
Burgess, Anthony, 174
Burnham, Forbes, 15, 24, 212
Burnett, Mackie, 267
Burrowes, ER, 14–5
Burton, Gary, 241, 243, 245, 249
Bustamante, Sir Alexander, 81
Byron, George Gordon, Lord, 230

Cadenas, Rafael, 37
Callender, Timothy, 139, 261
Calling the West Indies, 6–7
Cambridge University, 1, 10, 19, 35, 39, 42, 48
Camden Arts Centre, 290–1
Campaign Against Racial Discrimination (CARD), 27, 45, 91, 257, 290
Campbell, Clifton, 29, 87, 97, 99–101, 108–9, 123, 135, 150–2, 182, 194, 259
Campbell, Theo, 22
Campion College, Kingston (St Peter and St Paul), 208
Camus, Albert, 51
Carew, Jan, 11, 17, 30, 32, 152, 212, 216, 244, 295
Caribbean Commission Library, Port of Spain, 36
Caribbean Educational Association, Caribbean Educational and Community Workers Association (CECWA) 6, 247, 249, 252, 257, 294–5
Caribbean Quarterly, 42, 69, 99, 222
Caribbean Students Performing Group, 33, 158
Caribbean Voices, 5–6, 9–15, 19–21, 30, 34, 36, 42–4, 46, 50, 103, 114, 131, 165
Caribbean Writers and Artists Conference, 212
Caribbean Writers and Artists Convention, 212, 216–7, 253–6, 271, 306
Carifesta (Caribbean Festival of Arts), 216, 253–5, 259, 271–9, 280, 282, 307, 316
Carmichael, Stokely (Kwame Ture), 91–3, 119, 126, 136, 147, 164, 187, 220, 227
Carnegie, James, 207, 261
Carrena, Mercian Omodeinde, 316
Carpentier, Alejo, 110, 132, 157, 204, 257, 312–3, 321
Carter, Martin, 24–5, 109, 185, 240, 253, 255, 261, 272, 276
Cartey, Wilfred (Fred), 41, 86, 204
Casson, Sir Hugh, 18
Castro, Fidel, 143–4, 146
Cattouse, Nadia, 13
Central London Polytechnic, 5
Central Office of Information, 26, 162
Central School of Art, 58, 287
Centre of Contemporary Art, Kingston, 322
Centre for Contemporary Cultural Studies, Birmingham, 157, 162
Césaire, Aimé, 37, 85, 102, 109, 131–2, 137–9, 157–8, 167–8, 179, 182, 236, 238–9, 246, 257, 278, 312–4, 321
Chamberlain, Joseph, 245
Chang, Carlisle, 135
Chang, Victor, 320
Charles, Faustin, 29, 33, 51, 71–2, 83, 153, 157, 236, 250, 295, 298, 317
Chataway, Chris, 229
Chaucer, Geoffrey, 69
Chevannes, Barry, 219
Chin a Foeng, 278
Chorale de Francois, Martinique, 273
Chung, Denis Stafford, 250
Civil Rights Movement, 91, 313
Clarke, Austin C, 152
Clarke, Edith, 29
Clarke, Oliver, 29, 34, 87, 119, 126, 128–9, 151, 159, 185, 205, 223, 252, 306
Clarke, Sebastian, *see* Amon Saba Sakaana
Clark, John Pepper, 252
Cleverdon, Douglas, 61
Coard, Bernard, 294
Cohen, JM, 110
Coleridge, Samuel Taylor, 230
College of Arts, Science and Technology, Kingston, 190
Collins, Merle, 318
Collymore, Frank, 9, 60, 84, 139, 165, 210, 281
Columbia University, 86
Columbus, 100, 245
Commission for Racial Equality (CRE), 20
Commonwealth Arts Festival, 32, 60, 169
Commonwealth Biennale of Abstract Art, 32
Commonwealth Immigrants Act (1962), 26–8, (1968), 135
Commonwealth Immigration Act, 26, 300
Commonwealth Institute, 31–3, 115, 125, 152, 284–6

Compton, Jacques, 33, 239, 250
Comrie, Locksley, 29, 123, 154–6, 159, 164–5, 167, 172, 178, 183–5, 188–9, 227–9, 232, 236–7, 245, 251, 293
Congress of Black Writers, 191, 227
Congress on the Dialectics of Liberation, 91–2
Connor, Edric, 5, 18, 27, 32–3, 117
Connor, Pearl (Nunez Mogotsi), 5–7, 13, 18, 27, 32–3, 37, 61–2, 117, 153, 307, 316
Conrad, Joseph, 28, 276
Constantine, Sir Learie, 2
Contemporary Jamaican Artists Association, 219
Contemporary 12, 270
Coombs, Owen, 285
Cooper, Carolyn, 320
Co-operative Hall, Seven Sisters Road, 292, 294, 298, 309
Corsbie, Ken, 29, 119, 211–2, 280
Count Ossie, 267–8
Count Prince Miller, 302
Craig, Christine, 58, 259, 282, 317
Craig, Karl 'Jerry', 29, 58, 63, 80–1, 83, 87, 123, 127, 135, 142, 150–2, 179–80, 189, 223, 228–9, 232, 257, 259, 267, 274, 285, 296, 305, 318–9
Craig, Dennis, 261
Craig, Susan, 71
Crawford, Jeff, 156, 248
Creation for Liberation (CFL), 316, 319
Creative Arts Centre (CAC), UWI, Mona, Jamaica, 139, 218–9, 222, 259, 268–9
Critchlow, Frank, 258
Critchlow Labour College, Georgetown, 277
Critical Quarterly, 95
Cross, Thom, 269
Crosdale, Milton, 130
Croskill, Daryl, 140
Cuban Revolution, 143–50, 313
Cullen, Countee, 311, 313
Cultural Centre, Georgetown, 273
Cultural Congress of Havana, 74, 132, 137–8, 143–50, 153, 233, 308
Cultural Training Centre, Kingston, 269
Currey, James, 95, 112–3, 124
Currey, RN, 113

D'Andrade, 252
D'Aguiar, Fred, 320
Daily Telegraph, 110
Dalton, Eric, 158, 181, 185
Damas, Léon, 157, 232, 236–7, 243, 312–3, 321
Darbeau, Dave (Khafra Kambon), 211, 217–8
Dark and Light Theatre Company, Brixton, 288
Dash, Paul, 29, 159, 182, 230, 283–6, 289, 318
Dathorne, OR, 216
Davidson, John, 159
Davidson, RB, 238
Defoe, Daniel, 246
De Lisser, Herbert G, 104
Dem Two, 280
Dennison, Daphne, 285
Dépestre, René, 137, 227, 238
Derry, Art, 17–8, 80, 87, 90, 109, 123, 150–2, 229, 285, 318–9
Desnoes, Edmundo, 74, 137
De Vries, Erwin, 270
De Wynter, 15
Dickens, Charles, 22
Digby Stuart College of Education, 135
Dillons Bookshop, 90, 91, 159
Diop, David, 252
Dizzy, Ras, 262, 265
Dobru (Ravales), Robin, 278
Doiley, June C, 250
Dolphin, Celeste, 271
Dolphin, Lynette, 253, 255, 271, 273
Dominica, The Star of, 110, 125
Dostoevsky, Fyodor Mikhail, 149
Du Bois, WEB, 136, 227
Dumas, Alexandre, 85
Duvalier, 'Papa Doc', 133
Durrant, Faye, 204
Drayton, Arthur, 205
Dylan, Bob, 182

Edwards, Adolph, 61
Egbuna, Obi, 32, 125, 156
Egonu, Uzo, 31, 316
Eliot, TS, 56
Enquiry, 111
Evans Brothers, 91, 158, 181
Evora, Tony, 239
Expo 67, 109
Expression, 253

Faber & Faber Ltd, 30, 44, 65, 75, 91, 95, 105
Fanon, Frantz, 52, 66, 92, 182, 197, 199, 314
F B A Galleries, 152
Faraday Hall, 293
Fatoba, Femi, 239, 250, 252, 289–90, 316
Fernandez, Pablo Armando, 60, 74, 137
FESTAC, 316
Festival of Britain, 37
Festival of Negro Arts, Dakar, 32, 51, 168
Figueroa, John, 12, 34, 60, 261
Figueroa, Peter, 34, 71–2, 87, 109, 130, 153, 176
Focus, 9
Ford-Smith, Honor, 269
Forster, EM, 65
Forum Quarterly, 9
Franco, Jean, 131–4, 142, 307
Fraser, Peter, 29, 250, 316, 321
Free University Press, 192
French, Stanley, 116–8, 197–8
French Revolution, 84
Friends' House, Euston Road, 125
Froude, JA, 212–3
Full House, 301, 306
Furé, Rogelio Martinez, 138

Gallery, The, Kingston, 219
Gallery Barrington, Kingston, 270
Garden Theatre, Kingston, 268

Garlake, Margaret, 16
Garvey, Amy Ashwood, 20, 156
Garvey, Marcus, 20, 84, 102, 153, 156, 184, 199, 227, 302, 313, 315
Gayelle, 316
Genet, Jean, 208
George Padmore Supplementary School (George Padmore Community School), 249, 303
Gerald, Carolyn F, 249
Gibbons, Rawle, 269, 280
Giglioli, George, 288
Gilkes, Michael, 160
Gill, Edmund, 135, 159, 179, 181
Giovanni, Nikki, 249
Girvan, Norman, 39, 42, 192, 195
Glasgow Herald, 3
Golding, William, 45
Goldsmiths College, 181
Gonzalez, Anson, 264
Gonzalez, Ralph, 191–2
Goodison, Lorna, 22, 281–2, 319
Goulbourne, Jean, 281
Goulbourne, Harry, 302
Goveia, Elsa, 4, 39, 86, 97–9, 101–4, 106, 108, 111–3, 116, 118, 120–1, 123, 135, 141, 149, 158, 161, 196, 203–5, 215, 236, 244–5, 254, 307, 310, 321
Grabowski Gallery, 32
Granger, Geddes (Makandal Daaga), 217–8
Gray, Cecil, 193, 261, 267
Greenwich Theatre, 208
Greaves, Stanley, 273
Green, Earl, 245
Gregory, Colin, 208
Guardian, The (Manchester), 3, 131, 299
Guevara, Che, 146, 199, 231
Guillén, Nicolás, 37, 131–2, 261, 297, 312–3, 321
Guyana Graphic, 212, 217
Guyana Chronicle, 9, 95

Hall, Douglas, 98, 143, 147, 152, 192, 321
Hall, Ian, 273
Hall, Stuart, 10, 20, 157–9, 162–5, 167–8, 176, 298, 308
Hamilton, Norma Fay, 139, 193
Hamish Hamilton, 295
Hammersmith College of Art and Design, 29
Hammersmith Galleries, 17
Hampshire College, Amherst, Massachusetts, 302
Hansbury, Lorraine, 13
Hamambee Theatre, Kingston, 269
Harlem Renaissance, 4, 57, 104–5, 311–4
Harper Wills, Doris, 29, 109, 271, 274, 278, 307
Harris, Margaret (Burns), 26
Harris, Wilson, 24–6, 30, 33, 38, 43–5, 47, 62–8, 72–4, 85, 90, 95, 102, 106, 137, 152, 157–8, 160–1, 165–6, 171–6, 177–8, 180, 185–6, 188–9, 196, 211–6, 221–2, 230, 232, 239–40, 244, 253, 272, 276–7, 295, 304–5, 309–10, 313, 318, 320, 322
Harrison College, Barbados, 10, 19
Hasfal, Frank, 268–9, 296
Hawkins, Coleman Randolph, 19
Haynes, Antony, 19, 48–51
Haynes, Jim, 58–9
Hearne, John, 11, 30, 75, 77–9, 139–40, 152, 161, 174, 193, 261, 272
Heartman, Ras Daniel, 296
Heath, Roy AK, 271, 299
Heinemann Educational Books (HEB), 91, 95, 112–3, 124, 237
Helps, Althea, 296
Hendriks, AL (Micky), 261
Henriques, Pauline, 60
Henry, Roy, 127–8, 159
Herbert, George, 177
Hernton, Calvin, 62, 109, 152–3, 156, 158, 249, 313
Hill, Errol, 13, 41, 158
Hill, Robert (Bobby), 137, 193, 227, 302
Hill, Sheila, 198
Hinds, Donald, 21, 79, 202, 224–6, 237–8, 250, 252, 256, 282, 288–91, 298, 300, 306
Hines, Jack, 241, 245, 247, 249
Hockney, David, 286
Hodge, Merle, 232, 236–7, 239, 241, 243, 281
Holder, Ram John, 32, 115–7, 119, 234, 236
Hornsey College of Art, 17
Howard University, Washington DC, 91
Howe, Darcus, 294, 316
Hug, Tony, 249
Huggins, Nathan, 311
Hughes, Langston, 1, 115, 249, 311, 313
Huntley, Eric, 24, 99, 156
Huntley, Jessica, 24, 156, 250, 286, 289, 296, 303, 307
Hurston, Zora Neale, 311
Hussey, Dermot, 125
Hustler, The, 115, 159, 188
Hutchinson, Alfred, 284
Hutchinson & Co Ltd, 191
Hyde, Eugene, 219, 220
Hynam, Winston (Pony) K, 20, 86, 123, 284

Ideal Home Exhibition, 81
Immigration Act (1971), 300
Indigéniste Movement, Haiti, 312–4
Institute of Race Relations (IRR), 257, 301
Institute of Social and Economic Research, UWI, 109, 194
International African Institute, 84
International Book Fair of Radical, Black and Third World Books, 303, 316, 322
International Festival of Poetry (Poetry International), 60, 239
Institute of Contemporary Art (ICA), 80, 125, 15–4
Institute of Jamaica, 14, 112
Invader Steel Band, 72
Ionesco, Eugene, 140
Irish, JG (James), 204, 205, 218
Ishmail, Ibrahim Ibn, 152–3
Ismond, Patricia, 320

Is We, 280
Itabo, 117
Ital, 262

Jackson, Carl, 303
Jagan, Cheddi, 15, 24, 111, 239, 240
Jamaica Broadcasting Corporation (JBC), 208
Jamaica Gleaner, 9, 31, 95, 140, 192–3, 208, 268–9
Jamaica Journal, 140, 270
Jamaica National Dance Theatre Company (JNDTC), 198, 293, 322
Jamaica Playhouse, Kingston, 140, 198
Jamaica School of Art, 268, 319
James, Canute, 301
James, CLR, 1–2, 22, 26–7, 33–4, 41, 51, 61, 81, 83–6, 91, 93, 96, 98, 101–4, 107, 109, 113, 125, 134, 127–38, 144–7, 153, 204, 213, 215, 227, 232, 246, 250, 274–5, 321
James, Louis, 41–2, 49, 51, 54–5, 58, 61, 63–4, 66, 83, 86–7, 89, 96, 104–8, 110–1, 119–20, 122, 124, 126–7, 129–30, 142–3, 159, 161, 168, 183, 204, 223, 225, 231, 260, 286, 320–1
James, Horace, 13, 97, 108, 125, 128, 250
James, Selma, 23, 61, 84
Jeanetta Cochrane Theatre, Holborn (Cochrane Theatre), 58–9, 61
Jeffreys, Lionel, 26
Jegede, Emmanuel, 297
Jerry, Bongo (Robin Small), 227–8, 237, 262–3, 265, 276, 282, 302, 317
John, Augustine (Gus), 155, 241, 247, 249, 301
John, Errol, 13, 60
John, Frank (Nkemka Asika), 244, 299
John Peartree Gallery, Kingston, 220
Johnson, Millard, 6
Johnson, Linton Kwesi, 29, 297–8, 302, 314, 316–7, 319
Jones, Althea Lecointe, 294
Jones, Bridget, 51, 282
Jones, Claudia, 20–2, 27, 34, 45, 237
Jones, Evan, 14, 50–1, 60, 63, 86, 115–9, 157–8, 166, 223–4, 295, 302
Jones, Le Roi (Amiri Baraka), 313
Jonson, Bari (Barrington Johnson), 4, 13, 33, 87, 97–8, 108–9, 125, 127, 184, 208, 223, 250

Kabaka of Buganda, 6
Kaie, 271, 274
Kairi, 259, 280
Kairi House, 259, 280, 210, 316
Kalipha, Stephen, 230
Karenga, Ron, 250
Kayiga, Kofi (Ricardo Wilkins), 285
Keane, E McG (Shake), 33, 109, 297
Keens-Douglas, Paul, 280
Kennedy, John F (Jack), 147, 190
Kelshall, Jack, 14
Kenyatta, Jomo, 7
Keskidee Centre, 290, 296–8, 300, 309
Khan, Naseem, 159, 176, 316
King, Audvil, 262–3, 268, 282, 296, 317
King, Bryan, 19, 47–8, 80, 84, 86, 179, 187, 232
King, Lloyd, 202, 205
King, Martin Luther, 27–8, 45, 136, 143, 146–7, 152–3, 155
Kingsley, Charles, 103
Kingston Chorale, St Vincent, 273
Kipling, Rudyard, 92
Kizerman, Rudolph, 230, 299
Kustow, Michael, 153–4
Kwayana, Eusi (Sydney King), 240
Kyk-over-al, 9, 25, 42, 53, 253, 271

La Fortune, Knolly, 18, 27, 33, 98, 109, 133, 135, 158, 176, 295–6, 308
Laird, Christopher, 29, 68, 126, 176–9, 188, 225–6, 230–1, 256, 259, 280, 283, 289, 298, 316
Laird, Judith (McEachrane), 29, 176, 226, 259, 280, 290, 298, 316
Lamming, George, 9, 11, 18–9, 21, 30, 33, 45, 47, 56, 60, 67, 75, 85, 95, 97–8, 107–9, 112, 114, 137, 139, 152, 161, 165, 172, 196, 212, 232, 238, 244, 260–1, 274–7
Laryea, Tony, 302
La Rose, Irma, 24, 36, 179
La Rose, John (Antony), 1, 23–4, 26, 35–8, 42–3, 46–7, 49, 51, 58, 60–3, 67, 70–2, 75, 83, 86–7, 90–3, 97, 107–8, 110–1, 114–5, 122–5, 127–9, 132–5, 137–8, 142, 144–6, 148–50, 153–4, 156–7, 159, 161, 164, 168–72, 176, 179–80, 182–3, 185, 189, 191, 202, 211–2, 214–6, 218, 223–31, 234, 237–9, 241, 243–50, 251–8, 274, 280, 281, 283–4, 288–91, 295–304, 306–7, 309–10, 313–5, 317, 319, 322
Lashley, Cliff, 202
Las Villas University, Cuba, 232
Lawrence, DH, 28
Laye, Camara, 76
League of Coloured Peoples, 2, 6
Leech, Christopher, 150
Légitime Défense, 312
Le Maitre, Cris, 93, 156, 250
Lennox, Bill, 95
Léro, Etienne, 312
L'Etudiant Noir, 312
Lewis, Gordon K, 157–8
Lewis, W Arthur, 5, 36
Liberty's, 18, 80
Lincoln's Inn Students Union, 232
Lindo, Archie, 268
Lindo, Cedric, 6, 10–2
Lindo, Sir Lawrence, 150
Lindo, Locksley, 204
Linton, Joyce, 159, 176–7, 230
Literary Garveyism, 311, 314
Little Carib Theatre, Port of Spain, 5, 197, 284
Liyong, Taban Lo, 205, 252
Lloyd, Errol, 29, 80–1, 83, 87, 109, 135, 150–2, 156, 159, 179–81, 223, 229–30, 250, 285, 288, 296, 316, 318–20, 322
Locke, Donald, 212, 285
London College of Printing, 18, 29
London Magazine, 95, 112

London School of Economics (LSE), 4, 28–9, 50, 52, 135–6, 176, 183
London Traverse Theatre Company, 58–9
London University, 1, 4–5, 11, 28–9, 43, 45, 49, 62, 97, 131, 141, 155, 236
Longmans Green Ltd (Longman Group), 91, 95, 158, 207, 231
Look Lai, Wally, 29, 33, 71–2, 161
Lopez, Basil, 139
Lord Kitchener, 109
Losey, Joseph, 50
L'Ouverture, Toussaint, 153
Lovelace, Earl, 85, 102, 104, 110, 216, 318
Lowhar, Syl, 264
Lowry, Malcolm, 173
Lucie-Smith, Edward, 47–50, 62–3, 95, 124, 157–9
Luck, Ray, 273, 290
Luckhoo, Sir Lionel, 110
Lukàcs, Georg, 174
Luthuli, Chief Albert, 153
Lynch, George, 285
Lynch, Hollis, 202

McAndrew, Wordsworth, 70
McBurnie, Beryl, 5, 33, 62, 197, 216, 284
McCarran Act, 8
McDonald, Ian, 10, 19, 295
McFarlane, Douglas, 88
McGavan, Carol, 156
McGibbon & Kee Ltd, 9
McKay, Claude, 104–5, 130, 161, 267, 311, 313
McKenzie, Herman, 282
McKinney, Anthony, 150
McLean, Raymond, 33
McNair, Eugene, 197
McNeill, Anthony, 261, 265–7
McNish, Althea, 18, 80–1, 87, 135, 150–2, 229, 285, 302, 307, 319
McTair, Roger, 211, 264
Macmillan Company Ltd, 95
Maddy, Yulisa (Pat) Amadu, 289, 297
Mair, Lucille Mathurin (Walrond), 4, 111, 207, 266, 281
Mais, Roger, 30, 57, 139, 161, 178, 183, 244, 276
Makerere University, Uganda, 297
Malangatana, 253
Malcolm X (Al Hajj Malik al-Shabazz), 28, 105, 147, 187, 199, 236, 244, 249
Malik, Abdul (Delano de Coteau), 264, 280
Malik, Abdul (Michael de Freitas, Michael X), 227
Mangrove Restaurant, Notting Hill, Mangrove Nine, 258, 293, 299, 301
Manley, Edna, 9, 14, 18, 112, 180, 273
Manley, Norman, 6, 19
Marcus, Lowell A, 159, 175, 183, 185, 232, 293
Markham, EA (Archie), 29, 293, 295, 299
Marlowe, Christopher, 230
Marriott, Louis, 288, 293, 298
Marsden-Smedley, Hester, 167
Marshall, Paule, 202
Marshall, Sir Roy, 219
Marson, Una, 6, 267, 281
Martin, Tony, 230, 311
Matthews, Marc, 230–1, 261, 263, 266, 280, 293–5, 314, 319, 322
Matthews, Tony, 237, 244, 249–50, 295
Matos, Luis Pales, 37
Matura, Mustapha, 293, 298, 301
Maxwell, Marina Ama Omowale, 29, 108–9, 115–6, 118–20, 126–30, 133, 142, 151, 183, 190, 193–200, 204–5, 208, 217, 221, 244, 268, 279–80, 293, 295, 306–7
Melville Herman, 173, 276
Melville Joseph Ltd, 9
Miles, Judy, 281
Millette, James, 218
Mills, Sonia, 140
Minority Arts Advisory Service (MAAS), 316, 319
Minshall, Peter, 135
Mitchell, Adrian, 87, 153–4, 299
Mittleholzer, Edgar, 11–2, 30, 44, 165, 170–1, 212, 288
Modisane, Bloke, 62
Mohammed, Elijah, 187
Moko, 197
Monteith, Charles, 44–5
Moody, Harold Arundel, 2, 6–7, 45
Moody, Helene (Coppel-Cowan), 2, 31
Moody, Ronald, 1, 7, 17, 30–2, 62–3, 80, 82, 87, 110, 125, 150–2, 159, 179, 181, 202, 204, 229, 259, 269–70, 285, 296, 299, 304, 320
Moore, Gerald, 62, 75–78, 157, 159, 169–70, 187, 260, 321
Moore, Philip, 273
Moore, Robert (Bobby), 158, 170, 202
Moreau, Daniel, 182
Morejon, Nancy, 138
Morris, Mary, 16
Morris, Mervyn, 13, 60, 125, 139–40, 152, 157, 193–4, 261, 267–8, 295, 303
Morrison, Hugh, 199
Morton, Jelly Roll, 135
Movement for Colonial Freedom, 27, 45
Mullard, Chris, 300
Munro, Carmen, 13, 33
Munro College, Jamaica, 11
Murray, Dave, 211
Muttoo, Henry, 280
Mystic Revelation of Reastafari Orchestra, 267, 271

Naipaul, VS, Sir (Vidia), 10–2, 30, 33, 40, 44, 46–7, 67, 85, 103, 113, 131, 161, 166, 170–2, 215, 244, 246, 260, 271–2, 276–7, 299
NAM, St Vincent, 210
Narain, Denise de Caires, 320
Nasta, Susheila, 320
Nation, The, Barbados, 210
Nation, the, Trinidad, 23, 33
National History and Arts Council, Guyana, 253, 271
National Theatre Trust, Jamaica, 208, 268

Negrismo (Afro-Cubanism, Neo-Negritude), 132–4, 145, 147, 149, 312–4
Negritude, 51–2, 105, 132, 171, 227, 237–8, 241, 243–4, 312, 314
Negro Theatre Workshop, 32, 117
Negro Welfare, Cultural and Social Association, Trinidad, 37
Negro World, 311, 315
Neruda, Pablo, 108
Neto, Agostinho, 252
Nettleford, Rex, 42, 99, 195, 198, 242, 293, 322
New Beacon Books (Publications), 36, 58–61, 90, 110, 112, 114, 124, 161, 176, 242, 244, 250–1, 294, 301–3, 306–7, 310, 316, 320–1
New Beacon Books (Book Service, Bookstall), 90–1, 110, 123, 129, 135, 182, 249, 250–1, 284, 295, 298, 301, 303, 307, 316, 321
New Left Review, 20, 34, 51, 162
New Negro Movement, 311
New Statesman and Nation, 95
New Vision Centre Gallery, 17
New Vision Group, 16–7
New World Group, 39, 41, 194–5, 211, 254, 264, 322
New World Quarterly, 42, 200–1, 203–4, 263
Newsletter, CAM, 69, 84, 86, 89, 91, 99, 107, 122–3, 125, 127–9, 139–40, 142–3, 157, 188, 198, 204, 225–6, 231, 233, 237, 247, 252, 256, 276, 315, 322
Ngugi Wa Thiong'o (James Ngugi), 48, 51, 205, 252, 269, 297
Nigerian Society of African Artists, 316
Nkrumah, Kwame, 7, 39
Noel, Keith, 268
Norman, Alma, 207, 267
North London West Indian Association (NLWIA), 248, 257
Northwestern University, Illinois, 302
Norton, Graham, 229
Notting Hill Festival, 115–6
Nottingham CAM, 130–1, 143, 182–4, 231

Observer, 95, 237
Odlum, George, 69
Ogilvie, WG, 22
Okai, John, 253
Okara, Gabriel, 56, 252
Okigbo, Christopher, 252
Old Vic Theatre, 87
Olympia International Art Centre, Kingston, 270
Omo Ajini (Children of Guinea/Africa) Dance Group, UWI, Mona, 269
Onuora, Oku (Orlando Wong), 282
Orr, Peter, 127
Ové, Horace, 234, 298–9, 301–2
Owuor-Anyumba, Henry, 205
Oxford Council for Racial Integration, 247
Oxford University, 10, 13–4, 28–9, 54, 113, 159
Oxford University Press (OUP), 30, 59–61, 112–3, 131

Padmore, George, 3, 7, 84, 102, 156, 184
Palmer, Opal, 281
Papas, Williams, 257
Parboosingh, Karl, 219, 270
Pascall, Alex, 33
Pasuka, Berto, 4
Patterson, Nerys, 51, 54, 75, 125, 307
Patterson, H Orlando, 28, 30, 34, 49–55, 63, 65–6, 70–1, 74–9, 90–1, 125, 137, 139, 152, 171–2, 190, 193, 202, 220, 244, 298, 304, 318
Patterson, Patricia (Patsy), 109, 207
Patterson, Sheila, 238
Payne, Audrey, 176, 188, 230
Paz, Octavio, 108
p'Bitek, Okot, 207, 252, 297
Peacock, Thomas Love, 78
Penrose, Sir Roland, 80
Perkins, Elaine, 139
Perse, St–John, 85, 102, 109
Phillips, Anthony (Tony), 96, 207, 310
Phillips, REK (Reg), 130
Phoenix Literary and Debating Society, Arima, Trinidad, 38
Pieterse, Cosmo, 159, 175, 249–50, 252
Pike, Frank, 95, 105
Pilgrim, Frank, 271, 278
Pilgrim, Philip, 212
Pinter, Harold, 140
Pioneer Press, 8, 22
Piquion, René, 202
Pitt, Lord David, 27
Pivot (Unit 16), 211
Planno, Mortimo, 199
Playogg, R, 150
Poetry Book Society, 124
Pool, Rosey E, 143
Powell, Enoch, 28, 136, 141, 146–7, 154–5, 163–4, 232, 257
Présence Africaine, 95, 182, 314
Press, John, 48
Price-Mars, Jean, 312
Public Opinion, 9

Queen's College, Georgetown, 24, 212, 273
Queen's Royal College, Port of Spain, 10
Questel, Victor, 211, 261, 264, 280, 320

Race Today, 303, 316
Racial Action Adjustment Society (RAAS), 258
Radical Students Alliance, 144
Radio Jamaica Rediffusion (RJR), 125
Radio Times, 302
Rahim, Jennifer, 320
Ramchand, Kenneth, 28, 50, 53–4, 63, 66, 75–6, 78–9, 88, 96, 101, 104–5, 126, 130, 157, 159, 167, 172–5, 190, 200–6, 215, 226, 254, 260, 266–7, 272, 274–5, 281, 295, 320
Ramkissoon, Kaywal, 83
Ramsaran, John, 171–2, 176–7
Rand, Jimi, 299
Rasta Voice, 262

Rastafarian Drummers, Jamaica, 267
Read, Sir Herbert, 80
Reade, Charles, 22
Readers' and Writers' Guild, Port of Spain, 18
Rebelo, Jorge, 249, 252
Reckord, Barry, 13, 198, 200, 232, 261, 293, 296
Reckord, Lloyd, 13, 97, 99, 108, 115–7, 139, 194, 198, 208, 268, 293
Redcam, Tom (Thomas H Macdermot), 104, 267
Redfield, Robert, 120
Reid, VS (Vic), 139, 161, 244, 260
Reinders, Robert, 129, 130, 134–5, 161, 183
Revue Indigène, La, 312
Rhodes, Cecil, 245
Rhone, Trevor, 140, 197–8, 200
Rhys, Jean, 110, 113, 161
Rickards, Alain, 123
Rickards, Colin, 62
Rivera, Diego, 270
Rivers, Madge, 182–3, 188
Roach, EM, 60, 165, 211, 263–5, 272
Robeson, Paul, 3
Robinson, Celia, 115–7
Rodney, Walter, 141, 191–4, 207, 211, 217–9, 226–8, 242, 244, 250, 268, 292, 296, 301
Rohlehr, Gordon, 28, 41, 51, 54–6, 62, 68–71, 89–91, 107, 110, 124, 140, 142, 190, 198, 202, 204, 207, 210, 217, 244, 255, 260–1, 264, 274–7, 310, 319–20
Rose Bruford School, 29
Ross, Alan, 112
Roumain, Jacques, 37, 246, 312
Round House, Chalk Farm, 91–3
Roy, Namba, 8, 16–7, 31–2
Royal Academy of Arts, 31–2
Royal Albert Hall, 60, 169
Royal College of Art, 18
Royal Commonwealth Society, 182
Royal Court Theatre, 13, 33, 60
Royal Festival Hall, 239
Royal Institute Galleries, 88
Royal Opera House, Covent Garden, 87
Rugg, Akua, 320
Russian Revolution, 125

St Andrew's Junior School, Kingston, 208
St David's College, Lampeter, 29
St John, Bruce, 261, 263, 280
St Martin's School of Art, 16, 29
St Mary's College, Port of Spain, 23, 37
St Omer, Dunstan, 18, 40
St Omer, Garth, 95
Saakana, Amon Saba (Sebastian Clarke), 29, 230–1, 244, 253, 295, 309, 314, 317
Salkey, Andrew, 1, 11, 21, 30, 33, 35, 43–7, 49–51, 54, 58, 60–1, 63, 71–4, 79–81, 86, 99, 103, 109, 111, 122, 124, 127, 131–2, 137–8, 142, 144–8, 153–4, 156, 159–62, 165, 167, 169–72, 177, 179, 184, 186, 188, 191, 193, 198, 202, 204–5, 211–2, 214–8, 223–32, 237–9, 241, 244–7, 249–55, 257–8, 262, 266–7, 272, 274, 281, 283–4, 286–7, 289, 291, 295–302, 306–8, 314, 317, 319, 322
Salkey, Pat, 45, 307
Samaroo, Brinsley, 28, 77, 159, 321
Sardinha, Dennis, 297, 321
Sarduy, Pedro Perez, 138
Sartre, Jean-Paul, 314
Saul, Kelvin (Kelly), 252
Savacou, 105–6, 124, 198, 200–20, 222, 259, 261–7, 270, 274, 281–2, 298, 300–1, 307, 316–7
Savory, Ronald, 150–2, 211, 274
Schuler, Monica, 204, 219
Scope, 192–3
Scott, AD, 14, 270
Scott, Dennis, 70, 106, 139, 152, 261, 266–7, 269, 295
Scott, Sir Walter, 22
Sealey, Clifford, 211
Sealey, H, 150
Seeton, Marie, 2
Sejour, Victor, 134
Selvon, Sam, 9, 11, 30, 47, 50, 55–6, 62, 68, 157, 161, 165, 193, 211–2, 238, 244, 253, 256, 260–1, 274, 295, 302, 310, 313, 318
Senior, Olive, 282
Senghor, Léopold Sédar, 236, 252, 312, 314
Seymour, Arthur J, 9, 25, 165, 212, 215, 253, 255, 273–4, 278
Shakespeare, William, 230, 246
Shearer, Hugh, 192, 237
Shears, Gillian, 90–1, 159
Sheppard, Jill, 210
Sherlock, Sir Philip, 192
Shinebourne, Janice (Lowe), 253
Sibley, Inez, 166
Sierra Leone Dance Company, 234
Simon, Keith, 83, 285
Simmons, Harry, 14, 40
Singh, Vishnudat, 28, 111, 124, 159
Singham, Archie, 204
Sir John Cass College, 29
Sir George Williams University, Montreal, 93, 217, 232
Sivanandan, Ambalavaner, 257
Slade School of Fine Art, 29, 176, 287
Sloley, Denis, 199
Slory, Michael, 278
Small, Jerry, 197
Small, Richard, 27, 29, 34, 125, 128, 143, 154–6, 159, 164–5, 170, 183–9, 192, 211, 224, 226–9, 232, 236, 245, 249, 257, 293
Small, Robin *see* Bongo Jerry
Smith, Basil, 230–1, 237, 244, 249–50, 261, 295
Smith, Sir Leonard, 230
Smith, Michael (Mikey), 282, 319
Smith, N J, 150
Sobers, Sir Gary, 81
Sobers, Yvonne, 71
Society of Authors, 70
Society of Portrait Sculptors, 17, 31
Soyinka, Wole, 87, 239, 252
Sparrow, The Mighty, 21, 68–71, 83, 107, 261, 276, 310, 320
Spillers, Hortense, J, 223, 249

Stallworthy, Jon, 60, 112, 114
Stanley, McDonald, 92
Star The, Jamaica, 268
Stockbridge, John, 12
Stow, Randolph, 59, 62
Strindberg, August, 140
Student Non-Violent Co-ordinating Committee (SNCC), 91, 136, 137
Students Centre (see West Indian Students Centre)
Styron, William, 163
Sugar Hill Club, Mayfair, 44
Sunday Times, 62, 95
Swanzy, Henry, 6, 10–2, 19, 95, 113, 157, 159, 165–77, 169, 171–2, 177, 179, 182, 188

Tapia, 264
Tate Gallery, 320
Teitelbaum, Irving, 144, 146
Theatre Guild, Guyana, 39, 117, 253
Theatre Royal, Stratford, 87
Theatre Workshop, Trinidad, 293
Theatre 77, Jamaica, 140
Thomas, Dylan, 61
Thomas, Ewart, 250
Thomas, JJ, 36–7, 39, 70, 102, 212–3, 246, 256
Thomasson, Frank, 116–7
Thomson, George, 228
Thompson, Dudley, 7
Thorpe, Marjorie, 281
Thunder, 24
Times, The, 232
Times Educational Supplement, The, 295
Times Literary Supplement, The, 51, 271
Tong, Vernon, 285
Tootal, 80
Torch, 207
Toynbee, Arnold, 166–7
Trench Town Comprehensive School, Kingston, 153
Trinidad February Revolution, 217–8, 261, 292
Trinidad Guardian, 9, 10, 103, 188, 263
Trinidad All Steel Percussion Orchestra (TASPO), 37
Trinidad Folksingers, 125
Trinidad and Tobago Art Society, 14, 18
Trinidad and Tobago Television, 316
Trinidad and Tobago Youth Council (Movement), 33, 37
Tulloch, Courtney, 115, 116, 153, 159

United African Jamaica All-Star Steelband, 267
United Coloured Peoples Association, 126
Universal Negro Improvement Association, 84, 311
University of Birmingham, 28, 157, 162
University of Dar-es-Salaam, 141
University of Edinburgh, 28, 50, 75, 159, 206
University of Essex, 143, 155
University of Ghana, 86
University of Guyana, 158, 212, 255
University of Hull, 29, 54, 133
University of Kent at Canterbury, 42, 49, 55, 62, 94, 96, 109, 111, 124, 129, 143, 156–7, 167, 225, 305, 320–1
University of Leeds, 75, 129, 155
University of Leicester, 15
University of Manchester, 301
University of Nairobi, 205–6, 269
University of Nottingham, 129
University of Surrey, 155
University of Sussex, 28–9, 34, 42, 75, 129, 159, 172, 190, 321
University of Swansea, 171
University (College) of the West Indies (UCWI, UWI), Cave Hill, Barbados, 1, 96, 210; Mona, Jamaica, 1, 12, 28, 39, 41–2, 52, 97–8, 111, 125, 139–42, 190–6, 205–6, 209, 218–9, 259, 269, 281–2, 320–1; Extra-Mural Department, St Lucia, 40–41; St Augustine, Trinidad, 190, 210–1, 217, 320
University of Woodford Square, Port of Spain, 111, 305
University of York, 28, 209
University Players, UWI, Mona, 268
U'Tamsi, Tchic'aya, 253

Van Sertima, Ivan, 24–6, 149, 158, 162, 170–2, 179–8, 185, 189, 211, 239–40, 253, 255–6, 274, 276, 295, 321
Vaz, Noel, 140
Verity, Jeremy, 112–3, 119
Verity, Robert, 112
Voice of Youth, 38
Voices, 211

Wake, Clive, 158–9, 167
Walcott, Derek, 13, 41, 56, 59–60, 67, 70, 85, 105–7, 117, 131, 140, 152, 161, 175, 195, 197, 204, 244, 261, 265, 272, 276, 293
Walcott, Roderick, 40
Walmsley, Anne, 95, 110–1, 158, 162, 207, 210, 223, 231, 252, 267, 283, 286, 288–90, 295, 307, 321–2
Walrond, Eric, 4, 204, 311
Walter Rodney Bookshop (see Bogle-L'Ouverture)
Warner Lewis, Maureen, 28, 209, 269, 282
Wasafiri, 321
Watson, Barrington, 219, 270
West India Committee, 228, 230
West Indian Gazette, 20–2, 34, 45–6, 224, 237
West Indian Review, 9
West Indian Society, Cambridge, 19
West Indian Society, LSE, 135
West Indian Society, Oxford, 20
West Indian Standing Conference, 20, 27, 91, 128, 156
West Indian Students Centre, 13, 20, 27, 33–5, 48–9, 61–4, 71, 80, 86–8, 90, 94–5, 115, 123, 125, 128, 142–4, 150–6, 159, 181, 188, 226, 229, 233, 239, 241, 243–4, 246–7, 249–51, 283–5, 289, 295, 297, 305

West Indian Students Union (WISU), 5, 20, 26, 64, 123, 128, 155–6, 236, 241–7, 249–51, 308
West Indian World, 292
West Indies Chronicle, 111
Whannel, Paddy, 162
White, Eric Walter, 124, 159, 179
White, Lavonnie A, 130
White, Sarah, 43, 51, 58, 60, 110, 124, 129, 159, 182, 249, 283, 289, 295, 307
Whitehall Players, Port of Spain, 38
Whitelock, William, 229
Whylie, Dwight, 62, 151
Wickham, John, 36, 210
Williams, Aubrey, 15–7, 23, 31–2, 50–1, 57–8, 72–5, 80–3, 86–7, 96, 99–101, 109, 123, 135, 137, 150–2, 159, 161, 164, 171, 182, 204–5, 211–2, 214, 219–22, 229, 242–3, 253–6, 259, 271, 273–4, 277, 283, 285–8, 290, 299, 304, 309, 317–9, 321
Williams, Denis, 110, 169, 277, 287–8
Williams, Eric, 23, 26, 37, 111, 113, 161, 275, 277, 305
Williams, Eve (Lafargue), 16
Williams, Milton, 216, 240
Williams, Nigel, 301
Williamson, Karina, 159, 172, 176–9
Wilson, Betty, 34, 62, 190, 208
Wilson, Don, 28, 34, 62, 69, 71, 78, 89, 111, 115, 125, 142, 190, 194, 206–7
Wilson, Frank Avray, 32
Wilson, Harold, 135
Wilson, T-Bone, 293, 295, 298–9, 302
Windward Islands Broadcasting Service, 40
Wint, Nancy, 36
Wint, Pam, 296
Wong, Ansel, 29, 155–6, 245, 249–51
Wood, Donald, 321
Woodstock Gallery, 30–1, 152
Woolf, Leonard, 3
Woolford, Gordon, 12
Working Peoples Art Group, Guyana, 14–5
Writers Union of Trinidad and Tobago, 280
Wynter, Sylvia, 11, 30, 212, 218, 266

Xavier, Llewellyn, 285

Yambo, Ouloguem, 252
Yard Theatre, 197, 199–200, 219, 259, 262, 267–9, 293, 307, 310, 316
Yates, Frances, 177

Zirimu, Pio, 297